Antis he Holocaust

Anthony McElligott • Jeffrey Herf
Editors

Antisemitism Before and Since the Holocaust

Altered Contexts and Recent Perspectives

palgrave
macmillan

Editors
Anthony McElligott
University of Limerick
Limerick, Ireland

Jeffrey Herf
University of Maryland
College Park, Maryland, USA

ISBN 978-3-319-84034-5 ISBN 978-3-319-48866-0 (eBook)
DOI 10.1007/978-3-319-48866-0

Cover image © Godong / Alamy Stock Photo
Cover design by Henry Petrides

Printed on acid-free paper

This Palgrave Macmillan imprint is published by Springer Nature
The registered company is Springer International Publishing AG
The registered company address is: Gewerbestrasse 11, 6330 Cham, Switzerland

Robert Solomon Wistrich, 7 April 1945–19 May 2015 in memoriam

Acknowledgments

First and foremost, the editors and contributors to this volume owe a debt of gratitude to Holocaust Education Trust Ireland, who had the original idea and who organized the conference on Antisemitism and Holocaust Denial in Dublin in November 2010, from which this volume emerges, and whose enthusiasm for the project has never diminished.

The editors also thank the contributors to the volume for their patience and support. Our thanks, too, go to Kristin Purdy, our former editor at Palgrave Macmillan, for her forbearance and continued confidence in this project. We graciously acknowledge the three anonymous readers, whose criticisms and suggested change of title have contributed to making this a better volume. The Dublin Conference itself would not have taken place had it not been for the support and sponsorship of the Irish Department of Foreign Affairs; Irish Department of Education and Skills; Irish Office of the Minister for Integration; Failte Ireland; Embassy of Israel, Dublin; Embassy of the United States of America, Dublin; Embassy of France, Dublin; Embassy of the Federal Republic of Germany, Dublin; the Fondation pour la Mémoire de la Shoah, Paris; Trinity College Dublin; University College Dublin; and the Herzog Centre, Trinity College Dublin. The event was co-sponsored by the United Nations Department of Public Information with a message of goodwill from the Under-Secretary-General, Kiyo Akasaka. Finally, we sadly record the death of our friend, colleague, and mentor, Robert Wistrich, who passed away in the course of bringing this volume to fruition and to whose memory it is dedicated.

Contents

Notes on Contributors

Werner Bergmann is a sociologist and Professor at the Center for Research on Antisemitism, Technical University Berlin. His fields of research include the sociology and history of antisemitism, racism, and interethnic violence. His recent publications include "Is There a 'New European Antisemitism'? Public Opinion and Comparative Empirical Research in Europe," in: Lars Rensmann/Julius H. Schoeps (eds.), *Politics and Resentment. Antisemitism and Counter-Cosmopolitism in the European Union* (Brill, 2010); with Ulrich Wyrwa, *Antisemitismus in Zentraleuropa. Deutschland, Österreich und die Schweiz vom 18. Jahrhundert bis zur Gegenwart* (Darmstadt: Wissenschaftliche Buchgesellschaft, 2011); "Anti-Jewish Violence in Nineteenth and Twentieth Century Europe: Some Theoretical Considerations," in: *Jahrbuch für Antisemitismusforschung,* Bd. 21. 2012. Recently, he has been a member of an expert group preparing a "Report on Antisemitism" for the German Parliament (Bundestag).

Pierre Birnbaum is Emeritus Professor of History and Political Science at the University of Paris. His publications include *Sur un nouveau moment anti-Semite: Jour de colere* (Paris: Fayard, 2015); *Leon Blum: Prime Minister, Socialist, Zionist* (Yale University Press, 2015); *Les deux maisons: essai zur la citoyennete des Juifs en France et aux Etats-Unis* (Paris: Gallimard, 2012); *Geography of hope: Exile, the Enlightenment, Disassimilation* (Stanford University Press, 2008); *The Antisemitic Moment: A Tour of France in 1898.* (Hill and Wang, 2002; University of Chicago Press, 2011); *The Jews of the Republic: A Political History of State Jews in France from Gambetta to Vichy* (Stanford University Press, 1996); and *Anti-Semitism in France: A Political History from Leon Blum to the Present* (Blackwell, 1992).

Jeffrey Herf is Distinguished University Professor in the Department of History, University of Maryland, College Park. His publications in modern German history include *Nazi Propaganda for the Arab World* (Yale University Press, 2009); *The*

Jewish Enemy: Nazi Propaganda During World War Two and the Holocaust (Harvard university Press, 2006); *Divided Memory: The Nazi Past in the Two Germanys* (Harvard University Press, 1997); *Reactionary Modernism: Technology, Culture and Politics in Weimar and the Third Reich* (Cambridge University Press, 1984); and *Undeclared Wars with Israel: East Germany and the West German Far Left, 1967–1989* (Cambridge University Press, 2016).

Tony Kushner is Professor of History and, since 1986, the Director of the Parkes Institute for the Study of Jewish/non-Jewish Relations in the History Department at the University of Southampton. Educated at the University of Sheffield (BA and PhD) and the University of Connecticut (MA), he was formerly the historian for the Manchester Jewish Museum. His publications include *The Holocaust and the Liberal Imagination: A Social and Cultural History* (Blackwell, 1994); *The Holocaust: Critical Historical Responses* (with Donald Bloxham, Manchester University Press, 2005); *Remembering Refugees: Then and Now* (Manchester University Press, 2006); and *Anglo-Jewry since 1066: Place, Locality and Memory* (Manchester University Press, 2009). His most recent book is *The Battle of Britishness: Migrant Journeys since 1685* (Manchester University Press, 2012). He is co-editor of the journal *Patterns of Prejudice* and deputy editor of *Jewish Culture and History.*

Deborah E. Lipstadt is the Dorot Professor of Modern Jewish History and Holocaust Studies at Emory University in Atlanta. In 1996 David Irving brought a libel suit against her in the High Court in England for calling him a Holocaust denier and extremist. After a 12-week trial, the court ruled in Lipstadt's favor and declared Irving a denier and deliberate falsifier of the facts. She recounts that event in *History on Trial: My Day in Court with a Holocaust Denier* (Ecco: 2005). That book has been adapted for a movie, *Denial,* with a screenplay by David Hare. She is also the author of *Beyond Belief: The American Press and the Coming of the Holocaust* (The Free Press, 1986), *Denying the Holocaust: The Growing Assault on Truth and Memory* (The Free Press, 1993), *The Eichmann Trial* (Nextbook/Schocken, 2011), and *Holocaust: An American Understanding* (forthcoming with Rutgers University Press, 2016). She is currently writing a book on contemporary antisemitism.

Meir Litvak is an associate professor at the Department of Middle Eastern History and Director of the Alliance Center for Iranian Studies at Tel Aviv University. He is the author of *Shi'i Scholars of Nineteenth Century Iraq: The Ulama of Najaf and Karbala* (Cambridge University Press, 1998) and co-author of *Iran: From a Persian Monarchy to an Islamic Republic* (Ra'anana: Open University Press, 2014). His book *From Empathy to Denial: Arab Responses to the Holocaust*, co-authored with Esther Webman, was the recipient of the Washington Institute for Near East Policy's book prize for 2010. He has edited six books on modern Middle Eastern history and has published articles on modern Iranian and Shi`i history as well as modern Islamic movements and Palestinian nationalism.

Anthony McElligott is the founding professor of history and chair of the Department of History at the University of Limerick. He has written and edited extensively on the history of the Weimar Republic and the early years of the Third Reich, including *Working Towards the Fuhrer: Essays in Honour of Sir Ian Kershaw* (edited with Tim Kirk, Manchester: Manchester University Press, 2003); *Weimar Germany* (Oxford: Oxford University Press, 2010); and recently a major study, *Rethinking the Weimar Republic. Authority and Authoritarianism, 1916–1936* (London: Bloomsbury, 2014). He is currently writing a book on the destruction of the Jewish community of Rhodes titled *The Last Transport: The Holocaust in the Eastern Aegean* and a study of Himmler's chief statistician, Richard Korherr. He was elected a fellow of the Royal Historical Society in 1999 and a member of the Royal Irish Academy in 2015.

Robert Jan van Pelt has taught at the University of Waterloo School of Architecture since 1987 and held appointments at institutions of higher education in Europe, Asia, and North America. His publications include with Deborah Dwork, *Flight from the Reich: Refugee Jews, 1933–1946* (W.W. Norton, 2009); with Deborah Dwork, *Holocaust: A History* (W.W. Norton, 2002); *The Cast for Auschwitz: Evidence from the Irving Trial* (Indiana University Press, 2002); with Deborah Dwork, *Auschwitz, 1270 to the Present* (W.W. Norton, 1996); and with Carroll William Westfall, *Architectural Principles in an Age of Historicism* (Yale University Press, 1991). His work was featured in the BBC-Horizon program "Blueprints of Genocide." He was a senior consultant to the BBC/PBS series *Auschwitz: Inside the Nazi State* and served as an expert witness for the defense in the libel case of David Irving versus Penguin and Deborah Lipstadt.

Bassam Tibi is a professor emeritus of International Relations at the University of Göttingen, where he taught from 1973 to 2009. He is a native Syrian born in Damascus in 1944 and has been a German citizen since 1974. In 2010, he served as the Resnick Scholar for the study of antisemitism at the Center for Advanced Holocaust Studies/CAHS at the United States Holocaust Memorial Museum in Washington, D.C., and in 2011, he was visiting Koret Foundation Fellow at Stanford University. Tibi has published extensively on Islam. His recent publications include *Political Islam, World Politics and Europe*, 2nd edition (Routledge, 2014); *Islamism and Islam* (Yale University Press, 2012); *Islam in Global Politics: Conflict and Cross-Cultural Bridging* (Routledge, 2012); and *The Shari'a-State: Arab Spring and Democratization* (Routledge, 2013). His magnum opus was published in 2009 under the title *Islam's Predicament with Modernity. Religious Reform and Cultural Change*, also by Routledge Press.

Esther Webman is the head of the Zeev Vered Desk for the Study of Tolerance and Intolerance in the Middle East and a senior research fellow at the Dayan Center and the Stephen Roth Institute in Tel Aviv University. Her research is focused on Arab discourse analysis, mainly Arab antisemitism, and Arab perceptions of the Holocaust. Her publications include with Meir Litvak, *From Empathy to Denial: Arab Responses to the Holocaust* (Hurst & Co., and Columbia University Press 2009), recipient of the Washington Institute for Near East Policy's Gold book prize for 2010, Hebrew edition in 2015; "The 'Jew' as a Metaphor for Evil in Arab Public Discourse," *Journal of the Middle East and Africa*, vol. 6 (2015), 275–292; and "Mixed and Confused—Egyptian Initial Responses to the Holocaust," in Hilary Earl and Karl Schleunes (eds.), *Lessons and Legacies XI: Expanding Perspective on the Holocaust in a Changing World* (North Western University Press, 2014), pp. 335–354.

Mark Weitzman is the Director of Government Affairs for the Simon Wiesenthal Center. He is a member of the US delegation to the International Holocaust Remembrance Authority (IHRA) where he chairs the Committee on Antisemitism and Holocaust Denial. He was the lead author of the IHRA's Working Definition of Holocaust Denial and Distortion. His publications include with Michael Feinberg and Shimon Samuels, eds., *Antisemitism, the Generic Hatred: Essays in Memory of Simon Wiesenthal* (Vallentine Mitchell, 2007), winner of National Jewish Book Award in 2007. His publications from the Vidal Sassoon International Center for the Study of Antisemitism include *Jews and Judaism in the Political Theology of Radical Catholic Traditionalists* (2015); *Magical Logic: Globalization, Conspiracy Theory* (2008); with Steven Leonard Jacobs, *Dismantling the Big Lie: the Protocols of the Elders of Zion* (2003); and "Antisemitism and the Radical Catholic Traditionalist Movement," in Alvin Rosenfeld, ed., *Deciphering the New Antisemitism* (Indiana University Press, 2015), 242–286.

Juliane Wetzel is a senior research fellow at the Center for Research on Antisemitism, Technical University, Berlin, and managing editor of its *Jahrbuch für Antisemitismusforschung* (Yearbook for Research on Antisemitism). She is a member of the Board of the Vienna Wiesenthal Institute for Holocaust Studies. She is also a member of the German Delegation of the IHRA, co-coordinator of the Independent Expert Board on Antisemitism of the German Parliament, and co-author of its report: *Antisemitismus in Deutschland—Erscheinungsformen, Bedingungen, Präventionsansätze* (2011). Her publications include *Moderner Antisemitismus unter Muslimen in Deutschland* (Springer VS, 2014); with Wolfgang Benz, *Antisemitismus und radikaler Islamismus* (Klartext, 2007); with Werner Bergmann, *Manifestations of anti-Semitism in the European Union* (Center for Research on anti-Semitism, Technical University, Berlin, 2003); and *Waiting for Hope: Jewish Displaced Persons in Post-World War II Germany* with Angelika Konigseder (Northwestern University Press, 2001).

Christian Wiese holds the Martin Buber Chair in Jewish Thought and Philosophy at the Goethe University in Frankfurt am Main. His publications include *Challenging Colonial Discourse: Jewish Studies and Protestant Theology in Wilhelmine Germany* (Brill, 2005); *The Life and Thought of Hans Jonas: Jewish Dimensions* (Brandeis University Press, 2007); and with Walter Homolka and Thomas Brechenmacher, *Jüdische Existenz in der Moderne: Abraham Geiger und die Wissenschaft des Judentums* (De Gruyter, 2013). His edited volumes include *Redefining Judaism in an Age of Emancipation: Comparative Perspectives on Samuel Holdheim (1806–1860)* (Brill, 2007); with Andre Gotzmann, *Modern Judaism and Historical Consciousness: Identities—Encounters—Perspectives* (Brill, 2007); *Years of Persecution, Years of Extermination: Saul Friedländer and the Future of Holocaust Studies* (Continuum, 2010); and with Martina Urban, *German-Jewish Thought Between Religion and Politics: Festschrift in Honor of Paul Mendes-Flohr on the Occasion of his Seventieth Birthday* (with Martina Urban, De Gruyter, 2012). He is currently writing a biography of the journalist and politician Robert Weltsch.

Robert Wistrich was one of the world's most distinguished scholars of antisemitism, winning many international accolades, including an award for Lifetime Achievement from the *Journal for the Study of Antisemitism* and election to the British Academy. Until his death in May 2015, he held the Neuburger Chair for Modern European History at the Hebrew University of Jerusalem and was the head of the University's Vidal Sassoon International Center for the Study of Antisemitism. His major publications include *From Ambivalence to Betrayal: The Left, the Jews, and Israel* (University of Nebraska Press, 2012); *A Lethal Obsession: Antisemitism—From Antiquity to the Global Jihad* (Random House, 2010); *Laboratory of World Destruction. Germans and Jews in Central Europe* (University of Nebraska Press, 2007); *Antisemitism: The Longest Hatred* (New York, 1991); and *The Jews of Vienna in the age of Franz Joseph* (Oxford University Press, 1989).

Elhanan Yakira is a professor emeritus in the Department of Philosophy at the Hebrew University of Jerusalem. His main fields of research are early modern European philosophy, political philosophy, and twentieth-century French phenomenology. His extensive publications include *Spinoza and the Case for Philosophy* (Cambridge University Press, 2015); *Post-Holocaust, Post-Zionism: Three Essays on Denial, Forgetting and the Delegitimation of Israel* (Cambridge University Press, 2009); *La causalite de Galilee a Kant* (Presses universitaires de France, 1994); *Leibniz' Science of the Rational* (Franz Steiner Verlag, 1998); and recent essays on antisemitism, anti-Zionism, and Holocaust Denial.

List of Figures

List of Tables

CHAPTER 1

Antisemitism Before and Since the Holocaust: Altered Contexts and Recent Perspectives

Anthony McElligott and Jeffrey Herf

Within two months of the ending of the Second World War and in the aftermath of the worst state-perpetrated genocide ever to occur, an unpublished report by Nora Katzenstein noted the 'unmistakable signs of a growth in anti-Semitism, more or less virulent, throughout Europe in almost every country, with very few exceptions, even in such countries where anti-Semitism was practically unknown before the war'.[1]

Indeed, following the ending of the war in many places of Europe, Jews were frequently met with either fear or loathing or violence as they returned to their homes. The pogrom at Kielce in Poland, in which more than 40 Jews were murdered by Christians in July 1946 after false allegations of kidnap had been made by a nine-year-old boy, is perhaps the most graphically violent illustration of this postwar antisemitism.[2] There were many less dramatic examples of violence against individuals or, more usually, against Jewish property in the 20 years after liberation, such as

A. McElligott (✉)
University of Limerick, Limerick, Ireland

J. Herf
University of Maryland, College Park, MD, USA

A. McElligott, J. Herf (eds.), *Antisemitism Before and Since the Holocaust*, DOI 10.1007/978-3-319-48866-0_1

the desecration of the Jewish cemetery in Munich, formerly Hitler's 'city of the movement', or the anti-Jewish riots in the north English town of Prestwich in Lancashire; each leaving their own particular trauma on Europe's Jews.[3] Survivor testimonies frequently record the antipathy they faced as they came back from the camps.[4] There are numerous accounts of Jews returning to their homes only to either find strangers in possession of their homes or deprived of their personal effects that had been left in the hands of neighbors for safekeeping.[5] When Walter Fried and his father returned to their home town of Topolčany in Slovakia in the summer of 1945, neighbors to whom they had entrusted their valuables now denied any knowledge of these bar a few items of clothing. 'They didn't want us to come back', Walter told his interviewer, 'so they wouldn't have to settle their accounts with us and look us in the eye and say, "we don't owe you anything"'.[6] Such accounts are commonplace. When the 5,500 or so Jewish survivors of the death camps began returning to the Netherlands from 1945, many of them, granted not all, were met with grudging indifference and sometimes barely concealed hostility from former neighbors.[7] As Eva Schloss (né Geiringer) and her mother found as they tried to return to Amsterdam following their liberation from Auschwitz, 'the end of the war was not an end to prejudice—far from it'.[8]

This hostility took place in spite of efforts by various European governments to quickly restore 'unrestricted equality of rights' to Jews as they returned from the death camps. Katzenstein's observation points to a disparity between official and popular attitudes toward Jews in the aftermath of the Holocaust. Scholars who follow public opinion on this issue conclude that nearly eight decades later the divergence between governments addressing the crime of Nazi genocide of the Jews and popular antisemitism is still as wide as ever in many parts of Europe, while throughout the Muslim world there is a close convergence between the two.[9] At the very latest since the Stockholm Declaration in 2000, when 46 states agreed that the 27 January—the day Auschwitz was liberated by Soviet troops—should henceforth be a day of international commemoration of the victims of Nazi genocide—governments in Europe have made great efforts to integrate the Holocaust into their educational programs in order to raise broader awareness of the violent potentials of (racial) prejudice, albeit with varying degrees of success.[10] In spite of efforts, antisemitism continues to manifest itself—usually in the form of vandalism against Jewish property or in anti-Jewish expressions conveyed through the new media—but also on occasion more ominously against persons, as with the horrific attack at a Jewish school in Toulouse in southwest France in March 2012, in which a rabbi and three small children were killed and the equally murderous gun attack killing four people at the Jewish Museum in Brussels in May 2014 testify.[11]

In recent years, the Arab–Israeli conflict in the Middle East has come to serve as a surrogate platform among some groups and individuals for airing views that are either blatantly antisemitic or border on this.[12] One result of the hostile discourse surrounding the conflict (as well as the conflict itself) has been an increase in both verbal and physical attacks against Jews and Jewish institutions. Indeed, both of the attacks in France and Belgium were carried out by Muslims who had been radicalized by the conflict in the Middle East. During the summer of 2014 in Europe, anti-Israeli and antisemitic rhetoric assumed new levels of vitriol. In some countries, crowds shouted 'Jews to the gas'.[13] And while such incidents are at present rare—in Europe at least, nevertheless the trend is a recrudescence of violent antisemitism. While the conflation of anti-Zionism with antisemitism is clear to see in Holocaust denial among parts of the Arab world, there seems to be a paradox in the West, wherein enormous attention is devoted to 'learning' from the Holocaust, countered by public and popular expressions of hostility to Israel that spill over into animus of Jews.

Divided into five discrete sections, the present volume not only broaches the issue of Islamist denial of the Holocaust in the Middle East but also attempts to understand the Western paradox by looking at antisemitism before and since the Holocaust in Europe and the USA. It thus offers both a historical and contemporary perspective.[14] This volume begins and ends with observations by four leading scholars in the fields of Holocaust and antisemitism: Deborah Lipstadt, the late Robert Wistrich, Elhanan Yakira and Robert Jan van Pelt draw on professional practice and personal experiences to deliver powerful, even controversial chapters as in the case of Wistrich and Yakira who are reporting from the 'frontline', so to speak. Between these 'book-ends' a section containing three chapters by Christian Wiese, Mark Weitzman and Bassam Tibi offer a discussion on the relationship between Christianity and Islam; this is followed by five chapters that tackle historical and contemporary issues of antisemitism in the USA (Pierre Birnbaum), Europe (Werner Bergmann and Tony Kushner) and the Middle East (Jeffrey Herf and Meir Litvak); in the fourth section two chapters by Esther Webman and Juliane Wetzel look at the role of metaphor and discourse of Holocaust, its appropriation and inversion and how these contribute consciously or otherwise to contemporary antisemitism.

The 14 contributions to this volume do not necessarily provide a unity of argument—nor should they. Instead, they expose the plurality of positions within the academy and reflect the robust discussions that took place during the conference on which they are based.[15]

The link between the manifestations of antisemitism and Holocaust denial per se is not always immediately clear (although in this volume it is exposed in the contributions by both Lipstadt and van Pelt). The ideology of antisemitic terrorist organizations such as Hamas and Hizbollah and those groups closely associated with them, as well as until recently Iran's government, deny both the Holocaust and Israel's right to exist as a state.[16] Beyond this conflict zone, the relationship between the two phenomena is not always clear-cut (although as we have noted, the Arab–Israeli conflict since the second intifada at the latest, and particularly against the background of events during the summer of 2014 in Gaza, has resulted in a rise of antisemitism globally). More frequently, in what scholars refer to as 'inversion', the Holocaust and its imagery are invoked to attack the state of Israel's policy vis-à-vis Palestinians in the West Bank; and this occurs universally across borders. In such instances, the 'ownership' of the memory of the Holocaust is contested and expropriated, as Robert Wistrich, Esther Webman and Juliane Wetzel show in this volume. A recent example of this can be found in a review essay of a number of publications mostly critical of Israel in the weekend supplement of Ireland's national daily *The Irish Times* where its reviewer, US-born journalist Lara Marlowe, referred to Israel's policies of 'ethnic cleansing', 'dispossession' and 'extermination', language integral to the Jewish experience of Holocaust. The implication of Marlowe's piece as one reads on is an association with the Nazi racial state and its policy of planned genocide, even though she falls short of employing 'Holocaust' in her review.[17] In this piece of writing, by no means an isolated case as Esther Webman shows in her chapter, the specificity of the Holocaust, its uniqueness to the Jewish experience and identity, is removed through its inversion (this phenomenon is also reflected upon by Elhahan Yakira in this volume).

While it is true to say that 'Jewish identity' is not solely tied down to the Holocaust and its memory, it is nonetheless a key element as most of the authors here would agree. The denial or weakening of that memory has become an integral part of the so-called new antisemitism since the ending of the Cold War at the beginning of the 1990s.[18] As some of the contributors to this volume argue, traditional Jew-hatred and European modern antisemitism now coalesce with wider geopolitical conflicts, notably that in the Middle East and the re-emergence of radical Islamic politics.[19] Indeed, as Wistrich and Yakira point out, much of the criticism leveled at Israel too frequently serves as a screen for a thinly veiled antisemitic sentiment within 'middle-ground' society and particularly, though not exclusively, on the left of the political spectrum.[20] Much of the recent debate on the 'new antisemitism' has been held either within cognate disciplines of political sciences, sociology and social-psychology or has taken place in the full glare of the media. But while antisemitism or Judeophobia has a long, and according to Wistrich, unbroken history, Holocaust denial by definition or relativizing the Holocaust through its conflation with the Arab–Israeli conflict, is a recent part of this longer and continuous history.[21]

Robert Wistrich argues that the novelty in the 'new antisemitism' lies in what he calls its 'shift of gravity' from Europe to the Middle East, especially since the Iranian Revolution of 1979 and the growing prominence of radical Islam before and after the attacks on the Twin Towers in Manhattan on September 11, 2001. Since the mid-twentieth century, antisemitism, for centuries primarily a component of Europe's Christian culture as the contributions from Christian Wiese and Mark Weitzman attest, found added impetus within the modern tradition of Islamism and, according to Jeffrey Herf predates the founding of the state of Israel. Meanwhile, Tony Kushner taking a different approach, both contextualizes antisemitism as part of a wider societal difficulty of accommodating difference in an era when exclusive nationalism is on the rise; he also counters the idea of the 'new antisemitism', at least in its British sphere. Kushner argues that in Britain traditional antisemitism has today been superseded by islamophobia and racism more generally. Some might argue that the British case is exceptional. For Kushner, it is precisely where the exception challenges the rule that one needs to address the 'new antisemitism'; a point also touched on by Juliane Wetzel in her discussion of trivialization of the Holocaust on the worldwide web and by Werner Bergmann in his quantitative analysis of racist violence in contemporary Germany. A convergence in the different approaches to the question of antisemitism can be found, however, in a broad agreement that its contemporary manifestations are frequently triggered by the ongoing conflict in the Middle East. As Charles Asher Small has noted, the Arab–Israeli conflict serves has been adopted by (mostly) left intellectuals in Western Europe in a broad critique of colonialism/imperialism in which Israel is the stand-in for the USA.[22] And while antisemitism's gravity may have shifted to that region of the globe, it has also found its way back to Europe, notably among the remnants of the New Left in France in particular, as Yakira argues powerfully in his contribution.

In Europe in recent years, and notably since 9/11, a public discourse that equates Islam with terrorism, has only served to marginalize mostly young Muslims, thus fuelling a turn to Islamic radicalism and racism against Muslims among a materially and socially desiccated white youth. This twin phenomenon is captured graphically by Bergmann in his reading of recent data generated by the German authorities. While white extremist violence is more common, violent acts by politicized Muslims have frequently grabbed the headlines, thus promoting an air of unease among Jews, as, for example, in the UK where in fact violence directed against Jews is infrequent according to Tony Kushner in this volume. Nonetheless, 9/11 and the Middle East conflict have exposed a layer of antisemitism hovering below the surface of European attitudes that is not so much particular to marginal groups but the common property of mainstream society, as Wetzel shows. While Kushner's observation may hold true for the UK, and in part appears to share some common characteristics as revealed by the data marshaled by Bergmann, a different picture emerges in the Near East. Here Bassam Tibi and Meir Litvak show in their respective discussions the deeply violent antisemitism that characterizes militant Islam, and in particular in Iran under its former president, Mahmoud Ahmadinejad.

Some notable exceptions notwithstanding, what has been remarkable about recent scholarly discussions on the emergence of the 'new antisemitism', particularly in Europe, has been the almost absence of historians in the debate. It is noteworthy, for instance, that historians were sparsely represented at the international conference on global antisemitism hosted by the (now defunct) Yale Initiative for the Interdisciplinary Study of Antisemitism and the International Association for the Study of Antisemitism in 2010. This volume does not claim to, nor can it, fill the gap in the historiography; nevertheless it combines historical, philosophical and political and social science approaches in an effort to tackle the phenomenon of antisemitism and its relationship to Holocaust denial both in the past and in the present.

During the discussions triggered by the emergence of political antisemitism in the last decades of the nineteenth century, an historian of the stature of Theodor Mommsen could state in an interview in 1893 that it was pointless to try and debate with antisemites: 'the mob remains a mob and antisemitism is the disposition of the mob'.[23] This has by and large also been the position of the historical profession to date: reluctant to legitimate Holocaust deniers by engaging in a fruitless debate, with some justification as we will see below.

In the 1890s, political antisemitism expressed in the works of Georg von Schönerer in Austria, Édouard Drumont in France, Adolf Wagner in Germany and Edmond Picard in Belgium focused on the alleged relationship between Jews and capitalism; their tracts were overlain with racial language, but in themselves were not necessarily violent. None of the exponents of this 'first wave' political antisemitism argued for the material dispossession or civil divesting of the Jews, or demanded their expulsion or called for their murder. It simply depicted Jews as a 'people apart'.[24] At best, before 1914 political antisemitism remained on the margins albeit with growing influence, as the Dreyfus Affair in France demonstrates; but it was the Great War itself, or rather the way it ended in parts of Europe, that fuelled political antisemitism in its increasingly lethal manifestation. Paradoxically, the years after 1918 briefly saw the culmination of the process of legal emancipation of Jews in many (though not all) parts of Europe that ran in tandem with the climax of interwar political liberalism and which can be viewed as both the culmination and crisis of modernity; a process mirrored in an inflamed political antisemitism. This had its parallel in the USA, and is tackled by Pierre Birnbaum in this volume where he looks at the role of elite Jews in the process of state-building embarked upon by Roosevelt in the New Deal (and here making striking comparison to the Third Republic in France). Drawing comparisons with the French Third Republic (1871–1940), Birnbaum shows how the attempt to construct the modern welfare state in North America during the Depression was vilified by conservatives and the extremist right as a project of Jewish vested interests exemplified by the presence in key positions in FDR's administration of a number of leading personalities who *happened* to be Jews. But Birnbaum goes further in his chapter, showing also that Jews in America as in France placed trust in the benign role of the modern state: in some ways representing the positive culmination of Enlightenment thinking and its relationship to Jewry.[25] As was the case with nationalist political discourse in Weimar Germany and later in Nazi rhetoric, Birnbaum shows how Roosevelt's New Deal was presented by the radical right traditionally opposed to 'big government' and joined by elements within the Catholic Church as both an artifact of Jews and an artifice to spread their influence (the Catholic Church in North America is also dealt with in detail by Mark Weitzman in his contribution). In Europe, and above all in Germany, this emancipatory moment quickly passed with the turn to regimes driven by popular antisemitism.[26]

The decade following the ending of the Second World War also proved to be a dismal one for Jews almost everywhere. The Communist, Arab and third world propaganda offensive against Israel during the Cold War were one whose advocates insisted that anti-Zionism was not a form of antisemitism. Yet the obsessive focus on Israel's misdeeds in a world of sinners raised and continues to raise doubts that the two antagonisms can be so clearly distinguished from one another. At the beginning of the twenty-first century, those who levy their critique against Israel will also say that they do not wish to see Jews dispossessed of their human rights and so on, but argue, as Marlowe does in her review, that Israel reduces the rights of others and worse that its very existence rests on an immoral foundation of racism, aggression and expulsion. This is an argument that recalls Picard's claim that 'We [antisemites] don't want to reduce their [Jews] rights, but we don't want them to reduce ours'.[27] In another words, the Jews pose the original group danger and this calls for a response; a familiar trope in the arsenal of antisemite writers worldwide.[28] The lethal logic of this position in contemporary politics is discussed by Elhanan Yakira.

The origin of this volume, an international conference in Dublin in November 2010 convened by the Holocaust Education Trust Ireland, was a response to what we have been discussing thus far as it relates to Ireland—a country where *informed* debate on the Arab–Israeli conflict or historical consciousness in relation to Holocaust is conspicuous by their absence, and where expressions of antisemitism, intended or otherwise, are never too far from the surface of public discourse. In 2009, at the height of the notorious Holocaust denier Bishop Williamson affair, a prominent Irish journalist, Kevin Myers, wrote an ill-conceived column in which he not only defended the bishop's right to 'free speech' but also proceeded to engage in a bizarre if not nonsensical semantic game of what constitutes 'Holocaust' and its denial. Although the newspaper had to issue a public apology for the piece, the journalist himself remained unrepentant, further quibbling with the idea of Holocaust denial in a later issue of the newspaper.[29] Myers' articles exposed him as a charlatan in matters connected to this episode in history. But at the same time, his confused views also can be taken as symptomatic of a wider confusion over the issue of Holocaust denial, its trivialization and its relationship to current forms of antisemitism.

Ostensibly in the cause of 'free speech', Myers used the Williamson controversy to in fact attack what he clearly sees as the authoritarian traits of European liberalism. His real intention was not to have an intelligent discussion on the issue of Holocaust denial but merely to piggyback onto the public interest in Williamson in order to promote a different (mainly anti-European Union) agenda. While Myers, like many of his generation who have moved from student left-wing radicalism to the libertarian right, strenuously countered any direct or indirect allegation that he was in fact a Holocaust denier (in spite of his choice to state this very fact in the article), his article betrays all the hallmarks of what Juliane Wetzel in her contribution sees as an increasingly common practice of trivializing the Holocaust through its appropriation in aid of other causes that in so doing ultimately borders on a form of 'soft denial', to borrow the term coined by Deborah Lipstadt. Myers is not the first journalist to play with fire. Within months of publishing his article, and after two abortive attempts by student debating bodies at Trinity College Dublin (mid-1980s) and University College Cork (2009) to invite the notorious and convicted British Holocaust denier David Irving to speak, Irish national television provided Irving with a platform on its late evening talk show, hosted by the popular radio and television presenter Pat Kenny. For balance, the distinguished historian Robert Gerwarth, newly arrived at University College Dublin, was also invited onto the show to 'debate' with Irving, a skilled obfuscator of the truth. Irving displayed the classic trait of 'perpetrator' (in this instance of lies about the Holocaust) cast as 'victim' of illiberal free speech laws designed to protect the interest of 'international Jewry'.[30] It is not our concern to judge the outcome of this so-called debate, but we should note that a number of the comments posted on the web media site 'Youtube' demonstrated sympathy with Irving's views and some even expressed rampant Jew-hatred.

What Myers' article (and to a lesser extent the television encounter between Irving and Gerwarth) demonstrates is that while antisemitism since the defeat of Nazi Germany in 1945 had traditionally been associated with neo-Nazis and other extremist groups on the political fringes, more recently albeit in veiled form it has moved closer to the middle ground in some European societies. In North America in particular, it is not unusual for some campus professors such as the now retired psychology professor Kevin Macdonald from the University of California at Long Beach to abuse the platform of academic freedom to churn out thinly disguised but clever anti-Jewish propaganda under the mantel of 'scholarly research', mostly published over the worldwide web.[31] With the development of the Internet, classic conspiracy theories and lies about the 'Jewish conspiracy' are disseminated around the globe with unprecedented speed. Indeed, it is probably the case that the Internet now is the main vehicle for the spread of both antisemitism and islamophobia. Pernicious material is easily made available by radical right groups consciously targeting youth.[32] Juliane Wetzel explores some of the issues arising from this development, arguing that it is the responsibility of web platforms to pursue a more rigorous policy to block such material. In addition to this, there has also been a shift in the nature of expressions of both antisemitism and Holocaust denial. Today, antisemitism is expressed via surrogate discourses, not least that pertaining to the Israeli–Palestinian conflict. Like Irving, who has been exposed in a British court of law as a denier, Myers, who claims not to be a denier, is nonetheless loathe to employ the term 'Holocaust' when talking about the Nazi genocide of European Jewry since according to him the event does not correspond to the original meaning of the word. This tendency to dilute language, to veer toward a linguistic relativism, is increasingly common in practices of Holocaust denial, intentional or otherwise, as Wetzel argues.[33]

Modern political antisemitism is recent; its first incarnation allegedly minted by the journalist Wilhelm Marr in the late nineteenth century. But Judeophobia and Jew-hatred have a long and multifaceted lineage. Thus while Birnbaum sees its emergence as a consequence of modern nation-building, its roots cannot be pinpointed to any single factor. Christian Wiese and Mark Weitzman in their contributions draw attention to Christian sources of antisemitism and its relationship to Holocaust denial. In so doing, they both reflect and add to a large body of scholarship of recent decades that draws renewed attention to the importance of anti-Jewish themes in Christianity for Jew-hatred in Nazi ideology before and during the Holocaust.[34] Weitzman offers a fascinating and disturbing discussion of the anti-Semitism in the theology of radical Catholic traditionalists in the Society of Saint Pius X (SSPX) including Bishops Bernard Fellay and Richard Williamson and in the writings of the Irish priest Denis Fahey whose views continue to influence members of the SSPX. Weitzman suggests that the rejection of antisemitism to emerge from the Second Vatican Council in 1965 is a development that faces a continuing challenge from the weight of centuries of theological doctrine.[35] In a similar vein, Christian Wiese's contribution addresses 'the profoundly disturbing recognition that this genocide occurred in a heartland of Christian Western culture—which from a purely Christian perspective is a cause for profound shame and dismay'. He argues that this fact alone means the Christian Churches have to adopt a more assertive role in resisting apologetics about the past and to counter the still present tendency to relativize historical guilt. This requires, according to Wiese, a self-critical approach in countering entrenched ideas within the Christian tradition that veer toward a 'teaching of contempt'. As Wiese points out, the Churches have so far failed to address these issues and have until now not come to terms with their 'failure in the face of the inhumanity of the Nazi regime'.

Historians have not lost sight of the role Christians played in the anti-Nazi resistance within Germany and in the opposition to Nazism in the USA, Britain and in Occupied Europe before and during the Second World War. Nor do they overlook the fact that many Christians risked their lives (and indeed, gave their lives) to save Jews in the face of the Nazis' uncompromising genocidal persecution. Nevertheless, Wiese and Weitzman are among scholars who in recent decades have rightly drawn our attention to the Christian theological continuities that in their radicalized form underpinned the antisemitism that culminated in the Holocaust. In the face of this scholarship, historians who neglect the contribution of Christianity ideology to Jew-hatred in twentieth-century Europe might rightly be criticized for offering a complacent view of the multiple continuities of European Christianity.

But as we have noted, the realm of antisemitic ideology also has its concrete material contexts and sometimes it is difficult to distinguish between the two, as Pierre Birnbaum, in his chapter on the role of Jews in FDR's administration, shows. As we saw, the rhetoric of anti-'big-government' ideology dovetailed with a barely concealed antisemitism that was also articulated through an extreme Christian ideology, notably through such organizations as the America First Movement and its notoriously antisemitic leader and propagandist Father Coughlin. Since the final decade of the twentieth century, at the very latest, this Christian-based antisemitism has been superseded by the emergence of radical Islamic politics infused with an unremitting antizionism. Bassam Tibi traces the intellectual lineage of radical Islamic antisemitism from its Judeophobic origins to its present violent form to offer a robust dismissal of acceptance in some quarters of what he calls a 'palliative' response among left liberals to Islamic outrage over Israel. As Tibi shows, such an approach only serves to delegitimize Israel, and by extension, Jews, a conclusion supported by the philosopher Elhanan Yakira in his 'five reflections' in the final section to the volume. Nevertheless, the origins of modern Islamic antisemitism are to be found in the Second World War, as Jeffrey Herf argues in his contribution.[36] Here a convergence of Arab nationalism hostile to Zionism and traditional tropes common to Western antisemitism, such as Jewish conspiracy for world dominion, have become intertwined. The Mufti of Jerusalem, Haj Amin al-Husseini, has been the pivotal (if sometimes overrated) figure in this development.[37] The modern problem of Palestine/Israel dates to these turbulent years, with many of the arguments and suggested solutions, such as a bistate answer to resolving the conflict, having already been aired in 1943 by Hannah Arendt.[38] The irony here is that such calls for an accommodation between Arab and Jew at the height of the Holocaust has been wholly subverted with the inversion of the historical reality of the Holocaust as Israel's critics and enemies, Esther Webman argues, appropriate its memory to serve the vilification of Israel with the outcome being its ultimate denial through destruction.

***

As the German political scientist Manfred Gerstenfeld notes the '"new" anti-Semitism is more a continuation and development, than an innovation. Few people realize how rampant anti-Semitism and discrimination of the Jews were in post-Holocaust Europe, and how the legacy of that period laid the basis for today's resurgence of European anti-Semitism. When exposing the persistent anti-Semitic character of many current European attacks on Israel, examples taken from Europe's recent history must play a major role'.[39]

Gerstenfeld's observation draws attention to the long history of contemporary antisemitism in the shadow of the Holocaust: and the two cannot be easily segregated, nor should they be. The presence of antisemitism today, especially in its radical Islamist version with its anti-Israel/anti-Zionist tinge, is European in origin and dates from the Second World War.[40] Thus Katzenstein's observation with which we opened this introduction deserves further consideration in its own right, even if it is beyond the scope of the present volume. Her report anticipates Deborah Lipstadt's opening comments to this volume where she calls for continued vigilance and for greater educational awareness. Holocaust denial from its earliest incarnation as Nazi subterfuge (through both linguistic means and physical erasure of evidence) to its current forms of either 'hard' or 'soft' denial, to Holocaust 'inversion', to calls for the destruction of Jews' right to self-determination in their own state, is concomitant to the original crime of genocide. The trivialization of its memory for contemporary social and political purposes that frequently attack the liberal state also call for greater historical awareness of the immensity of the original crime; awareness of the complex relationship between Islam and Judaism now overlain by geopolitical concerns and ideological struggles that distort that relationship also call for greater understanding. But the lesson is also of another type. Robert Jan van Pelt in his personal reflections on Holocaust denial shows how the need to engage the pseudo-scholarship of Holocaust deniers stimulated him to dig deeper into the minute details of the technical processes of mass murder, reaffirming beyond doubt the existence and purpose of the crematoria in Auschwitz. Acting as an expert witness for the defense in the landmark Irving v. Lipstadt libel case heard in the English High Court led to both a deepening and a sharpening of his own awareness as an historian. Van Pelt, like Pierre Vidal-Naquet in his confrontation with Holocaust denial in France in the 1970s, sees his response to Holocaust denial as a crucial reaffirmation of the commitment of scholars to establishing facts and finding truths about the past. This desideratum should serve as a foundation for an understanding of the present in order to forge a better informed and more enlightened future.

In the period since the contributors to this volume gathered in Dublin in 2010, Holocaust denial has continued to persist in some quarters and especially in Iran and the Arab countries; and while blatant denial has become rarer in terrestrial Europe (but not on American campuses!), it remains rampant in the new alternate world of the web. Meanwhile the boundary between antagonism to Israel and antisemitism has become ever more blurred, rendering liberal 'middle ground' or leftist criticism of Israeli government policy a surrogate antisemitism. The contributions to this volume represent an exploration of the past as well as contemporary events; their conclusions might point to that better world.[41]

Notes

1. Wiener Library, London, MF Doc 54/Reel 8, Doc., 525: N. Katzenstein, 'Report of Jews in the Liberated Countries, July 1945', p. 2. See also: Koppel S. Pinson, 'Antisemitism in the Post-War World', *Jewish Social Studies*, Vol. 7, No. 2 (Apr., 1945), pp. 99–118, and the informative case study by János Kovács, 'Neo-Antisemitism in Hungary', *Jewish Social Studies*, Vol. 8, No. 3 (Jul., 1946), pp. 147–160.

2. Jan T. Gross, *Fear. Anti-Semitism in Poland after Auschwitz. An Essay in Historical Interpretation* (Princeton and Oxford, 2006), p. 93, gives the figure 42 of those buried, see pp. 81–117 passim. Bozena Szaynok, 'The Jewish Pogrom in Kielce, July 1946—New Evidence', in: *Intermarium* Vol. 1, Nr. 3 (1997), cites 'over forty' killed, http://ece.columbia.edu/files/ece/images/kielce.html, accessed 12/05/2015. David Engel, "Patterns of Anti-Jewish Violence in Poland, 1944–1946," *Yad Vashem Studies* Vol. XXVI (Jerusalem, 1998), pp. 43–85.
3. Anne Applebaum, 'Cruelty and injustice in postwar Europe' in *The Jewish Chronicle Online*, accessed at: http://www.thejc.com/comment-and-debate/comment/90035/cruelty-and-injustice-postwar-europe; Daniel Trilling, 'Britain's last anti-Jewish riots: Why have the 1947 riots been forgotten?', *New Statesman*, 23 May 2012.
4. As well as Gross, *Fear*, pp. 31–80, see David Bankier (ed.), *The Jews Are Coming Back* (Jerusalem: Yad Vashem, 2005).
5. There are also examples where this was not the case and home and property was returned to their rightful owners, Eva Schloss, *After Auschwitz* (London: Hodder & Stoughton).
6. Cited in Laurence Rees, Auschwitz. *The Nazis and the 'Final Solution'* (London, BBC Books, 2005), p. 350.
7. Ido de Haan, 'Paths of Normalization after the Persecution of the Jews: The Netherlands, France, and West Germany in the 1950s', in Richard Bessel and Dirk Schumann eds., *Life after Death. Approaches to a Cultural and Social History of Europe during the 1940s and 1950s* (Cambridge, Cambridge University Press, 2003), p. 72.
8. Schloss, *After Auschwitz*, p. 163. See also the essays dispelling the myth of a tolerant Europe in Manfred Gerstenfeld, *Europe's Crumbling Myths: The Post Holocaust Origins of Today's Anti-Semitism* (Jerusalem: Jerusalem Center for Public Affairs/Yad Vashem/World Jewish Congress, 2003).
9. http://www.coe.int/en/web/commissioner/-/europe-still-haunted-by-antisemiti-1. See also: Charles Asher Small (ed.), *Global Antisemitism: A Crisis of Modernity. Volume IV: Islamism and the Arab World* (New York, 2013).
10. www.holocausttaskforce.org/about-the-itf-declaration.html. For two succinct introductory overviews in English and in German see

Steven Beller, *Antisemitism: A Very Short Introduction* (Oxford: Oxford University Press, 2007) and Werner Bergmann, *Geschiche des Antisemitismus*, third edition (Munich: C.H. Beck, 2006).

11. There had been an earlier similar attack on the synagogue in Brussels—with a copycat attack in Paris—in September 1982, *Lakeland Ledger* 19 September 1982. There was also a similar gun attack at the US Holocaust Memorial Museum in Washington on June 10, 2009.
12. Arthur Arnheim, 'Anti-Semitism after the Holocaust—Also in Denmark' in *Jewish Political Studies Review* 15:3–4 (Fall 2003) accessed at http://www.jcpa.org/phas/phas-arnheim-f03.htm. Manfred Gerstenfeld 'The Academic Boycott Against Israel' in *Jewish Political Studies Review* 15:3–4 (Fall 2003) accessed at http://www.jcpa.org/phas/phas-gersten-f03.htm
13. http://www.bbc.com/news/world-europe-24857207; for individual examples: http://www.israelnationalnews.com/News/News.aspx/158095#!; http://greece.greekreporter.com/2014/05/31/vandals-desecrate-jewish-cemetery-in--thessaloniki/; http://www.jpost.com/Jewish-World/Jewish-News/Vandals-desecrate-Jewish-cemetery-in-Russia; http://www.jpost.com/Jewish-World/Jewish-Features/Two-British-13-year-olds-arrested-in-major-cemetery-desecration-360882
14. The only comprehensive approach to this so far is the international conference on Global Antisemitism: A Crisis of Modernity convened by the Institute for the Study of Global Antisemitism and Policy at Yale University in August 2010, and whose papers were subsequently published in five slim volumes edited by Charles Asher Small, the Institute's director. It is a pure coincidence that this conference took place more or less contemporaneously to the Dublin Conference.
15. These can be followed via podcasts at the Website of the Holocaust Education Trust Ireland: http://www.hetireland.org
16. http://nctc.gov/site/groups/hamas.html. Jeffrey Herf, ed. *Convergence and Divergence: Anti-Semitism and Anti-Zionism in Historical Perspective* (Oxford and New York: Routledge/Taylor and Francis, 2007), pp. x–xix.
17. Laura Marlowe, 'Fear and Loathing: Palestinians pay the price of history', *The Irish Times*, Saturday, September 13, 2014, p. 11.

18. Jonathan Judaken, 'So what's new? Rethinking the 'new antisemitism in a global age', in: *Patterns of Prejudice*, Vol. 42, Nos. 4–5 (2008), pp. 531–560; Robert Fine, 'Fighting with phantoms: a contribution to the debate on anti-Semitism in Europe', Patterns of Prejudice, Vol. 43, No. 5 (2009), pp. 459–479.
19. For a challenging view, see Brian Klug, 'Is Europe a lost cause? The European debate on antisemitism and the Middle East conflict', *Patterns of Prejudice*, Vol. 39, No.1, (2005), pp. 46–59.
20. Meir Litvak and Esther Webman, 'Israel and Antisemitism' in Albert S. Lindemann and Richard S. Levy (eds.), *Antisemitism: A History* (Oxford and New York: Oxford University Press, 2010), pp. 237–249; Jehuda Reicharz, Monika Schwarz-Friesel, Evytar Friesel (eds.), *Akueller Antisemitismus—Ein Phänomen der Mitte* (Berlin, New York: de Gruyter, 2010); Stephen H. Norwood, *Antisemitism and the American Far-Left* (Cambridge: Cambridge University Press, 2013). Jocelyn Hellig, *The Holocaust and Antisemitism: A Short History* (Oxford: Oneworld Publications, 2003). For a more alarmist and sensationalist approach, see Daniel Goldhagen, *The Devil That Never Dies: The Rise and Threat of Global Antisemitism* (New York: Little, Brown and Company, 2013). For further recent examples of antisemitism see the interesting blog site: http://antisemitism-europe.blogspot.ie/2014_08_01_archive.html
21. See Robert Wistrich, *A Lethal Obsession: Antisemitism—From Antiquity to the Global Jihad* (New York: Random House, 2010); Richard J. Evans, *Lying about Hitler* (New York: Basic Books, 2002) and Robert Jan van Pelt in this volume.
22. Charles Asher Small, 'Introduction', *Global Antisemitism: A Crisis of Modernity, Vol. III: Global Antisemitism: Past and Present* (New York, 2013), p. 13; see also the contributions to idem (ed.), *Global Antisemitism: A Crisis of Modenrity Volume II: The Intellectual Environment* (New York, 2013).
23. Hermann Bahr, *Der Antisemitismus* (Berlin: Fischer Verlag, 1894), pp. 28–9. See above all, Peter Pulzer, *The Rise of Political Anti-Semitism in Germany* (New York, 1964).
24. David Vital, *A People Apart. The Jews in Europe 1789–1939* (New York and Oxford, 1999), See the useful summary by Kenneth L. Marcus, 'The Definition of Antisemitism' in Charles Asher

Small (ed.), *Global Antisemitism: A Crisis of Modernity, Volume I: Conceptual Approaches* (New York, 2013), pp. 99–111; and the stimulating essay by Catherine Chatterley, 'The Antisemitic Imagination' in ibid., pp. 79–83.

25. On the negative role of Enlightenment modernity, see Zygmunt Bauman, *Modernity and the Holocaust* (Cornell: Cornell University Press, 1989, 2000).
26. For Germany, see Peter Pulzer, 'Jews and Nation-Building in Germany 1815–1918', in *Year Book of the Leo Baeck Institute*, 41 (1996), pp. 199–224.
27. Ibid., interview with Edmond Picard, p. 165.
28. On this point, see Robert Pois, 'Kevin MacDonald: Separation and Its Discontents: Toward an Evolutionary Theory of Anti-Semitism', in *IDEA: a journal of social issues* November 1, 1998, vol. 3 no. 4, http://www.ideajournal.com/articles.php?id=18, accessed 20/09/2013; and George Michael, 'Professor Kevin MacDonald's Critique of Judaism: Legitimate Scholarship or the Intellectualization of Anti-Semitism?' in *Journal of Church & State* 48 (4), 2006, pp. 779–806. For an early socio-psychological analysis: Gustav Ichheiser, 'The Jews and Antisemitism, in *Sociometry*, Vol. 9, No. 1 (Feb., 1946), pp. 92–108.
29. Kevin A. Myers, 'I'm a holocaust denier, but I also believe the Nazis planned the extermination of the Jewish people', The Irish Independent, 4 March 2009, and 'The victims of the Nazi programme of genocide are dead. They cannot be 'offended', The Irish Independent, 1 April 2009.
30. http://www.youtube.com/watch?v=DMk2yyetJaQ
31. Macdonald appeared on behalf of the Holocaust denier David Irving during his lawsuit against Deborah Lipstadt in 2000. See van Pelt in this volume.
32. Ralf Palandt (ed.), *Rechtsextremismus, Rassismus und Antisemitismus in Comics* (e-book, Archiv der Jugendkulturen, 2012).
33. Myers' semantic contortion should not be confused with a legitimate discussion among scholars on the use of Holocaust or Shoah when referring to the Nazi genocide of the Jews.
34. See, for example, Doris Bergen, *The Twisted Cross: The German Christian Movement in the Third Reich* (Chapel Hill: University

of North Carolina Press, 1996); Robert P. Erickson, *Complicity in the Holocaust: Churches and Universities in Nazi Germany* (Cambridge and New York: Cambridge University Press, 2012); Saul Friedländer, *Nazi Germany and the Jews, 1933–1945, Abridge Edition* (New York: Harper, 2009); Susannah Heschel and Robert P. Erickson, eds., *Betrayal: German Churches and the Holocaust* (Augsburg Fortress, 1999); Susannah Heschel, *The Aryan Jesus: Christian Theologians and the Bible in Nazi* Germany (Princeton: Princeton University Press, 2010); Michael Phayer, *The Catholic Church and the Holocaust, 1930–1965* (Bloomington, IN: Indiana University Press, 2001); Christopher Probst, *Demonizing the Jews: Luther and the Protestant Church in Nazi* Germany (Bloomington, IN: Indiana University Press, 2012); Richard Steigmann-Gall, *The Holy Reich: Nazi Conceptions of Christianity, 1919–1945* (Cambridge and New York: Cambridge University Press, 2004); Robert Wistrich, *A Lethal Obsession: Anti-Semitism from Antiquity to the Global Jihad* (New York: Random House, 2010).

35. On the challenge to long-standing Catholic doctrine about the Jews, see John Connelly, *From Enemy to Brother: The Revolution in Catholic Teaching on the Jews, 1933–1965* (Cambridge, MA: Harvard University Press, 2012). For a more polemical look at the role of the Catholic Church see: Daniel Goldhagen, *A Moral Reckoning: The Role of the Catholic Church in the Holocaust and its Unfulfilled Duty of Repair* (New York: Vintage, 2007).
36. For a useful discussion and key literature, see Norman A. Stillman, 'Antisemitism in the Arab and Islamic World' in Lindemann and Levy (eds.), *Antisemitism*, pp. 212–221, here 219–20.
37. Klaus Gensicke, *The Mufti of Jerusalem and the Nazis: The Berlin Years* (London and Portland Or.: Vallentine Mitchell, 2011) orig. 2007; Klaus-Michael Mallmann and Martin Cüppers, *Halbmond und Hakenkreuz: das Dritte Reich, die Araber und Palästina* (Darmstadt: Wiss. Buchgesellscahft, 2006), pp. 114–118.
38. Hannah Arendt, 'Kann die jüdisch-arabische Frage gelöst werden?' in *Aufbau* 17 and 31 December 1943 reprinted in *Vor Antisemitismus ist man nur noch auf dem Mond sicher* (Munich, Zurich, 2004), pp. 117–125.

39. 'Europe's crumbling Myths' at: http://www.jcpa.org/mg-myths.htm
40. Stillman, 'Antisemitism in the Arab and Islamic World', op.cit.
41. See the insightful comments by Charles Asher, 'Introduction', in: *Global Antisemitism Volume III: Global Antisemitism: Past and Present*, op. cit., pp. 14–15.

PART I

Two Preliminary Observations

CHAPTER 2

A Few Observations on Holocaust Denial and Antisemitism

Deborah Lipstadt

I begin with a cautionary remark. My observations should not be construed as a suggestion that Holocaust denial is a clear and *present* danger. Currently it is a small but persistent phenomenon. It is engaged in by disparate groups and individuals. Far more individuals worldwide engage in the study of the Holocaust than engage in its denial. But the latter does, however, have potentially potent implications for the future. This is particularly so because deniers have become exceptionally adept at the use of the Internet. Moreover, the Internet is particularly well suited for the dissemination of conspiracy theories, Holocaust denial among them.[1] In these preliminary observations to this volume, I would like to explore the inexorable connection between Holocaust denial and anti-Semitism and argue that denial is nothing other than a form of anti-Semitism. In addition, it contrasts traditional Holocaust denial, which I call "hard-core" denial, with a newer variant, which I call "soft-core" denial. Therefore, I offer my observations not as a cry of alarm, but rather as a call for sustained and serious caution.

D. Lipstadt (✉)
Emory University, Atlanta, GA, USA

A. McElligott, J. Herf (eds.), *Antisemitism Before and Since the Holocaust*, DOI 10.1007/978-3-319-48866-0_2

The Basic Premises of Hard-Core Denial

The basic premises of traditional or "hard-core" Holocaust deniers, people such as David Irving, Robert Faurisson, and even Iran's former leader Mahmoud Ahmadinejad, include:

1. There was no attempt by the Third Reich to wipe out the Jews of Europe.
2. Some Jews may have suffered and even been killed but they were not singled out for mass annihilation.
3. Those Jews who were persecuted were deserving of what was done to them. German Jews were engaged in such nefarious activities that the German regime's hostility toward them was legitimate. Those Jews who were killed by the *Einsatzgruppen* were guilty of being spies and partisans.[2]
4. Those Jews who were incarcerated in concentration camps were placed there by the Germans for their own protection, to save them from the righteous anger and hostility of German "Aryans."
5. The number 6,000,000 is an exaggeration which was fabricated by Jews in the postwar period.
6. Gas chambers are a scientific impossibility. Therefore, the claims that they existed are false.
7. People who purport to be survivors of the concentration and death camps are sociopaths, liars, or doing this for financial gain.

As is evident from these assertions, hard-core deniers are those who deny the facts—the well-established and documented facts—of the Holocaust.[3] In short, they are saying, "It did not happen. The Jews perpetrated this myth."

Responding to Holocaust Deniers: A Rational Perspective

One can expose the irrationality—if not absurdity—of deniers' claims in a variety of ways. One can "follow the footnotes" back to their sources. This is what my legal team and I did in the *David Irving vs. Penguin UK and Deborah Lipstadt*, when the Holocaust denier David Irving brought a libel case against me in London in 1996 that ended four years later with a resounding judgment in my favor.[4] With the help of outstanding historians, we demonstrated to the court that David Irving's claims were, in the words of our lead historical witness, Cambridge historian Richard Evans, "a tissue of lies." Evans told the court

> Not one of his books, speeches or articles, not one paragraph, not one sentence in any of them, can be taken on trust as an accurate representation of its historical subject. All of them are completely worthless as history, because Irving cannot be trusted anywhere, in any of them, to give a reliable account of what he is talking or writing about. It may seem an absurd semantic dispute to deny the appellation of "historian" to someone who has written two dozen books or more about historical subjects. But if we mean by historian someone who is concerned to discover the truth about the past, and to give as accurate a representation of it as possible, then Irving is not a historian.[5]

We demonstrated to the court that, as regards evidence, deniers fabricate, invent, distort, and blatantly misinterpret its clear-cut meaning. In a 350-page decision, the judge affirmed our contentions about Irving and his misuse of historical evidence.

There is, however, another way to demonstrate the irrationality and fallacies in Holocaust denial without relying on documents. When addressing the topic with my students, I ask them: "In order for deniers to be correct in their contention that the Holocaust was a myth, who must be wrong?"[6] Using a deductive approach, they quickly produce a list of suspects. They generally begin with the victims, those who say "This is my story; this is what happened to me." They know there are inconsistencies in survivors stories but recognize that the witnesses to any traumatic event will often be confused about the ancillary details, but not about the core event. Salman Rushdie, in his memoir on his years in hiding because of Muslim threats on his life, recalled being told by a high-ranking British intelligence officer: "'When there is no variation in the story then we are one hundred percent certain it's a fake.' Human beings telling the truth never told the story quite the same way twice."[7] Moreover, the victims' arrival at places such as Auschwitz-Birkenau was designed to be chaotic and unnerving.

Deniers try to raise questions about survivors' reports, not just by focusing on inconsistencies in them but also by arguing that the Germans were so efficient and meticulous in their work that, had they actually been intent on wiping out the Jews, they would have ensured that none lived to tell the tale. Germany would never have allowed the survival of witnesses. After sharing this assertion with my students, I ask them to isolate the irrational in it. With noticeable alacrity, they observe that the Germans were also intent on winning the war and yet they did not succeed at that. In fact, one could legitimately contend, they were even more intent on winning the war than on the immediate annihilation of the Jews. Military victory would have enabled them to complete the killing of not only the Jews but also a myriad of other groups they were intent on eliminating. If they did not win the war, why then should we assume that they would have succeeded at everything else they intended to do, including killing survivors of the death camps?

But, the students recognize, that it is not only the victims who must be wrong in order for deniers to be right. The "bystanders," people such as the Poles in villages around the camps and the Polish train engineer whom Claude Lanzmann interviewed in his epic documentary, *Shoah* watched or, in the case of the engineer, drove the trains into the camp day after day and came away empty. They knew that there was not enough room in those camps to absorb all those being brought to the camps. Those who lived nearby could smell the burning flesh. They, of course, were not the only bystanders who offered information. There were Poles such as Jan Karski who, after sneaking into both a ghetto and an extermination camp, brought his eyewitness report to both London and Washington.[8] There were Germans such as the industrialist Eduard Schulte, the head of a mining company which had a branch near Auschwitz and who learned from SS officers what was taking place in the camp. He gave the information on the gassing to the representative of the World Jewish Congress in Switzerland, Gerhard Riegner.[9] Another "bystander" was the renegade SS officer, Kurt Gerstein, who witnessed a gassing in Belzec and then told a Swedish diplomat about it.[10]

At this point, I urge my students to think yet of others who must be wrong for the deniers' assertions to be right. I tell them that, from a deductive or forensic perspective, this last source may be the most critically important. Not only have those in this category not denied the killings but also they have affirmed that they happened. Students soon realize that the answer for this category is the perpetrators. They are the best situated to challenge the deniers' claims. At no war crime trial since the end of World War II has a defendant ever tried to defend himself (and in a few rare cases, herself) by arguing that the Holocaust did not happen. They have offered a variety of other justifications: "I did not do it." "I was just following orders." "I had no option but to participate." Such was the case at the Eichmann trial (1961), the Frankfurt Auschwitz trials (1963), and at every other World War II war criminal trial. Simply put, perpetrators, both those who did the actual killing and those who gave the instructions to kill, have never even suggested that it did not happen. Yet deniers, who were not there, do so.

Deniers, ever resilient, have an explanation for the perpetrators' failure to deny the Holocaust. These defendants, they observe, were being tried by their former enemies. The latter made it quite clear that, had the defendants refused to "admit" to these crimes, they would have been punished severely. Such contentions ignore a basic question. What could the defendants gain by falsely admitting to participating in a horrendous crime, one which might well bear the death penalty? Confessing to such wrongdoings would have only guaranteed that they would be dealt severe punishment, possibly death.

It is not only individual perpetrators who admitted to this wrongdoing. Germany [West] accepted responsibility for its impact in the form of reparations. Why would a nation admit to such a crime, particularly one that was destined to force it to wear an unparalleled historical badge of shame? Deniers contend that the Jews were so successful in spreading the myth of the Holocaust and in planting evidence that Germany had no choice but to acquiesce to its supposed guilt *despite being innocent*. Acknowledging guilt for this horrific crime was the only way Germany could be readmitted to the "family of [civilized] nations." Had it denied its complicity, it would have earned an even greater degree of the world's contempt and been relegated to pariah status. In order to avoid this, Germany had to shoulder both a moral and a financial burden. It had to pay financial reparations to the victims as well as the State of Israel and, possibly even more significantly, accept abiding responsibility for this nefarious deed.

I point out to my students that the myriad of documents which attest to the mass killing of Jews, by both shooting and gassing, could not, despite claims to the contrary by deniers, be easily forged. German official documents bore extensive identification numbers, file designations, and a series of other markings. A forged document would have had to bear a number that corresponded to those that preceded it and followed it in the file and the "genuine" document which bore that number would have to be eliminated. The forged document would have had to be in the same typeface and have been typed in the same strength typewriter ribbon. Moreover, copies of the same document would have had to have been planted in other files. For example, a letter would have had to have been placed in the recipient's file and a copy of the letter in the sender's file. In short, documents of this nature cannot be created out of thin air and produced en masse.

Holocaust Denial: Age-Old Anti-Semitism in New Clothing

The "explanation" by deniers as to why Germany accepted responsibility for this massive crime when, in fact, it never committed it, deftly draws on enduring anti-Semitic stereotypes. Deniers claim that Jews created this hoax in order to win the world's sympathy which they then used to secure reparations from Germany and establish the State of Israel.[11]

At the heart of these deniers' claims is the notion that Jews are not the victims but the victimizers. They compelled Germany to pay billions in reparations, forced the world to grant them a state, and displaced another people. Behind the scenario that Jews created this vast myth in order to get a state and enrich themselves is the traditional anti-Semitic depiction of Jews: Jews engage in secret, behind-the-scenes manipulations in order to win political and financial benefit even if it comes at the expense of the majority population. This stereotype finds its roots, of course, in the story of the crucifixion of Jesus as portrayed by the *New Testament*. That event became the template for millennia of anti-Semitic charges which incorporated elements of the deicide myth: a small number of Jews harm a large number of Christians (or any other ethnic or religious group) for the purpose of their own material and financial gain.[12]

Someone who is inclined to believe that these stereotypes are rooted in reality, might consider the charge that Jews have connived to create this myth in order to wrest great sums of money from Germany and to dispel a people from their land to be rational. It would "make sense" to the anti-Semite. This is precisely the modus operandi *used* by deniers to spread their wares. In fact, one could argue that it essentially argues that the Jews were not murdered by the Germans but, given their evil ways, were deserving of having been killed.

Denial: A Wolf in Sheep's Clothing

For many years, most Holocaust denial arguments were crudely presented. Reminiscent of Third Reich era publications, they were filled with Nazi symbols and included pornographic drawings of Jews. They were worthy of the Nazi publisher Julius Streicher and seemed designed to appeal to skinheads, fascists and neo-Nazis. Then in the late 1970s, deniers adopted a dramatically different and far more efficacious tactic, one designed to draw to denial a more educated and sophisticated audience and to present denial, particularly to its detractors, as a balanced claim that deserved serious consideration. While this new tactic might not convince the detractors of denial, it would, deniers assumed, make it harder for them to dismiss it out of hand as anti-Semitic canards.

Rather than depict themselves as neo-Nazis who wished to defend—if not resurrect—the Third Reich deniers cast themselves as scholars engaged in a reasoned pursuit of historical truth. They were "revisionists" dedicated to ferreting out mistakes in history and revising accepted but incorrect truths. This change in strategy was associated with the founding of the California-based Institute for Historical Review (IHR). The institute's primary funder was Willis Carto, who was also the founder of Noontide Press, a company which published pseudo-scholarly books on the superiority of white people as well as anti-Semitic works.[13] The conferences organized by the IHR were structured to project the aura of legitimate academic enterprises. The IHR published a journal which mimicked the appearance of mainstream academic journals. The IHR cast itself as a proponent, not of denial, but of historical revisionism, a long-standing and respected methodology. Historical revisionists question accepted historical conclusions. This is a common and well-accepted practice. Historians engage in this process based on, among other things, the discovery of new evidence or the course of subsequent events. However, even the most basic perusal of IHR materials gave the lie to this claim of being interested in a broad array of topics. They were devoted almost in toto to Holocaust denial and other anti-Semitic diatribes. Moreover, when one dissects their claims and the evidence they offer for them, it becomes abundantly clear that their premise is based on fabrications and distortions.

Soft-Core Denial

In contrast to traditional deniers, soft-core deniers are those who do not overtly deny the facts of the Holocaust but who raise questions about it in a more covert fashion. They make false comparisons with the Holocaust and often do so for political ends. Their denials are "squishier," that is, they are harder to precisely define and consequently. Therefore, they are often more insidious. The terms "hardcore" and "soft core" are, of course, generally associated with pornography. It is not by chance that I choose these terms. From an historical, scholarly, and ethical perspective, denial is a form of pornography. I am reminded of what US Supreme Court Justice Potter Stewart said when deciding a case of pornography. "I cannot define it but I know it when I see it."[14] So too to some extent is the case with soft-core denial. Often it includes parallels between the Holocaust and other tragedies in a way that diminishes the former and aggrandizes the latter. I am not suggesting—in any manner, shape, or form—that one cannot compare and contrast the Holocaust to other tragedies. One can and one must make comparisons when studying history.[15] I disagree with those who argue that the comparing Holocaust to other tragedies diminishes its singularity. Such a stance makes historical inquiry impossible. My opposition to these kinds of false comparisons is not an argument about the unprecedented nature of the Holocaust. It is rather a question about whether the comparisons are historically valid.

These kind of false comparisons have permeated comments about Israel and the Palestinians. One can totally disagree with Israel's policies vis-à-vis the Palestinians and feel that much of the unrest there is Israel's fault. However to speak of a *genocide* of the Palestinians, as critics of Israel often do, is to misconstrue the reality of the political situation. Furthermore, one can feel that the Israeli army has acted in an unethical fashion. However, to speak of the "Nazi-like" behaviors of the Israeli army is to deny the reality of what is taking place today and, even more, to draw an utterly false comparison to what happened 70 years ago.

Other false comparisons may not necessarily fall into the category of denial. Rather than deny, they trivialize the Holocaust. Environmental activists (both those who are convinced by the idea of global warming and those who are not) have fallen back on Holocaust analogies. Opponents of abortion speak of the "abortion Holocaust." Animal activist compare the conditions in which animals are kept to concentration camps and, when they are consumed by humans, of a "Holocaust on your plate." Muslim leaders in Canada have compared governmental efforts to ban veils at citizenship hearings to laws against Jews in Nazi Germany.[16]

Even Jewish groups, fervently religious ones, have been guilty of this trivialization. In 2011, a group of *Haredim*, fervently religious Jews, pinned on yellow stars, put their children in striped uniforms, and paraded in the streets of Jerusalem protesting the government's attempt to stop gender separation on public transportation. They may believe that they have been discriminated against, but their analogizing their claim with the Holocaust was so beyond the pale that it brought down upon them a storm of criticism.[17] Jews at the other end of the cultural and religious spectrum have engaged in the same kind of trivialization. A number of years ago, the Jewish Museum in New York, arguably one of the premier Jewish cultural institutions in the world, mounted a show "Mirroring Evil." The exhibit included a concentration camp made out of Legos and the picture of a well-fed man holding a Diet Coke while surrounded by concentration camp victims.[18] While these cases are certainly not acts of denial per se, they can lead to a form of diminution of the seriousness of the Holocaust. If the Holocaust is used as an example for this wide variety of issues, it not only cheapens the significance of the event itself but also leads to a clouding of its importance as a marker in world history.

There are additional examples I wish to offer. One is supported by legitimate governments and the other by nameless and faceless groups on the Internet. In the former Soviet bloc countries, ultranationalist groups have successfully managed to equate Nazism with communism and have persuaded the European Union to do the same. They brought charges against Jews who escaped the ghettoes and joined Soviet-based resistance groups. This is not to suggest the peoples of Eastern Europe did not suffer—mightily so—under communism. They did. I do, however, question whether the Nazi attempt to annihilate the Jews is the equivalent of communism's horrendous mistreatment of the populations of these countries. Moreover, the groups pushing for the equation of the two are often the direct heirs of the very nationalist groups, for example, Latvians, Lithuanians, and Estonians, who cooperated with the Nazis in the annihilation of the Jews. By equating the two and asserting that the core of the Communist party was comprised of Jews, they are suggesting that what happened to the Jews was, in some fashion, a deserved punishment.[19]

The final example of Holocaust denial relies on the Internet for dissemination. A recent four-minute video typifies this kind of material. It begins with a shot of three-dimensional model of the gas chambers at Treblinka with the roof peeled back showing drawings of cadavers thrown around helter-skelter. A narrator speaks in a low, rather flat voice: (Bold is used to indicate emphasis by the narrator.)

> *Here's a model of the gas chamber. At Treblinka alone 750,000 allegedly died in a building like this in a period of roughly six months. To put it in perspective a large university has 30,000 students. The amount of people who went through this building is 25 times that. You would think that would* ***at least*** *warrant a double door.*

At this point two red flashing arrows point at the door.

And entering a hallway first? Why design it like ***that****? And then to take a hard right turn and go into a gas chamber and go into a gas chamber the size of a medium size bedroom?*

How about these design changes? ***SCRAP THE HALLWAY.*** *Get rid of these wall partitions. Make it into two large chambers: one here and one here.* [Squiggly lines erase the hallway and the part ions and two redlines show how the place could be divided into two large rooms. DL] *Put a set of double doors here and here. Make it on ground level.* ***NO STAIRWAY.*** *You could have guards out here and out here. Rather than here in this five foot hallway where the guards would have to put backs against the wall would have to put their guns to their chest just to let people get by.*

Yellow lines outlining double doors appear on the front of the structure. Red lines cross out the steps and X's are placed where the guards would stand.

Lastly make the building bigger so that it could hold the two thousand people which is the amount of people who would come into the camp in one transport. The model we've been looking at is the second gas chamber designed for the three camps (Belzec, Sobibor, and Treblinka) …

While a page of Raul Hilberg's, *The Destruction of European Jews,* is shown on the screen, the narrator notes that Hilberg described these as "massive structures" and then goes on to say in an "aside," "*well hardly massive structures as we have seen.*" A picture of Yitzchak Arad's book open to the page where he discusses this building is shown as the narrator continues.

And Yitzchak Arad writes in his book that "the new gas chambers that had been built in Belzec … were the model in the other two camps." So this design and all the problems that have been pointed out is supposedly the culmination of a lot of testing and experience. ***Hard to believe isn't it?***

The second segment of the video is entitled "Comparing Treblinka with the Population of San Francisco." The narrator observes, while a map of San Francisco is shown, "*so what they're saying is that the numerical equivalent to everyone in this city ascended that 3.5 foot narrow stairway, went into that narrow hall, and then went into one of the six bedroom sized gas chambers.*" (Meanwhile the camera pans across an aerial view of SF.) *But as you look at this expanse of San Francisco keep in mind the big picture that according to the story all these people were gassed then buried. Later they were dug up and cremated on outdoor fires.* ***It's kind of hard to believe isn't it?***[20]

This video and most of the over nine hours of other videos on the same site rarely, if ever, mention denial, make any overtly anti-Semitic statement, or aggrandize Nazism, anti-Semitism, or Hitler. Yet a person watching it could easily wonder whether the historical assertions about these gas chambers make any sense. I recently showed the video to a group of lawyers all of whom had been singled out as outstanding in their fields. None of them had a connection with deniers or sympathy with them. Yet a number asked me afterwards about the "problems" with the gas chamber structure and whether that might not "mean that the historians got it wrong." Their reaction exemplifies the efficacy of this soft-core approach. It has the potential to confuse even well-meaning people, who may not have the necessary background knowledge to this issue.[21]

Conclusion

Holocaust denial, as we have seen, can take many forms and can exist in the netherworld between trivialization and outright hard-core denial. In the coming years, as the time since the Holocaust grows longer and the number of eyewitnesses to the event grow far smaller, there is reason to believe that deniers will persist in their efforts. In fact, there is no reason to believe that the battle against denial can ever be fully "won." Anti-Semitism has persisted and, in certain locales, flourished even after one out of three Jews worldwide was murdered. Even today, Holocaust denial, as a variant of anti-Semitism, promises to have the same lengthy, if not unending, shelf life as some of the contributions that follow demonstrate.

Notes

1. Michael Whine, "Cyberhate, Anti-Semitism, and Counterlegislation," *Post-Holocaust and Anti-Semitism*, No. 47, August 2006; *Transparency and Conspiracy: Ethnographies of Suspicion in the New World Order*, Harry G. West and Todd Sanders, eds. [Durham: Duke University Press, 2003].
2. Because the reports prepared by the *Einsatzgruppen* leaders are so specific and plentiful, deniers cannot dismiss them as forgeries. Instead, they seek to justify the killing of the Jews by claiming that they were partisans, spies, war profiteers, and the like. *The Einsatzgruppen Reports: Selections from the Dispatches of the Nazi Death Squads' Campaign Against the Jews July 1941–January 1943*, Yitzhak Arad, Shmuel Krakowski, Shmuel Spector, eds. [translated by Stella Schossberger]. (New York, N.Y.: Holocaust Library, 1989).

3. This is not to suggest, of course, that there are not numerous aspects of the Holocaust which are debated by scholars and about which there is serious difference of opinion, for example, the date of the decision for the Final Solution or how the decision to murder the Jews came about.
4. Richard J. Evans, *Lying about Hitler: history, Holocaust, and the David Irving trial* (New York: Basic Books, 2001); Deborah Lipstadt, *History on Trial: My Day in Court with a Holocaust Denier,* (New York: Harper Collins, 2005); Robert Jan van Pelt, *The case for Auschwitz: evidence from the Irving trial* (Bloomington: Indiana University Press, 2002).
5. Richard Evans, "David Irving, Hitler and Holocaust Denial: Electronic Edition," http://www.hdot.org/en/trial/defense/evans/6. See also his: *Lying about Hitler.*
6. My appreciation to the late Paula Hyman for suggesting this approach.
7. Salman Rushdie, "Joseph Anton: A Memoir." Random House, 2012-09-18. iBooks, Chapter III, "Year Zero."
8. Jan Karski, *Story of a Secret State* (Boston: Houghton Mifflin Co., 1944).
9. Walter Laqueur & Richard Breitman, *Breaking the Silence* (New York: Simon and Schuster, 1986).
10. Saul Friedländer, *Kurt Gerstein: The Ambiguity of Good* (New York: Alfred A Knopf, 1969); Paul A. Levine, *Raoul Wallenberg in Budapest: Myth, History and Holocaust* (London; Portland, OR: Vallentine Mitchell, 2010).
11. Note that there is legitimate historical question as to whether the Holocaust led directly to the establishment of the State of Israel. There is good reason to argue that there would have been some form of a state without the Holocaust. Before World War II and the Final Solution, the British Peel Commission (1936) proposed the creation of a Jewish political entity. It is historically questionable, therefore, to link the establishment of the State of Israel to the Holocaust. However, the popularly accepted belief is that the two are directly linked and it is upon that popular belief that deniers premise their assertions.]
12. The fact that everyone in the deicide story was Jewish with the exception, of course, of the Romans who did the actual crucifixion, is immaterial to popular perceptions. Franklin H. Littell, *The*

Crucifixion of the Jews: The Failure of Christians to Understand the Jewish Experience (Macon, Ga.: Mercer University, 2000).

13. http://noontidepress.com//
14. Justice Potter Stewart, concurring opinion in Jacobellis v. Ohio 378 U.S. 184 (1964), regarding possible obscenity in *The Lovers.*
15. http://sdiencyclopedia.wikispaces.com/Holocaust+Trivialization; Alvin Rosenfeld, *The End of the Holocaust* (Bloomington: Indiana University Press, 2011).
16. http://www.canadafreepress.com/index.php/article/43228
17. http://www.adl.org/ADL_Opinions/Holocaust/120109_JTA.htm; http://www.thedailybeast.com/articles/2012/01/03/in-jerusalem-the-holocaust-is-trivialized.html
18. http://www.city-journal.org/html/eon_4_3_02sk.html
19. Dovid Katz, "Halting Holocaust obfuscation," *The Guardian*, January 8, 2010. http://www.guardian.co.uk/commentisfree/2010/jan/08/holocaust-baltic-lithuania-latvia
20. www.onethirdoftheholocaust.com
21. On this, see Robert Jan van Pelt, Auschwitz.

CHAPTER 3

Antisemitism and Holocaust Inversion

Robert Solomon Wistrich

Already in 1971, the French philosopher Vladimir Jankélévitch predicted the increasingly ominous connection between Israel, antisemitism, and the Shoah, which has come to haunt the contemporary European mind. He remarked on the extraordinary shadow which the Holocaust had cast over the events of the Second World War and modernity as a whole—a kind of invisible cloud of remorse. This was the "shameful secret" ("ce secret honteux") behind the apparent "bonne conscience contemporaine"—the hidden anxiety which seized so many Europeans at their belated realization of the enormity of the crime in which they were so deeply implicated.

How then could one be freed from such a terrible incubus? Jankélévitch suggested that "anti-Zionism" was likely to provide the providential and unexpected opportunity for much-needed relief: for it offered the freedom, the right, and perhaps even the duty to be "antisemitic" in the name of democracy![1] Anti-Zionism, he argued, would become the new "justifiable" and democratized antisemitism of the future, and finally placed it within the reach of Mr. and Mrs. Everyman. And what if the Jews themselves were no better than Nazis? Why, that would be just wonderful.

†The author was deceased at the time of publication.

R.S. Wistrich (✉)
Vidal Sassoon International Center for the Study of Antisemitism, Hebrew University of Jerusalem, Jerusalem, Israel

A. McElligott, J. Herf (eds.), *Antisemitism Before and Since the Holocaust*, DOI 10.1007/978-3-319-48866-0_3

One would no longer have to feel sorry for them—after all, "they would have deserved their fate." What better alibi could there be for forgetting the unspeakable crime or diluting European responsibilities and thinking about happier things?

Today, in light of the hostility to Israel that has become a significant aspect of parts of European intellectual life, such observations come more naturally and may even seem self-evident, though they were much less clear at the time. At least some of the new European Judeophobia, as well as the antagonism toward Israel, functions psychologically as a kind of overcompensation mechanism for discharging latent and often unavowed guilt feelings about the Jews. In fact, those who brand Israel as a Nazi state, kill two birds with one stone. They may point the finger at the erstwhile victims who are no better than "we, Europeans" (in fact they are worse, since they did not try to learn from their history); and they are then free to express in a "politically correct" anti-Zionist language those sentiments which are no longer respectable among educated people—namely dislike of Jews. The Star of David is thereby visually metamorphosed into the swastika, the victims mutate into perpetrators and Jews (or others) who defend the "Nazi" State of Israel can expect to be vilified as "racists," "fascists," and "ethnic cleansers." Indeed, in many European countries, scholars report that it is becoming increasingly difficult to even discuss the Shoah without balancing it by appropriate references to Palestine, intended to offset the horrors of Nazi Germany with those of the Palestinian *naqba* (catastrophe) since 1948.[2]

For several decades now, the Shoah has ceased to be a taboo subject. On the contrary, it is at the heart of contemporary Western consciousness—a subject of constant interdisciplinary research and media interest—integral to the culture, pedagogy, and politics of the new Europe.[3] Yet this preoccupation (which has at times assumed an obsessive quality) also has its perverse side effects. The most obvious distortion is, of course, straightforward Holocaust denial. I mean the patently false claim that there was no "extermination" of the Jews, that there were no gas chambers, that the Jews and/or Zionists (with some help from the Western Allies or the Communists) simply *invented* the "hoax of the century." As Alain Finkielkraut once put it, the classical antisemites screamed: "A mort les Juifs" (Death to the Jews) but the Holocaust deniers added something new—"Les Juifs ne sont pas morts" ('the Jews did not die').[4] This was and is a double assassination. It begins with the genocidal antisemitism that produced the mass murder of European Jewry and is followed by the denial that the six million were even here, on our planet; that they ever existed. To quote Per Ahlmark: "First the antisemites take Jewish lives; a few decades later they take their deaths from them too."[5]

Thus Holocaust denial in its purest sense is precisely this effort of the Jew-haters to destroy memory. Beyond that, by accusing Jews and/or Zionists of "inventing" the Shoah to extract billions of dollars and blackmail postwar Germany or the West, the deniers have added a peculiar conspiracy theory to the arsenal of millennial antisemitism and transformed the victims into superlatively cunning and fraudulent perpetrators. The main purpose of this, as Ahlmark notes, has been "to clear Nazism from its criminal stigma and rehabilitate antisemitism."[6] Hence this type of denial is primarily an expression of neo-Nazi, far-right and so-called revisionist politics in Europe, North America, and other parts of the world. To quote Irwin Cotler on this classic Orwellian cover-up of a true international conspiracy:

> [T]the Holocaust denial movement whitewashes the crimes of the Nazis, as it excoriates the crimes of the Jews. It not only holds that the Holocaust was a hoax, but maligns the Jew for fabricating the hoax.[7]

Nowhere has this imposture been more transparent and widespread than among militant Muslims. For example, at the turn of the millennium, the leader of Iran, the Ayatollah Ali Khameini, brazenly condemned the "exaggerated statistics on Jewish killings" and emphasized the close symbiosis between Zionists and the German Nazis.[8] The Lebanese Hizbollah, like its Iranian paymasters, sees the "Auschwitz lie" as an integral part of its general delegitimization of Israel and use of antisemitic discourse. Its spiritual leader Sheikh Fadlallah never tired of referring to the six million victims as a "pure fiction," a mark of Zionist cunning and rapacity; and a testament to the ability of Jews to squeeze the West and manipulate its guilt feelings, as a result of their stranglehold over the capitalist economy and mass media.[9] This media control allegedly permits Israel to persecute all those—like the French Holocaust denier Roger Garaudy—who dare to challenge its founding myths.[10] Islam and the Palestinians are naturally regarded as the prime victims of the "Zionist" hoax.

Back in 2000, the then-Mufti of Jerusalem Sheikh Ikrima Sabri, like many Palestinian clerics and intellectuals to the present day, eagerly seized on Holocaust denial to assert that the Zionists used this issue "to blackmail the Germans financially" and to protect Israel.[11] The dark shadow of

Shylock is never far from such "revisionist" discourse. As one Palestinian professor at the Islamic University in Gaza City put it nearly 15 years ago,

> [T]he Jews view it [the Holocaust] as a profitable activity so they inflate the number of victims all the time. ... As you know, when it comes to economics and investments, the Jews have been very experienced even since the days of *The Merchant of Venice*.[12]

At the same time, while slandering Jews and denying the reality of the Holocaust, some Arab and Muslim commentators have come to stress that Israel—the so-called heir of Holocaust victims—has committed far worse crimes than those of the Nazis. Since the war between Israel and Hamas that began in late December 2008, the negationist efforts to substitute the Naqba for the Shoah or to deny that the Holocaust even occurred, have in fact multiplied among Israeli Arabs as well as Gaza or West Bank Palestinians.[13]

The growing centrality of Holocaust denial and inversion in contemporary Arab discourse was already revealed in May 2001 by the Arab forum on historical revisionism that took place in Amman—replacing the aborted conference scheduled for Beirut two months earlier.[14] At this gathering of Arab journalists and members of professional associations opposed to "normalization" with Israel, speakers enthusiastically praised the French "revisionists" Roger Garaudy and Robert Faurisson.[15] They also argued that Zionism was much worse than Nazism, denounced the handful of Arab intellectuals who were critical of Holocaust denial, and insisted that "revisionism" was not a reactionary ideology at all but a well-documented research project.[16]

The case of Roger Garaudy was particularly significant. As a prominent left-wing French intellectual (Catholic, Stalinist, then dissident) who converted to Islam, he became a cult hero in the Arab world after his trial and conviction in a Paris court in 1998 for antisemitic incitement and *négationnisme*.[17] Garaudy's completely unoriginal thesis that there was no Nazi extermination policy or gas chambers, his charge that Zionists had collaborated with the Nazis, and that Israel fabricated the Holocaust to justify its occupation of Arab lands, proved to be a source of deep satisfaction for many Arab intellectuals.[18]

If such European "revisionist" charlatans as Henri Rocques, Wilhelm Stäglich, and Gerd Honsik could be regarded as respectable historians in the Arab world, it is small wonder that Garaudy's *The Founding Myths of*

Israeli Politics struck such a responsive chord among Muslims. Among Garaudy's most fervent advocates was former Iranian President Ali Akbar Hashemi Rafsanjani, the same cleric who proclaimed on "Jerusalem Day" 2001 in Teheran that "one atomic bomb would wipe out Israel without a trace."[19] It is all-too-revealing of this radical Islamist mind-set that the real Nazi Holocaust should be so vehemently denied by those determined to repeat it.

A discussion on Al-Jazeera TV on 15 May 2001 revealed just how widespread such genocidal passions had become.[20] During the debate, Hayat Atiya, the female translator of Garaudy into Arabic, shouted before the cameras (while brandishing the photograph of an Arab child accidentally killed during the intifada): "Here is the Holocaust. ... There is no Jewish Holocaust! There is only one Holocaust, that of the Palestinians!"[21] Among the statements appearing on the Al-Jazeera website and announced before the end of the debate was one to the effect that

> Nothing will dissuade the sons of Zion, whom our God described as descendants of apes and pigs, except a real Holocaust which would exterminate them in a single blow.[22]

At the end of this so-called debate, it emerged from an internet survey conducted by the channel that 85% of Arab spectators watching this program believed that Zionism was indeed worse than Nazism. Nothing much has changed since then.

Observers of Arab politics and journalism have concluded that Arab Holocaust denial, unlike its Western counterparts, long ago became mainstream. In Egyptian government-subsidized newspapers like *Al-Akhbar*, deniers regularly treat the Holocaust as a "swindle," supposedly proven by French and British "revisionists" (such as Garaudy and David Irving). Some openly regret that Hitler did not succeed in carrying it the Nazi "Final Solution" through to completion.[23] The deniers endlessly manipulate figures to pretend that there were less than a million Jewish victims all told; that the Jews were a fifth column in Germany, that they were traitors and spies who had in any case to be eliminated; that the Zionists originally inspired Hitler's racism while deliberately stoking up antisemitism (as stated in the doctoral dissertation of Palestinian leader Abu Mazen [Mahmoud Abbas]).[24] Such a bewildering tissue of contradictions has led to an abyss of trivialization, distortion, and hatred.[25]

This culture of hatred has carried over into European countries with large Muslim populations, such as France (and to a growing extent Belgium, Holland, Sweden, and Great Britain) where Holocaust denial or relativization fuses all too easily with pro-Palestinism, anti-Zionism, and anti-Americanism.[26] The situation in French state schools emerged as especially alarming after 2000, with pupils from the Maghreb often rejecting any attempt to teach them about the Shoah. The subject was negatively identified by the young *Maghrébins* with the established order, with the "Zionist enemy" and the political self-interest of the Jewish community. In this immigrant milieu, far from having a beneficial pedagogical effect, the very mention of the Holocaust has, on occasion, seemed to elicit violence and threats to exterminate or burn the Jews. The importance given to the subject, if anything, "confirmed" the widespread Muslim belief in the world Jewish conspiracy or Jewish control of the Western media. European and French sensitivity to the Shoah is to this day frequently linked by young Muslims to "Jewish money" and the power of the Zionist lobby. Hence the paradox that antisemitism has risen to unprecedented levels in France, Britain, and Europe as a whole (particularly among Muslims but not exclusively by any means) at a time when the Shoah has never been so widely recognized and integrated into cultural consciousness.[27] Surely this fact should inspire greater prudence and soul-searching among those who believe that Holocaust education, in and of itself, can dam up the rising antisemitic wave. On the contrary, I would argue, there is ample evidence that a highly politicized focus on the Holocaust may act as a potentially dangerous boomerang against Israel and Diaspora Jewry.

If this is increasingly true in the school classroom, it is even more painfully evident at the level of public discourse that invokes the Holocaust for political ends. No doubt some of this malaise has its roots in the earlier postwar years, and in the case of Eastern Europe, it reflects transparent communist manipulations of the national memory.[28] Serious debate on the centrality of Nazi Germany's anti-Jewish policy was delayed in the former Soviet bloc until the 1990s. But in the West, Holocaust education and growing interest in the Shoah have been a reality for a considerable period of time. There is no convincing evidence, however, that educating young people about the Shoah will prevent attacks on Jews or will lead to a better world, let alone reduce racism and antisemitism.

Equally troubling for the future is the relativization and banalization of the Holocaust through false analogies, especially with the current policies of the Jewish State. Increasingly, we see the bitter fruit of this syndrome across Europe, as well as on other continents. Examples of the "Nazi-Zionist" amalgam abound on the internet, television, radio, in the press and the arts. The instances I will mention are only the tip of a huge iceberg. The tone was set already in April 2002, when the pro-Government Center Left Greek publication *Eleftherotypia* featured a caricature of a Nazi soldier, labeled with a Star of David, threatening an Arab, dressed up like a Jewish concentration camp prisoner. The headline read "Holocaust II" and the caption said: "The War machine of Sharon is attempting to carry out a new Holocaust, a new genocide."[29] Such caricatures are frequent in Greece. Their prevalence helped feed the rising tide of support for the neo-Nazi movement, *Golden Dawn*, which enjoyed a substantial share of the vote at the last Greek elections—won by an extreme Left movement which was itself very nationalist.

Europe's elite avant-garde of intellectuals and artists from the Portuguese Nobel Prize winner, the late José Saramago, to the recently deceased German literary titan Günter Grass, have been no less guilty of Holocaust inversion. Writing in the Spanish daily *El País* over a decade ago, Saramago grotesquely compared the West Bank capital Ramallah to Auschwitz. With astounding obtuseness and contempt, he described Israelis as

> educated and trained in the idea that any suffering that has been inflicted, or is being inflicted, or will be inflicted on everyone else, especially the Palestinians, will always be inferior to that which they themselves suffered in the Holocaust. The Jews endlessly scratch their own wound to keep it bleeding, to make it incurable, and they show it to the world as if it were a banner.[30]

More recently, on 4 April 2012, a leading German daily *Süddeutsche Zeitung* published a no less scandalous prose "poem" by another Nobel Prize laureate Günter Grass, entitled "What Must Be Said." In this ugly little text, the German Social Democrat Grass posed as a possible victim of Jews, claiming that while Iranian President Ahmadinejad was a mere "loudmouth," Israel sought to "annihilate the Iranian people." In a key sentence Grass suggested that "Israel's atomic power endangers an already fragile world peace," yet this real threat could supposedly not be discussed because of accusations of antisemitism.[31]

For Grass, as for many European intellectuals of the "progressive" persuasion, it was almost "normal" to invoke the Shoah and denounce the alleged Jewish–Zionist "blackmail" behind any charges of antisemitism. In so doing, they could continue to demonize Israel and call the Jews to account. Grass's anti-Israel slurs should be seen against the background of a 2011 study by the University of Bielefeld on behalf of the German Friedrich Ebert Foundation. This survey demonstrated that in seven European countries, over 40% of respondents viewed Israel as having "genocidal" intentions toward the Palestinians. This was particularly true of Germany itself, Great Britain, Hungary, and Portugal. No less than 63% of Poles thought Israel was actually conducting a "war of extermination" against Palestinians—tantamount to calling it a Nazi State. Such antisemitic defamation of Israel has by now thoroughly permeated the European mainstream.[32]

This is no less true of Great Britain, despite the fact that Holocaust education in the past 15 years made considerable progress—almost in tandem with extreme forms of Israel-bashing. At the beginning of the twenty-first century, the Irish poet and Oxford University professor, Tom Paulin, had slandered the Israel Defence Forces as "the Zionist SS," the most brutal of Hitler's executioners, in a vicious little poem called "Crossfire," which provoked considerable controversy.[33] Prominent British journalists like A.N. Wilson, Brian Sewell, and Richard Ingrams, also made similar slurs with very little public opposition. As elsewhere in Western Europe, discussions of Israeli actions are quite frequently overladen by the specter and vocabulary of Auschwitz—only this time the Jews are in the role of perpetrators.[34] Moreover, during the past decade, there is little doubt that the notion of the "Zionist State" as a mirror image of Nazism (or else as a racist "apartheid" state) has assumed a prominent place in the pro-Palestine BDS movements on British university campuses, in South Africa, Canada, and the United States.[35]

The academic boycott movement in the West is, of course, more respectable in tone than the crassly antisemitic Holocaust denial of the Arab world, of neo-Nazis, or radical right-wing extremists in Europe and America. The Holocaust "inversion" in which it indulges reflects a human rights terminology—which while wallowing in double standards, explicitly repudiates the Nazi legacy, publicly deploring all forms of racism, antisemitism, warmongering, empire, and power politics. It evokes the Holocaust more as a stick with which to beat the Jewish State in the name of "universal humanity" and the rights of the "Other"—who, for some strange reason, has become almost exclusively Muslim or Palestinian. Since the Palestinian "other," in particular, is assumed to be the *abso-*

lute victim of Jewish injustice, then Israel—according to this logic—must be the *absolute perpetrator*, the ultimate configuration of evil—literally a "Nazified" State. This is a more subtle though no less insidious way of deforming the Holocaust. It has little connection to anachronistic visions of blackshirted skinheads in jackboots yelling "Sieg Heil!" It is a post-Auschwitz "progressive" version of antisemitism which has constructed its own Manichean and "essentialist" view of Israel as the very incarnation of racism.[36]

Finally there remains the case of Iran—the one postwar nation to have turned Holocaust denial (including inversion and relativization) into a fully fledged state doctrine. The Iranian regime has never hidden its historic admiration for Germany and its identification with Germans as victims of a Holocaust "hoax" invented by money-grubbing Zionists, Western imperialists, and Jews. Iran is unique today, not only in its open, unabashed, and unrelenting calls for the annihilation of Israel but also in its unrestrained use of a Nazi vocabulary about the Zionist entity as a "festering tumor" or "filthy microbe" that must be eradicated from the Middle East.[37] At the same time, it mocks, denies, or utterly trivializes the Shoah, even organizing—as in the spring of 2015—a contest of Holocaust caricatures in Tehran to this effect. Indeed, for the first time since 1945, Holocaust denial in all its forms has become an integral part of the national-religious identity of a powerful State that repeatedly proclaims its aim to wipe out six million Jews in the contemporary State of Israel.[38] With this macabre dance of death, driven by radical Islamist antisemitism, we have come full circle. Holocaust denial fuses with its inversion to ideologically prepare the ground for a nuclear genocide in the Middle East.

Notes

1. Vladimir Jankélévitch, *L'Imprescriptible: pardonner dans l'honneur et la dignité* (Paris 1996; 1st ed. 1971), p. 188.
2. A good illustration of this syndrome is Belgium; see Joël Kotek, *La Belgique et ses Juifs: De l'antijudaïsme comme code culturel, à l'antisionisme comme religion civique* (Les Études du Crif, no. 4, June 2004). See also Georges Bensoussan, *Antisemitism in French Schools* (The Vidal Sassoon International Center for the Study of Antisemitism, *Acta* no. 24, 2004, Hebrew University of Jerusalem) and Robert S. Wistrich, *A Lethal Obsession. Anti-Semitism from Antiquity to the Global Jihad* (New York, 2010), pp. 295–302.

3. See *Stockholm International Forum on the Holocaust* (Proceedings of the Conference on Education, Remembrance and Research in Stockholm, 26–28 Jan. 2000).
4. Alain Finkielkraut, *L'avenir d'une negation: Reflexion sur la question du genocide* (Paris 1982).
5. See the remarks of Per Ahlmark in the workshop on "Facing Denial in Society and Education," *Stockholm International Forum*, p. 235.
6. Ibid. See also Wistrich, *A Lethal Obsession*, op. cit., pp. 632–644.
7. See the remarks of Irwin Cotler on this phenomenon, in *Stockholm International Forum*, p. 242.
8. Quoted in *Jerusalem Post*, 25 Apr. 2001.
9. Esther Webman, "Die Rhetorik der Hisbollah: die Weiterführung eines antisemitischen Diskurses," *Jahrbuch für Antisemitismusforschung*, no. 12 (Berlin 2003): pp. 47–49.
10. Goetz Nordbruch, *The Socio-Historical Background of Holocaust Denial in Arab Countries. Reactions to Roger Garaudy's* The Founding Myths of Israeli Politics, ACTA series, no. 17 (Jerusalem: Vidal Sassoon International Center for the Study of Antisemitism, Hebrew University of Jerusalem, 2001). For a more recent discussion, see Meir Litvak and Esther Webman, *From Empathy to Denial: Arab Responses to the Holocaust* (London, 2009).
11. Interview, *New York Times*, 26 Mar. 2000.
12. *Holocaust Denial in the Middle East. The Latest Anti-Israel Propaganda Themes* (New York: Anti-Defamation League, 2001), p. 12.
13. See Gilbert Achcar, *Les Arabes et la Shoah* (Paris, 2009), pp. 383–403. The Lebanese-born S.O.A.S. professor in his highly polemical though significant book did recognize the reality of Arab and Iranian Holocaust denial, along with its Islamist, antisemitic roots, while maintaining a virulent anti-Israel stance that mars many of his judgments.
14. The driving force behind that aborted conference was Swiss Holocaust denier, Jürgen Graf, founder of The Truth and Justice Association; it was co-sponsored by the California-based Institute of Historical Review—at the time, the leading "revisionist" organization in the world. Among those originally scheduled to speak were French deniers Garaudy and Robert Faurisson, and the German neo-Nazi ideologue Horst Mahler. Lebanese President Rafiq Hariri (subsequently murdered) cancelled the Conference

under intense prodding from the US State Department and an open letter of protest by 14 Arab intellectuals. However, after severe criticism for having conceded too much to the "Zionist" narrative of the Shoah, several of these intellectuals retracted, including Edward Said and Mahmud Darwish.

15. *Free Arab Voice Online* (*FAV*) 15, 28 Apr., 22 May 2001; *Jordan Times Online*, 15 May 2001.
16. Ibrahim Alloush, "Why is the 'Holocaust' Important to Palestinians, Arabs and Muslims?" *FAV*, 28 Apr. 2001; and the interview in the California-based *Journal of Historical Review* (May/June 2001).
17. Nordbruch, *Socio-Historical Background*, 3–5, 9–13, 27; for details of the affair in France, see Valérie Igounet, *Histoire du Négationisme en France* (Paris 2000), pp. 472–83.
18. The Arab reaction to Garaudy was overwhelmingly favorable. None of those who protested on his behalf questioned his claim that the Holocaust was a Zionist invention. His supporters included the now deceased Sheikh Muhammad Al-Tantawi of Al-Azhar University, Rafiq Hariri, former prime minister of Lebanon, Egyptian Nobel Laureate Nadjīb Mahfouz, and the famous Arab political commentator Muhammad Hassanin Haikal. The Arab Lawyers Federation and Palestinian Writers Association also wrote protest letters in his favor. For the contrast between the French and Arab reaction, see Mouna Naim, "Critiqué, jugé, sanctionnné pour ses theses en France, l'ancien théoricien du PC, Roger Garaudy, est décoré et louangé dans les pays arabes," *Le Monde,* 1 Mar. 1998. For a critical account, see the previously mentioned work of Litvak and Webman, *From Empathy to Denial* (2009).
19. *Holocaust Denial in the Middle East,* pp. 8–9.
20. See *Memri*, no. 225, 6 June 2001, for the details; Raphaël Israeli, "L'antisémitisme travesti en antisionisme," *Revue d'histoire de la Shoah*, Le monde juif, no. 180, special issue on "Antisémitisme et Négationnisme dans le monde Arabo-Musulman: La Dérive." (Jan.–June 2004): pp. 109–71.
21. Israeli, ibid., p. 151.
22. Ibid. For the phenomenon of annihilationist Arab antisemitism and anti-Zionism, including Holocaust denial as well as inversion, see Wistrich, *A Lethal Obsession*, op. cit., pp. 647–779.
23. *Al-Akhbar* (Egypt), 29 Apr. 2002; Memri, special report no. 375, 2 May 2002; no. 231, 20 June 2001.

24. Abu Mazen's doctoral thesis was defended in Moscow in 1982 and published in Arabic two years later in Amman under the title *The Secret Ties between the Nazis and the Leadership of the Zionist Movement*; on Abu Mazen's "moderation," see Israeli, "L'antisémitisme travesti en antisionisme," pp. 165–68, and Wistrich, *A Lethal Obsession* (2010), op. cit., pp. 723–4.
25. Clemens Hemi, *Antisemitism: A Specific Phenomenon* (Berlin, 2013), pp. 212–299, provides many examples from Germany of the links between antisemitism, terrorism, Islamism, and Holocaust distortion in current polemics.
26. Pierre-André Taguieff, *Rising from the Muck: The New Anti-Semitism in Europe* (Chicago 2004), pp. 97–100, and his important study, *La Judéophobie des Modernes* (Paris, 2008), pp. 407–451.
27. Georges Bensoussan, *Antisemitism in French Schools* (2004), op. cit., pp. 18–19, 26–7.
28. See Manfred Gerstenfeld, *Europe's Crumbling Myths. The Post-Holocaust Origins of Today's Anti-Semitism* (Jerusalem 2003), pp. 10–92.
29. *Eleftherotypia*, 1 Apr. 2002.
30. Quoted in Phyllis Chesler, *The New Antisemitism* (San Francisco 2003), p. 119. On Saramago, see also Wistrich, *A Lethal Obsession* (2010), op. cit., pp. 7–8.
31. It should be noted that Grass hid the fact that he had been a member of the Waffen-SS in 1945 for over 60 years, while claiming to be the "moral conscience" of postwar Germany. Among the many commentaries, see that of Jeffrey Herf, "The Odious Musings of Gunter Grass," April 5, 2012, http://www.Fnr.com/article/books-and-arts/102417/grass-poem-anti-semitic-gunter (visited 5 May, 2012).
32. See Manfred Gerstenfeld, *Demonizing Israel and the Jews* (New York, 2013).
33. Quoted in Winston Pickett, "Nasty or Nazi? The Use of Antisemitic Topoi by the Left-Liberal Media," in Paul Iganski and Barry Kosmin (eds.), *A New Anti-Semitism? Debating Judeophobia in 21st-Century Britain* (London 2003), pp. 155–57.
34. A notorious example was the short play by Caryl Churchill, *Seven Jewish Children,* performed at London's Royal Court Theatre in 2009. See Robert Wistrich, *From Blood Libel to Boycott. Changing*

Faces of British Antisemitism (Hebrew University of Jerusalem, 2011), pp. 11, 21–22.

35. Alvin H. Rosenfeld, *Anti-Zionism in Great Britain and Beyond. A "Respectable" Anti-Semitism?* (New York: American Jewish Committee, 2004); Wistrich, *From Blood Libel*, op. cit.; and most recently, Cary Nelson and Gabriel Noah Brahm (eds.), *The Case Against Academic Boycotts of Israel* (Chicago and New York, 2015).
36. See Robert S. Wistrich (ed.), *Holocaust Denial. The Politics of Perfidy* (Berlin/Jerusalem, 2012), pp. 1–26.
37. Matthias Küntzel, *Germany and Iran. From the Aryan Axis to the Nuclear Threshold* (New York, 2014), pp. 171–179, 241–54.
38. Robert S. Wistrich, "Deadly Comparisons," *The Jerusalem Post*, 25 April 2015.

PART II

Religion

CHAPTER 4

The Political Dimensions of Theology: Christianity and Antisemitism

Christian Wiese

> We will not [...] be capable of 'thinking the Shoah,' albeit inadequately, if we divorce its genesis, and its radical enormity from theological origins.
>
> George Steiner[1]

I

In his book on *Anti-Judaism: The Western Tradition*, historian David Nirenberg, reflecting upon the roots of the Shoah, comes to the conclusion that the Nazi genocide, even though it can certainly not be seen as an inevitable result of the long history of the obsessive thinking about Jews and Judaism in Western culture, "was inconceivable and is unexplainable without that deep history of thought." The history he writes is

This is an abbreviated and updated version of a previously published article: Christian Wiese, "An 'Indelible Stigma': The Churches between Silence, Ideological Involvement, and Political Complicity," in *Years of Persecution, Years of Extermination: Saul Friedländer and the Future of Holocaust Studies*, eds. Christian Wiese and Paul Betts (London and New York: Continuum, 2010), pp. 157–192. The article is used here by permission of Bloomsbury Publishing Plc.

C. Wiese (✉)
Goethe University, Frankfurt am Main, Germany

A. McElligott, J. Herf (eds.), *Antisemitism Before and Since the Holocaust*, DOI 10.1007/978-3-319-48866-0_4

that of the pervasive influence of anti-Judaism—in its various and changing forms—throughout two millennia, a history that "had encoded the threat of Judaism into some of the basic concepts of Western thought" and thus shaped the mentality that, under specific historical circumstances, enabled an unprecedented crime.[2] Christianity and Christian concepts and images of the Jews were, as he convincingly describes, an integral part of this tradition. Therefore, the awareness of the fateful consequences of the long tradition of Christian anti-Jewish hatred, its indissoluble interaction with the history of antisemitism, and of the role Christian theology and the Christian churches played within the context of the discrimination, persecution, abandonment, and murder inflicted on a large proportion of European Jewry necessarily belong to the fundamental elements of Christian theological self-reflection after World War II and the Shoah. The painful insight into the enormous dimension of Christianity's involvement in and co-responsibility for the Nazi genocide, first only acknowledged by a few theologians who allowed themselves to be fully exposed to the shock engendered by the crimes associated with the symbolic name of Auschwitz and who realized that their own tradition could not remain unchanged by them, became, during the last few decades, a crucial element of the critical reorientation of Christian theology in the course of the Jewish–Christian dialogue since the 1970s and 1980s. The long—and still unfinished—process of recognizing and historically elucidating the Christian guilt, which has found expression in important theological declarations and historical works, has advanced the awareness that Christian tradition's fundamentally anti-Jewish orientation and the repression and distortion of Jewish self-understanding in the history of Christian Europe—including the "catastrophic violence"[3] against Jews connected with this—have caused infinite suffering and forms part of the history of the murderous antisemitism of the Nazis. As a result, the Churches, in Germany and in other parts of the world, while still at risk of falling back into the traditional stereotypes of their theology and practice, have gradually proceeded on the path of overcoming what Jules Isaac has once called the "teaching of contempt." However, the historical interpretation of the contribution of Christian anti-Jewish ideas, stereotypes, and actions to the horrific events of the twentieth century and the precise analysis of Christian complicity with Nazi antisemitism continue to be controversial, among Jewish and non-Jewish historians alike. The following thoughts are devoted to a differentiated look into some of the conflicting views and to an attempt to explore the vexing questions related to the political dimensions of Christian theology with regard to Jews and Judaism.

II

> Christianity is a religion that consecrated at its core and, historically, spread throughout its domain a megatherian hatred of one group of people: the Jews. It libelously deemed them—sometimes in its sacred texts and doctrine, to be Christ-killers, children of the devil, desecrators and defilers of all goodness, responsible for an enormous range of human calamities and suffering. This hatred—Christianity's betrayal of its own essential and good moral principles—led Christians, over the course of almost two millennia, to commit many grave crimes and other injuries against Jews, including mass murder. The best-known and largest of these mass murders is the Holocaust.[4]

This passage, quoted from Daniel J. Goldhagen's book *A Moral Reckoning* (2002) is characteristic of the attempt of part of contemporary historiography to define the relationship between Christianity and antisemitism by pointing to the long destructive tradition of Christian Jew-hatred and by analysing the concrete part played by Christian theology and ecclesiastical politics in the persecution and destruction of European Jewry. With the Catholic Church as an example, the book represents a type of historical interpretation—practiced by Jewish and non-Jewish researchers alike—that assumes the unequivocal complicity of Christianity with genocide,[5] and the undeniable continuity between religious forms of Jew-hatred since antiquity and particularly the Middle Ages, modern antisemitism in the second half of the nineteenth century, and the racial antisemitism of the Nazis. In his massive attack on the Roman Catholic Church, which evolved from a review of recent writing about the problematic role of Pope Pius XII during the Shoah, Goldhagen postulates the existence of an "eliminationist antisemitism," deeply rooted in Church history, that did not demand the mass murder of Jews and even explicitly rejected violent solutions. Nevertheless, due to the centuries-old religious demonization of Jews and Judaism and its political implications, it "was, however unintended, compatible with or implied eliminationist solutions, including perhaps extermination"[6]: "Anti-Semitism led to the Holocaust. Anti-Semitism has been integral to the Catholic Church. The question of what the relationship is between the Church's anti-Semitism and the Holocaust should be at the center of any general treatment of either one."[7]

Goldhagen's critique of the Catholic Church begins with an assessment of the tradition of Christian Jew-hatred as a fundamental theological and ethical failure at the heart of Christianity and a detailed reconstruction of the Church's historical guilt up to the Nazi period. It continues by accusing the Church of a lack of repentance and critical self-reflection after Auschwitz, and it ends by demanding a radical reorientation of the Church's theological traditions. Ultimately, it is an explication of the moral subtext of his no less controversial book *Hitler's Willing Executioners* (1997), in which he claimed that the "ubiquitous demonizing, racial anti-Semitism"[8] dominated the ideas of German society and its elites, including the Churches, during the Nazi era, to such an extent that the overwhelming majority of Germans became willing, enthusiastic followers of National Socialism, among whom it was easy to recruit the real murderers. This hatred dated back to the Middle Ages and the Early Modern period; in Germany, it had acquired a dominant political and cultural significance by the nineteenth century.[9] There were several interrelated types of "eliminationism." The first was the moderate, liberal type of the progressive forces, who regarded the Jews in Germany as an alien element, but one that was capable of becoming assimilated and truly German by accepting German culture in general and Christianity in particular. This amounted to an elimination of the Jews by assimilation and conversion. The second type of "eliminationism" was the more radical antisemitism of those nationalists who wanted to restore the situation that had pertained in Germany before the Jews were emancipated and granted equal rights. The even more extreme third type was represented by those who wanted to drive out the Jews, as the medieval rulers of western and central Europe had done. Finally Goldhagen describes in great detail the murderous type of "eliminationism," which had developed into the antisemitism of the Nazis in the twentieth century. According to Goldhagen, almost the entire German nation, whether passively or actively, willingly participated in the project of the destruction of the Jewish people because German society was totally steeped in this "eliminationist" mindset. The Christian tradition as well as the Protestant and Catholic Churches in Germany play a central part in Goldhagen's contention that the antisemitism of the Nazi period was an "axiom of German culture" and "just a more accentuated, intensified, and elaborated form of an already broadly accepted basic model."[10] He claims that, throughout the history of European civilization, Christian culture had turned the Jews into a "central cultural symbol," in fact "the symbol of all that was awry in the world"[11]—a structure that had persisted throughout the transformations and intensifications of Christian prejudice. Of course, he recognizes historical change in the cultural and ideological manifestations of Jew-hatred and he grants that antisemitism in its extreme racial and *völkisch* form has invalidated traditional Christian elements that had limited anti-Jewish violence. However, he interprets it as a mere modernization of a Manichaean construction and a demonization of Judaism created by Christianity and inherent in its very core teachings. Despite the deficiencies and the lack of historical differentiation in Goldhagen's judgement,[12] the challenging question he raises is whether there is indeed *one* continuous line from traditional Christian Jew-hatred—which is already discernible in texts of the New Testament, by way of medieval Jew-hatred, Martin Luther's anti-Jewish diatribes, the ambivalent judgements on Judaism during the Enlightenment period and the nationalism of German romanticism—to modern antisemitism, and whether the history of Jewish suffering all the way to the Shoah was not a direct consequence of Christian ideas about Judaism. As long as the Churches fail to admit this truth, Goldhagen says, the road to a genuine change of direction and a reconciliation between Judaism and Christianity will remain barred.[13]

A completely different image emerges from the document *We Remember: A Reflection on the Shoah*, published in 1998 by the "Holy See's Commission for Religious Relations with the Jews." It solemnly condemns all forms of antisemitism, deploring the "unspeakable tragedy" of the Holocaust and demanding a "moral and religious memory and, particularly among Christians, a very serious reflection on what gave rise to it." However, it consistently avoids mentioning any guilt on the part of the Church and, by drawing a sharp dividing line between anti-Judaism and antisemitism, as well as placing a strong emphasis on Catholic objections to the policies of the Nazis, finally reaches the conclusion: "The *Shoah* was the work of a thoroughly modern neo-pagan regime. Its antisemitism had its roots outside Christianity and, in pursuing its aims, it did not hesitate to oppose the Church and persecute her members also." Even the concession that Christianity's religious stereotypes might have prevented the development of Christian sensitivity to the persecution of the Jewish minority ends with an apologetic interpretation, which claims that ultimately it was not the Church as an institution, but at the most "some Christians" who had incurred the guilt of hostility towards Jews and Judaism and "indifference" to the fate of the hard-pressed Jewish people.[14] As is well known, this half-hearted and trivializing examination by the Catholic Church of its own past was sharply criticized not only by Jewish authors but also by Christians engaged in the dialogue with Judaism who had arrived at much more radical conclusions.[15] In its reply to the Vatican's document *We Remember*, the International Jewish Committee for Interreligious Consultations issued a warning against an uncritical separation of "anti-Judaism" and "antisemitism," and demanded an honest recognition of the link between both phenomena despite all the justifiable historical distinctions:

> The implication that while Christians have been guilty of anti-Judaism antisemitism is a contradiction of the teaching of the Church is dubious and it is unfortunate that it is put forward in generalities that could well mislead many for whom this document is intended. There was indeed a change in the main emphases of antisemitism in the late nineteenth century from a religious basis to a more secular prejudice with a pseudo-racialist base. However can it be said that the latter was not influenced by the long centuries of Church conditioning? [...] Thus the statement that this was 'an anti-Judaism that was essentially more sociological and political than religious' plays down the fact of the unbroken line of Christian anti-Judaism/antisemitism and its impact throughout Europe. After all, the Jew was still the deicide and the traditional anti-Jewish stereotypes were not changed or renounced and were absorbed into the new antisemitism. The Catholic attitude toward the Jews was unchanged and its influence cannot be excluded. This is why the suggestion of a complete dichotomy between 'anti-Judaism' and 'antisemitism' is misleading. One shades into the other. It was Christian anti-Judaism that created the possibility of modern pagan antisemitism by delegitimizing the Jews and Judaism. [...] It is true that the National Socialist regime adopted a pagan ideology which rejected the Church—although this did not mean that all Churchmen and believers rejected National Socialism. It may be noted that Hitler, Himmler and the other Nazi leaders were all baptized Christians who were never excommunicated. The same is true of the vast apparatus of killers, the product of Christian Europe. The Church is not accused of direct responsibility for the Shoah but of its legacy of sixteen centuries of conditioning which had created an environment in which a Shoah became possible and many Christians would feel no compunction in collaborating.[16]

Interestingly enough, the controversy about the historical effect of Christian antisemitism and the shared responsibility of the Churches for the Shoah is not restricted to Christianity's internal discourse. It also plays an important part in the current dialogue between Christians and Jews and it leads to very different judgements even among Jewish dialogue partners. This is corroborated by a look at a fiercely disputed passage of the declaration *Dabru Emet: A Jewish Statement on Christians and Christianity*,[17] a declaration drafted by a group of Jewish scholars in 2000 and signed in the USA by more than 200 rabbis and intellectuals. The document was intended by its initiators to respond to changes in the attitude of the Churches towards Judaism in past decades and to dispel the reservations within the Jewish public against active participation in the Christian-Jewish dialogue. A central argument of the document is devoted to counteracting the construction of a direct line of continuity between Christian Jew-hatred and the Holocaust and to make appropriate historical distinctions:

> Nazism was not a Christian phenomenon. Without the long history of Christian anti-Judaism and Christian violence against Jews, Nazi ideology could not have taken hold nor could it have been carried out. Too many Christians participated in, or were sympathetic to, Nazi atrocities against Jews. Other Christians did not protest sufficiently against these atrocities. But Nazism itself was not an inevitable outcome of Christianity. If the Nazi extermination of the Jews had been fully successful, it would have turned its murderous rage more directly to Christians. We recognize with gratitude those Christians who risked or sacrificed their lives to save Jews during the Nazi regime. With that in mind, we encourage the continuation of recent efforts in Christian theology to repudiate unequivocally contempt of Judaism and the Jewish people. We applaud those Christians who reject this teaching of contempt, and we do not blame them for the sins committed by their ancestors.

Unlike *We Remember*, this passage does not aim at an exoneration of Christianity but at a differentiated treatment of historical reality. There is no doubt that the text is based on the results of recent historical debates. This does not alter the fact that the authors are not historians and that the statement is a highly problematic shorthand for complicated historical distinctions. The authors themselves realized this and anticipated the criticism of some Jewish commentators who feared that the formulations concerning antisemitism might be used by Christians to avoid the painful confrontation with Christian historical guilt. They argued that what was intended was something completely different, that is, a fair assessment of history which recognized that Christianity also included some central values that contained the potential for resistance against the Nazi ideology and in some cases had actually led to solidarity with the persecuted Jews. This negation of the unavoidable involvement of Christianity in the crimes of the Nazis, they claimed, provided the basis for a Jewish–Christian dialogue by indicating the possibility of overcoming Christian anti-Judaism.

Michel Signer in particular also stressed the pedagogical and psychological function of the passage: to suggest topics for a dialogue that will enable Christians to "discover" the anti-Judaism of their own tradition and to "choose" an alternative route. By acknowledging the rescue of Jews by Christians, recognizing the attempts of post-1945 Christian theology to reject the contempt for Judaism and the Jewish people, and refraining from generalizing accusations against contemporary Christians, the document had been intended not to promote "forgiveness" but to provide an answer to Christian "metanoia" that would encourage greater efforts to reform the relations of Christians with Judaism.[18] Not least, Jewish interpreters such as David Rosen have engaged in hermeneutical reflections about the particular context of *Dabru Emet*, stressing that the entire explanation was not addressed to Christians but must be understood in the context of a debate between Jews in the USA which is strongly affected by the awareness of the connection between Christian Jew-hatred and the Shoah:

> Of course, if this had been a Christian statement, then we would have expected some extensive soul searching and greater acknowledgement of the sin of Christian antisemitism. But *Dabru Emet* is a Jewish statement that is explicitly directed at Jews. The Jewish community does not need persuading as to the case of Christian historic guilt and responsibility for antisemitism—on the contrary! As a modern Jewish leader in the dialogue with Christianity has put it, the Jewish community often tends to indulge in a "triumphalism of pain."[19]

Insofar as *Dabru Emet* aims above all to counteract the monolinear identification of Christianity, antisemitism, and the Shoah in the American-Jewish context, it requires not only a general historical commentary but also an intensive critical exegesis of both the overall structure and individual formulations of the text. This shows that the reflection about the shared responsibility of Christianity for the Shoah not only oversimplifies the historical discourse but also in part misses the point and therefore holds more dangers than opportunities. At first sight, the text contains several elements that—considered in isolation—even seem to have structural similarities to the Vatican document *We Remember*, despite the completely different motivation. The radical thesis "Nazism was not a Christian phenomenon," which would be historically incorrect without recourse to differentiated reflections about the interplay of Christian and non-Christian elements in modern antisemitism and the receptivity of Christian theologies to Nazi ideology, does not, in principle, preclude the disastrously trivial interpretation implied in the view that antisemitism has "its roots outside of Christianity." The next sentence—"Without the long history of Christian anti-Judaism and Christian violence against Jews, Nazi ideology could not have taken hold nor could it have been carried out"—implies the sharing of responsibility by Christianity. However, owing to its linguistic structure, which suggests a rather passive effect of Christian discourse about Judaism, it fails to articulate what a Christian reception must urgently stress in a self-critical way: that Christian theology and the policy of the Churches, as well as a widespread social mentality determined by demonizing stereotypes of the "alien," dangerous Jew actively and often consciously prepared the ground for the National Socialist policy of disenfranchisement and—a few exceptions apart—contributed to the fate of the Jewish minority through consistent desolidarization and quiet surrender. It is true that the text of *Dabru Emet* refers to a violent relationship between Christians and Jews and does not deny the participation of Christians in the "atrocities" of the Nazis. However, with its rather simplistic use of language and argument, it seems unable to counter the suppression of the concrete historical affinity of anti-Jewish thought patterns and the National Socialist ideology by documents such as *We Remember*. At any rate, a Christian reception would have to state unequivocally that the unprecedented monstrosity of the crime was "not only, although it was the first, German nightmare of European history, but also the real culmination of a European fantasy of destruction sown by Christians."[20] It would also have to acknowledge that a wealth of historical writings demonstrates the extent to which anti-Jewish theology and racial antisemitism mutually influenced and reinforced each other; the spectrum of Christian guilt and shared responsibility for the Shoah, Christians will have to keep in mind, extended from active ecclesiastic and theological complicity to the failure even of those in the resistance movement against the Nazi regime who were Christian-motivated to feel, let alone to express solidarity with the persecuted Jews. Not least, it would be necessary to point to the phenomenon of a racially infected antisemitic current within the Church—namely the Protestant "German-Christian" theology, whose radical representatives aimed to conquer the Church for National Socialism and who tried to cleanse Christianity of all Jewish traces.[21]

In any case, the historical facts revealed by the research into antisemitism and the Holocaust are much more complex than *Dabru Emet*—arising as it does from the context of the attempts at a religious dialogue—is able to explain. The proposition "Nazism was not a Christian phenomenon" initially only articulates a historical distinction that is also frequently supported by Jewish scholars, but it can be weighted in different ways. The historical classification and interpretation is often determined as soon as the controversial question is raised of whether or not to make a conceptual and functional distinction between "anti-Judaism" and "antisemitism" and further types of Jew-hatred. In today's historical research, the term "antisemitism" is frequently applied to all the periods and varieties of Jew-hatred, while distinguishing, say, "religious," "political," or "racial" antisemitism.

The distinction between "anti-Judaism" and "antisemitism" is, of course, classic and still widespread. It usually refers to the fact that the term "antisemitism," used as a self-description, did not appear till the second half of the nineteenth century. As is well known, the term was originally intended to indicate that the antisemites were not concerned with religious prejudice, or the conflict between Christians and Jews, but with the allegedly objective contrast between the "Aryan" and the "Semitic race." "Antisemitism," according to this distinction, is a phenomenon of the nineteenth century and differs substantially from the traditional theological conviction that the Jews had been driven out of their country as a punishment for allegedly murdering the Son of God and that, as a consequence, they were now living scattered and deprived of rights—as a sign of the truth of Christianity—among the nations, while the status of the chosen people had been transferred to the Church as the "new Israel." Critics quite rightly point out that the distinction between "anti-Judaism" and "antisemitism" is strongly susceptible to the trivialization of religious Jew-hatred and frequently inclined to conceal the political dimension of theological issues. It tends to overlook that theological anti-Judaism has never been a "purely theological" phenomenon, but has always influenced the political relations with the Jewish minority through its images and myths, be it directly or by imprinting a mentality that regarded the persecution, disenfranchisement, and violent treatment of Jews as a matter of course and justified. Religious, cultural, and political–social or economic reasons have always been closely interwoven, and theological ideas about Jews and Judaism never failed to have an immediate existential effect on the objects of those ideas. That is why Goldhagen warns against a distinction between anti-Judaism and antisemitism, which in his view "is itself founded on a fiction, a sanitized account of the Church's so-called anti-Judaism," and assumes an indissoluble connection between them.[22] His view, therefore, leads to the question of whether there is such a thing as an "eternal Jew-hatred" that has pervaded the history of the Western world since the beginning of Christianity and assumed in Germany in particular "eliminatory" features until the catastrophe occurred between 1933 and 1945; or whether it is necessary to assume clear ruptures and transformations which endowed Jew-hatred with a completely new quality.

III

The question regarding the nature and degree of the influence of Christian antisemitism on later racial or Nazi antisemitism has, however, been the topic of intense disagreement, with historians providing very different answers.[23] Hannah Arendt, for example, in *The Origins of Totalitarianism* rejected the concept of the continuity of an "eternal antisemitism" of Christian provenance and demanded a strict distinction between the murderous hatred of modern antisemitism since the nineteenth century and the traditional Christian Jew-hatred.[24] George Mosse, in his *The Nationalization of the Masses*, similarly stated that the Nazis, like the intellectual "forefathers" of racial antisemitism in general, completely changed the character of anti-Jewish prejudice by secularizing, albeit not abandoning the "basic form" of Christian anti-Judaism.[25] Michael Burleigh echoes this interpretation when he argues that Christianity's "fundamental tenets were stripped out," even though "the remaining diffuse religious emotionality had its uses."[26] In contrast to this line of argument, Leon Poliakov—like Raul Hilberg in his seminal book *The Destruction of the European Jews*[27]—in the Preface to his comprehensive *The History of Antisemitism*, argues that "antisemitism" must be understood as an ancient phenomenon which has remained unchanged, not in its forms of expression but in its essence.[28] And Lucy Dawidowicz in her portrayal of the Shoah likewise traces modern racial antisemitism to "Haman's advice to Ahasuerus," even though she is aware that it has more recent roots in the nineteenth century: the German variant of modern antisemitism was "the bastard child of the union of Christian antisemitism with German nationalism."[29] Other historians such as Steven T. Katz contradicted this assumption of an essential continuity between Christian and National Socialist antisemitism and—without trivializing the dehumanization and demonization of the Jews by Christian theology—pointed out that Christian thinking was able to live with contradictions, including the continuing existence of Judaism despite its alleged divine "rejection," or defer the resolution of the contradiction to the end of history. On the other hand, secular racist ideologies raised the "solution of the Jewish Question" to the level of a human task and thus aimed to disenfranchise and expel, and in their extreme *völkisch* form destroy the Jews.[30] It is true that Katz too notes a "decisive element of continuity"—namely the construction of the "otherness of Jews"—but unlike Goldhagen he comes to the conclusion that, instead of being primarily a consequence of traditional prejudice, antisemitism resulted from the "Aryan myth," together with its counter-myth of the biologically inferior and destructive character of the Jews and its dualistic outlook that explained the entire course of Western history with reference to the alleged German-Jewish racial differences.[31]

The definition of the precise historical link between the centuries-old ecclesiastical tradition of Jew-hatred and the murderous antisemitism of the Nazis is, therefore, one of the most complex and controversial questions not only of the critical self-reflection of Christendom after the Shoah but also of the history of antisemitism. The distinction between the two phenomena necessarily balances on a ridge between an important historical differentiation and an improper trivialization of what seems to be a "merely theological" anti-Judaism. The argument that theological antagonism to Judaism essentially belongs to Christianity but must not be made responsible for antisemitism and the Shoah was and is to this day one of the most common strategies for avoiding recognition of historical guilt. For instance, about a decade ago, I was witness to a panel discussion in the town of Weimar when a serious German Church historian made an extremely telling, completely thoughtless, irresponsible, and possibly cynical comparison between Martin Luther's anti-Judaism and the trains leading to Auschwitz. He argued that just as these trains were, in themselves, completely neutral and only became instruments of genocide when used by the Nazis for their deportations, so Christian anti-Judaism only became part of the history of the Holocaust after being instrumentalized by racial antisemitism.[32]

From my point of view as a historian, the theoretical differentiation between racial, political, economic or cultural antisemitism, and theological anti-Judaism can, if used with caution, be a legitimate instrument of critical analysis when aiming at a precise historical understanding of anti-Jewish motives and motivations; it is, however, constantly at risk of becoming a meaningless and irresponsible trivialization of "merely" anti-Judaistic images of Judaism when failing to understand the profound political implications of negative theological images of Judaism.[33] It is necessary to recognize the interaction between the two phenomena and to closely examine the way in which traditional Christian patterns of thought continued to be active in the new, often secular contexts of the nineteenth and twentieth centuries.

In contrast to a simplistic dichotomy between anti-Judaism and antisemitism as well as an undifferentiated assumption of simple continuity, scholars of antisemitism such as Yehuda Bauer and, above all, Saul Friedländer, have pleaded for a more nuanced approach. Bauer, for instance, describes the "latent or overt non-murderous antisemitic attitudes in the general population" as a consequence of a Christian antisemitism "that had sought to dehumanize the Jews for many centuries," but was never "translated into a genocidal program" by Christian society. Thus, the tradition of Christian antisemitism was not directly responsible for the Nazi persecution, even though it had a disastrous effect on the development of hateful mentalities and "prevented any serious opposition to the Nazis once they had decided to embark on the murder of the Jews."[34] And Friedländer, who rejects Goldhagen's teleological reconstruction of the continuity of an "eliminationist" antisemitism with a laconic remark,[35] suggests that "the majority of Germans, although undoubtedly influenced by various forms of traditional anti-Semitism and easily accepting the segregation of the Jews, shied away from widespread violence against them, urging neither their expulsion from the Reich nor their physical annihilation."[36]

Friedländer's interpretation of the relationship between Christian Jew-hatred and modern antisemitism is part of his comprehensive analysis of the specific character of Nazi antisemitism. In the first volume of *Nazi Germany and the Jews,* his starting point is a differentiated connection between traditional and modern motives, according to which the biological–racist antisemitic ideology of the Nazis did, indeed, use traditional antisemitic images and stereotypes, but radicalized them. In contrast to a strict separation of radical and more moderate variants of anti-Jewish ideology, Friedländer stresses the relevance of two aspects for the new racial antisemitism: "the survival of traditional religious anti-Semitism and the related proliferation of conspiracy theories in which the Jews always played a central role."[37]

The fact that radical antisemites with their fantasies of being under threat as well as their visions of the exclusion and expulsion of the Jews were able to invoke Christian Jew-hatred as a matter of course is, in his view, a result of the *longue durée* of the perhaps most deeply rooted prejudice in Christian Europe, that is, the fact that "in dogma, ritual, and practice, Christianity branded the Jews with what appeared to be an indelible stigma. That stigma had been effaced neither by time nor by events, and throughout the nineteenth and the early decades of the twentieth centuries, Christian religious anti-Semitism remained of central importance in Europe and in the Western world in general."[38] At the same time, Friedländer contradicts the analysis of those historians for whom the "rootedness" and the "very permanence of Christian anti-Judaism" represents the only foundation of all forms of modern antisemitism. In so doing, he refers mainly to Jacob Katz's argument that modern antisemitism was merely "a continuation of the premodern rejection of Judaism by Christianity, even when it [modern antisemitism] renounced any claim to be legitimized by it or even professed to be antagonistic to Christianity." Friedländer considers this interpretation "excessive,"[39] but agrees in principle that modern antisemitism is unimaginable without the profound influence on European societies of the religious antagonism to Jews and Judaism. He believes, however, that the murderous racial antisemitism that led to an unprecedented crime in Nazi Germany possessed a new quality in comparison to traditional Jew-hatred.

Friedländer aptly calls this "redemptive anti-Semitism" because it made the redemption of "Germanness" and the Aryan world dependent on liberation from the Jews and was, therefore, consistently inclined to racial struggle and strategies of extermination. The insight that, according to the historian, is crucial for a differentiated evaluation of the historical impact of Christian elements on modern antisemitism refers to the fact that the tradition of Christian Jew-hatred, with its language, its images, and its construction of the Jews as the "others" in European civilization formed the background and the indispensable arsenal of the more radical, "eliminationist" versions. In Friedländer's felicitous words:

> the very notion of "outsider" applied by modern anti-Semitism to the Jew owed its tenacity not only to Jewish difference as such but also to the depth of its religious roots. Whatever else could be said about the Jew, he was first and foremost the "other," who had rejected Christ and revelation. Finally, perhaps the most powerful effect of religious anti-Judaism was the dual structure of the anti-Jewish image inherited from Christianity. On the one hand, the Jew was a pariah, the despised witness of the triumphal onward march of the true faith; on the other, from the Late Middle Ages onward, an opposite image appeared in popular Christianity and in millenarian movements, that of the demonic Jew, the perpetrator of ritual murder, the plotter against Christianity, the herald of the anti-Christ, the potent and occult emissary of the forces of evil. It is this dual image that reappears in some

major aspects of modern anti-Semitism. And, its threatening and occult dimension became the recurrent theme of the main conspiracy theories of the Western world.[40]

Nevertheless, although according to Friedländer, the "centrality of the Jews" in the "phantasmic universe" of paranoid racial antisemitism can be explained "only by its roots in the Christian tradition," the spread of a radical variant of this ideology, which led to the murderous antisemitism of the Nazis, represents a new phenomenon that contradicts simplistic assumptions of continuity. In Friedländer's view, the specifically German contribution to this ideology in the wake of the social and economic crises after World War I consisted in the development of a radical current of racial antisemitism that "emphasized the mythic dimensions of the race and the sacredness of Aryan blood."[41] This "redemptive anti-Semitism," as he calls it, represents a novel mutation of racially motivated Jew-hatred, which hoped for an intellectual, moral, and physical redemption of the "Aryans" by cleansing both the individuals and society of the "decomposing" presence of the Jews. Friedländer discusses two types of racial antisemitism. One is based on the results of pseudo-scientific research in the late nineteenth century, such as in the areas of racial biology, social Darwinism and eugenics, the other on a "decidedly religious vision" where "the struggle against the Jews is the dominant aspect of a worldview in which other racist themes are but secondary appendages."[42] The second type arose from the fear of "miscegenation," the apprehension about a Jewish infiltration of German society and the dream of a German rebirth, which would be the result of liberation from the Jews by expulsion or something worse. The distinguishing marks of this new quasi-religious ideology that was shaped by racial biology, social Darwinism and eugenics were the assertion of the biologically inferior and destructive character of the Jews and a dualistic outlook that explained the course of Western history, including the social, political, and intellectual conflicts of the time, in terms of the alleged Germanic-Jewish racial difference. Friedländer's convincing portrayal of the National Socialist variant of racial antisemitism thus manages to integrate the elements of continuity and discontinuity in the German ideology through the ages. The combination of Christian Messianic hopes and traditional anti-Jewish motives had already given rise to an enormously powerful Jew-hatred, which now was joined—and not only in Germany—by modern pseudo-science and the mystical Messianic promise of the redemption of the "Aryan race" from contamination by the Jewish counter-race. This account shows strong affinities with Israeli historian Uriel Tal's studies of the type of radical *völkisch* antisemitism that consistently developed into a religion which, despite remaining dependent on Christian antisemitism, also turned against Christian religion's Jewish origins and demanded the programmatic Germanization and "de-Judaization" of Christianity.[43]

Friedländer does not claim that "redemptive anti-Semitism" was an ubiquitous conviction but that it was based on the history of the late nineteenth and early twentieth centuries. He describes how it gained ground—particularly in the Weimar years—in parts of the public sphere in Germany. "Redemptive antisemitism" thus becomes a key concept for understanding not only the Nazi ideology as such but also the enormous attraction it had for the German elites (including the Protestant and Catholic Christian Churches) and the population as a whole. By combining the old Christian antisemitic prejudices and the social-Darwinistic theses of modern science with Messianic hopes and expectations, National Socialism created a powerful instrument for its struggle for the approval of the German people. At the same time, it should be noted that racial antisemitism, including the variant of "redemptive antisemitism"—albeit already in evidence, above all among the intellectual elites, before the Nazis came to power—was a marginal phenomenon initially rejected even by convinced representatives of a nationalistic antisemitism that was widespread in the Churches.[44] Friedländer notes that the general approval of the antisemitic measures of the Nazi regime up to 1938, which aimed at the exclusion of the Jews from German society and which pressed ahead fast with their dispossession and stigmatization, was ultimately based on the proliferation of a non-radical, non-murderous Jew-hatred among the German population. Only during the war, thanks to an intensive propaganda campaign, the Nazis managed to convert "redemptive antisemitism" from the quasi-religious belief of a small minority into an opinion which—assisted by the current "moderate" antisemitism—was accepted by more and more people. Friedländer offers no explicit explanation as to how this rapid transformation occurred, but the portrayal of the development itself seems more than plausible.

As far as the relationship between continuity and change in antisemitism in the nineteenth and early twentieth centuries is concerned, Friedländer's interpretation ultimately produces a certain synthesis between two influential interpretative models found in recent research into antisemitism. These have resulted into rather different evaluations of the significance of religious elements in the context of "modern" variants. One model, which stresses the political and social causes and contexts of antisemitism, interprets "modern antisemitism" in Germany as the expression of a crisis in modern liberal bourgeois society and culture, which led many people to project everything frightening and contradictory onto the Jews by depicting them as a dangerous alien power from which Germany had to be liberated, at least by restricting or abolishing their civil rights. Initially the religious tradition of Jew-hatred does not seem to have played a particular part in this form of antisemitism, whose function has been interpreted as providing the "cultural code" of a secular, anti-liberal, anti-democratic, and anti-pluralist ideology which turned the Jewish minority into a symbol of the crises of the liberal capitalist economic order.[45] Therefore, at first glance, in an age of increasing secularization, the political, social, and economic causes of antisemitism appear much more significant than religious thought patterns that are patently unable to explain the novelty of modern antisemitism.

In contrast to this, the second model, by accentuating the significance of cultural history and the history of mentality, places greater emphasis on the long continuity of Jew-hatred in the Christian West and rightly stresses that the Jewish minority became a symbol of hatred because Jews had always been negative symbols, that is, embodiments of the "Other." The traditional stereotypes and religious prejudices remained effective even under increasingly secular conditions. Images and myths of a religious kind about Jews and Judaism, such as charges of deicide and ritual murder or fantasies of well poisoning and host desecration, were deeply anchored in the collective consciousness even after the Enlightenment and far into the twentieth century and could be activated for racially motivated campaigns of hatred, albeit in new, modernized clothes.[46] Thus, as is well known, the charge of ritual murder was transformed into the image of Jewish "Mammonism," materialism, or Jewish "bloodsucking" (i.e. capitalism) and the accusation of "deicide" into the claim of the dangerous alien and demonic qualities of Judaism, which was considered to be capable of any and every crime against non-Jewish society. This allegedly "rational" antisemitism, as it claimed to be, was altogether more consistent than the traditional Jew-hatred because the "Jewish question" had to be "solved" in one way or another. At the same time, racism and *völkisch* ideas penetrated deep into Christian theology and ecclesiastical life: This was possible chiefly because one of the fundamental structures of anti-Jewish discourse was preserved despite all modernization: Judaism served throughout as a counter-image to the self-understanding of non-Jewish society. Conservatives and liberals, orthodox Christians and radical critics of religion, *völkisch* nationalists and early socialists all regarded Judaism as the antithesis of their ideological aims—as unbelievers, as representatives of capitalism, as enemies of the world, as counter-race. That is why Nazism's strategic "usurpation and colonization of Christian theology, especially its antisemitism," as Susannah Heschel has described it in her book on *The Aryan Jesus*, was so successful in the 1930s.[47] Conversely, this is the reason why Christian anti-Judaism remained compatible with political forms of Jew-hatred and why there were reciprocal influences and partly an adoption of racial antisemitism by the Church.

Any analysis of the relationship between Christianity and antisemitism needs to confront the silence and complicity of the Christian Churches during the Shoah: their theological contribution to the antisemitic discourse of the 1930s and 1940s; their assent to the discrimination of German Jewry; their political failure in the face of the dramatic and murderous intensification of the Jewish policy of the Nazis from the pogrom of November 1938 and the outbreak of World War II; and their general inability to respond to the genocide in a way that would have corresponded to the ethical claims of Christianity. Here, as before, a brief comparison between Goldhagen's and Friedländer's interpretations will be instructive. It is not surprising that Goldhagen, in *Hitler's Willing Executioners*, talks about the "moral bankruptcy of the German Churches"[48] and devotes a large space in his arguments to their share of the ideological and political responsibility for the Shoah, since he believes Christian antisemitism to have been the nucleus of the "eliminationist" ideology of the Nazis and the attitude of the Churches emblematic for the entire German people. The "attitude of the Churches serves as a crucial test for evaluating the ubiquity and depth of eliminationist antisemitism in Germany,"[49] he asserts, and the detailed reasons he gives for his view that both the Protestant and the Catholic Church not only kept silent when Jews were discriminated against, persecuted, driven out of their homes, deported, and murdered[50]—as if all moral commands had been cancelled and Jews were not part of humanity—but also "cooperated wholeheartedly" in the Nazis' murderous policies,[51] supply the proof of his book's fundamental argument:

> If the ecclesiastical men, whose vocation was to preach love and to be the custodians of compassion, pity, and morality, acquiesced or looked with favour upon and supported the elimination of the Jews from German society, then this would be further and particular persuasive proof of the ubiquity

> of eliminationist antisemitism in Germany, an antisemitism so strong that it not only inhibited the natural flow of the feeling of pity but also overruled the moral imperatives of the creed to speak out on behalf of those who have fallen among murderers. As studies of the Churches have shown, it cannot be doubted that antisemitism did succeed in turning the Christian community—its leaders, its clergy, and its rank and file—against its most fundamental tradition.[52]

Friedländer's analysis is much more cautious, but its moral force is by no means less than that of Goldhagen. On the contrary, the subtler tone of Friedländer's examination of the silence and ideological complicity of the Churches, based on a detailed study of the relevant research, not only produces a more nuanced image but also, in its sober clarity, confronts the reader at least as forcefully with the frightening insight into the full dimension of the moral and political failure of the Christian Churches in Germany and in the whole of Nazi-occupied Europe. In his view, no Christian self-reflection after the Shoah can avoid acknowledging that the role of the Christian Churches "was, of course, decisive in the permanence and pervasiveness of anti-Jewish beliefs and attitudes in Germany and throughout the Western world."[53] This was all the more the case because the Christian faith continued to exert a strong influence within German society—despite the often hostile attitude of the Nazi party to the Christian tradition and the organized Church—and because it was precisely this deeply rooted religious anti-Judaism that made many Christians receptive to the antisemitic propaganda of the Nazis, facilitated their assent to anti-Jewish measures, and calmed their conscience over the discrimination and persecution inflicted on the Jewish minority. Without wishing to generalize, Friedländer arrives at some fundamental conclusions: the first concerns the pervasiveness of Christian antisemitism, that is, the "stigmatizing intrinsic to Christian dogma or tradition," which did not entail a uniform eliminationist ideology, as Goldhagen assumes, but which in their often very different forms and nuances "found their way into the minds and hearts of tens of millions of believers, Protestant or Catholic" and "offset any urges of compassion and charity, or even fuelled aggressive antisemitism."[54] The second refers to the shocking silence in the face of the Jews' sufferings and the Nazis' genocidal intentions: "Although some sporadic protests by some Catholic bishops or Protestant religious leaders did take place, the vast majority of Protestant and Catholic authorities remained publicly silent in the face of the deportations of the Jews and the growing knowledge of their extermination."[55] Unlike Goldhagen, Friedländer does not insinuate that the Christian Churches actively assented to the genocide as an ultimate fulfilment of their obsessive eliminationist fantasies, but he doesn't spare Christianity the challenging question whether or not it was the general European "religious anti-Jewish culture" that contributed "to the passive acceptance, sometimes to the occasional support, of the most extreme policies of persecution, deportation, and mass murder unfolding in the midst of Europe's Christian populations."[56]

***

"What is the value of religion, and in particular of Christianity, if it provides no defence against brutality and can even become a willing participant in genocide?" This question raised by historian Doris Bergen in the introduction to her book *The Twisted Cross*[57] leads to most challenging reflections on the involvement of Christianity and the Christian Churches in the history of the unprecedented genocide of the Jews. The profoundly disturbing recognition that this genocide occurred in a heartland of Christian Western culture—which from a purely Christian perspective is a cause for profound shame and dismay—has become a shared Christian and Jewish challenge and a motive for a reflection, carried out in a dialogue about the human condition, religion, and ethics after Auschwitz. In an age of ongoing violence and genocides, this theme raises universal issues of the relationship between religion and barbaric violence, as well as the potential of religions to counteract inhumanity.[58] For the Christian Churches, one element of this reflection will have to continue to be to resist the temptation of apologetics concerning the past, to overcome the still rather widespread compulsion to deny or relativize historical guilt,[59] and, instead, to engage, with greater historical honesty, in a self-critical dialogue with those disastrously influential theological thought patterns that belong to the heritage of Christianity and have been among the causes of its catastrophic failure in the face of the unprecedented inhumanity of the Nazi regime.

Notes

1. George Steiner, "Through that Glass Darkly," reprinted in Steiner, *No Passion Spent: Essays 1978–1996* (New Haven and London: Yale University Press, 1996), pp. 328–347, here at p. 336.
2. David Nirenberg, *Anti-Judaism: The Western Tradition* (New York and London: W. W. Norton & Company, 2013), p. 459.

3. For the importance and continuity of Christian violence against Jews in Germany from the early modern period to the Shoah, see Helmut Walser Smith, *The Continuities of German History: Nation, Religion, and Race across the Long Nineteenth Century* (Cambridge: Cambridge University Press, 2008), chapter 3; for the concept of "catastrophic violence," see particularly p. 7; pp. 75–77; 83; pp. 101–103.
4. Daniel J. Goldhagen, *A Moral Reckoning: The Role of the Catholic Church in the Holocaust and Its Unfulfilled Duty of Repair* (London: Abacus, 2002), p. 9.
5. According to Goldhagen, the genocide was "one logical, though not the only logical or an inevitable, policy extension of the antisemitism they had propagated and the earlier eliminationist policies they had supported. Even if the churchmen disapproved of this most extreme eliminationist punishment, their antisemitism was such that it was hard to rouse themselves in sympathy for the Jews" (ibid., p. 149).
6. Ibid., p. 32. Equally drastically, philosopher Karl Jaspers drew a line of continuity from Martin Luther to Auschwitz, claiming—in view of Martin Luther's infamous anti-Jewish recommendation to the authorities in 1543: "What Hitler has done, had been recommended by Luther, with the exception of the murder in gas chambers"; see Karl Jaspers, "Die nichtchristlichen Religionen und das Abendland," in idem, *Philosophie und Welt: Reden und Aufsätze*, 2nd ed. (Munich: Piper, 1963), pp. 156–166, here p. 162.
7. Ibid., p. 49. Goldhagen emphasizes, of course, that he could have written the same moral verdict on the Protestant churches and that his analysis is meant to be "exemplary" for the German and European churches in general (p. 34).
8. See Daniel J. Goldhagen, *Hitler's Willing Executioners: Ordinary Germans and the Holocaust* (London: Abacus, 1997), p. 442.
9. See the argument of chapter 1, in ibid., pp. 27–48.
10. Ibid., p. 32.
11. Ibid., p. 67.
12. For the discussion on Goldhagen's book, see Julius H. Schoeps (ed.), *Ein Volk von Mördern? Die Dokumentation zur Goldhagen-Kontroverse um die Rolle der Deutschen im Holocaust* (Hamburg: Hoffmann & Campe, 1996); Yisrael Gutman, Goldhagen—His Critics and His Contribution,' in *Yad Vashem Studies*. Vol. 26

(1998), pp. 329–364; Robert A. Shandley (ed.), *Unwilling Germans? The Goldhagen Debate* (Minneapolis: University of Minnesota Press, 1998); Geoff Eley (ed.), *The "Goldhagen Effect": History, Memory, Nazism—Facing the German Past* (Ann Arbor: University of Michigan Press, 2000); Yehuda Bauer, *Rethinking the Holocaust* (New Haven and London: Yale University Press, 2001), pp. 93–111; for the debate on his portrayal of Catholicism, see John K. Roth, "Goldhagen and the Moral Reckoning," in *Menora*, vol. 14 (2003), pp. 71–75; Olaf Blaschke, "Hitlers willige Katholiken?: Goldhagens Moralpredigt gegen die katholische Kirche aus der Sicht eines anderen Kritikers ihres Antisemitismus," in *Zeitschrift für Geschichtswissenschaft*, vol. 50, No. 12 (2002), pp. 1099–1115; Olaf Blaschke, "Goldhagen und Hitlers willige Katholiken zwischen Sensationshascherei und Wirklichkeit. Ein ernstes Themenfeld droht zu verbrennen," in *Menora*, vol. 14 (2003), pp. 163–193; Julius H. Schoeps (ed.), *Goldhagen, der Vatikan und die Judenfeindschaft* (Berlin: Philo, 2003); Ronald J. Rychlak, 'Goldhagen vs. Christianity,' in Patrick J. Gallo (ed.), *Pius XII, the Holocaust and the Revisionists: Essays* (Jefferson, NC: McFarland&Co, 2006), pp. 167–180.

13. See the chapter "Repairing the Harm," in Goldhagen, *A Moral Reckoning*, 243–372.
14. See http://www.jewishvirtuallibrary.org/jsource/Holocaust/poperep.html; the document responds to the question, "Did Christians give every possible assistance to those being persecuted, and in particular to the persecuted Jews?," in a way that distorts historical reality and seems clearly motivated by apologetics: "Many did, but others did not. Those who did help to save Jewish lives as much as was in their power, even to the point of placing their own lives in danger, must not be forgotten. During and after the war, Jewish communities and Jewish leaders expressed their thanks for all that had been done for them, including what Pope Pius XII did personally or through his representatives to save hundreds of thousands of Jewish lives. Many Catholic bishops, priests, religious and laity have been honoured for this reason by the State of Israel."
15. As a critique of the document's unhistorical character from a historian's point of view, see Michael R. Marrus, "We Remember: The Vatican and the Holocaust in Historical Context," in Judith H. Banki and John T. Pawlikowski (eds), *Ethics in the Shadow of the*

Holocaust: Christian and Jewish Perspectives (Franklin, Wisconsin: Sheed & Ward, 2001), pp. 117–133. For critical comments from a Catholic theologian involved in Catholic-Jewish Dialogue, see John T. Pawlikowski, "The Vatican and the Holocaust: Putting 'We Remember' in Context," in *Dimensions*, vol. 12, No. 2 (1998), pp. 11. The US Catholic Conference implicitly contradicted the Vatican document in its 2001 statement "Catholic Teaching on the Shoah: Implementing the Holy See's *We Remember*": "Christian anti-Judaism did lay the groundwork for racial, genocidal anti-Semitism by stigmatizing not only Judaism but Jews themselves for opprobrium and contempt. So the Nazi theories tragically found fertile soil in which to plant the horror of an unprecedented attempt at genocide" (cited in http://www.usccb.org/beliefs-and-teachings/ecumenical-and-interreligious/jewish/upload/Catholic-Teaching-on-the-Shoah-Implementing-the-Holy-See-s-We-Remember-2001.pdf). As a comparison to the apology of the French episcopate in 1997, see Patrick Henry, 'The Art of Christian Apology: Comparing the French Catholic Church's Apology to the Jews and the Vatican's 'We Remember',' in *Shofar*, vol. 26, No. 3 (2008), pp. 87–104. Goldhagen, *A Moral Reckoning*, accuses the Catholic Church of erecting "an iron curtain between the Church's own virulent antisemitism and the virulent antisemitism that led the Germans and those who helped them to persecute and then slaughter Jews" (ibid., p. 90).

16. See the response of the International Jewish Committee on Interreligious Consultations (accessed at http://www.jcrelations.net/en/?item=1016)
17. For the text of the declaration, see http://www.jcrelations.net/Dabru_Emet_-_A_Jewish_Statement_on_Christians_and_Christianity.2395.0.html; for the genesis of the document as well as the public discussion on its different elements, see the contributions in Rainer Kampling und Michael Weinrich (eds), *Dabru Emet—Redet Warheit: Eine jüdische Herausforderung zum Dialog mit den Christen* (Gütersloh: Gütersloher Verlagshaus, 2003); Erwin Dirschel (ed.), *Redet Wahrheit—Dabru Emet: Jüdisch-christiches Gespräch über Gott, Messias und Dekalog* (Münster: Lit, 2004); Hubert Frankemölle (ed.), *Juden und Christen im Gespräch über "Dabru Emet—Redet Wahrheit"* (Paderborn: Bonifatius, 2005). As a more comprehensive commentary on the entire

document, see Tykva Frymer Kensky, David Novak, Peter Ochs, David Fox Sandmel and Michael A Signer (eds), *Christianity in Jewish Terms* (Boulder, CO: Westview Press, 2000).

18. See Michael A. Signer, 'Some Reflections on Dabru Emet' (access at http://www.jcrelations.net/en/?item=781).
19. David Rosen, "*Dabru Emet*: Its Significance for the Jewish-Christian Dialogue" (access at http://www.jcrelations.net/Dabru+Emet%3A+Its+Significance+for+the+Jewish-Christian+Dialogue.1504.0.html?L=3).
20. Ekkehard Stegemann, 'Theologie zwischen Antisemitismuskritik und alten Vorurteilen,' in Christina Tuor Kurth (ed.), *Neuer Antisemitismus—alte Vorurteile?* (Stuttgart et al.: Kohlhammer, 2001), pp. 199–215, here 200.
21. See Peter von der Osten-Sacken (ed.), *Das mißbrauchte Evangelium: Studien zu Theologie und Praxis der Thüringer Deutschen Christen* (Berlin: Institut für Kirche und Judentum, 2002).
22. Goldhagen, *A Moral Reckoning*, p. 104.
23. See, for example, Gavin Langmuir, *Toward a Definition of Antisemitism* (Berkeley: University of California Press, 1990), pp. 57–99; Paul Lawrence Rose, *Revolutionary Antisemitism in Germany from Kant to Wagner* (Princeton: Princeton University Press, 1990); John Weiss, *Ideology of Death: Why the Holocaust Happened in Germany* (Chicago: Ivan R. Dee, 1996).
24. Hannah Arendt, *The Origins of Totalitarianism* (New York: Harcourt, Brace and Company, new ed. with added prefaces, 1978), pp. xi–xvi; p. 3–120; and see Hannah Arendt, "Approaches to the German Problem," in *Partisan Review*, vol. 12, No. 1 (1945), pp. 93–106, here p. 96: "Nazism owes nothing to any part of the Western tradition, be it German or not, Catholic or Protestant, Christian."
25. George L. Mosse, *The Nationalization of the Masses: Political Symbolism and Mass Movements in Germany from the Napoleonic Wars through the Third Reich* (New York: Howard Fertig, 1975), p. 80.
26. Michael Burleigh, *The Third Reich: A New History* (Basingstoke and Oxford: Macmillan, 2000), p. 256.
27. See Raul Hilberg, *The Destruction of the European Jews*, vol. 1, 3rd ed. (New Haven and London, Yale University Press, 2003), pp. 1–27.

28. Leon Poliakov, "Foreword," in: *The History of Antisemitism*, vol. 1: *From the Time of Christ to the Court Jews* (Philadelphia: University of Pennsylvania Press, 2003), pp. vii–xi.
29. Lucy Dawidowicz, *The War Against the Jews: 1933–1945* (London: Weidenfeld and Nicolson, 1975), p. 23.
30. See Steven T. Katz, *Kontinuität und Diskontinuität zwischen christlichem und nationalsozialistischem Antisemitismus* (Tübingen: J. C. B. Mohr, 2001), esp. pp. 43–45.
31. Ibid., pp. 41–43 and pp. 59–61. For the 'Aryan Myth,' see Leon Poliakov, *The Aryan Myth: A History of Racist and Nationalist Ideas in Europe* (New York: Barnes and Noble Books, 1996).
32. For Luther's views on Jews and Judaism, see Heiko A. Oberman, *The Roots of Antisemitism in the Age of Renaissance and Reformation*, trans. James I. Porter (Philadelphia: Fortress Press, 1984); Peter von der Osten-Sacken, *Martin Luther und die Juden: neu untersucht anhand von Anton Margarithas "Der gantz Jüdisch glaub" (1530/31)* (Stuttgart: Kohlhammer, 2002); Thomas Kaufmann, Luthers 'Judenschriften'. Ein Beitrag zu ihrer histprischen Kontextualisierung (Tübingen: Mohr Siebeck, 2011); idem, *Luthers Juden* (Ditzingen: Philipp Reclam jun. Verlag, 2014).
33. For research on Protestant antisemitism, see for example, Marikje Smid, "Protestantismus und Antisemitismus 1930–1933," in Jochen-Christoph Kaiser and Martin Greschat (eds), *Der Holocaust und die Protestanten: Analysen einer Verstrickung* (Munich: Kaiser, 1988), pp. 38–72 and Heinz E. Tödt, "Die Novemberverbrechen 1938 und der deutsche Protestantismus: Ideologische und theologische Voraussetzungen für die Hinnahme des Pogroms," in *Kirchliche Zeitgeschichte*, vol. 2, No. 1 (1989), pp. 14–37. The conceptual distinctions are based on the assumption that the varied manifestations and motives of Protestant Jew-hatred cannot simply be understood with the aid of the concept of antisemitism but have to be interpreted by using different conceptual categories. In contrast to racial antisemitism, whose biologist–determinist views do not permit the Jews to escape their alleged racial characteristics, "anti-Judaism" aims explicitly at "the rejection of Judaism as a non-Christian religious community on biblical and theological grounds" (Smid, 'Protestantismus und Antisemitismus,' p. 41). In contrast to this, the most common type of social and cultural Jew-hatred was characterized by moral, social, and cultural distance

from the Jewish minority, but could also adopt both racial and religious elements; see Marikje Smid, *Deutscher Protestantismus und Judentum 1932/1933* (Munich: Kaiser, 1990), pp. 200–201. Tödt, "Die Novemberverbrechen 1938," 32 assumes a "synergy of anti-Jewish attitudes" and argues that these ideal–typical motives never existed in their pure form but interacted and reinforced each other. The differentiation between "anti-Judaism" and "anti-Semitism," I would argue, is only meaningful as an instrument that contributes to a critical analysis of theological traditions (such as parts of cultural Protestantism in Germany) which, although actively rejecting antisemitism in the political realm, continued to pass on anti-Jewish theological images of Judaism without reflecting upon their political impact; see Christian Wiese, *Challenging Colonial Discourse: Jewish Studies and Protestant Theology in Wilhelmine Germany* (Leiden and Boston: Brill Publishers, 2005).

34. Bauer, *Rethinking the Holocaust*, p. 105.
35. Saul Friedländer, *Nazi Germany and the Jews, 1933–1939: The Years of Persecution* (New York: HarperCollins, 1997), p. 387 n. 53: "An interpretation of the events assuming the widespread presence in German society at large, throughout the modern era, of an 'eliminationist anti-Semitism,' craving the physical annihilation of the Jews, is not convincing on the basis of the material presented in this study."
36. Ibid., p. 4.
37. Ibid., pp. 82–83.
38. Ibid. Similar is the interpretation by Philippe Burin, *From Prejudice to the Holocaust: Nazi Anti-Semitism* (New York and London: The New Press, 2005), who emphasizes the "internal diversity and the relative novelty of Nazi-Judeophobia" (p. 6), but also the "extent to which the new [antisemitic] discourse in fact substantially perpetuated the Christian tradition of stigmatizing the Jews" (p. 20). Similarly, Peter Pulzer writes in the introduction to the revised edition of his classic study on antisemitism: "I am more strongly convinced than I was when I wrote the book that a tradition of religiously-inspired Jew hatred [...] was a necessary condition for the success of antisemitic propaganda, even when expressed in non-religious terms and absorbed by those no longer religiously observant"; see Peter Pulzer, *The Rise of Political Antisemitism in*

Germany and Austria, 2nd ed. (Cambridge, MA: Harvard University Press, 1988), p. xxii.

39. Friedländer, *Nazi Germany and the Jews, 1933–1939*, p. 83. The quotation from Katz is to be found in Jacob Katz, *From Prejudice to Destruction: Anti-Semitism 1700–1933* (Cambridge, MA: Harvard University Press, 1982), p. 319. Katz continues: "No anti-Semite, even if he himself was anti-Christian, ever forwent the use of those anti-Jewish arguments rooted in the denigration of Jews and Judaism in earlier Christian times." See the similar argument in Burin, *From Prejudice to the Holocaust*, p. 24.
40. Friedländer, *Nazi Germany and the Jews, 1933–1939*, p. 84.
41. Ibid., pp. 85–86.
42. Ibid., pp. 86–87.
43. See Uriel Tal, "Religious and Anti-Religious Roots of Modern Anti-Semitism," in idem, *Religion, Politics and Ideology in the Third Reich: Selected Essays*, ed. Saul Friedländer (New York: Routledge, 2004), pp. 171–190; and see idem, *Christians and Jews in Germany: Religion, Politics and Ideology in the Second Reich, 1870–1914* (Ithaca, NY and London: Cornell University Press, 1975), pp. 223–389.
44. See Geoff Eley, 'What Are the Contexts for German Antisemitism?,' in *Studies in Contemporary Jewry*, vol. 13 (1997), pp. 100–132, here p. 122; and see the chapter on 'Eliminationist Racism' in Walser Smith, *The Continuities of German History*, pp. 167–210.
45. See Shulamit Volkov, "Antisemitism as a Cultural Code: Reflections on the History and Historiography of Antisemitism in Imperial Germany," in *Leo Baeck Institute Yearbook*, vol. 23 (1978), pp. 25–46.
46. See, for example, Christhard Hoffmann, "Christlicher Antijudaismus und moderner Antisemitismus. Zusammenhänge und Differenzen als Problem der historischen Antisemitismusforschung," in Leonore Siegele-Wenschkewitz (ed.), *Christlicher Antijudaismus und Antisemitismus: Theologische und kirchliche Programme Deutscher Christen* (Frankfurt am Main: Hain, 1994), pp. 293–317.
47. Susannah Heschel, *The Aryan Jesus: Christian Theologians and the Bible in Nazi Germany* (Princeton, NJ: Princeton University Press, 2008), p. 8.

48. Goldhagen, *Hitler's Willing Executioners*, p. 107. See his detailed analysis within the context of his chapter on "Eliminationist Antisemitism," particularly pp. 107–114.
49. Ibid., p. 434.
50. Se ibid., pp. 436–437: "Throughout the period of Nazi rule, as the government and people of Germany were subjecting the Jews of Germany and those of the conquered countries to an increasingly severe persecution that culminated in their physical annihilation, the German Protestant and Catholic churches, their governing bodies, their bishops, and most of their theologians watched the suffering that Germans inflicted on the Jews in silence. No explicit public word of sympathy for the Jews, no explicit public condemnation or protest against their persecution issued from any of the authoritative figures within the churches."
51. Ibid., p. 111.
52. Ibid., pp. 434–435. The reason for this is the fact that "even in the Christian Churches, racist antisemitism overlay, and to a large extent, replaced the traditional religious enmity to Jews" (p. 436).
53. Saul Friedländer, *The Years of Extermination: Nazi Germany and the Jews, 1939–1945* (New York: HarperCollins, 2007), p. 55 See ibid., pp. 190–1911: "The anti-Jewish measures were accepted, even approved, by the population and the spiritual and intellectual elites, most blatantly so by the Christian Churches. What was tacitly approved by the French Church was explicitly welcomed by the Polish clergy, enthusiastically supported by part of German Protestantism, and more prudently so by the remainder of Christian churches in the Reich. Such religious support for or acceptance of various degrees of anti-Jewish persecution helped of course to still any doubts, particularly at a time when among most Europeans the influence of the Churches remained considerable and their guidance was eagerly sought."
54. Ibid., p. 575.
55. Ibid., p. 574. Friedländer emphasizes that "a clear distinction was systematically established between the tiny minority of converted Jews and the quasi totality of the 'ordinary' Jews" (ibid.). He acknowledges that some Christian institutions took risks in hiding Jews, however not without pointing out that "proselytism and conversion were major, albeit very elusive elements in granting such help, particularly in the hiding of children. In some places

conversion may have been considered essential for better camouflage, but generally it was an aim in itself. This of course changes the historical assessment of Christian assistance, notwithstanding risk, compassion, or charity" (ibid., p. 577); this remark is especially significant given Friedländer's own biographical experience.

56. Ibid., 576.
57. Doris Bergen, *Twisted Cross: The German Christian Movement in the Third Reich* (Chapel Hill: The University of North Carolina Press, 1996), p. xii.
58. See Doris Bergen, "Religion and Genocide: A Historiographical Survey," in Dan Stone (ed.), *The Historiography of Genocide* (London: Palgrave Macmillan, 2008), pp. 94–227; Omer Bartov and Phyllis Mack (eds), *In God's Name: Genocide and Religion in the Twentieth Century* (New York: Berghahn, 2001).
59. For the question concerning guilt in the discourse on the Shoah, see Dan Diner, "On Guilt Discourses and Other Narratives: Epistemological Observations," in Gulie Ne'eman Arad (ed.), *Passing into History: Nazism and the Holocaust beyond Memory: In Honor of Saul Friedländer on His Sixty-Fifth Birthday* (Special Issue of *History & Memory*, vol. 9, No. 1&2 [1997]) (Bloomington: Indiana University Press, 1997), pp. 301–320.

CHAPTER 5

"Every Sane Thinker Must Be an Anti-Semite": Antisemitism and Holocaust Denial in the Theology of Radical Catholic Traditionalists

Mark Weitzman

The radical Catholic traditionalist movement surged into the headlines when Pope Benedict XVI announced, on January 21, 2009, that he was lifting the excommunications of four bishops associated with the breakaway Society of Saint Pius X (SSPX). This was immediately followed by

My thanks to Mary Christine Athans, who generously shared her important work on Denis Fahey and Charles Coughlin, as well as her encouragement and incisive criticism on an earlier version of this chapter, which was presented at the conference Global Antisemitism: A Crisis of Modernity, Yale University on August 23–25, 2010. My thanks as well to Jeffrey Herf, Anthony McElligott, and Alvin Rosenfeld whose incisive comments on different versions of this chapter have been extremely helpful. Finally, I would also like to acknowledge the deep interest and encouragement of my good friend, the late Robert Wistrich, whose untimely passing is an inestimable loss to all who engage in the study of and work against antisemitism.

The title is taken from an article by the radical Catholic John Sharpe, Judaism and the Vatican, where he quotes Father Denis Fahey as the author of that statement. Sharpe's article was accessed at http://webarchive.org/web/20031012011638/http://www.sspx.ca/Angelus/2003_June/Judaism.html

M. Weitzman (✉)
Simon Wiesenthal Center, New York, NY, USA

A. McElligott, J. Herf (eds.), *Antisemitism Before and Since the Holocaust*, DOI 10.1007/978-3-319-48866-0_5

the airing, on Swedish television, of an interview with one of the bishops, Richard Williamson, in which he questioned the Holocaust saying "I believe that the historical evidence is strongly against, is hugely against six million Jews having been deliberately gassed in gas chambers as a deliberate policy of Adolf Hitler"[1] and "I think that 200,000 to 300,000 Jews perished in Nazi concentration camps, but none of them in gas chambers."[2] The resulting controversy dominated the media and has since, in different manifestations, become a recurring story.

Since then, the radical Catholic movement has seldom been far from the headlines, yet for many, the reality behind the headlines is still blurry. How large is the movement, and who belongs to it? What exactly do they believe, and is Holocaust denial and antisemitism an essential core element of their belief system? Does Williamson's view reflect a larger constituency, or is he just a lone wolf? Are these groups isolated and limited in their influence and impact, or do they merit serious attention and concern? Was the controversy over Williamson a brief flare-up that has since faded, or is there something deeper than the wild statements of one individual that should still command our attention?

While a full scale study of these groups is beyond the scope of this chapter, I will suggest that a closer examination will demonstrate that Williamson was not an isolated aberration, that antisemitism is indeed a foundational aspect of the core beliefs of the radical movement, and that while their numbers are not overwhelming, they do deserve our attention because of their continued influence to both the Catholic Church and the general public discourse on these issues. Finally, as we confront the threat posed to the West and Islam by the resurgent violence jihadist mentality, the remaining evidence of extremist exclusionary Catholicism is a reminder that Western tradition also contains radical religious roots that have left their tragic mark on the shaping of our modern world.

To date, there has been very little scholarly attention paid to these groups. Michael Cuneo's 1999 sociological study, *The Smoke of Satan*, has been the only full-length treatment of this movement in the USA and is in need of both updating and enhancement. However, Cuneo's work has been useful in defining radical Catholic traditionalists as those who have rejected the reforms of Vatican II and "entered into schism from the institutional church" a definition that I will follow.[3]

An unambiguous display of the rejection of Vatican II occurred on November 12, 2013. That evening, a group of young Catholics began to disrupt a service of Jews and Catholics who had gathered in the

Metropolitan Cathedral of Buenos Aires to commemorate the 1938 Kristallnacht pogrom in Nazi Germany in a ceremony inaugurated by Cardinal Jorge Mario Bergoglio, who in 2013 became Pope Francis. The protesters were "shouting the rosary and the 'Our Father' prayer ... (and) saying 'followers of false gods must be kept out of the sacred temple.'"[4] According to Buenos Aires Rabbi Abraham Skorka (who coauthored a book with the future pope on modern faith and family), the protestors "began to hand out little pieces of paper saying that Jews were blaspheming the place," and also made comments such as "the Jews killed Jesus."[5] The day after the event, the Reverend Christian Bouchacourt, the South American leader of the SSPX, identified the protesters as members of his organization, justifying their actions as "a reaction of faithful who are scandalized ... the protesters have a right to feel outraged when rabbis preside over a ceremony in a Catholic cathedral."[6]

The Israeli historian, Israel J. Yuval, recently wrote that "The Christian-Jewish debate that started nineteen hundred years ago, in our day came to a conciliatory close. ... In one fell swoop, the anti-Jewish position of Christianity became reprehensible and illegitimate. ... Ours is thus the first generation that can and may discuss the Christian-Jewish debate from a certain remove ... a post-polemical age."[7] Yuval based his optimistic assessment on the strength of the reforms in Catholicism that stemmed from the adoption by the Second Vatican Council in 1965 of the document known as "Nostra Aetate" which has been described as "the revolutionary" document that signified "the Catholic church's reversal of its 2000 year tradition of anti-Semitism."[8]

Yet recent events in the relationship between Catholics and Jews could well cause one to wonder about the optimism inherent in Yuval's pronouncement. For while the established Catholic Church is still officially committed to the teachings of Nostra Aetate, the opponents of that document and of "Modernity" in general have continued their fight and, in spite of their presumed marginal status, appear to have gained, if not a foothold, at least a hearing in the Vatican today. And, since in the view of these radical Catholic traditionalists "International Judaism wants to radically defeat Christianity"[9] using tools like the Freemasons, it is in their views on Jews and Judaism that we can find the most profound expression of their radical rejection of Nostra Aetate, Vatican II and the modern virtues of democracy and tolerance, and their retention of the traditional "teachings of contempt."[10]

In this chapter, we will see how Williamson's Holocaust denial reflects a deeper antisemitism that is fundamental to the theology of these radicals. We will also trace that theology of antisemitism back to the teachings of an Irish priest, Father Denis Fahey, and to the USA, showing the long-standing links between these Catholic antisemitic traditionalists and American right-wing extremists.

This loose constellation of groups and sympathizers makes an accurate assessment of the exact numbers of radical Catholics very difficult. In 1998, estimates were, for approximately one million followers, loosely divided into those who were official adherents of a number of different groups and other sympathizers not officially affiliated but still retaining membership in the Church.[12] However, a Catholic source in 2004, relying on "official Vatican figures," claimed nearly one million adherents for the SSPX itself.[13] According to the SSPX, they now maintain chapters in 37 different countries.[14] By contrast, the Houses of the Priestly Fraternity of Saint Peter, a traditionalist group that has accepted many of the Vatican II reforms and is in good standing with the Church, lists chapters in 15 countries.[15] And more recently, one traditionalist author described the current picture as "slow growth in Europe" but more spectacular progress in North America.[16]

***

The SSPX has become the locus of the extreme Catholic traditionalist world. It was created in 1970 by Archbishop Marcel Lefebvre, who first came to attention when he refused to sign the Vatican II statement on Religious Liberty and the Church in the Modern World.[11] In 1970, he created a traditionalist seminary in Econe, Switzerland, and in the same year he founded the SSPX. Lefebvre was ordered to close down his Swiss seminary in 1974 by Pope Paul VI but refused, and as a result in 1976 his priestly functions were suspended. Eight years later, Pope John Paul II reintroduced, under some conditions, the Tridentine (Latin) Mass as a gesture of conciliation to the traditionalists. But Lefebvre and the traditionalists were not reconciled, and in 1987, Lefebvre again threatened to consecrate a successor. This time, the Vatican responded by entering into negotiations with the group, and on May 5, 1988, Lefebvre signed an agreement acknowledging his loyalty to the Vatican and accepting the new Mass as legitimate. In return, the SSPX was to be recognized and allowed to continue to use the Tridentine Mass in its services. The very next day, Lefebvre repudiated the agreement, and on June 30, 1988, he consecrated four bishops in defiance of Rome's authority. This time, the Vatican responded forcefully, excommunicating Lefebvre and his priests and putting the SSPX into a state of schism.[12] Lefebvre died in 1991, but by then the SSPX had become well established. Swiss born Bishop Bernard Fellay was elected as Superior General in 1994 and was reelected in 2006.

The most recent controversy erupted in January of 2009 when Bishop Richard Williamson, who was one of the four consecrated in 1988, denied the Holocaust on the same day that Pope Benedict XVI lifted the excommunications; on that day in an interview aired on Swedish TV, Williamson said "I believe that the historical evidence is strongly against, is hugely against six million Jews having been deliberately gassed in gas chambers as a deliberate policy of Adolf Hitler"[13] and "I think that 200,000 to 300,000 Jews perished in Nazi concentration camps, but none of them in gas chambers."[14]

The reaction from outraged Jews and others was immediate and grew upon exposure of Williamson's history of antisemitic comments that included a belief in the accuracy of the notorious forgery, *The Protocols of the Elders of Zion*.[15] The resulting torrent of criticism caused the Vatican to insist upon Williamson's renunciation of his Holocaust denial, which he refused to do. However, in a February 2009 letter, he wrote that "Observing these consequences I can truthfully say that I regret having made such remarks" but never indicated a recantation of his views.[16] The negative reaction to Williamson's comments, coming amid the ongoing reconciliation discussions with the Vatican, was not lost on the SSPX leadership. Fellay tried to distance the SSPX from Williamson's Holocaust denial by issuing a statement that said "It's clear that a Catholic bishop cannot speak with ecclesiastical authority except on questions that regard faith and morals. Our Fraternity does not claim any authority on other matters. Its mission is the propagation and restoration of authentic Catholic doctrine, expressed in the dogmas of the faith. It's for this reason that we are known, accepted and respected in the entire world. The affirmations of Bishop Williamson do not reflect in any sense the position of our Fraternity. For this reason I have prohibited him, pending any new orders, from taking any public positions on political or historical questions."[17]

Yet Williamson's antisemitism was neither new nor hidden. In a letter that was posted on the SSPX's seminary website, dated February 1, 1991, Williamson reflected on the (first) Gulf War. First he claimed that the war was instigated by Russia in an attempt to "kill with one stone ... obstacles to the advance of International Socialism," that would then allow "Russia to march through the now unguarded gateway to Europe." But hidden behind the Russian advance was, according to Williamson, another more sinister cause. "However, behind the Gulf War, and even behind Russia, may one not, thirdly, fear the looming figure of the Anti-Christ?" The war was a creation of "the many friends of Israel in the USA … whooping for the United States to break the Arab strong man."[18] Finally, Williamson placed these comments into a clear theological perspective "Until (the Jews) recover their true messianic vocation (by accepting the Church) they may be expected to continue fanatically agitating, in accordance with their false messianic vocation of Jewish world domination. … So we may fear their continuing to play their major part in the agitation of the East and the corruption of the West."[19]

In another letter to his supporters, written on the letterhead of the SSPX's Saint Thomas Aquinas Seminary in Winona, Minnesota, just a few months later, while discussing the media's debilitating influence on society (referring specifically to the Supreme Court's confirmation hearings of Clarence Thomas), Williamson quoted the notorious *Protocols of the Elders of Zion* approvingly "it is indispensable to stir up the people's relations with their governments in all countries so as to utterly to exhaust humanity with dissension, hatred, struggle, envy … so that the goyim see no other course open to them than to take refuge in our complete sovereignty in money and all else."[20] Williamson's belief in the Protocols remained consistent. A decade later, in a letter of May 1, 2009, he wrote "God puts in men's hands the '*Protocols of the Sages of Sion*' … if men want to know the truth, but few do."[21]

Williamson's letters demonstrate not only his antisemitism but also overt racism and sexism—thus the unrest that occurred in France in 2005 resulted in his view "when white men give up on saving Jews, looking after other races and leading their womenfolk, it is altogether normal for them to be punished respectively by the domination of Jewish finance, by the refusal to follow of the non-white races and by rampant feminism."[22] As we noted, Williamson has been consistent in his beliefs. In his letter of November 1991, he combined two of his favorite themes; responding to criticism of his September letter in which he condemned women for wearing trousers and jocularly comparing it to criticism of his Holocaust denial, he wrote "Few of you will be surprised to learn that the September letter appealing to the women not to wear trousers caused a strong reaction, comparable only to the reaction of the Seminary letter which referred to scientific evidence that certain famous 'holocaust gas-chambers' in Poland cannot have served as gas-chambers at all."[23]

It is clear that Williamson's antisemitism was already evident and publicly disseminated to the membership of the SSPX for at least 18 years prior to Fellay's statement. Thus, Fellay was being disingenuous at best when he claimed that "The affirmations of Bishop Williamson do not reflect in any sense the position of our Fraternity." Ultimately, Williamson was expelled from the SSPX in 2012, not because of any stated discomfort or disagreement with his doctrinal positions but because in the words of the official SSPX statement of his "having distanced himself from the management and the government of the SSPX for several years, and refusing to show due respect and obedience to his lawful superiors."[24] As one prominent Catholic blogger stressed "It must be emphasized that the conflict between Bishop Williamson and his former superiors was not over doctrine but about policy."[25]

Although Williamson was expelled from the SSPX, he continued, and continues, to be active in far-right circles, having just ordained a bishop, an act which again made headlines and earned him his second excommunication from the Church.[26]

In fact, the SSPX and the extremist Catholic traditionalist movement in general are shot through with antisemitism to such an extent that it is possible to consider antisemitism as one of the foundational doctrines of the movement. If we return to Lefebvre, we see that his record on Jews and Judaism was also highly questionable. In a letter, dated August 31, 1985, to Pope John Paul II, he was quoted as having spoken approvingly of "both the World War II-era Vichy Regime in France and the far-right National Front, and who identified the contemporary enemies of the faith as 'Jews, Communists and Freemasons.'" In that letter, Lefebvre also criticized "all the reforms carried out over 20 years within the church to please heretics, schismatics, false religions and declared enemies of the church, such as the Jews, the Communists and the Freemasons."[27] Lefebvre also gave an interview to the journal of the National Front in France, suggesting that Catholic opposition to a residence of Carmelite nuns at the site of the Auschwitz concentration camp was instigated by Jews.[28]

Lefebvre's followers often share this outlook. One of the four bishops ordained by him in 1988, Bernard Tissier de Mallerais, who is the official SSPX biographer of Lefebvre, said in 1997 "The church for its part has at all times forbidden and condemned the killing of Jews, even when 'their grave defects rendered them odious to the nations among which they were established.' ... All this makes us think that the Jews are the most active artisans for the coming of Antichrist."[29] Nor has the SSPX's record been confined simply to making statements. In 1989, Paul Touvier, a Nazi collaborator and fugitive from French justice charged with ordering the execution of seven Jews in 1944, was arrested in a priory of the Fraternity of Saint Pius X in Nice. The fraternity stated at the time that Touvier had been granted asylum as "an act of charity to a homeless man." When Touvier died in 1996, a parish church operated by the fraternity offered a requiem Mass in his honor.[30] And more recently, in October 2013, a priest who had been connected to (and later expelled from) the SSPX officiated at the funeral of another convicted Nazi war criminal, Erich Priebke. That priest, Father Florian Abrahamowitz, was also described as the unofficial chaplain of Italy's far-right political party, the Liga Nord.[31]

Shortly after the controversy over Williamson exploded, two articles on the SSPX's website that summed up their theology regarding Jews and Judaism were removed. In one essay, the Vatican II teaching that "the Jews should not be spoken of as rejected or accursed as if this followed from Holy Scripture" is described as "outrageous."[32] The other essay claims that "Judaism is inimical to all nations in general, and in a special manner to Christian nations" and that "the unrepentant Jewish people are disposed by God to be a theological enemy, the status of this opposition must be universal, inevitable, and terrible." There are claims that "the Talmud, which governs Jews, orders enmity with Christians" and that the "Jewish people persecute Christendom," "conspire against the Christian State," commit "usury," and even "are known to kill Christians"! Thus, the essay defends the notion that Jews should not be "given equality of rights" but rather should be forced into ghettos ("isolated into its own neighborhoods").[33]

Decades earlier, Lefebvre's close ally, Bishop Gerald Sigaud, wrote in a 1959 letter that "Money, the media, and international politics are for a large part in the hands of Jews," Sigaud added "Those who have revealed the atomic secrets of the USA were … all Jews. The founders of communism were Jew (sic)" This letter was also posted on the SSPX website.[34] The Southern Poverty Law Center also noted that "as of early February, 2009 … the Canadian SSPX website still hosted an archive of Williamson's anti-Semitic letters, one of which complains that 'Jews have come closer and closer to fulfilling their … drive toward world domination.'"[35]

These positions are not original to the SSPX or other current extremist Catholic traditionalists; indeed, they bear a striking similarity to the writings of an otherwise obscure Irish priest named Father Denis Fahey, whose work is one of the most, if not the most frequently cited by the members of the SSPX and similar believers. Mary Christine Athans, in her important book, *The Coughlin-Fahey Connection: Father Charles E. Coughlin, Father Denis Fahey, C. S. SP., and Religious Anti-Semitism in the United States, 1938–1954*, thoroughly explored Fahey's life and thought and how his theology of antisemitism made its way from Ireland to the USA.[36]

Fahey was born on July 2, 1883, in Kilmore, Golden, County Tipperary, Ireland. In 1900, he was a novice of the Holy Ghost Congregation in France, which was still dealing with the impact of the Dreyfus Affair and French government's anti-clerical actions. At that time, France was an incubator of ecclesiastical antisemitism. As David Kertzer wrote "In the cauldron of Catholic resentment toward the republican state in the 1880s, the Jews, visible in national politics, in the civil service and in the economy, served as a lightning rod, all that was wrong with modern French society."[37]

***

In 1908, Fahey went to Rome and obtained two doctorates there (philosophy and theology).[38] Ordained in 1911, Fahey returned to Dublin in 1912, where he stayed (except for 1916–1920, when he was in Switzerland for health reasons) as a professor at the Holy Ghost Seminary until his death on January 24, 1954. Fahey maintained a high profile in Ireland, and upon his death, Irish Prime Minister Eamon de Valera attended his evening funeral Mass.[39] While there is a question as to the extent of the impact that Fahey had during his lifetime, there is no doubt that antisemitic beliefs, such as those espoused by Fahey, were commonplace in segments of Irish society at that time. Mervyn O'Donnell, in his research on Jewish immigration to Ireland in 1933–1939, has pointed out that during this period "Many Irish civil servants betrayed negative preconceived notions about the Jews."[40] Although de Valera's position toward Jews was viewed as moderate, and his attendance at the funeral Mass might have been a matter of protocol, his presence certainly reflected positively on Fahey's stature.

In Rome, Fahey was heavily influenced by Father Henri l'Floch, who was the Superior of the Seminaire Francaise where Fahey lived. Mary Athans described l'Floch "as an exponent of conservative right-wing French and Italian Catholic thought in those anti-Modernist years. ... L'Floch had substantial influence on Fahey. ... He was later removed from his position as Rector because of his relationship to the controversial and anti-Semitic *Action Francaise* movement which was finally condemned by Pius XI in 1926."[41] L'Floch was also a revered mentor to Lefebvre. Athans, who interviewed a number of Fahey's students and younger colleagues in

Ireland, wrote that "Some (priests) believe that L'Floch's influence can also be seen in Archbishop Marcel Lefebvre … founder of the dissident traditionalist movement … known as the Fraternity of SSPX."[42] Another resident of the French Seminary was the future Archbishop of Dublin and Primate of Ireland John Charles McQuaid who studied under Fahey. McQuaid's biographer, John Cooney, has also asserted that L'Floch's "combination of theological rigidity and political conservatism rubbed off on the seminarians, among them … Marcel Lefebvre."[43] Having been nurtured in the same intellectual milieu, it is no surprise that Fahey, Lefebvre, and McQuaid shared much of the same *weltanschauung*.

Fahey also drew on the journal *Revue International des Societes Secretes*.[44] This journal was founded in 1912 by Father Ernest Jouin, who was described by Kertzer as "The main champion of the *Protocols of the Elders of Zion*, and the best known exponent of Catholic antisemitism in the 1920s" in France.[45] Jouin and his work were not isolated on the fringes of Catholic life. Pope Benedict XV gave Jouin the title of "Prelate of His Holiness," which he used to add papal authority to his works, and he received further blessings from Vatican Secretary of State Gasparri in 1919 and later from Pope Pius XI as well. Jouin even claimed credit for originating the term "Judeomasonic" in 1920 and claimed to have been told by Pius XI to "Continue your *Review* … for you are combating our mortal enemy."[46]

Fahey was a prolific writer, publishing over 20 books and pamphlets, many with repetitive titles and similar themes that reflected his obsessions, such as his late work "*The Kingship of Christ and the Conversion of the Jewish Nation* (1953). In his works, Fahey viewed the world as a very simple, but also very dangerous place. In his Manichaean perspective he believed that God was only accessible through the Catholic Church which in turn was 'supra-national and supernatural'"; however, at the same time, God was locked in a cosmic struggle with Satan, which was, for Fahey, a very real antagonist. Although Judaism was the chief antagonist, Satan's agents included "Bolshevism, as the most recent development in the age-long struggle waged by the Jewish nation against the Supernational Messias, our Lord Jesus Christ, and his Mystical Body, the Catholic Church." This was because Judaism, through their rejection of Jesus as Christ, was attempting to "recast (the world) in the mould of Jewish national life." Fahey asserted that this rejection "cannot but mean the complete undoing of the catholic organization of society" which required destroying the ordained appropriate order.[47] Thus Communism was just a tool used by the Jews. "The real forces behind Bolshevism in Russia are Jewish forces. ... Bolshevism is really an instrument in the hands of the Jews for the establishment of their future Messianic kingdom."[48]

This contrast between Judaism and Catholicism moved from the theological to the social and political. For example, in his tract *The Rulers of Russia* (3rd ed., 1940), Fahey spells out the differences between Jews and Catholics regarding what he terms "citizenship." "Here it will be well ... to contrast the Jewish idea of citizenship with the Catholic idea. ... As members of their own 'messianic' nation, they must strive for the domination of their nation over others, as thus they alone, they hold, justice and peace can be achieved on earth. The Jew would fail in his duty to the Messias to come if he did not subordinate the interests of other nations to is own. ... But the Catholic Church, being supra-national and supernatural, does not aim at the obliteration of national characteristics and qualities by the imposition of a national form, but at their harmonious development by the elimination of the defects due to original sin."[49] This reading of history views Judaism as a religion committed to ruling over the nations, while Catholicism by its nature (and despite the historical evidence to the contrary) is seen as less restrictive and thus deserves to be the proper dominant authority in society.

Fahey further believed that human society peaked in the thirteenth century, when the Church was dominant. However, that idyllic state did not last long. For Fahey, religious liberty was a tool of the devil that was used to seduce state and society away from the true worship of the Church. This belief was echoed years later by Williamson. In comments on Pope Benedict's December 2005 Address to the Curia, Williamson wrote that "What is wrong with freeing States from any obligation to Christ the King is that *implicitly you are denying that Jesus Christ is God*. ... Religious liberty means in effect, a declaration of independence from God, which is directly opposed to the first Commandment. ... However, where Catholics are in a sufficient majority, the State may physically prevent the *public* practice of false religion while tolerating their practice in private."[50] This was a fundamental tenet of Lefebvre's belief as well. In his biography by de Mallerais, he is quoted as saying that the acceptance of the doctrine of religious liberty is "a scandal to Catholic souls (that) cannot be measured. The Church is shaken to its very foundation."[51]

In January 2008, a SSPX theologian repeated this theme in a *Catechism of the Crisis of the Church* addressed to the church membership. After posing the question "Is there, then, no right to the free exercise of religion?"

he offers the following answer "The true religion possesses the absolute right to develop and to be practiced freely, for no one can be impeded from serving God in the way He Himself has prescribed. It is an exigency of the natural law. The false religions, to the contrary, have no real right to be practiced precisely because they are false and erroneous. Error can never have any right; only the truth has rights."[52] The same *Catechism* succinctly summed up the SSPX's stance on tolerance; tolerance, it claimed, was simply "the patient endurance of an evil."[53] For Fahey and similar thinkers, political freedom, along with religious freedom, can only be found in, and thus only given by the Church; and so the right order is one in which the Church reigns supreme and delegates those freedoms as she desires and for her benefit; outside of the Church there are no rights and no freedom; and all in opposition or in non-belief are agents of Satan. This essentialist position mirrors that of radical Islamists; only the specifics of the doctrinal basis are changed.

Fahey's theology began with the original fall of humanity in the Garden of Eden, followed by more recent events, such as the Reformation and the French Revolution, with equally disastrous results. As he wrote, the "Protestant Reformation ... broke the unity of European subjection to the supranational, supernatural Church of Christ. ... It did not however install a naturalistic international organization. ... That was reserved for the French Revolution ... (which began) the domination of the world by Masonic Naturalism. ... Behind Masonry, however (was) the other naturalistic force of the once chosen people. ... The Jews everywhere made use of Freemasonry to secure the rights of becoming citizens of the once Christian states."[54] Even the Holocaust did not shatter Fahey's deep-rooted antisemitism. The revulsion of the world to the horrors of the Shoah made it necessary for him to attempt to draw a distinction between unacceptable antisemitism, which was defined as "hatred of the Jewish nation" and "opposition to the Jewish and Masonic naturalism," which was a source of evil because it inevitably led to rejection of belief in God or any other form of supernaturalism, and thus stood in defiance to essential Catholic dogma.[55] In the foreword to *The Kingship of Christ and the Conversion of the Jewish Nation* published in 1953 (the body of the book was written before the war), he wrote of "the confusion created in minds owing to the use of the term 'anti-semitism.' The Hitlerite naturalistic or anti-supernatural regime in Germany gave to the world the odious spectacle of a display of Anti-Semitism, that is hatred of the Jewish Nation. Yet all the propaganda about that display of Anti-Semitism should not have made Catholics forget the existence of age-long Jewish Naturalism and Anti-supernaturalism. Forgetfulness of the disorder of Jewish naturalistic opposition to Christ the King is keeping Catholics blind to the danger that is arising from the clever extension of the term 'Anti-Semitism' with all its war connotation to the mind of the unthinking."[56]

In the body of that book, Fahey went so far as to theologically justify the Nazi actions against the Jews. In Fahey's words "One can readily conclude that the National-Socialist reaction against the corroding influence of Jewish Naturalism on German national life leads, not only to measures of repression against the Jews but to a dire persecution of the Catholic Church. The deified German race has attacked the rival natural deity, the Jewish race, directly, and has proceeded systematically to get rid of it as corrupting the very fount of deity, German blood. ... We have seen that the Nazi movement in Germany is one of a number of national reactions against the naturalistic Internationalism of the Jewish Nation and of Freemasonry."[57] Thus, in Fahey's vision of the Third Reich, innate Jewish "naturalism" was a danger that led to a defensive reaction, which eventually crystallized as the Holocaust.[58]

Fahey, like most conspiratorial antisemites, relied uncritically on highly questionable sources, for example, drawing upon *The Protocols of the Elders of Zion*. Athans has compared Fahey's attitude to the *Protocols* to that of Henry Ford, Charles Coughlin, and Nesta Webster (antisemitic figures admired by Fahey) who "all admitted that (while) they could not prove the veracity of the *Protocols* ... (but) what was described in the *Protocols* was what was going on in the world."[59]

Fahey was also prone to seeing conspiracies of Jews everywhere. In one of his books, he even claimed that the Jews were attempting to eliminate any religious meaning from the celebration of Christmas. The proof for this insidious plot was "Christmas cards that show a 'row of dogs and a few birds (that) have nothing to remind the recipient of what the rejoicing is for. ... In this process of eliminating the supernatural Messias from the celebration of the anniversary of his birth the largest firm of Christmas card manufacturers, have certainly played a great part. ... All three directors appear in the communal Directory of the Jewish Year Book' (and other Jewish communal activities)."[60] Thus "the Jews," through the ownership of a greeting card company by three Jews, were intent on stripping Christmas of its sacral meaning! In other works, he published lists of Jews in the Russian/Communist leadership, as well as a list of "Members of the Jewish Nations in the United Nations Organization. ... As of last year

(1951) this tiny but powerful group of Zionist nationalists hold the following key posts." This list comprised 86 names, spread over five pages.[61] A forerunner of many extremists today, Fahey wrote that "The real purpose of the UN is to pave the way for a 'World Government' to which all nations (but one?) surrender their sovereignty and independence."[62]

For Fahey, this Jewish threat meant that the Church had to fight back by all available means, including depriving Jews of their civil rights (denying them the latitude and freedom they were using to undermine society) as well as not allowing Jews their own national aspirations. He believed that "A step to be taken to undo the naturalism of the French Revolution and, at the same time, prevent onslaughts on the Jews, is to withdraw citizenship of other States from all of them, and limit them to citizenship of some other State, their own. That State must not be Palestine, for the Jewish claim to Palestine is implicitly a denial that they have disobeyed God and missed their vocation by the rejection of the True Supernatural Messias."[63] Finally, after the Holocaust, he was worried that Catholic sympathy for Jews because of their terrible suffering would create a lessening of Catholic anti-Jewish vigilance. And, despite the growing awareness of the Nazi Holocaust, those crimes did not begin to compare to the ancient Jewish crime of deicide, which result should have ordained history and the structure of society ever since. "Some Catholics seem to forget that the Jews who, in their terrible opposition to God … were intent on the most awful crime ever committed, the crime of deicide."[64]

Fahey's theology was clearly formed in and reflective of the reactionary Church of the late nineteenth century. However, as that church began to change after World War II, his teachings might well have faded into obscurity but for the fact that he found a powerful ally in the USA in the person of Father Charles Coughlin who brought Fahey to the attention of a receptive audience across the Atlantic. As Coughlin's aura dimmed, Fahey's teachings seemed to also wane but in reality they were only waiting for the right circumstances to flower.

***

M.C. Athans in her book on *The Coughlin-Fahey Connection* and in other writings has demonstrated how "the 'theologian' Coughlin quoted most frequently was … Father Denis Fahey."[65] Coughlin did not just quote Fahey or even base his thought on the Irish priest's writings, but he took an even more active role, reprinting and distributing Fahey's tract *The Rulers of Russia* through his Social Justice Publishing Company. Published in 1940, when Coughlin was at the height of his powers, this distribution ensured Fahey's introduction to a mass American audience. Coughlin even boasted in a 1940 letter to Fahey that he had circulated 350,000 copies of the pamphlet, thus ensuring Fahey's introduction to a mass American audience.[66]

Coughlin was easily the most prominent Catholic and antisemite in the USA at that time. As one of his biographers wrote "Coughlin ... dominated among antisemitic public figures in these years. ... Not only did he reach millions with his weekly radio broadcasts, but he also disseminated his extremist messages through his widely read magazine *Social Justice*, which claimed 200, 000 subscribers."[67] The result was that he popularized an antisemitism that had a significant impact on US popular discourse, even spurring antisemitic acts by his followers that threatened public safety.[68] As Athans has clearly demonstrated, by bringing Fahey's writings to an American audience, Coughlin allowed Fahey to become a bridge between the French and papal reactionary Catholic antisemitism of the early twentieth century and right-wing extremists in America.[69] Coughlin did so, as one historian has written, by translating "the struggles of the Christ and Antichrist into contemporary terms, in which Christianity and America represented Christ, and Communists and bankers represented the Antichrist. And conveniently, the two evils were linked together in the Jewish race."[70]

Some of Coughlin's followers were involved in a radical group called the Christian Front that was implicated in a series of disruptive and violent antisemitic acts in the late 1930s and early 1940s. These disturbed the peace and threatened the security of Jews throughout cities with a large Irish Catholic presence such as Boston and New York. In both cities, the wave of antisemitism was often ignored by sympathetic Catholic policemen and eventually had to be countered by official action by Massachusetts Governor Leverett Saltonstall and New York Mayor Fiorello LaGuardia.[71] Even before the wave of antisemitism became overt, the antisemitic discourse had become sufficiently heated and the issue became politically sensitive enough that it reached the White House. In a 1941 memorandum to Myron Taylor, his personal representative to the Vatican, President Franklin D. Roosevelt wrote "I forgot to mention that when you get the chance, you might express the thought that there is a great deal of anti-Jewish feeling in the dioceses of Brooklyn, Baltimore and Detroit and this feeling is said to be encouraged by the church. The point to make is that if anti-Jewish feeling is stirred up, it automatically stirs up anti-Catholic feeling and that makes a general mess."[72] Taylor did raise the issue but found the Vatican non-responsive; the Vatican's resident American expert, Father Joseph Patrick Hurley, who himself was a virulent antisemite, advised the Vatican to ignore Coughlin's antisemitism.[73]

While the Coughlin-Fahey correspondence continued in the same vein even after Coughlin's official silencing, the lack of a public voice in America certainly lowered Fahey's profile in the USA.[74] However, by then, Coughlin's influence had introduced Fahey to a new audience. Among Coughlin's associates and allies were Gerald Winrod and Gerald L.K. Smith, who were foundational figures in American right-wing extremism. Smith was in direct contact with Fahey, exchanging letters in the late 1940s and early 1950s. Fahey wrote in one letter to an Irish follower "the programme of Gerald L K Smith as taken from his paper *The Cross and the Flag* … declares unflinchingly and unequivocally for the Rights of Christ the King. Are his detractors and smearers for Christ the King or against Him? The Judaeo-Communists tried to brand every man who stood for American nationalism and against Communism during the war as pro-Nazis."[75] Coughlin influenced Willis Carto, arguably the most important figure on the American far right in the last half-century; Carto recalled Coughlin as a seminal figure from his childhood.[76] As a youth, Carto claims to have never heard of right-wing extremists "with the exception of Father Coughlin, to whose broadcasts he would listen with the whole family" describing him as "a spellbinding orator."[77] Carto remembered "Coughlin as a genuine populist" and cited "opposition from Jewish organizations … as evidence of Coughlin's bona fides as a true American hero."[78]

This nexus between extremist traditionalist Catholics and the far right has continued to the present. Returning to Bishop Williamson, he too has found himself taken up by various members of the movement. Thus among those who have adopted the Bishop's cause are the notorious neo-Nazi and professional Holocaust denier, Mark Weber, the director of the Institute for Historical Review (founded by Carto and the center of organized Holocaust denial in the USA) who, in a March 2009 article entitled "*Bishop Williamson and 'Holocaust Denial': Why the Uproar*," concludes "The Williamson affair underscores a well entrenched Jewish-Zionist bias in the cultural life of modern Western society, and reminds us, once again, of the power behind that bias."[79] Robert Faurisson, the French academic Holocaust denier, who squabbled with Weber over the future of Holocaust denial, also sprang to Williamson's defense. According to a posting on his blog, "The height of his enemies misfortune, and for the traditionalist Catholic he is ... if he ever did fall to his knees before the new Inquisition he would immediately remind everyone of Galileo, the man whom science and history ended up acknowledging to be right despite his abjuration. Even if he wound up losing, Richard Williamson would thus have won."[80]

The links between the Holocaust deniers and Catholic extremists are not limited to Williamson. In 1993, the *Journal of Historical Review*, the house organ of the Institute of Historical Review (IHR), published in its September/October issue three short entries under the title "*The Holocaust Issue: Three Christian Views.*" Two were by traditionalist Catholics (including the late Joseph Sobran, fired by William Buckley from his journal *National Review* for antisemitism) and the other by Bishop Louis Vezelis, described as the "editor of *The Seraph*, a traditionalist Catholic monthly." According to Vezelis "the preponderance of objective and factual evidence shows the promoters of the Holocaust story to be libelous frauds."[81] Sobran was defended by the IHR as far back as 1987 and later spoke at the IHR's 2002 conference.[82]

Although the activities of the IHR have greatly diminished over the past few years, and its journal is now available only electronically, Holocaust denial and distortion continue to be an ongoing issue. Early in spring 2015, Weber participated in a meeting in London that was described in the press as a gathering of "Nazi sympathisers, (and) Holocaust deniers." The "host" of the meeting was Jeremy ("Jez") Bedford-Turner, a 45-year-old veteran of the British far-right scene, who, together with another activist, Derek Holland, is also involved in the radical traditionalist movement.[83]

While Sobran may have been marginalized because of his overt antisemitism, his friend, Patrick Buchanan, is a decidedly major figure in US political discourse. Shifting between mass media and high political office, including his service in the Nixon, Ford, and Reagan administrations, where during the Reagan presidency, he lobbied in defense of Nazi war criminals, Buchanan has made no secret of his often controversial views on many issues, such as stating "that it was impossible for 850,000 Jews to be killed by diesel exhaust fed into the gas chamber at Treblinka."[84]

Upon the ascension of Pope Benedict to the papacy, Buchanan wrote in 2007 that Benedict "acted to advance a reconciliation with traditionalists out of communion with the Holy See, including the 600,000 followers of the late Archbishop Marcel Lefebvre, excommunicated in 1988, who belong to his Society of Saint Pius X." Buchanan was describing a process where "The current head of SSPX, Bishop Bernard Fellay, has welcomed papal restoration of the Latin Mass. But he has called it a first step toward addressing all doctrinal disputes dating to Vatican II. Among these are the issues of ecumenism and religious liberty. If the true church is one, holy, catholic, and apostolic, then not all churches are equal." Buchanan has recently even contributed an article to the April 2015 edition of *American Free Press*, a publication that was founded by Willis Carto and is considered one of the leading antisemitic and radical voices. It was the combination of words and associations like these that forced the late William F. Buckley, the patriarch of American political conservatism (and a non-radical traditionalist Catholic himself; as one friend observed, Buckley was "a devout Roman Catholic, [and] he loved the Latin mass") to denounce both Sobran and Buchanan as antisemites.[85]

Another major political figure in the USA who has links to the radical Catholic extremists is former Congressman and two-time Republican Presidential candidate Ron Paul. In October 2013, Paul spoke at a meeting of the antisemitic, Holocaust denying Fatima Center, another radical traditionalist group organized by a defrocked Catholic priest, Father Nicholas Gruner.[86] Two of Paul's associates, Daniel McAdams (the Executive Director of the Ron Paul Institute for Peace and Prosperity and cohost of the Ron Paul Liberty Report) and Jim Condit (a self-described Catholic political activist and former Paul campaign worker who blamed the failure of Paul's 2008 presidential campaign on "Jewish neoCon criminals." Condit is also an acolyte of Denis Fahey), have also participated in radical Catholic extremist activities.[87]

Meanwhile, Fahey's influence extends to the Asia SSPX's website which has a piece posted from March–April 2000 by Bishop Salvador L. Lazo entitled *My Return to The Traditional Latin Mass: Autobiography of a Traditional Catholic Bishop*. In it, Lazo lists some of the books that inspired him on his spiritual journey. They include Fahey's *The Kingship of Christ and The Conversion of the Jewish Nation*, as well as others about the dangers of Freemasonry. Lazo wrote that "Reading these books gave me a better idea of the crisis and confusion in the Church today. It became clear to me who are the real enemies of the Catholic Church. Father Denis Fahey pinpointed them when he wrote: 'The enemies of the Catholic Church are three. One invisible, Satan, and two visible: (a) Talmudic Judaism, and (b) Freemasonry.'"[88] Williamson himself has been explicit about the stature in which he holds Fahey, writing in a 1983 letter to his followers that "Catholics should … keep to sound doctrine and proven authors, for instance the excellent Fr. Denis Fahey."[89]

Finally, it must be recognized that Fahey's baleful inspiration is alive today not only in the SSPX but also among similar-minded Catholics and within academia. E. Michael Jones, who has been an inflammatory figure in the radical Catholic movement, over the past few decades, relies on Fahey's distinctive definition of antisemitism. Jones' antisemitism has led him into similar company—such as the radical Palestinian-American activist Hesham Tillawi, on whose cable TV show Jones appeared in 2008. Tillawi's show has become a forum for numerous antisemites, including such notorious figures as David Duke, Mark Weber, and fellow Holocaust deniers Bradley Smith, Frederick Toben, and Willis Carto.[90] Williamson even found a defender in the former university lecturer and 9/11 conspiracy theorist, Kevin Barrett, who converted to Islam and posted an article defending Williamson on the radical Islamist site *"Ascertain the Truth."*[91]

Fittingly enough, the SSPX and other antisemitic traditionalists also found themselves defended by what is probably the USA's most pseudo-academic far-right website, *The Occidental Observer*. The *Occidental Observer* is an offshoot of the *Occidental Quarterly* which is edited by and reflects the views of the controversial former California State University professor, Kevin MacDonald. MacDonald, a psychologist, has written extensively on Jews and Judaism from what he calls "an evolutionary perspective," most notably in a trio of books.[92] The scholar of right-wing extremism in the USA, George Michael, has described MacDonald's work as having "been well received by those in the racialist right, as it amounts to a theoretically sophisticated justification for anti-Semitism."[93] MacDonald's article, "The Church and anti-Semitism—again" was originally published in February 2009, and in it he defended the SSPX and other extremist Catholic traditionalists by describing how "the Catholic Church has played the role of ethnic and cultural defense in the past. It is certainly not surprising that Jewish organizations are alarmed by any suggestion that it might be returning to its historic self-conception." And he concludes, by hoping that "the traditionalists don't give in to what will be a furious onslaught to prevent any glimmer of the resurgence of traditional Catholicism."[94]

Conclusion

The SSPX has been quite open about their goals. Speaking about the current efforts by Rome to bring the group back into the Church, Bishop Tissier de Mallerais was blunt, saying "we do not change our positions, but we have the intention of converting Rome, that is to lead Rome towards our positions."[95] Rome's recent response was summed up by an article in the semi-official Vatican newspaper *L'Osservatore Romano* (December 1, 2011) that "The interpretation of the innovations taught by the Second Vatican Council must therefore reject, as Benedict XVI put it, 'a hermeneutic of discontinuity and rupture,' while it must affirm the 'hermeneutic of reform, of renewal within continuity.' The same article did stress, more than once, that 'there remains legitimate room for theological freedom' thus accommodating some of the traditionalists concerns."[96]

However, these attempts were once again rejected by the SSPX. Fellay, in a statement from early December, continued to place all responsibility for the schism on the Church. "They claim ... everything that was done at the Council is faithful to Tradition ... whether it be ecumenism or religious liberty. ... And so what we decide to do, besides answering that it is not possible, is to tell them: Wouldn't you like to look at things a bit differently? Wouldn't you like to try to understand that the Society is not the one that is a problem. There is indeed a problem in the Church, but it is not the Society."[97] And all the while this was going on, Williamson and the head of the French SSPX chapter Régis de Cacqueray together accused the Jews of deicide. "How can anyone entertain the thought that God will be pleased with the Jews who are faithful to their fathers, who crucified the Son of God and deny the Triune God?" asked de Cacqueray in a communiqué "Published with the approbation of Bishop Bernard Fellay"![98] Despite this, there are still those today who would claim that the issue of antisemitism is only limited to Williamson and still hold out hope for reconciliation.[99]

The announcement in the fall of 2012 that the Vatican had broken off talks with the SSPX signified the complete failure of this effort; the October statement by Archbishop Gerhard Müller, head of the Congregation for the Defense of the Faith, that "We cannot give away the Catholic faith. ... [T]there will be no compromises here; I think there will be no new discussions" seemed unambiguous in signaling the end of negotiations. While Pope Francis did authorize some discussions in the fall of 2014 between Archbishop Muller and Bishop Fellay, he has also indicated his commitment to Vatican II and Nostra Aetate.

However, it is no secret that within the Church there still remains some significant sympathy for the radical traditionalists and their rejection of Nostra Aetate. This was noted by Cardinal Kurt Koch, the President of the Pontifical Council for Christian Unity, who, in a May 2015 interview on Vatican Radio, warned "The same groups, they are against ecumenism, against interreligious dialogue, against the religious freedom declaration." Koch reaffirmed the Vatican's commitment that "We must go on the basis of the Second Vatican Council with the high authority of the Catholic Church."[100] Yet just one month before Koch's statement, Cardinal Mario Poli of Buenos Aires recognized the local branch of the SSPX as an "association of diocesan right," in other words, giving them formal status in Catholicism, an act which meant for "first time that the breakaway traditionalist group has been officially recognized by a Catholic diocese."[101]

As long as the Vatican appears to hold open the possibility of accepting back into its good graces, those who refuse to accept Nostra Aetate or the Declaration on Religious Liberty, and who use theology and language as a tool to demean other beliefs, it will allow Jews and others to question the Church's commitment to those issues. The only way for the Church to overcome those doubts is to make clear to the radical Catholic traditionalists that their antisemitism is indeed, as Pope John Paul II declared, "a sin against God and humanity."[102]

Notes

1. http://news.bbc.co.uk/nol/ukfs_news/hi/newsid_7870000/newsid_7878500/787580.stm
2. http://www.telegraph.co.uk/news/worldnews/europe/vaticancityandholysee/4317996/Pope-to-cancel-excommunication-of--rebel-bishops.html).
3. Michael Cuneo, *Smoke of Satan* (Baltimore: Johns Hopkins University Press, 1999), 6.
4. Michael Warren, "Saint Pius X Catholic Group Protests Kristallnacht Interfaith Memorial in Argentina, Challenging Pope Francis," Huffington Post, 11/13/2013, http://www.huffingtonpost.com/2013/11/13/catholic-protests-kristallnacht-argentina_n_4267655.html?ref=topbar, accessed 3/24/14. A video of the disruption posted by a traditionalist sympathizer can be found at "SSPX Priest Disrupts Vatican II New Religion Interfaith Service," YouTube, 11/23/2013, http://www.youtube.com/watch?v=HbfN8JQLzFk.
5. Michael Warren, "Catholic Fringe Disrupts Kristallnacht Ceremony," 11/13/2013, http://news.yahoo.com/catholic-fringe-disrupts-kristallnacht-ceremony-170954080.html. See also Jorge Mario Bergoglio and Abraham Skorka, http://www.ama-

zon.com/Sobre-cielo-tierra-opiniones-Francisco-ebook/dp/B007KD7D4Q Sobre el cielo y la tierra (Buenos Aires: Editorial Sudamericana, 2010), published in English as On Heaven and Earth: Pope Francis on Faith, Family, and the Church in the Twenty-First Century, trans. Alejandro Bermudez and Howard Goodman (New York: Image, 2013).

6. "Buenos Aires Rosary Protest: The Facts," Society of Saint Pius X, 11/13/2013, http://sspx.org/en/news-events/news/buenos-aires-rosary-protest-facts-2799.
7. Israel J. Yuval, *Two Nations in Your Womb: Perceptions of Jews and Christians in Late Antiquity and the Middle Ages*, (Berkeley and Los Angeles, 2008) pp. 20–21.
8. Michael Phayer, *The Catholic Church and the Holocaust*, 1930–1965, (Bloomington, 2001) p. 203.
9. Letter of Bishop Gerald Sigaud to Cardinal Tardini, Aug. 22, 1959, posted under the title *What Vatican II Should Have Done,* http://www.sspx.org/MISCELLANEOUS/whatvaticaniishould have done.htm
10. See Jules Isaac's seminal work, *The Teachings of Contempt* (New York, 1964).
11. Cuneo, *Smoke of Satan*, p. 91.
12. Ibid., pp. 91–92.
13. http://news.bbc.co.uk/nol/ukfs_news/hi/newsid_7870000/newsid_7878500/787580.stm
14. http://www.telegraph.co.uk/news/worldnews/europe/vaticancityandholysee/4317996/Pope-to-cancel-excommunication-of-rebel-bishops.html).
15. http://www.catholicherald.co.uk/articles/a0000226.shtml. Also see Steven L. Jacobs and Mark Weitzman, *Dismantling the Big Lie: the Protocols of the Elders of Zion* (Hoboken and Los Angeles, 2003) for current use of the Protocols, as well as a detailed refutation of the text.
16. http://news.bbc.co.uk/2/hi/europe/7915022.stm)
17. Jan 26, 2009, http://www.commonwealmagazine.org/blog/?p=2721
18. Williamson's language here is reminiscent of the earlier comments by another radical Catholic traditionalist, the politician and commentator Pat Buchanan, who said on TV in 1990 "The only two groups that are beating the drums for war in the Middle East—the

Israeli Defense Ministry and its amen corner in the US" (http://www.infoplease.com/spot/patbuchanan1.html).
19. http://www.sspxsemianry.org/publications/letter/1991/February/February/.shtml
20. Williamson, letter of Nov. 3, 1991, copy in my possession.
21. (Williamson, May 1, 2000, http://www.sspx.ca/Documents/Bishop-Williamson/May1-2000.htm
22. Williamson, Denial of Christ Creates Chaos, http://www.daily-catholic.org/issue/05Nov/nov14lit.htm).
23. See note 13 above.
24. http://www.dici.org/en/news/communique-of-the-general-house-of-the-society-of-saint-pius-x-october-23-2012/
25. *Why was Bishop Williamson Expelled from SSPX*?, Michael J. Miller, The Catholic World Report, Oct. 25, 2012, http://www.catholic-worldreport.com/Blog/1694/why_was_bishop_williamson_expelled_from_sspx.aspx. Williamson's post-expulsion activities will be discussed below.
26. http://www.catholicnewsagency.com/news/automatic-excommunication-for-bishop-over-illicit-ordination-55021/
27. *Lefebvre movement: long, troubled history with Judaism*, Thomas C. Fox, Jan. 26, 2009, NCR Online, http://ncronline.org/node/3180
28. Ibid.
29. Ibid.
30. On Touvier and his connection to the SSPX see his obituary in the NY Times, July 18, 1996 at http://www.writing.upenn.edu/~afilreis/Holocaust/touvier-obit.html
31. http://www.huffingtonpost.com/2013/10/15/erich-priebke-funeral_n_4101902.html. For Abrahamowitz as the «unofficial chaplain », see http://www.huffingtonpost.com/2009/02/04/angela-merkel-attacks-pop_n_163843.html
32. *Can it truly be said that the Jewish race is guilty of the sin of deicide and that it is consequently cursed by God, as depicted in Gibson's movie on the Passion?* Featured in the Q and A section, *The Angelus* magazine, March 2004. *The Angelus* is the SSPX's official magazine.
33. *Of the Jewish People in History*, by Frs. Michael Crowley & Kenneth Novak—Originally printed in the April 1997 issue of *The Angelus* magazine.

34. *Intelligence Report* Winter 2007—a copy of this letter is in my possession.
35. Heidi Beirich, *Behind the Bishop: The Anti-Semitism of the SSPX*, posted in the *radical traditionalist Catholic blog*, Feb. 26, 2009.
36. Mary Christine Athans, *The Coughlin-Fahey Connection: Father Denis Fahey, C. S. SP., and Religious Anti-Semitism in the United States, 1938–1954* (New York, 1991).
37. David Kertzer, *The Popes Against the Jews*, (New York 2001) p. 170.
38. Athans, 'A New Perspective on Father Charles E. Coughlin', in *Church History*. Volume: 56. Issue: 2.: 1987, p. 226.
39. Athans, *Coughlin-Fahey*, p. 59.
40. Mervyn O'Donnell, 'The 'Jewish Question'', Irish Refugee Policy and Charles Bewley, 1933–1939', in *Racial discrimination and ethnicity in European history*. ed. Guðmundur Hálfdanarson. (Pisa 2003), p. 148.
41. Athans, *Coughlin-Fahey*, pp. 22–23,Oscar L. Arnal, A*mbivalent Alliance: The Catholic Church and the Action Francaise, 1899–1939*, (Pittsburgh, 1985), p. 68 describes how L'Floch (and others) shared support of the *Action Francaise* with Pope Pius X.
42. Athans, *Coughlin-Fahey,* pp. 62–63, n. 25 cf. Yves Congar, *Challenge to the Church: The Case of Archbishop Marcel Lefebvre* (n.p., U.S.A., 1976), pp. 16, 88–90 and see also http://www.catholicity.com/commentary/rutler/07849.html
43. John Cooney, *John Charles McQuaid: Ruler of Catholic Ireland,* (Dublin, 1999) p. 53.
44. Ibid. p. 129.
45. Kertzer, p. 267.
46. Ibid. pp. 267–269.
47. Fahey, *Rulers of Russia*, (Detroit, 1940) pp. 44–45.
48. Fahey, *Rulers,* p. 22.
49. Ibid., p. 72.
50. http://www.cfnews.org/bw-dec22.htm).
51. Quoted in Rome-SSPX, Background to the Doctrinal Discussions, http://cfnews.org?SSPX-DD.htm, which is a traditionalist website).
52. *CATECHISM OF THE CRISIS IN THE CHURCH, Fr. Matthias Gaudron, Angelus Press. P. 16,* January 2008, Volume XXXl, Number 1.

53. Ibid.
54. Fahey, *Rulers*, pp. 50–51, section titled "Democracy" versus "Fascism").
55. Fahey, *What Really is Anti-Semitism*, posted on the SSPX website at http://www.salvationisfromthejews.com/sspx_what_really_is_anti_semitism.html. The description that he quoted approvingly was taken from a review of his book *The Kingship of Christ and the Conversion of the Jewish Nation* published in La Civilta Cattolica, March 1947.
56. Fahey, *The Kingship of Christ and the Conversion of the Jewish Nation*, pp. 5–6.
57. Ibid., pp. 44–45, 57.
58. For a convincing review of the Nazis overwhelming obsession with and reliance on antisemitism as a driving force for World War II and the Holocaust, see Jeffrey Herf, *The Jewish Enemy* (Cambridge, 2006).
59. Athans. *Coughlin-Fahey*, p. 103.
60. Fahey, *The Kingship of Christ and the Conversion of the Jewish Natio*n p. 51.
61. Ibid, pp. 169–173.
62. Ibid., p. 174.
63. Fahey, *Rulers,* p. 75.
64. Fahey, *The Kingship of Christ and the Conversion of the Jewish Natio*n p. 53.
65. Athans, *Coughlin-Fahey*, p. 224.
66. Coughlin to Fahey, 20 March 1940, Fahey Papers, cited in Enda Delaney, "Political Catholicism in Post-War Ireland: The Revd. Denis Fahey and *Maria Duce*, 1945–54," *Journal of Ecclesiastical History*, 52, no. 3 (July 2001): 495.
67. Donald Warren, *Radio Priest: Charles Coughlin, the Father of Hate Radio* (New York, 1996), pp. 188–189, 305, cited in Joseph W. Bendersky, *Dissension in the Face of the Holocaust: The 1941 American Debate over Antisemitism*, in *Holocaust and Genocide Studies* 24, no. 1 (Spring 2010, p. 96).
68. See, among many, David Bennett, *The Party of Fear*, (New York, 1995) pp. 263–266.
69. Athans, *Coughlin-Fahey.*
70. Esther Yolles Feldblum noted that "a number of the hierarchy were displeased with Coughlin's ravings, he, nevertheless, found a

receptive and supportive audience in the diocesan press. One of his key supporters in the eastern press was the [Brooklyn] *Tablet.* In a typical defense of Coughlin's ant-Semitism, the editor (Patrick Scanlon) remarked "Fr. Coughlin has fearlessly and courageously discussed the Jewish problem that others would pass by in cowardly silence … [no Catholic can honestly criticize] Fr. Coughlin's very temperate reference to the part that a Jewish *Weltanschauung* contributed to the untoward world conditions." Brooklyn *Tablet*, Feb. 4, 1939, cited in Esther Yolles Feldblum, *The American Catholic Press and the Jewish State 1917–1959*, (New York, 1997) p. 46.

71. Leonard Dinnerstein, *Antisemitism in America*, (New York, 1995) pp. 120–123, 132–133. Philip Jenkins, *Hoods and Shirts: The Extreme Right in Pennsylvania 1925–1950* (Fchapel hill, 1997) examines the Christian Front and similar groups in one state.
72. FDR Papers, President's Secretary's File, 1941, Box 51, FDR Archives, Hyde Park, N.Y.
73. Charles R. Gallagher, *Vatican Secret Diplomacy: Joseph P Hurley and Pope Pius XII* (New Haven 2008) pp. 68–70 and see also his article 'A Peculiar Brand of Patriotism: The Holy See, FDR, and the Case of Reverend Charles E. Coughlin' in David B. Woolner and Richard G. Kurial, *FDR, the Vatican, and the Roman Catholic Church in America, 1933–1945* (New York, 2003) pp. 272–275. Gallagher also points out that Hurley "became the only bishop of the entire Second Vatican Council to officially and publicly protest the signing of Nostra Aetate".
74. For example, see Coughlin's letter to Fahey "while anti-Semitism is to abhorred in so far as it is related to hatred for the Jews as individuals and racials, nevertheless, *anti-Judaism, which means opposition to the Judaic concept of life, is not to be so condemned* … I cannot understand how so many amongst our hierarchy and clergy are demonstrating tolerance towards Judaism", Coughlin to Fahey, March 5, 1941, Quoted in Athans, 'New Perspectives', pp. 188–189.
75. Fahey. Letter of May 3, 1949, in Athans, art. p. 213.
76. Ibid. p. 74.
77. Ibid. p. 10.
78. Ibid. p. 154.
79. http://www.ihr.org/williamson_march09.html)

80. http://robertfaurissonblogspot.com/2009/04/mark-weber-must-resign-from-institute.html
81. Loius Vezelis, *Examine All the Evidence* in *Journal of Historical Review,* September/October, 1993, Volume 13, Number 5, pp. 34–35. Buckley's opinion of Sobran's antisemitism can be found in his *In Search of Anti-Semitism* (New York, 1992. His conclusion there (pp. 118–119) was that Sobran had indeed "written anti-semitic articles."
82. Mark Weber, *Joseph Sobran and Historical Revisionism*, accessed at http://www.ihr.org/jhr/v07/v07p373_Weber.html, and Sobran, *For Fear of The Jews*', accessed at http://www.ihr.org/conference/14thconf/sobranconf.html.
83. For the meeting, see http://www.dailymail.co.uk/news/article-3045115/Nazi-invasion-London-EXPOSED-World-s-Holocaust-deniers-filmed-secret-race-hate-Jews-referred-enemy.html. Turner has hosted Williamson at his Iona Forum in London, see http://www.searchlightmagazine.com/archive/holocaust-denying-bishop-speaks-at-iona-london-forum-meeting, as well as the audio recording at http://www.blogtalkradio.com/renegadebroadcasting/2014/10/22/voice-of-albion-jez-turner-of-the-london-forum.-iona?AID=CJSource&utm_source=CJ&PID=6157437. Holland is described by Roger Griffin as a "British fascist" in Roger Griffin, *The Nature of Fascism* (London: Routledge, 2013) is a partner in an antisemitic American radical Catholic publishing venture called IHS Press and an interview with him is offered for purchase at another extremist traditionalist site—http://isoc.ws/interviews/#derek-holland.
84. "Is Pat Buchanan Anti-Semitic?," Newsweek, 12/22/91, accessed at http://www.newsweek.com/pat-buchanan-anti-semitic-201176.
85. Lowell Ponte, "Memories of William F. Buckley Jr.," Newsmax, 2/28/2008, http://www.newsmax.com/LowellPonte/William-Buckley/2008/02/28/id/323027/. For Buckley's judgment on Sobran, see Buckley, In Search of Anti-Semitism, 119 where he concludes "as for me, it was enough he had written anti-Semitic articles". Buckley's judgment of Buchanan was "I find it impossible to defend Pat Buchanan against the charge that what he did and said during the period under examination amounted to anti-

Semitism." (44) The book originated as an extended essay that occupied a whole issue of Buckley's journal, National Review (Dec. 30, 1991).

86. http://www.huffingtonpost.com/bruce-wilson/ron-paul-to-speak-at-holo_b_3881363.html. Other topics discussed at the meeting included climate change as an Israeli plot and denial of the earth's rotation of the sun. For more on Gtruner and the Fatima Center, see Cuneo, *Smoke of Satan*, esp. pp. 137–152.
87. McAdams and Condit were listed as speakers at The Catholic Restoration Conference VII, Sept. 11–13, 2015. For more details, see http://catholicrestorationconference.com/speakers/#dr-peter-e-chojnowski. Condit's analysis of the 2008 presidential campaign can be found at http://freedomportal.net/forum/index.php/topic,9657.msg78368.html?PHPSESSID=8b2543c34974dc1c8a7c739d2ae44854#msg78368.
88. http://www.sspxasia.com/Newsletters/2000/March-April/Autobiography.htm)
89. The letter, a response to a question about reading a book by a Protestant author, was posted on the website of the SSPX's seminary in Winona, Minnesota, and accessed at http://www.leofec.com/bishop-williamson/64.html, accessed 1/28/2017.
90. See Mark Weitzman, *Magical Logic: Globalization, Conspiracy Theory and the Shoah*, published in the series *Posen Papers in Contemporary Antisemitism*, no. 10, Vidal Sassoon International Centre for the Study of Antisemitism, (Jerusalem 2008), p. 18, where I discuss efforts amongst extremists to bridge the gap between the far left, the extreme right and radical Islam.
91. Kevin Barrett, Holocaustism vs. Islam, accessed at http://www.ascertainthetruth.com/att/index.php?option=com_content&view=article&id=213:holocaustism-vs-islam&catid=61:where-religions-differ&Itemid=103. Barrett, who taught at the University of Wisconsin, has also questioned the Holocaust, saying that he "could not dismiss the arguments of … Irving, and even Zundel" and that the Holocaust had to be "characterized … as a hideously destructive myth," although he later rejected the label of Holocaust denier, claiming that it was only "polemical chain-pulling" in a series of email exchanges. The entire story can be found at http://

blogs.phoenixnewtimes.com/bastard/2007/moonbattery_acid_denier_key.php.

92. Kevin MacDonald, *A People That Shall Dwell Alone: Judaism As a Group Evolutionary Strategy, With Diaspora Peoples* (Westport: Praeger 1994), *The Culture of Critique: An Evolutionary Analysis of Jewish Involvement in Twentieth-Century Intellectual and Political Movements* (Westport: Praeger 1998) and *Separation and Its Discontents Toward an Evolutionary Theory of Anti-Semitism* (Westport: Praeger, 1998). MacDonald, now retired from his teaching position, is devoting his time to the extremist movement. He was a professor of psychology at the California State University, Long Beach. Both the University Senate and his own department have formally disassociated themselves from his positions.

93. George Michael, *Professor Kevin MacDonald's Critique of Judaism: Legitimate Scholarship or the Intellectualization of Anti-Semitism?* in *Journal of Church and State*, (2006) pp. 779–806, available online at http://www.kevinmacdonald.net/JC&S48-2006.pdf. Macdonald also appeared as a defense witness for David Irving in Irving's unsuccessful libel suit against Deborah Lipstadt.

Kevin MacDonald, 'The Church and anti-Semitism—again', in *Occidental Observer*, http://www.theoccidentalobserver.net/articles/MacDonald-SSPX.html. MacDonald in his article refers approvingly to claims by James C. Russell which asserted that, in MacDonald's paraphrasing, "the Church was influenced by German culture." Russell's writings recently became a matter of public controversy; he won the Republican and Conservative parties nomination to run against a long-term Democratic Congressional incumbent in a suburban New York district, however, when one of his articles that was published in the *Occidental Quarterly* in 2001 became a matter of the public record, the Republicans tried to drop him as their candidate. See Leah Rae, *Westchester GOP drops candidate over inflammatory essay, The Journal News*, September 22, 2010 and related stories available at http://www.lohud.com/article/20100922/NEWS01/9220350/Westchester%20GOP%20drops%20candidate%20over%20inflammatory%20essay.

94. Kevin MacDonald, "The Church and anti-Semitism—again," *Occidental Observer*, February 2, 2009, http://www.theoccidentalobserver.net/articles/MacDonald-SSPX.html.
95. http://rorate-caeli.blogspot.com/2009/02/tissier-de-mallerais-speaks.html
96. On adhesion to the Second Vatican Council, http://www.news.va/en/news/on-adhesion-to-the-second-vatican-council
97. http://www.dici.org/en/news/sermon-of-bishop-bernard-fellay-superior-general-of-the-society-of-saint-pius-x-on-the-solemnity-of-the-immaculate-conception-december-8-2011-in-econe/
98. The English translation was accessed at http://rorate-caeli.blogspot.com/2011/09/sspx-on-assisi-2011.html. For the original French text, see http://laportelatine.org/district/france/bo/cacqueray_assise110912/scandale_assise2011.php, which is the official site of the French SSPX chapter. Williamson's remarks are on his subscriber-only blog *Eleison Comments* and are carried on the site of the professional antisemite and Holocaust denier, Michael Hoffman, http://revisionistreview.blogspot.com/2011/10/how-can-pope-benedict-let-go-of-ancient.html. A radical traditionalist blog published a letter Fellay sent to Williamson right after those remarks threatening "the starting of the canonical procedure leading to exclusion from the SSPX", http://mauricepinay.blogspot.com/2011/10/letter-from-bishop-fellay-to-bishop.html.
99. See for example, the remarks by Dr. Jeff Mirus "Since Bishop Richard Williamson of the Society of Saint Pius X has yet again made a number of anti-Jewish statements, various Jewish leaders are calling for the Pope to suspend talks with the SSPX. This is an unfair reaction. The head of the SSPX, Bishop Bernard Fellay, has long since made it clear that Bishop Williamson's attitudes are not those of the Society as a whole", *The SSPX, Jews, and Authority* (Oct 21, 2011), posted on the influential blog, *Catholic Culture*, http://www.catholicculture.org/commentary/otc.cfm?id=880.
100. http://www.zenit.org/en/articles/cardinal-koch-recalls-impact-of-nostra-aetate

101. http://www.catholicculture.org/news/headlines/index.cfm?storyid=24607
102. For one example of this oft-repeated theme, see *Address Of His Holiness John Paul II To The Members of The British Council For Christians And Jews*, Nov. 16, 1990, accessed at http://www.fjp2.com/id/yohanes-paulus-ii/perpustakaan-oonline/speeches/11539-to-the-members-of-the-british-council-for-christians-and-jews-november-16-1990. It can also be found in the collection of statements by Pope John Paul II, *Spiritual Pilgrimage: Texts on Jews and Judaism 1979–1995*, edited by Eugene J. Fisher and Leon Klenicki, (NY, 1995), pp. 139–140.

CHAPTER 6

Religion, Prejudice and Annihilation. The Case of Traditional Islamic Judeophobia and Its Transformation into the Modern Islamist Antisemitism

Bassam Tibi

In this paper, I examine contemporary anti-Jewish prejudice that is spreading in Islamic civilization. I pose two core questions. First, is this Jew-hatred recent or traditionally inherited? Second, is it simply a Judeophobia or is it a new variety of antisemitism? Based on the work of Hannah Arendt, I distinguish between two evils: Judeophobia and antisemitism. I also challenge two, in my view, ideologically blinkered interpretations. The first, deflects interpretations that point to the empirical evidence of Islamist antisemitism by calling them examples of Islamophobia. The second, minimizes or even excuses this antisemitism as a justifiable response of Islamic outrage to grievances caused by the Middle East conflict and Western policy more generally. In short, these two interpretations deny the existence of an Islamist antisemitism whose origins lie primarily in the core elements of Islamist ideology. The paper draws attention to denial in a different context, not the now famous denial of the Holocaust in and by

B. Tibi (✉)
University of Göttingen, Göttingen, Germany

A. McElligott, J. Herf (eds.), *Antisemitism Before and Since the Holocaust*, DOI 10.1007/978-3-319-48866-0_6

Europeans, but the denial of the reality of antisemitism in its Islamist form by observers of recent trends in the Middle East.

As a result of the Islamization of European antisemitism in contemporary history a new antisemitism has emerged. It presents elements that should not be conflated with the religion of Islam itself.[1] That said, Islamist antisemites seek to prevent criticism of their hatreds by describing it as a blasphemous attack on the religion of Islam.[2] In fact, Islamic theology has honored Jews as monotheists and it prescribes respect for them, in their capacity as *ahl al-kitab*, that is as people of a world religion. On the other hand, it also has viewed and downgraded Jews and Christians to *dhimmi*, that is as second class believers.[3] In reality Jews both thrived and suffered in Islamic history. As Bernard Lewis has observed, classical Islam did not produce an antisemitism similar to the Christian-European form.[4] True, hostility to Jews and Judaism has a place in the history of Islam, but this prejudice did not assume genocidal proportions. Islamism, in contrast to the mainstream of the religion of Islam, has introduced antisemitism to Islam in modern times in a way that never existed before. The following two core assumptions underpin the present study:

1. The thesis of an "Islamization of European antisemitism" challenges four flaws in the prevailing scholarly narrative in the West[5]: First, it takes issue with the conflation of secular pan-Arab Nationalism that dominated Arab politics in the decades preceding the Six Day War of 1967 with the Islamist currents and intensification of religion in the region's politics in the succeeding decades. Second, it challenges a with the confusion of prejudice against Jews in the longer span of Islamic history with either contemporary Arab-nationalist, or with Islamist antisemitism. This confusion emerges from a larger confusion of Islam and Islamism. Third, it challenges denials of the existence of an Arab or Islamist antisemitism which present it as the result of anti-Zionism and Muslim grievances under globalization. Finally, it challenges the view that
2. Contemporary Middle Eastern and Islamist antisemitism is a result of Israeli politics in Palestine and in the Middle East conflict. However, what I view as the unjust policies of the state of Israel towards the Palestinians and emergence of Islamist antisemitism are two fully different issues not related to one another. A solution of the Israeli-Palestinian conflict would not automatically lead to a subsiding of Islamist antisemitism.

Based on the foregoing assumptions I put forward the following four arguments:

First: The Islamization of European antisemitism constituted and constitutes an effort rendering the adoption of European ideas authentic in an indigenous Islamic context, that is, to make it look home-made. This effort has taken the form of offering an Islamist, that is, theological rationale for antisemitism. Islamism is not only distinguished from secular pan-Arab nationalism by its religious foundation. That foundation also leads to a different view of the nation. Where Arab nationalism professedly embraced the European idea of the nation, Islamism stressed and stresses that non-Muslim other: Secular Nationalism was thus one of those ideas despised as "hulul mustawradah/ Imported solution" and were and are pejoratively compared to the presumably authentic "al-hall al-Islami/Islamic solution."[6] Hence, where secularist nationalists remain in a Westphalian world of multiple nation states, Islamists argue that the globe is divided into one fundamental binary between Islam and the non-Islamic world. The Jews and their supposed "Jewish-masterplan" have played a central role in the Islamist imagination, one that therefore declares Jews to be Islam's eternal enemy.

There are prominent figures in the Islamist tradition, most importantly the Mufti of Jerusalem Amin al-Huseini who combined Islamism with secular nationalism. That said, the distinctions matter. Islamist antisemitism is more dangerous than the secular one since its religionized ideology is more appealing because it is not the ideology of Westernized elites and because a politics driven by religion makes political conflicts intractable. The nationalist Palestinian PLO/Fatah negotiated with Israel the Oslo-Peace. In contrast, Hamas enshrines already in its Charta the holiness of *filastin Islamiyyah* (Islamic Palestine) to deny the Jews the right of existence of their own state Israel. On these grounds Hamas repeats that no peace should ever be negotiated with "the Jews".

Second, making a distinction between Islam and Islamism forms a central part of our argument. It is that Islam is a 16 centuries old faith, cult and cultural system, while Islamism is a contemporary political ideology born 1928 along with the foundation of the Movement of the Muslim Brothers (MB) by Hasan al-Banna. As Bernard Lewis has argued, antisemitism as an ideology of extermination was historically alien to Islam. To be sure, there was prejudice against Jews in Islamic history, but in my view this did not constitute antisemitism. Therefore, I take sharp issue with Andrew Bostom who speaks in general of "Islamic"—not of "Islamist" antisemitism and believes that this evil can be traced back to the birth of Islam.[7] Ironically Boston's argument that Islam is inherently antisemitic concurs with the Islamist ideology that also views Islam as in a state of eternal enmity with the Jews.[8]

Third, pan-Arab nationalists and Islamist antisemitisms were the results of either the conflict between Israel and the Arab states and Israel and the Palestinian people. Obviously both conflicts have bred and breed hatred, but they did not generate pan-Arab nationalist and Islamist antisemitism. Both, Arab Nationalism and Islamism—as well as the related views about the Jews—predated the creation of the state of Israel.

Fourth, there is a painful dark page in modern Arab history, namely the cooperation of pan-Arab nationalists with Nazi-Germany and the newly disclosed Islamist admiration for Hitler. In their 2006 work, *Halbmond und Hakenkreuz* (published as *Nazi Palestine: The Plan for the Extermination of the Jews of* Palestine), Klaus-Michael Mallmann und Martin Cüppers revealed that the SS had created an "Einsatzkommando" that was to be sent to work behind the lines of Rommel's "Afrika Korps " in the event of victory over the Allies in Egypt and would then execute plans for the murder of Jews in Palestine. As the SS had worked with non-German collaborators in Eastern Europe, so it anticipated that it would find Arab collaborators in the Middle East.[9] In his recent study, "Nazi Propaganda for the Arab World," Jeffrey Herf has offered evidence of Arab and Islamist collaboration with Nazi Germany's Arabic language radio and print propaganda.[10] In these years pan-Arab nationalism turned from liberal frankophilia to an admiration for Germany that I have previously called "Arab Germanophilia."[11] By then, Arab nationalists abandoned the French liberal idea of "la nation" and replaced it with the völkisch-German idea of Volk as an organic nation applied exclusively to ethnic Arabs as a "Kulturgemeinschaft". To be sure—and this is most important—this earlier Arab Germanophilia was based on an admiration for Herder and Fichte, not for Hitler. These German philosophers determined the nation as Kulturgemeinschaft in the understanding of an essentialized cultural entity independent from the nation-state. In its early stage Arab Germanophilia was a cultural attitude, thus definitely not an admiration of Nazi-Germany, but nonetheless, Arab-nationalist collaborators made use of it when they acted on behalf of Nazi-Germany. In those years they were in a position to count on very positive pre-existing Arab-sentiments toward Germany. Therefore, the research findings of the two different books on this subject can be related to one another to establish an indirect link between cultural Germanophilia and political collaboration with Nazi-Germany, though both need to be strictly distinguished from one another.

Islamist Jew-Hatred and the New Antisemitism

The bottom-line is that Islamism is not Islam. This insight is central to understanding contemporary antisemitism. Given the antisemitic character of the Islamist ideology, it is disconcerting to observe that in recent years there has been a shift in the assessment of political Islam—also named Islamism—in the West.[12] This sea-change can be both observed in scholarship (Islamic and Middle Eastern Studies) and in politics (the policy of the Obama administration). The new positive assessment of Islamism draws partly on third-worldist romanticisim[13] and the resulting tendency to see Islamism as "a cry of the oppressed peoples". Such observers neglect the centrality of antisemitic conspiracy thinking among Islamist ideologues. There is a need for a rethinking of Islamic studies, but this seems to derail in taking a wrong path, when Western scholars move from maligning to exoneration.[14]

It is most unfortunate that the Obama administration—despite all its aspiration to overcome the Bush legacy—adopted one flaw of the former policy: the confusion of Islam and Islamism. It then in a reserved manner embraced Islamist movements as possible partners. It is one of the greatest mistakes of Western policies to support the empowerment of the Islamist Muslim Brothers in Egypt in post-Arab Spring.[15] In the aftermath of 9/11 in the US and Islamist assaults in Europe in the period 2005–07 (Madrid, Amsterdam, London, Paris), hostility to Islam emerged in the West. The Arab Spring induced Western policies to move to other extreme of an exoneration. The distinction proposed by some observers between "moderate Islamists" and "jihadists" overlooked the facts that both share an Islamist antisemitism, as well as the concept of an Islamic state as a political order. There is a major distinction between institutional (peaceful) and jihadist (violent) Islamists, but it merely relates to the means employed—the options are: the bullet, or ballot-box. The ultimate goal: namely the Islamist shari'a state, is a shared goal. This is a fact and it should not be dismissed by the lumping together of various directions within Islamism.[16]

Scholars have offered convincing evidence of both hostility to Jews as well as of what Bernard Lewis called the "Jewish-Islamic symbiosis."

Yet though antisemitism was alien to Islamic tradition, an Islamization of antisemitism took place in the Islamist venture in modern history, most importantly in the Muslim Brotherhood.[17] To be sure there is also the Shi'i variety of Islamist antisemitism that, however, needs to be put in a different category. The majority of the world community of Islam (circa 90 percent) consists of Sunnis and for this reason antisemitism on the Sunni side matters more than the Shi'ite one represented by Iran. Nonetheless, this study keeps the focus on the Islamization of antisemitism launched by the Islamist movement of the Muslim Brothers.

The new Jew-hatred in Islamic societies results from the contemporary Islamization of European antisemitism. It adds tremendous obstacles in the way of a conflict resolution in the Middle East. Islamist antisemitism undermines the search for peace. As the notion of a "moderate" Islamism continues to find a place in academic and policy circles in Europe and the United States, a look at Islamism's ideological core is important.

What Is the Islamization of Antisemitism?

The new direction of an Islamist antisemitism in the Middle East conflict has been at first a Sunni phenomenon. Nonetheless, decades later, Ayatollah Khomeini connected an image of enmity regarding the US combined with Jew-hatred. In so doing, he established a Khomeinist Shi'i variety of antisemitism. In this variety that is incorporated into an anti-Americanism the ideology is based on the perception of "the Israeli conspiracy to destroy Islam" and the "Protocols of the Elders of Zion" are "referred to ... as evidence".[18] However, in the Shi'i variety of Islamist antisemitism the "Jews" act as a proxy for the US, not on their own. In this understanding, the Jewish state of Israel "was identified as an alien essentially Western colonial element in the region and a policeman".[19] This state policeman acts in the US interest, and for this reason Israel and the Jews are viewed by Iran as a proxy.

Even though the present study does not deal with the Shi'a and Iran, but rather with a Sunni phenomenon, it does not overlook the links existing between both. Hamas, for example, is supported both by the Sunni Muslim Brotherhood and the Shia government of Iran.[20] Experts on Iran acknowledge the "latent antisemitism ... that the Islamic Republic (of Iran) brought out."[21] In contemporary Sunni Islamism the anti-Jewish sentiments depict the Jewish state Israel as the "big Satan", no longer the little one acting on behalf of the US. In contemporary Sunni Islamism an

Islamization of European antisemitism takes place in a different presentation of the issue. As noted above, in contrast to earlier secular ideologies in the Middle East, Islamism claims an authenticity that derives its impact from its self-presentation as the expression of true Islam.[22] Islamists put on its agenda a program of purification that targets the Jews. In Islamist ideology the Jews are viewed as those who manipulate others—including the US—in a conspiracy to rule the world.[23] Hence, leading Islamists view the Jews as "evil" actors who contaminate the world and thus deserve to be annihilated. This is the core point for making a distinction between the older prejudice of a Judeophobia and the genocidal ideology of antisemitism.

Here again, the distinction between Islamism and Islam matters. "Islamization" suggests that the contemporary antisemitism prevailing in the world of Islam rests on an import from Europe. The Islamists equate what has been Islamized with what is authentic. Yet a proper understanding of the history of Islam suggested that Islamized antisemitism is not authentic in Islam. It is, instead, rather alien to it. The murderous ideology of Islamist anti-Semitism has been imported from Europe and then indigenized in an Islamization process. In contrast to Andrew Bostom's contention that "Islamic antisemitism" is "as old as Islam," my view is that Islamist antisemitism has been developing since the 1920s.

For an honest and fruitful dialogue between the West and Islamic civilization to take place, we need to determine which kind of Islam is open to partnership. In the United States, knowledge on this issue is poor. The distinction between Islam and Islamism has yet to fully enter into American academic and policy discussions.

Moreover, it is remarkable to observe that there are American scholarly works published by major scholarly presses that even support Islamist description of the American support for Israel as a contemporary form of "crusaderism" carried out by the West.[24]

In contrast to these approaches that dominate Ameican scholarship on contemporary Islamic politics, I have long drawn on Hannah Arendt's work on totalitarianism to understand Islamism. Arendt argued that antisemitism was an essential segment of any totalitarian ideology.[25] In this understanding I see in the basic features of the ideology of Sunni Islamism the most recent variety of totalitarianism.[26] This approach challenges the misperception that claims to find a "Moderate Muslim Brotherhood."[27] In fact, this "moderate" movement has been the source of the evil of

Islamized antisemitism. One of the few Westerners who know Egypt and its culture best, Raymond Stock, has correctly observed that the ideology of the Muslim Brotherhood today remains "anti-Western, anti-secular, anti-Christian, antisemitic, anti-female ... directly influenced by the Nazis ...". Nevertheless, he continues, some Westerners view the Muslim Brotherhood Islamists "not as they are, but as they wish them to be: moderate, liberal ... we have no evidence at all that they have changed so far."[28] Those who apply the moderation scheme to the Muslim Brothers dismiss the "no-change" statement as an expression of essentialism and thus view it as unacceptable. The facts indicate, however, no change in the Islamist ideology.

A recent reader on "Liberal Islam" includes the distortion that the Egyptian Muslim Brother Yusuf al-Qaradawi is a liberal.[29] Qaradawi is in fact the heir of Sayyid Qutb. What is liberal about the following statement from al-Qaradawi: "There is no dialogue between us and the Jews except by the sword and the rifle".[30] Qaradawi is representative of that current in Arab and Islamist politics that interprets events through the lense of a conspiracy pursued by a crusader instigated by "Jews" to destroy Islam. It is an idea rooted in Qutb's work.

In Europe as well, one notes in scholarly and political opinion an inclination to avoid the realities of antisemitism, a trend particularly strong in the European liberal left in recent decades. Rather than acknowledge the presence of antisemitism when it exists, there is a tendency to remain silent about it or to present it as an outrage about injustice or simply a contestation of Zionism as anti-Zionism. In fact, antisemitism cannot be so neatly separated from anti-Zionism.[31] Neither Qutb nor Hamas nor Islamists in general distinguish between Judaism and Zionism. They reject them both and see Zionism as the logical result of a Judaism that they find contemptible.

The Narrative of Islamist Antisemitism Told by Sayyid Qutb in His "Battle Against the Jews"

As there can be no Marxism without Marx and his work there evidently can be no Islamism without Sayyid Qutb and his rich pamphleteering.[32]

The Movement of the Muslim Brothers continues to adhere to his political thought, even in the aftermath of the Arab Spring. His supporters are not on the fringe of Islamist politics. Rather they are part of a powerful mass movement which continues to be inspired by Qutb's views on Jews and the US. Those American scholars who dismiss these facts with the fashionable criticism that pointing out these realities amounts to "essentialism" have been engaging in self-deception and foolery.

Sayyid Qutb's biography is now familiar. He lived in the United States from 1948 to 1950 and returned to Egypt with a profound hatred for American and Western life and culture and the conviction that the United States was rule by Jews. In the 1950s he continued to be a major figure of Islamism in his role as an ideological leader of the Muslim Brotherhood. Qutb transmitted his hatreds of the Jews and the United States into an Islamist idiom upon his return to Egypt, most notably in his 1950s essay, "Our Struggle with the Jews."

Today, the ideas of Sayyid Qutb have given Islamism its most authoritative imprint. All basic features of Islamism emanate from Qutb's work including his Jew-hatred. In contrast to secular pan-Arab nationalists Qutb does not confine his efforts to "translating" an antisemitism imported from Europe into a local articulation. He wanted more: an Islamization of antisemitism to give it, as he pretends, an authentic face. Qutb was executed in public in 1966, a year before the shattering military defeat in the Six-Days-War of 1967 took place. This defeat contributed to the end of pan-Arab nationalism and to the spread of Islamist ideas across the Middle East against the defeated secular regimes of that region. These authoritarian regimes mostly legitimized by secular pan-Arabism were delegitimated in the post-1967-developments.[33] It was in the context of reaction to the Arab defeat in 1967 that the Islamization of antisemitism pursued by the Islamists became most powerful. Though Islamism had been a factor in Arab and Muslim politics since 1928, it did not become visible and appealing to a broader audience until after the Arab defeat in the Six-Day War of 1967.

Qutb's execution on the orders of the most popular hero of pan-Arabism, Gamal Abdel Nasser in 1966 meant that he did not witness his success. In 1950, in "Our Struggle with the Jews," Qutb laid the foundations for the Islamization of antisemitism. First published by the Saudi regime, by 1989, the book had appeared in ten editions.

In "Our Struggle with the Jews," Qutb paid tribute to youth that join forces with this movement "not for the sake of any material benefits, but simply to die and sacrifice one's own life".[34] This glorification of death earlier emphasized by the founder of the Muslim Brothers Hasan al-Banna in his "Essay on Jihad" was a departure from the ethics of life in Islam.[35]

It became important for the glorification and justification of suicide terrorism. In the Islamist ideology of al-Banna and Qutb Muslims are supposed to die in a cosmic war waged against the Jews. According to Qutb, Muslims had no choice, because the Jews themselves wanted this war, one they had launched since the birth of Islam in Medina 622For Qutb the Jews are "evil" and therefore viewed as the major enemy of Islam since the beginning of its history. Qutb accused the Jews of using their "*La'ama*/wickedness" to destroy Islam. Qutb reassures that "this is an enduring war that will never end, because the Jews want no more no less than to exterminate the religion of Islam ... Since Islam subdued them (in Medina, B.T.) they are unforgiving and fight furiously through conspiracies, intrigues, and also through proxies who act in the darkness against all what Islam incorporates".[36] Such views indicate that the contemporary Jew-hatred by the Islamists and their view that American leaders are the executioners of a Jewish conspiracy will not end if and when there is a resolution of the Middle East conflict. The Islamists believe in an alleged cosmic war against Islam designed by the Jews to undermine the alleged claim of Islam to al-iyada/supremacy. One finds the notion on the Muslim Brotherhood logo. The cosmic war that Sayyid Qutb described did not only target the Jews. It was also to be waged against "America".[37] For Qutb, the cosmic war in point was also a "war of ideas".[38] This notion has appeared in Western discussions since 9/11. However, the coinage of *harb al-afkar* is Islamist in origin and much older than the Western one. As Qutb put it: "The Jews do not fight on the battlefield with weapons ... they fight in a war of ideas through intrigues suspicions, defamations and maneuvering", thus demonstrating their "wickedness and cunning".[39] Despite his claims to be authentic by drawing on Islamic sources, Qutb did not refrain from drawing on one European source, namely the fraudulent "The Protocols of the Elders of Zion." He quoted liberally from them to support his allegations. Subsequent Islamist authors have followed his example. However, Qutb reads the European antisemitism into Islamic history to give it through selective religious arguments an Islamic authentic shape. This feature results from reading a major European ideology to give it the design of an Islamized antisemitism. The narrative of Qutb's "*Ma'rakutna ma'a al-Yahud*/Our Struggle against the Jews" expresses this claimed authenticity. Given, according to Qutb that an Islamic-Jewish enmity has prevailed throughout all of Islamic history, it follows that this form of antisemitism is one source of the conflict Arab and Palestinian conflict with Israel. While modern Arab antisemitism also drew on Christians followed by Muslim secular pan-Arabists, who studied in Europe, their antisemitism was based on a pure copying of a European view. That is, it was an import. The Islamization of a murderous ideology that gives antisemitism an authentic Islamic shape is the work of Qutb. With Islamization, antisemitism in the Arab world was no longer restricted to secular Westernized elites.

Qutb was a well-educated Muslim, who knew the Qur'anic distinction between "*ahl-al-kitab*/people of the book" (Jews and Christians), who are acknowledged as believers, and the "*kuffar*/unbeliever". He speaks though of "*al-kuffar al-Yahud*/the Jewish unbeliever", which is by Qur'anic terms a contradiction in terms. Qutb legitimated this deviation from the religious doctrine with an outcasting of the Jews based on the allegation that they "who were originally in fact included in *ahl-al-kitab* community diverted, however, from the very beginning ... They committed *shurk*/unbelief and became the worst enemies of believers." With the support of this interpretation Qutb constructed an enmity between Islam and "the Jews" articulated in religious terms to justify a cosmic war against the Jews. This enmity allegedly began "from the very first moment, when an Islamic state was established at Medina, as it was opposed by the Jews, who acted against Muslims on the first day when those united themselves in one *umma*." Qutb continued this propaganda on two levels, the first of which is the history of Jews that he invented. This invention was related to the interaction of Jews with Islam in history. The second level of Qutb's antisemitism was determined by psychological and anthropological aspects, such as the description of "*simat al-Yahud*/the basic traits of the Jews." This was a pure essentialization. In this unequivocally antisemitic jargon expressed in a combination of an alleged "history" and of an "anthropology" of the Jews, Qutb laid the foundations for an Islamized antisemitism. He charged that the Jews were the source of all evils and that therefore their "annihilation" was a requirement for ending the "cosmic war." The result would be what Qutb called an "Islamic peace", in an understanding of *Pax Islamica* for the globe as a new world order.[40]

Qutb began his narrative with the foundation of an *umma*/community in Medina by the Prophet in 622. He wrongly labeled this "*dawla*/state" to serve as a model of a shari'a-state never known in the Islamic past. Yet the term "state" was never used in those times and it is neither among the vocabulary of the Qur'an, nor of *hadith*, the authoritative canonical records of the Prophet. The constructed war with the Jews should have been continued throughout Islamic history, which Qutb sums up in a phrasing that deserves being quoted at length. The text begins with asking a question about the source of the "evil" to answer this with one word: "*Yahudi*/a Jew". On these grounds, the following quote seems implicitly to legitimate a purification, a kind of a new Holocaust, which is still an imagined one because Islamists still lack the power instruments to implement their Islamist ideology. Qutb asks:

> "Who tried to undermine the nascent Islamic state in Medina and who incited Quraish in Mecca, as well as other tribes against the foundation of this state? It was a Jew! Who stood behind the *fitna*-war and the slaying of the third caliph Osman and all the tragedies that followed hereafter? It was a Jew! And who inflamed national divides against the last caliph and who stood behind the turmoil that ended the Islamic order with the abolition of shari'a? It was Ataturk, a Jew! The Jews always stood and continue to stand behind the war waged against Islam. Today, this war persists against the Islamic revival in all places on earth."[41]

Qutb's version of the history of Islam contradicts the well established historical record. Yet this erroneous tale has served to support the view that there never, ever can be a settlement, a reconciliation or a compromise with Jews. Qutb believed in his lifetime that the Jews "use all weapons and instruments employed in their genius of Jewish cunning." He added to this "*amqariyyat al-makr*/geniality of cunning", the pursuit of their "malicious conspiracy". In this mindset the Jews, not the Muslims, were those who waged this never ending cosmic war. Thus, fighting jihad is merely a defensive measure. It was and remains the Jews who are aggressors.

Qutb addressed the question as to why the Jews engaged in these "assaults" against Islam? The answer Qutb always provides is "the Jewish character" which Qutb describes as "evil" and "wicked." The logical conclusion is that the annihilation of the Jews was the solution and that therefore he consented to a Holocaust. Approval of the Nazi's genocide of European Jews is the obvious implication of his argument. Qutb repeats the prejudice that "they (the Jews) killed and massacred and even sawed the bodies of a number of their own prophets … So what do you expect from people who do this to their prophets other than to be blood-letting and to target the entire humanity!" The prejudice amounts to a consent to "liberate humanity" from this "evil". Such antisemitism was alien to classical Islam and it cannot be compared with any earlier existing Judeophobia. Therefore, the notion of an "Islamic legacy of antisemitism" is utterly wrong.

Again, the "Islamization" of a European ideology refers to an undertaking more dangerous than any secular precedents because the action authenticates an alien ideology that becomes an Islamized antisemitism. In this localized form, antisemitism was no longer an import from Europe and thus became more appealing to larger numbers of Muslims in Arab societies. This indigenization explained why the Islamized ideology was able to strike roots and to be enhanced as well as to be strengthened by popular anti-Americanism.[42] In this combination the ideology in question prevails today throughout the world of Islam. Islamists believe that the alliance between the US and Israel indicates a war named "crusader-Zionist *harban salibiyya-sahyuniyya*/war against every element of the roots of the religion of Islam." This view is not shared by the "Muslim enlightened thought" that recognizes Jews as equals and "open the way to a full respect for civic spheres in which Muslims can coexist as equal citizens with non-Muslims".[43] This is also the spirit of a trialogue of an "Encountering the Stranger". This encounter also implicates Jews and Muslims. Islamists do not share this spirit.[44]

The Islamist perception of "Islam under siege"[45] is underlined by a belief in a "conspiracy" against Islam hatched by "world Jewry" and "world Zionism" in alliance with the United States. In this perception there are many confusions and identifications: These Islamist ideologues identify and conflate "Zionists" and "the Jews." Contrary to Western observers who justify Islamist antisemitism as due to anti-Zionism, Qutb's successors did not and do not distinguish one from the other. Furthermore: Americans are for Islamists the "new crusaders". Qutb is deeply convinced that: "The Jews were the instigator from the very first moment. The crusaders followed only next." Thus the *salibiyyun* are downgraded to "executioners of the Jews". Those who speak of a moderate Islamism fail to address these prevailing images. To state that these images to persist is not an essentialist statement.

In short, the major ideological sources of Islamist antisemitism in the world of Islam are Qutb's writings and those of others in the related Islamist tradition. They are not due to the policies of the administration of George W. Bush combined with Israel's policies toward the Palestinians in the occupied territories.

The truth is, that the equation of "world Jewry" and "world Zionism" viewed as instigators of an US-war against Islam long predated the Bush administration and the Israeli occupation of the West Bank after the 1967 war. The source instead was the "Islamization of antisemitism" laid down by Qutb.

Articulated in policy-terms, the issue can be stated in this manner: Islamized antisemitism was introduced by the political thought of Sayyid Qutb. For countering one needs ventures like a trialogue. This is more promising than the failed and disastrous politics of an indiscriminate "war on terror" unsuccessfully pursued by the Bush administration and not really ended by the Obama administration.

Those who belittle the impact of Qutb, overlook his most powerful essentialization of "the Jews" as an "evil" combined with the implication of an imagined Holocaust viewed as the solution. Qutb's antisemitism is not a view of a minority. Qutbism has become a corner stone in the political-religious thought of most Islamist movements of our time. Qutb's thoughts have become the major source for the Islamist worldview on which Islamized antisemitism combined with an anti-Americanism rests.

Again and again, the reader is reminded of the most important distinction between Islam and Islamism. This distinction is of a great importance and therefore it is repeated due to its pertinence to Islamist antisemitism. This distinction is not only rejected by Islamists (they believe they are the "True Believers"), but unfortunately also in some US-Islamic studies often conducted under the impact of Saidism.[46] The Islamists dismiss the distinction in their war of ideas against the West in an act of purification enacted as a de-Westernization. In this war, the work of Qutb has a great impact. The reference that most Islamists make to the alleged "wickedness" of the Jews considered to be "evil-doer" who act in the pursuit of their "secret masterplan"—is based on an adoption from the work Qutb. This antisemitism is articulated in the language of an Islamic variety of the global phenomenon of religious fundamentalism. Political Islam, or Islamism declares a war of ideas on the US and Jews and is the Islamic name for this phenomenon for which Qutb in the past and the global TV Mufti Yusuf al-Qaradawi at present are the major ideologues.[47] The Islamist movement remains faithful to its ideology also after its empowerment in the course of the Arab Spring. Nonetheless Islamists engage in short-lived tactical coalitions, and even in mediation (e.g. Gaza November 2012), but they never abandon their power grab in pursuit of a shari'a-state.[48]

The call for a shari'a-state against the secular order of a nation-state is, as two Saudi professors, Jarisha and Zaibaq, tell us, a part of the fight against the Jews. They state:

> "The West waves the flag of secularism … invades with its new values the society of Islam to replace the Islamic values … We shall talk about Zionism, or world Jewry, in order to address the related masterplan pursued by the related secret societies for the destruction of the world".[49]

The alleged masterplan is then identified by those two Saudi professors as a "Jewish conspiracy". The quoted statement resembles a textbook-like definition of the Islamist anti-Westernism guided by antisemitism. The "Christian West", for which the US stands, acts against Islam as a proxy of the Jews. The overall context is a universal conspiracy aimed at destroying Islam. The fact of a full equation of the term "*sahyuniyya*/Zionism", and "*al-Jahudiyya al-alamiyya*/world Jewry", as included in the quoted statement not only indicates a continuation of the thinking of Qutb, but also belies all contentions to the contrary. This equation gives reason to argue that the allegation "anti-Zionism is not antisemitism" is baseless. This argument cannot only be falsified on intellectual grounds, it is also political in that it serves to cover and to legitimate a real antisemitism advanced in the name of a political contestation of Zionism that does injustice to Muslims. In the narrative of the Islamists, Islam is embattled; it is encircled by a secular Jewish-crusader alliance embodied today by the US. In this Islamist narrative "Islam is under siege" and Islamism is the response. The defense of the secular outlook[50] against Islamist antisemitism is also a defense of the secular world order against the one Islamists are poised to impose, at least in the present stage in the field of a "war of ideas".

Do not be mistaken, political Islam is not about extremism and terrorism. As John Kelsay's work evidences it is rather about "the very notion of governance".[51] Outb described the "Jews" as an "evil doer" in the context of political order. He believed that the Jews pull the strings to impose their vision of a world order against an Islamic polity for the world.

From Islamist Ideology to Jihadist Action: Sayyid Qutb's Executioners—Hamas

In an interpretation of Qutb's booklet "Our Struggle Against the Jews" one tends to see that Qutb imagined a new Holocaust in murderous Islamist antisemitism to "free" the world from the accused "evil-doers". This interpretation might be wrong, but the thinking of the program included in the Charter of the Palestinian Hamas is based on Qutb's deliberations.

A proper understanding of the Islamist movement of Hamas presupposes an understanding of its roots in the ideology of the Muslim Brotherhood. Hamas subscribes to this origin and acknowledges being its off-spring. One also needs to understand the overall context of the return of the sacred. In this context religion is advanced in a politicized shape to a component of world politics and it has its local varieties. 9/11 has been a watershed in this process. On these grounds the global religionization of conflict takes also a regional shape in the Middle East and elsewhere in the world of Islam (e.g. South and Southeast Asia). The religionization in point becomes a source of tensions.[52] At issue is a general phenomenon that materializes in regional and local conflicts and makes them intractable. This insight is highly important for understanding how "Islam's civil war" turns into a "geo-civil war".[53] The Middle East conflict is highly affected by this global development. Today, one can argue with a reference to this context, that the Arab-Israeli conflict as well as its Palestinian component are affected by political Islam as it replaces pan-Arab nationalism.[54] This religionized politics applies in an Islamization of Palestinian politics to Hamas which is not a nationalist movement. The earlier Palestinian secular nationalism lost its spell in a development that determines an inner-Palestinian struggle. It is between Islamists and secular Palestinian nationalists.[55]

Against this background Hamas acts in the overall context of transnational religion. The Palestinian Islamist Muhsin Antabawi in his tiny booklet of 58 pages explains in the booklet's title: "Why do we reject any peace with the Jews".[56] This is a publication written on behalf of the "Islamic Association of Palestinian Students in Kuwait" and articulates an Islamist public choice that heralds how a religionized conflict becomes intractable. In this specific Palestinian context one encounters the general, earlier cited contention of Qutb that "there can be no peace between Muslims and Jews". It is applied to the conflict over Israel/Palestine and it is the view of Hamas. Therefore, Hamas cannot be appeased, nor can Iran, the regional promoter of this Islamist movement. Iran has become—thanks to the US-Iraq war a regional power in the Middle East.

What matters here is Hamas commitment to an Islamized antisemitism. The "*al-Yahud*/the Jews" are clearly profiled in an antisemitic manner by the formula "*al-sahyuniyun*/the Zionists". Unlike the Iranian President Mohammed Ahmadinejad, who was at pains to cover his antisemitism as anti-Zionism in his well-known venture of 2007, the Palestinian al-Antawabi does not care about such a camouflage. All Jews are essentialized as an anti-Islamic Zionist entity. For Antabawi all Jews are permanently conspiring in a cosmic war against Islam. His conclusion is that Jews can therefore never be appeased. Antabawi's other conclusion is: "The solution for Palestine can only be brought by a generation mobilized against the Jews on the grounds of a combination of the Qur'an with the gun". The result of this mobilization seems to be the imagined Holocaust, since no middle-way seems to be admitted. This is the ideology of Hamas.

Clearly, Hamas represents the Palestinian variety of Islamism which is not a religious nationalism, as some argue. This movement is embedded in transnational religion. The root is also the transnational Movement of the Muslim Brotherhood and its discourse is based on the thought of Sayyid Qutb outlined above. I reiterate, that Qutb in his booklet "*Ma'rakatuna ma'a al-Yahud*/Our Struggle Against the Jews" laid the foundations for the new pattern of Jew-hatred in political Islam which is the origin of an Islamization of antisemitism. The statement made by Qutb that "the Jews continue to be perfidious and sneaky, and try to mislead the Islamic *umma* in diverting it away from its religion" is quoted again to remind of Qutb's allegation that all tragedies of the Muslim *umma* stem from "Jewish conspiracies" to justify a cosmic war against the Jews also fought by Hamas that sets forth Islamist tradition and transfers its views into a political agenda. Those EU-politicians and also the European opinion leaders who want to accommodate Hamas in an inclusive approach seem to lack knowledge about the political agenda of Hamas. In contrast, the German Political Scientist Matthias Küntzel provided a superb study on Islamism and Jew-hatred showcased on Hamas.[57] Küntzel notes aptly about the Hamas Charter in his study: "In every respect, Hamas' new document put the 1968 PLO Charter in the shade ... The Hamas Charter probably ranks as the one of contemporary Islamism's most important programmatic document and its significance goes far beyond the Palestine conflict." For this reason, Hamas' Charter deserves a closer scrutiny as a prominent example for Islamized antisemitism to be accomplished in this section. Even in the West, Hamas has received respectability and great attention. In Europe, Hamas is positively perceived by the liberal left as a liberation movement acting against "oppressors." The showing of Hamas in the election of January 2006 has been tainted by its terrorist action 2007. It continues to be an anti-American, and antisemitic organization as Andrew Levitt discloses in his earlier cited Hamas-study.

In the following I shall focus on the Hamas Charter as it demonstrates its roots in "The Movement of the Muslim Brotherhood" which is a transnational one. This movement represents today the most important one among the major networks of internationalist Islamism. Already in its first pronouncement of December 14, 1988, Hamas acknowledged to be "the armed hand of The Muslim Brotherhood". Furthermore, there is the Charter's[58] article 32 that identifies "world Zionism" as the enemy; here one fails to find the name of Israel. The reference makes it clear that Islamism relates the conflict over Palestine to a cosmic war against what Qutb termed "world Jewry". Hamas perceives of itself as "*ra's hurbah/* spearhead" in this cosmic war against "world Zionism". All Muslims who fail to share this view are vilified.

There are two references in the Hamas Charter indicative of its religionization of the conflict. The first draws on the "secret plans" included in "The Protocols of the Elders of Zion" to unveil the "wickedness of the Jews", while the second relates to the allegation that the "Zionist master plan/conspiracy" knows no boundaries, "today Palestine, tomorrow more expansion". The Charter outlaws on these religious grounds, i.e. in the name of shari'a, all Muslims who engage in any politics of a peaceful solution. This rejection includes the Oslo accords as well as the Peace of Camp David. The Muslims who engage in peace negotiations are accused of committing a "*khiyana uzma/*great treason". A comparison of the Charter text with the polemical pamphlet by Qutb against the Jews discussed at length in the first section reveals great borrowings. There is also a resemblance based on congeniality in the argumentation. In the text of the Charter there exists no distinction between Jews and Zionists. Altogether, they are the enemy. In an obvious antisemitic manner, article 22 vilifies Jews as the source of all evil. One may compare the following quotation with the very similar one brought from Qutb in the foregoing section of the present study. In its Charter Hamas states the Jews:

> "stood behind the French and the communist revolutions ... in the pursuit of the interests of Zionism ... they were behind the First World War that led to the abolition of the caliphate ... to get the Belfour Declaration ... Then they established The League of Nations to rule through it the world and hereafter they pulled the strings for the Second World War ... to establish the state Israel and to replace the league of nations by the UN and its security council. They rule the world ... There is no single war without the hidden hand of the Jews acting behind it....".

If this conspiracy-driven accusation of the Jews of pulling the strings in all affairs in world-politics does not smack of antisemitism, so what would it then be? One can demonstrate the idea of a religionization of conflict in the shift from the secular Palestinian nationalism of the PLO to the Islamism of Hamas. The task of drawing boundaries is fulfilled in Charter's article 27 in which the borderline is described in this phrasing: "Secular thought contradicts fully the religious idea ... We refuse the belittling of the place of religion in the Arab-Israel conflict and insist instead on the *Islamiyyat*/Islamicity of Palestine. We cannot replace this claim by secular thoughts. The Islamicity of Palestine is part and parcel of our religion". The outcome is a religionized conflict that leaves no more space for any negotiation, or for a compromising. The foremost implication of this unwavering religionization is the introduction of an understanding of political religion that also includes along these lines the new religionized antisemitism. Unlike the earlier pan-Arab nationalist antisemitism the new one is presented in a religionized shape.

Islamism is not a scriptural traditionalism; it is a modern religious fundamentalism. Nonetheless, the Hamas Charter makes ample references to the holy scripture with an arbitrary interpretation followed for instance by a quote from Hasan al-Banna, the founder of The Muslim Brotherhood made in this phrasing: "Israel stands and shall continue to stand until Islam eradicates it, as it did undo earlier similar entities." The goal is to "wave the flag of Allah over every inch in Palestine" (article 6). Such references impose wrongly the meaning that the "killing of the Jew" is "a religious obligation". This is the most perilous implication of the religionization of antisemitism. The deep impact of the political-religious thoughts of Qutb on the Hamas Charter is in this context clear. In this line the charter pronounces "a cosmic war" against the Jews viewed as zero-sum game.

In a commitment to the ideology of Hamas the Palestinian politician, opinion leader and writer Antabawi precludes "peace with the Jews". His argument is based on his belief that "this violates the shari'a". This is a standard Islamist argumentation.[59] In this line of reasoning the Hamas Charter declares Palestine in article 11 as "*waqf Islami*/divine property". The Charter adds "The shari'a rules that every land conquered by Muslims is their property until the "day of resurrection/*qiyama*". Then the text adds the phrase: "peaceful solutions contradict the commitment of Hamas to Islam. The abandonment of any piece of Palestine is an abandonment of the religion itself" (Article 13). It follows the conclusion: "There is no real solution to the conflict over Palestine except other than jihad … anything else is a wasting of time", as the same article 13 continues. All of these bellicose Islamist statements are done by Hamas with a reference to shari'a supplied with the definite article becoming "the shari'a" as the statement quoted above reveals.

According to authoritative Muslim scholars of the enlightened Muslim thought (see note 43) there is no such thing in Islam that allows speaking of an established standard named with the definite article "the shari'a".[60] One of those, Fazlur Rahman, tells us much of shari'a which "embodies moral and quasi-moral precepts" all of which are open to debate and different interpretations. Another authoritative Muslim scholar, Hamid Enayat, emphasized the historical fact that "there is no such thing as a unified Islamic system" named "that shari'a". The Islamist shari'atization of Islam results in a claim that there is one law, it is the law of the Islamist movement itself presented as "the shari'a". The consequence is to accuse those Muslims who disagree of heresy and non-Muslims of Islamophobia.

Conclusions

The core assumption of the present study is that Islamist antisemitism is not authentic, but rather rests on an Islamist (not Islamic) Islamization of European antisemitism. At issue is a contemporary phenomenon which is rooted in political Islam. Islamism includes the misconception that the Jews are instigators of a conspiracy directed against Islam, Historically, they believe, it was fulfilled on their behalf by "Western crusaders". If there were a lesson to learn from the history of the crusades—and of course—respectively—from the Islamic wars of Jihad named *futuhat* wars, then it would be that any religionized war is indiscriminately an evil for humanity. Yet, in the name of respect to Islam, Islamism is judged by benign Westerners positively by a standard different from the one applied to right-wing movements in the West. Earlier I quoted Raymond Stock, one of the best experts on Egypt, stating that the Muslim Brothers are "anti-Western and antisemitic" in their supremacist ideology (see note 28). Those opinion-leaders in the West who turn a blind eye to this Islamist antisemitism believe, as Stock continues, to see the Islamist "leaders not as they are but as they wish them to be, moderate, liberal ….". One wonders whether these people were surprised when the Egyptian MB-president Morsi fired in an unconstitutional action at the end of November 2012 the general prosecutor of the country. Morsi also abolished by edict the constitutional division of executive, legislative and juridical powers in Egypt. The edict placed the political decisions of the Muslim Brother president of Egypt "above juridical review",[61] parallel to doing away with the independence of the courts. This behavior was not only unconstitutional but also by all democratic standards an indication of a new autocracy. In his personal Decree president Morsi assigned to his person sweeping powers that irreversibly allowed him to rule without permitting any institutional or legal instance to check his authority. The edict also allowed him to override law and to establish an authoritarian personal rule. President Morsi thus put his presidency of an Islamic state above the rule of democracy. There are no names for this decree other than autocracy or even an Islamist dictatorship. It was highly impressive to see on TV-news angry Egyptians returning to the Tahrir square to protest against the new dictator. It was amazing to listen to Western commentators stating that not even Mubarak went that far to put himself this far above the law in the name of religion.

Under these new conditions the Middle East conflict becomes a religionized conflict and thus intractable. In the past, Israel was able to negotiate the conflict with the secular PLO and even to strike the Oslo peace[62] that was unfortunately destroyed. Nothing like negotiated peace could ever be repeated with the Islamists because for them politics is a divinity which is simply unnegotiable beyond any debate.

Some Western academic apologists view Islamism, though, as a liberation theology. It gets worse: Islamism is upgraded by some to the other modernity. The study of the six features of the Islamist ideology (one of which is antisemitism) reveals, however, that a right-wing ideology is at issue. What is named "anti-crusaderism" is today an anti-Western ideology, not a contestation of capitalism, nor is it an anti-globalization. There is a need for an enlightenment based on solid information to which this study aims to contribute. No doubt, one can and should criticize US- and Western policies in the world of Islam, in particular in the Middle East. Also the Israeli unjust occupation of Palestinian territory is a subject of a legitimate criticism. However, one should beware of endorsing an antisemitism as happens often in parts of the contemporary Western debates.

Therefore, it is—in a scholarly world that seems to be set upside down—most perplexing to see that not antisemitic Islamism is outlawed, but rather instead the contributions of those who criticize it. They are accused of Islamophobia while Islamism is celebrated as "liberation theology" of the oppressed. The accusation of Islamophobia outlaws criticism.

This happens in a scholarship that instead to enlighten about the reality sets it upside down. Some US university presses publish books that upgrade Islamists.[63] In these books Muslim critics of Islamism are vilified and called names, while Islamist movements, and even Islamist Iran, are praised.[64]

The analysis provided in this paper contradicts these views and is based on evidence that unveils an antisemitic Islamism. This feature continues to prevail in the aftermath of Arab Spring. Islamist rulers (e.g. President Morsi in the Gaza conflict 2012) may mediate for tactical reasons, but do not engage in an enduring resolution of the Middle East conflict to establish peace between Jews and Arabs. The needed resolution requires acknowledging the nationhood of the other as an equal and specifically the right of the Jews to their own state. Islamism rebuffs this requirement most vehemently. Islamist ideology reflects a de-humanization of the Jews in an Islamization of European antisemitism.

As a Muslim on all levels and faithful to the tradition of Islamic humanism[65] I acknowledge my leaning on Karl Popper and on his partisanship to civil society as "open society". I view Islamism as a major contemporary "enemy of open society". Also in the tradition of my academic Jewish teacher Max Horkheimer who survived the Holocaust I, in a commitment to the "enlightened Muslim thought" (see note 43), join forces against "all totalitarianisms". Based on my study of Islamism in the past three decades I come to the professedly unpopular conclusion that Islamism is "the new totalitarianism". One is reminded of Hannah Arendt's view that antisemitism is a major feature of any totalitarianism. The current Western "moderation-literature" on Islamism rightly advocates a process of democratization in Post-Arab Spring that also engages Islamist movements. This is not the problem. The problem is rather the confusion of engagement and empowerment after the breakdown of authoritarian regimes.

This study concludes with three pertinent questions that should not be silenced and to which I add an Islamic option. The first question is: Is a genuine democracy in an Islamist shari'a-state possible?, the second is: Could an ideology that features antisemitism be the grounds for a democratic peace?, third, is it an expression of Islamophobia to state the existence of an Islamist antisemitism?[66]

There is an alternative Islamic option to Islamism. It is the "enlightened Muslim thought" outlined by the Moroccan writer Abdou Filali-Ansary in the following quote:

> "In the enlightened view, religion is a historically situated expression of spiritual visions and ethical ideals ... The realization that Islam, properly understood, is not a system of social and political regulations, frees up space for cultures and nations ... This opens the way, in turn, to the acceptance of a convergence with other religious traditions and universalistic moralities. ... This acceptance and this respect are to enlightened Muslim minds matters of principle and not merely grudging tactical concessions of the sort some Islamists make."[67]

The outlined "enlightened Muslim thought" reflects a civil Islam based on the tradition of Islamic humanism mentioned above and outlined elsewhere.[68] This Muslim thought not only outlaws antisemitism, it also smoothes the way for an honest Jewish-Muslim mutual respect and mutual recognition. At present Muslim Arabs and Jews urgently need a new and better variety of the medieval "Muslim-Jewish symbiosis" in the context of an "Encountering of the Stranger" in this new century.[69]

Acknowledgment: The outstanding research assistance provided on all levels to all drafts by Thorsten Hasche is most thankfully acknowledged. The many earlier drafts of the present paper were completed 2007–2010 within the framework of two affiliations. One at Yale University (2008/9 at YIISA-the Yale Interdisciplinary Initiative on the Study of Antisemitism) and the other was a senior fellowship at the Center for Advanced Holocaust Studies/CAHS at the US Holocaust Memorial Museum (2008 and 2010). The unpublished paper was presented at the Dublin international conference on antisemitism in November 2010. The present chapter is a revised draft completed in 2012 for the present publication.

Notes

1. For more details see B. Tibi, *Islamism and Islam* (New Haven: Yale University Press, 2012), chapter three. In distinction from Islam, the book argues, Islamism is characterized by six specific features. One of them is the Islamization of European antisemitism.
2. See Paul Marshall and Nina Shea, *Silenced: How Apostasy and Blasphemy Codes are Silencing Free Speech Worldwide* (New York: Oxford University Press, 2012).
3. On this matter see Bat Ye'or, *Islam and Dhimmitude. Where Civilizations Collide* (Cranbury/NJ: Associated University Presses, 2002).

4. Bernard Lewis, *The Jews of Islam* (Princeton: Princeton University Press, 1984).
5. This thesis is based on research conducted at these institutions: Cornell and Yale Universities and the US Holocaust Memorial Museum. Next to the book referenced in note 1 the other related references to this research are B. Tibi, "Public Policy and the Combination of Anti-Americanism and Antisemitims in Contemporary Islamist Ideology". In: *The Current* (Cornell University) Vol. 12, 1 (Fall 2008), pp. 123–146 and B. Tibi, "From Sayyid Qutb to Hamas. The Middle East Conflict and the Islamization of Antisemitism". New Haven, *YIISA Working Paper*, Yale University 2010.
6. The primary source of this formula and its claim for authenticity is the work of Yusuf al-Qaradawi, *Hatimiyyat al-hall al-Islami*, 3 volumes. Vol. 1: *al-Hulul al-mustawradah* [The Imported Solutions] (Cairo: Mu'ssasat al-Risalah, reprint 1980). See also the chapter on authenticity in B. Tibi, *Islam's Predicament with Modernity* (New York: Routledge, 2009), pp. 237–264.
7. Andrew G. Bostom, Ed. *The Legacy of Islamic Antisemitism* (Amherst, NY: Promotheus, 2008).
8. Being a Muslim co-founder (along with the revered late Rabi Albert Friedlaender) of the Jewish-Islamic dialogue I strongly dismiss these views and the related sentiments that underpin them. If they were true, then how could one explain the attitudinal changes of Muslim-Arabs in their "Responses to the Holocaust: From Empathy to Denial", as Meir Litvak and Esther Webman state in the title of their significant book. See their major study: *From Empathy to Denial. Arab Reponses to the Holocaust* by Meir Litvak and Ester Webman (New York: Columbia University Press, 2009). For a trialogue see the contributions in Leonard Grob and John Roth, eds. *Encountering the Stranger. A Jewish, Christian, Muslim Trialogue* (Seattle: University of Washington Press, 2012).
9. Klaus Michael Mallmann and Martin Cüppers. *Nazi Palestine. The Plans for the Extermination of the Jews in Palestine* (New York: Enigma Books, 2010), p. 124 and p. 125.
10. Jeffrey Herf, *Nazi Propaganda for the Arab World* (New Haven: Yale University Press, 2009).
11. B. Tibi. *Arab Nationalism. Between Islam and the Nation-State* (London: Macmillan, 3rd edn. 1997, 1st 1980).

12. The Western support of Islamism in the name of democratization is among the great flaws. See for example the pre-Arab Spring books by Raymond Baker, *Islam Without Fear. Egypt and the New Islamists* (Cambridge: Harvard University Press, 2003) and Bruce Rutherford, *Egypt after Mubarak. Liberalism, Islam, and Democracy in the Arab World* (Princeton: Princeton University Press, 2008).
13. In this context see the chapter on third-worldism in B. Tibi, *Islam in Global Politics* (London: Routledge, 2012), pp. 140–160.
14. The contributions to Carl W. Ernst and Richard Martin, eds. *Rethinking Islamic Studies. From Orientalism to Cosmopolitanism* (Columbia/ S.C.: University of South Carolina Press, 2010) demonstrate such a development. The subtitle of this book contends a change from "Orientalism to Cosmopolitanism", but this promise is not delivered; some of its authors rather engage in an "Orientalism in Reverse".
15. B. Tibi, *The Shari'a-State. Arab Spring and Democratization* (London and New York: Routledge, 2013).
16. On the distinction between peaceful institutionalist and jihadist Islamists see Tibi, *Islam and Islam* (referenced in note 1).
17. The classic book on this movement is Richard Mitchell, *The Muslim Brothers* (London: Oxford University Press, 1969). For an overview see Nazih Ayubi, *Political Islam. Religion and Politics in the Arab World* (London: Routledge, 1991) and B. Tibi, *Political Islam, World Politics and Europe* (London Routledge, 2008).
18. Alireza Jafarzadeh, *The Iran Threat. President Ahmadinejad and the Coming Nuclear Crisis* (New York: Palgrave, 2007); Ervand Abrahamian, *Khomeinism* (Berkeley: University of California Press, 1993), pp. 124–125.
19. Graham Fuller, *The Center of the Universe. The Geopolitics of Iran* (Boulder/Col: Westview, 1991), p. 123.
20. See Matthew Levitt, *Hamas. Politics, Charity and Terrorism in the Service of Jihad* (New Haven: Yale University Press, 2006), pp. 172–178.
21. Fuller, *The Center* ... (see note 19), p. 123.
22. On Islamism and authenticity see B. Tibi, *Islamism and Islam* (note 1), Chapter 7; see also the reference in note 6. On pre-Islamist ideologies see B. Tibi, "Islam and Modern European Ideologies", in: *Islam and Globalization. Critical Concepts in Islamic Studies*,

four volumes, edited by Shahram Akbarzadeh (New York: Routledge, 2006), included as chapter 11 in vol. one, pp. 206–222.
23. See for example the views of the Saudi professors Mohammed Jarisha and Yusuf al-Zaibaq, *Asalib al-Ghazu al-fikri lil-alam al-Islami* [Methods of the Intellectual Invasion of the World of Islam] (Cairo: Dar al-I'tisam, second printing 1978).
24. Emran Qureshi and Michael Sells, eds, *The New Crusaders* (New York: Columbia University Press, 2003). This slogan is employed by Islamists in their inflammatory anti-Western war of ideas to identify the West with the formula of crusaderism/ *al-salibiyya*. The book by John Mearshheimer and Stephen Walt, *The Israel Lobby and US Foreign Policy* (New York: Farrer and Strauss, 2008) is most contentious. A troubling impact of the book is its support to Islamist contentions.
25. See Hannah Arendt, *The Origins of Totalitarianism* (New York: Harcourt Inc., 1951, new printing 1976). Arendt's work has been the source of inspiration for my study of the political nature of Islamism. See Chapter 8 "Islamism and Totalitarianism" and Chapter 9 "Civil Islam as an Alternative" in my Yale book *Islamism and Islam* (referenced in note 1). See also the earlier contributions B. Tibi, *Der neue Totalitarismus* (Darmstadt: Primus, 2004) and by the same author the article: "The Legacy of Max Horkheimer and Islamist Totalitarianism", in: *Telos* (2009) issue 148, pp. 7–15.
26. See B. Tibi, "The Totalitarianism of Jihadist Islamism", in: *Totalitarian Movements and Political Religions*, vol. 8, 1 (2007), pp. 35–54 and the references in the preceding note.
27. See the unconvincing assertions made by Robert Leiken and Steven Brooke, "The Moderate (sic!) Muslim Brotherhood", *Foreign Affairs*, vol. 86, 2 (April 2007), pp. 107–121. For a contrast see the article by Raymond Stock referenced in the following note 28.
28. Raymond Stock, "The Donkey, the Camel and the Facebook Scam: How the Muslim Brotherhood Conquered Egypt and Canned the World", *Foreign Policy Research Institute E-Notes* July 2012.
29. It is highly amazing to see the heir of Qutb, namely Yusuf Qaradawi, being upgraded to a "Muslim liberal" to be included in the most questionable reader by Charles Kurzman, ed., *Liberal Islam. A Sourcebook* (New York: Oxford University Press, 1998), pp. 196–204. The major work of Qaradawi, his book trilogy

al-Hall al-Islami [The Islamic Solution] (referenced in note 6 above) enjoys a great dissemination. For a criticism of Kurzman's reader see Abdou Filali-Ansary's contribution referenced in note 43 below.

30. Qaradawi, quoted by Walter Laqeuer, *The Changing Face of Antisemitism* (New York: Oxford University Press, 2006), Chapter Three, p. 199.
31. On these confusions see the clearing by Jeffrey Herf, ed., *Antisemitism and Anti-Zionism in Historical Perspective* (New York: Routledge, 2007) in particular the introduction by the editor Herf, pp. X-XIX and the chapter by Markovits, pp. 71–91. Confusions can also be found in Jonathan Laurence and Justin Vaisse, *Integrating Islam* (Washington/DC: Brookings Institution, 2006), p. 233.
32. As Roxanne Euben notes, "Qutb's influence is undisputed ... He has altered the very terms of Islamic political debates," in her , *The Enemy in the Mirror. Islamic Fundamentalism and the Limits of Modern Rationalism* (Princton/NJ: Princeton University Press, 1999), p. 55. Another scholar of Islam, David Cook, writes that „Qutb ... has founded the actual movement ... (He) was the very center of the Arab Muslim political, intellectual and religious debate ... His works have been cited by radical Muslims from the 1960s until the present and his influence upon the movement is significant." See his David Cook, *Understanding Jihad* (Berkeley: University of California Press, 2004), pp. 102–103. See also the important book by Matthias Küntzel, *Jihad and Jew-Hatred. Islamism, Nazism and the Roots of 9/11* (New York: Telos Press, 2007), part 2.
33. On the de-legitimation in the aftermath of the Six-Days-War of 1967 and on its repercussions (e.g. de-legitimation) see B. Tibi, *Conflict and War in the Middle East. From Inter-State War to New Security* (New York: St. Martin's Press, 2nd edition, 1998), chapters 3 and 4. On the history of Pan-Arab nationalism see B. Tibi, *Arab Nationalism.* (referenced in note 11 above).
34. Sayyid Qutb, *Ma'rakatuna ma'a al-Yahud* [Our Battle with the Jews] (Cairo: Dar al-Shuruq, 10th legal printing, 1989), p. 15. For the English translation see Sayyid Qutb, *Our Struggle with the Jews*, trans. Ronald Nettler in Ronald L. Nettler, *Past Trials and Present Tribulations: A Muslim Fundalmentalist's View of the Jews* (Oxford:

Vidal Sassoon Cetner for the Study of Antisemitism, Hebrew University of Jerusalem and Pergamen Press, 1987). I quote from the Arabic original; translation my own.

35. Hasan al-Banna, *Risalat al-Jihad* [Essay on Jihad] is the corner stone in the development of classical jihad to a jihadism. The essay is included in al-Banna's collection of essays: *Majmu'at Rasail al-Imam al-Shahid* [Collected Writings of the Martyr Imam] (Cairo: Dar al-Da'wa, legal edition, 1990), pp. 271–291.
36. These quotes are adopted from Qutb, *Ma'rakatuna*, (referenced in note 34), p. 33.
37. For more details on this see the book by the Islamist Salah A. al-Khalidi, *Amerika min al-dakhil bi minzar Sayyid Qutb* [America Viewed from Inside Through the Lenses of Sayyid Qutb] (al-Mansura/Egypt and Jedda/Saudi Arabia: Dar al-Manara, third printing, 1987).
38. Walid Phares, *The War of Ideas. Jihadism against Democracy* (New York: Palgrave, 2007), and more recent the volume by Eric Patterson and John Gallagher, eds., *Debating the War of Ideas* (New York: Palgrave, 2009).
39. The following quotes are adopted from Qutb, *Ma'rakatuna ma'a al-Yahud* (referenced in note 69), pp. 31–33.
40. Sayyid Qutb, *al-Salam al-alami wa al-Islam* [World Peace and Islam] (Cairo: Dar al-Shuruq, 10th legal edition, 1992).
41. This and the following quotes are from Qutb, *Ma'rakatuna* (referenced in note 69), p. 33, p. 32, p. 27 and p. 33, 23.
42. Peter Katzenstein und Robert Keohane, eds, *Anti-Americanisms in World Politics* (Ithaca/NY: Cornell University Press, 2007), p. 22. The volume includes a very weak chapter by Marc Lynch on "Anti-Americanisms in the Arab World." Lynch evades the connection of antisemitism/anti-Americanism which is - as cited - acknowledged by the editors. See also B. Tibi, "Public Policy and the Combination of Anti-Americanism and Antisemitism in Contemporary Islamist ideology" (referenced in note 5 above) and the interesting book by Andrei S. Markovits, *Uncouth Nation. Why Europe Dislikes America* (Princeton/NJ: Princeton University Press, 2007).
43. Abdou Filali-Ansary, "The Sources of Enlightened Muslim Thought". In: Larry Diamond and others eds. *Islam and Democracy*

in the Middle East (Baltimore, Johns Hopkins University Press, 2003), pp. 237–251, here 249–250.

44. On the idea of a "trialogue" see the volume edited by John Roth and Leonard Grob. *Encountering the Stranger* (referenced in note 8 above) which grew from a project conducted at The Center for Advanced Holocaust Studies/ CAHS, Washington D.C. The volume includes my contribution "The Place of non-Muslims in the Islamic Concept of the Other" in which I criticize Islamism as an anti-pluralist ideology.
45. On the misperception of Islam under siege see Graham Fuller and Ian Lesser, *A Sense of Siege. The Geopolitics of Islam and the West* (Boulder/Col.: Westview, 1995).
46. An example for this impact are the two volumes edited by Richard Martin. One is quoted in note 14 above and the other is: *Islamism. Contested Perspectives on Political Islam* (Stanford: Stanford University Press, 2010).
47. See the reference in note 6 above. The trajectory of Islamism is designed in the most influential book by Sayyid Qutb, *Ma'alim fi al-tariq* [Signposts along the Road] (Cairo: 13th legal edition, al-Shuruq, 1989). This political Islam is one variety of the global phenomenon of religious fundamentalism; see B. Tibi, *The Challenge of Fundamentalism* (Berkeley: University of California Press, 1998, updated edition 2001).
48. B. Tibi, *The Shari'a-State. Arab Spring and Democratization* (London and New York: Routledge, 2013).
49. Jarisha and Zaibaq, *Asalib* (referenced in note 23), pp. 3–4.
50. Paul Cliteur, *The Secular Outlook. In Defense of Moral and Political Secularism* (Chichester: Wiley and Blackwell, 2010).
51. John Kelsay, *Arguing for a Just War in Islam* (Cambridge/MA: Harvard University Press, 2007), p. 166.
52. On this religionization as a source of tensions see B. Tibi, Islam: Between Religious-Cultural Practice and Identity politics, in: Y. Raj Isar and Helmut Anheier, eds, *Tensions and Conflict. The Culture and Globalization Series, Vol. I* (New York: Sage, 2007), pp. 221–231.
53. John Brenkman, *The Cultural Contradictions of Democracy* (Princeton/NJ: Princeton University Press, 2007), pp. 165–69, also p. 158.

54. On Islam placed in the Middle East conflict see Rifaat S. Ahmed, *al-Islam wa qadaya al-sira' al-Arabi al-Israeli* [Islam and Conflict. Studies on Islam and the Arab-Israel conflict] (Cairo: Dar al-Sharqiyya, 1989), see also Beverly Milton-Edwards, *Islamic Politics in Palestine* (London: Tauris, 1999).
55. On Palestinian nationalism see Muhammed Mulish, *The Origins of Palestinian Nationalism* (New York: Columbia University Press, 1988). On the fight between Palestinian secularists and Islamists see Loren Lybarger, *Identity Politics and Religion in Palestine. The Struggle between Islamism and Secularism* (Princeton NJ: Princeton University Press, 2007) and Amal Jamal, *The Palestinian National Movement. The Politics of Contention* (Bloomington/Indiana: Indiana University Press, 2005).
56. Mushin al-Antabawi, *Limatha narfud al-Salam ma'a al-Yahud* [Why do we Reject on Peace with Jews] (Cairo: Kitab al-Mukhtar, no date). The following quotes are adopted (in my own translation) from this publication that was completed on behalf of the "Islamic Association of Palestinian Students" at the University of Kuwait, as stated in the booklet.
57. Küntzel, *Jihad and Jew-Hatred*, p. 109.
58. In the following I quote from the original text in Arabic of Hamas charter and translate it. The document is included in: Ahmed Izzuldin, *Harakat al-Mqawama al-Islamiyya Hamas* [The Islamic Resistance Movement Hamas] (Cairo: Dar al-Tawzi' al-Islamiyya, 1998), pp. 43–82.
59. Antabawi, *Limatha*, p. 49.
60. The following quotes are adopted from Fazlur Rahman, *Islam and Modernity* (Chicago: University of Chicago Press, 1982), p. 32 and Hamid Enayat, *Modern Islamic Political Thought* (Austin: University of Texas Press, 1982), p. 67. See also the chapter on Islamist shari'a in B. Tibi, *Islamism and Islam*, pp. 158–176.
61. See *New York Times* of November 23, 2012. The *NYT*-report also speaks of a "power grab". President Morsi himself keeps talking about shari'a and the democracy of an Islamic state. For more details see Chapter 4 in B. Tibi, *The Shari'a-State. Arab Spring and Democratization* (New York: Routledge, 2013 forthcoming).
62. See David Makovsky, *Making Peace with the PLO. The Rabin-Government's Road to the Oslo Accord* (Boulder/Col.: Westview, 1996). This peace is presented from a Palestinian perspective by

Mahmoud Abbas (Abu Mazen), *Through Secret Channels. The Road to Oslo* (Reading/UK: Garnet Publishers, 1995), and from an Israeli perspective by Uri Savir, *The Process. 1.100 Days that Changed the Middle East* (New York: Vitage Books, 1998).

63. See the reference to the Harvard University Press and Princeton University Press published books in note 12 above. Long before the empowerment of Islamism 2011/12 these books provided the Muslim Brothers with a legitimacy to rule. See also the most problemmatic publication: *The New Crusaders*, published by Columbia University Press (referenced in note 24 above).
64. See Ahmad Moussalli, *US Foreign Policy and Islamist Politics*, published by Florida University Press in 2008. See my review article in: *The International History Review*, vol. 31, 1 (March 2009), pp. 204–206. In the aftermath of the Arab Spring the US-policy seems to fulfill what this book demands.
65. See the reference in note 43 above. The article B. Tibi, "Islamic Humanism vs. Islamism", in: *Soundings* vol. 95, 3 (2012), pp. 230–254 is placed into this "enlightened Muslim thought".
66. The book by Paul Berman, *The Flight of the Intellectuals* (Brooklyn, NY: Melville House, 2011) was accused of Islamophobia because it courageously asked similar questions.
67. Abdou Filali-Ansary, "The Sources of Enlightened Muslim Thought" (referenced in note 43), here 249–250.
68. See the chapter on Islamic humanism in B. Tibi. *Islam in Global Politics* (New York: Routledge, 2012), pp. 85–110 and also Tibi's article "Islamic Humanism vs. Islamism" (referenced in note 65).
69. See the books by Bernard Lewis *The Jews of Islam* and the other by Grob and Roth which are referenced in note 4 and 8.

PART III

Historical and Contemporary Political Arenas

CHAPTER 7

Political Antisemitism, 'State Jews' and Roosevelt's New Deal

Pierre Birnbaum

The origins of political antisemitism from the late nineteenth century paralleled those of the emergent modern nation-state with its tendency towards interventionist government. Arguably, it first appeared in France as a reaction to the Third Republic, which, in the eyes of its detractors, was seen as a Jewish state threatening the identity of the Christian nation because of the prominent roles Jews were perceived to have in state-building. Its key spokesman was Edouard Drumont, who invented this new form of antisemitism, and who, with his thousands of followers, organised in mass movements, the so-called *ligues*, threatening the legitimacy of the republican state. Drumont and his followers openly sought to destroy the republican state seen as Jewish-controlled, although in the end, they failed. Such a movement with its populist antisemitic rhetoric was an entirely new phenomenon—the Dreyfus affair is its most significant articulation before 1914.[1]

The emergence of political antisemitism in France was soon followed elsewhere in central Europe and notably by Germany. But unlike in France, the fact that the German state never became a strong state, or an entirely secular state where Jews who had not otherwise converted to Christianity were mostly absent from leading positions in the various branches of the

P. Birnbaum (✉)
Professor of History, Political Science at the University of Paris, France

A. McElligott, J. Herf (eds.), *Antisemitism Before and Since the Holocaust*, DOI 10.1007/978-3-319-48866-0_7

state, meant it remained, relatively speaking, weaker. This changed dramatically with the Weimar Republic as Jews, converted and otherwise, rose to positions of visible power. The appointment of Walther Rathenau as foreign minister is but one example of this seismic change. His assassination in 1922 is also an illustration of the explosion of extreme political antisemitism directed against the German republic and its protagonists (to clarify the point: in spite of its vehemence, there were no similar murders of Jews in the Third Republic until the Vichy regime).[2] It was not uncommon for nationalist opponents of the republic and its liberal institutions to refer to it as the 'Jew republic'; in particular, their vitriol was reserved for the Prussian state—the largest and most powerful of the German states, seen as the puppet of domestic and foreign Jews. But this political antisemitism under the Weimar Republic only found its violent apotheosis after 1933 once Hitler came to power.

As we know, Hitler was influenced by the speeches of the pre-war First World War mayor of Vienna, Karl Lueger. Lueger was himself strongly influenced by Edouard Drumont's books and speeches. Hitler became obsessed with the idea of permanently destroying the Prussian state, after 1918 seen, for the first time, as a 'Jewish state'.[3] He expressed in *Mein Kampf* his hatred of Weimar's republican state for allowing Jews to enter the political and administrative structures as in France. Clearly influenced by the so-called *Protocol of the Fathers of Zion* (a forgery written with the French Third Republic in mind), Hitler became obsessed by what he (and others) claimed was Jewish power controlling the state from within and from without. His regime set about suppressing the state as an autonomous body, 'synchronising' its institutions and bringing it to heel under the Nazi jackboot. The result is what Ernst Fraenkel coined the 'dual state': based on paralleled institutions of the totalitarian Nazi Party and the traditional bureaucracy[4]; as Hans Buchheim has shown, the Hitler regime 'transformed the State, its enemy, into its own slave'.[5] The point here is that the German state, unlike that of the French Third Republic, was too 'unformed', and in the case of its Weimar incarnation too weak and 'illegitimate', to resist the force of political antisemitism with its twin target of Jews-state. In 1933, political antisemitism had achieved part of its destructive aim but was incomplete in terms of its totality. In this context and seen in the long term, the Shoah can be viewed as the ultimate consequence of the birth of political antisemitism in Germany.

The curtailed political antisemitism of the French Third Republic and the unbound extremism of the Third Reich are the two poles between which historians usually broach this subject. In this chapter, I wish to outline a third example, not usually associated with the phenomenon but nonetheless closely related to the European examples outlined here: namely that of the United States. The United States traditionally was characterised by a weak central state, which meant that where antisemitism reared its ugly head, it usually was social or religious. It never became 'political' until 1932, when President Roosevelt tried to create a *quasi*-strong state through the New Deal. Surrounded, as in France and to a lesser extent, in Germany, by Jews, this aspiring 'strong state' was seen immediately as 'Jewish', provoking a strong but short life of political antisemitism. In what follows, we shall look at the link between those I call 'state Jews', such as Felix Frankfurter, under the New Deal and political antisemitism in North America.

The presence of some 'state Jews' in Roosevelt's victory cannot be denied. On 7 November 1932, Felix Frankfurter sent a telegram to Franklin Roosevelt:

> Your campaign has educated the hopes of the nation and reinvigorated its faith ... After 4 March you will be able to mobilise the will of the nation as no other president has ever done since Wilson.

Three days later, on 10 November, he sent the following telegram:

> The end crowns all and a glorious end it is—a very great beginning. Apart from all else, you will carry to the White House an equipment of transcendent importance. No predecessor of yours, not even T.R. brought to the Presidency so extensive and intimate knowledge of his countrymen as you have. You will thus be the comprehending expression of diverse interests, feelings, hopes and thoughts of the multitude of forces which are unified into the nation.[6]

Frankfurter literally worshipped Roosevelt, comparing him throughout his life to Washington or Lincoln, the greatest heroes of American history. When he spoke of the president in later years, his eyes would fill with tears and he would be overcome by powerful emotion. A famous professor of Law at Harvard and a naturalised American Jew, for many years Frankfurter maintained close links with Roosevelt, who in 1939 nominated Frankfurter to the Supreme Court. Like the Jews who throughout their long history revered the state, Frankfurter reincarnated the Jewish figure who prayed for the health, happiness and success of their kings, emperors and heads of state.[7] Like them, his praise for Roosevelt was limitless and sometimes approached obsequiousness. One of his least favourable biographers considered him as a specialist in the art of adulation. Certainly, on occasions, he appeared excessively and unattractively flattering.[8]

Between the election in November 1932 and coming to power in March 1933, Roosevelt and Frankfurter communicated constantly in a stream of telegrams. Shortly before December 1932, Roosevelt invited Frankfurter and his wife Marion to 'speak of current matters'. They went on talking until the early hours as Roosevelt displayed his concern to grasp vital information on the abilities of his future collaborators. The next day, Marion, who was present for part of the meeting, noted: 'After all, he is the President-elect! [...] he was taking down notes almost as though he were in a seminar of yours'.[9] Enjoying Roosevelt's fullest confidence, Frankfurter refused the President's offer of the prestigious and influential post of Advocate General, insisting that his relations with the Supreme Court would be vital; having consulted Louis Brandeis, Advocate Justice at the Supreme Court, he preferred to stay in Harvard from where he could exercise an essential influence on future servants of the State. Thus, Frankfurter remained outside the machinery of the New Deal, at a distance from the State but close to the President, a kind of *éminence grise*—in his own words, its 'recruiting officer'[10]; he could very clearly be seen as tutor to the new administration.[11] One Yale professor later offered a description of the relationship between the two men: in his eyes, Frankfurter was 'a Michaelangelo of friendship ... Franklin Roosevelt is Frankfurter's best known work'.[12] This astonishingly close relationship dated back to 1924 and Roosevelt's election as governor of New York, but it remained informal because Frankfurter never at any time held an official position. Frankfurter remained at a distance, almost in the shadows, a personality of often determining influence without serving within the politico-administrative apparatus. In January 1936, the magazine *Fortune* described him as the most influential man in the United States. If he was seen as a conspirator, it was because his activities allegedly

> [...] had that faint odour of the cabal which the salon always exudes [...] Mr Frankfurter has done little more to place intelligent lawyers in contemporary Washington than he has been doing for the past twenty five years.[13]

Thus an enduring legend was born. And yet while Frankfurter saw himself as Roosevelt's man body and soul, the reason for this, as he wrote in 1937, was to further his overriding ambition for the improvement of public service through permanent careers that would attract the nation's finest intellects.[14]

The relationship between Frankfurter and Roosevelt, and the advent of so many brilliant young lawyers into public institutions, coincided with the New Deal. The New Deal itself marked a new situation characterised by a change in relations between the business world and the public sector. In terms of government institutions, the United States was seen as a weak state, its political and administrative elites largely existing in close symbiosis with the business world. In this sense, the New Deal represented a 'process of building governmental institutions where none existed, of choosing among various prescriptions for an expanded American State'.[15] Thus, this period saw the growing establishment of 'discrete elements of strong statehood', as new structures of independent administration were created, marking out its own identity and autonomy. However, this birth of a regulatory state had to struggle in the face of a long tradition of domination by an upper class which came largely from the business world.[16] It was a crucial turning point for an American society that was unfavourably disposed to national centralisation, but it was also part of an exceptional period when recourse to state intervention was inevitable, one of the consequences of the 1929 crisis. From then on, the traditional links which brought public power and the Jews together could once more be renewed. Against the background of unprecedented crisis of mass unemployment, the loss of traditional points of reference and the general collapse of social norms, a strengthening of the state reassured America's Jews who looked to the state to provide effective protection against the prejudices and violent behaviour of disorientated social groups in search of scapegoats. In some respects paralleling the situation of the French Third Republic, whose fragile institutions were threatened on several occasions by elites within the old order able to mobilise nationalist movements and radical antisemites, the New Deal offered a vital opportunity for many young lawyers with a public conscience but considered to be outsiders due to their ethnicity. As Abe Fortas' biographer Laura Kalman notes, the New Deal demanded a strong executive branch of government which Fortas advocated as a New Dealer [...] the New Deal's emphasis on meritocracy meant fresh opportunities for Jewish and Irish Catholic lawyers. Their intelligence won them access to new positions of power [...] Government service during the New Deal enfranchised Fortas and other outsiders.[17]

Among the many brilliant Harvard-trained jurists who found their way to Washington were Jews, often on the recommendation of Felix Frankfurter and his mentor Louis Brandeis. Again paralleling developments under the Third Republic, under the patronage of Frankfurter and Brandeis, a number of these jurists rose into the higher echelons of the administration.

This development meant that these so-called state Jews operated in a culture where servants of the weak state traditionally had little power or prestige, but now worked alongside Republican staff to ensure the triumph of public interest through the actions of the state. It signalled a shift which worked to the detriment of certain elite figures hostile to such growth or who feared their loss of control of the state, and thus provoked anger among populist elements of the Right. Whereas the traditional elites relied on wealth and status for influence and power, neither applied in the case of 'state Jews', and certainly not to Frankfurter, who was closer to the French style of 'state Jew', with administrative competence, a vocation to serve the state and a sense of public service as his sole assets. His relations with Franklin Roosevelt, like those of Brandeis or the other Jewish lawyers who participated in or were close to the Roosevelt administration, were in no way dependent on class status or fortune. In no way, therefore, did they resemble the nineteenth-century 'Court Jews' as claimed by some historians.[18] While it is true that unlike 'state Jews' he did not hold high public office, this was hardly surprising in a weak state in which the higher administration was small and lacked prestige. To some extent, as Professor of Law at Harvard, Frankfurter more closely resembled the nineteenth-century state Counsellor.

Roosevelt also revered Brandeis, whom he referred to respectfully as Isaiah, with a moral stature so great that he could be seen as the New Deal's 'oracle',[19] the President's 'black angel'.[20] Roosevelt consulted his 'oracle' at great length during the development of his economic policy in April 1922, in a long conversation at the White House. Nominated to the Supreme Court by President Wilson in 1916, Judge Brandeis had been seen for many years as the archetype of the quintessential wise man. His legitimacy and moral stature were beyond question, and he was considered irreproachable: a man of justice, law and equity. Brandeis for his part saw Frankfurter, who was 26 years his junior, as a 'half Brother, half Son' figure,[21] and from 1905, their intimacy, their bond of trust and the personal relationships that they sustained together were incomparable, their correspondence of rare intensity, evidence of an outstanding closeness. The first judge to occupy the 'Jewish seat' in the Supreme Court, from 1916, Brandeis was at the height of his prestige, enjoying an unrivalled reputation, not least because after his years in Boston, he was not afraid of confronting local patronage by standing up to it unflinchingly on behalf of unions and workers. He drew steadily closer to the working-class world, for example, during the strikes of 1910–1911, protesting against the prevailing poverty among workers, campaigning for better wages, rights and shorter working hours, winning new rights which brought democratic practices into the business world and abolished managerial despotism.

In his famous publication, *The Curse of Bigness*, in defence of small businesses and market laws, Brandeis compared big business to feudalism and condemned 'the reign of plutocracy', regretting that 'the big companies often show themselves capable of dominating the State'. During Wilson's presidency, Brandeis acted as chief economic adviser and, as we saw above, was behind the origins of anti-trust measures. He led the campaign against 'the big men' based on an individualist and democratic vision of the world, with an ethic hostile to money that was more than a function of true economic analysis: for him, 'bigness' was the 'mark of Cain, the sign of sin'.[22] Throughout his life he had only a single concern, 'to keep business out of government'.[23] To this end, speaking at several conferences also attended by Frankfurter, Brandeis would enjoin young jurists to abandon their defence of the business world and instead take up the cause of public interest.

Brandeis' protégé and loyal friend, Frankfurter shared this strong hostility towards the conservative and frequently antisemitic Protestant establishment. He wholeheartedly adopted Brandeis' scorn for the 'financial oligarchy' and distrust of the bankers whom he confronted frequently. Brandeis had come to be seen in some quarters as acting 'in the shadow' of Roosevelt while Frankfurter was now seen as 'his prophet'.[24] Frankfurter, perhaps even harsher than Brandeis in his excoriation of the world of wealth, constantly urged Roosevelt to confront the business world, to reduce the powers of the privileged and use taxation to put an end to their opposition. During the summer of 1935, he wrote to Brandeis that 'Roosevelt [...] seems keenly aware of the intentions of Big Business and Finance and also when I told him, very frankly 'your views are irrepressible conflict', he said 'he's got his finger on the crux of the situation'. He then went on to tell me his political dilemma—to baby them along for the present and wait for a fight or fight now [...] I replied that you wouldn't have him declare war, but recognise that here *is* and act on that assumption.'[25]

Frankfurter, like Brandeis, rejected any corporatist strategy implying cooperation with the business world; it was acknowledged that, in Brandeis' words, the corporate world was 'able sometimes to dominate the State'.[26]

In his first measures, however, Roosevelt kept his distance from this attitude. Indeed, his first reforms were aimed at conciliation between the State and private economic interests: in the face of the Depression, the first aim was to associate the business world with the functioning of the State, a perspective which defined and justified itself in the absence of a breeding ground of high functionaries and the traditional weakness of the federal state bureaucracy. The attempt was symbolised by the National Industrial Recovery Act (NIRA), introduced by leaders from the business world in a framework which presented no threat of anti-trust laws to big business. Business leaders and the world of labour would be free to work together to establish a code of loyal conduct; once accepted by the executive power, this would take active effect and acquire the force of law.

Roosevelt's 'Brains Trust', from which Frankfurter and Brandeis were excluded, conceived a Premier New Deal which was forcefully rejected by those who sought confrontation with the business world. Brandeis and Frankfurter challenged these efforts at conciliation which brought in corporative leaders, and did not conceal their hostility towards the business world in the form of monopolies, the role of the banks and the influence of money. From that time, in the eyes of Rexford Tugwell, who led this Brains Trust together with Adolf A. Berle, Brandeis 'was declaring war' on the New Deal.[27]

The communion of thinking between Brandeis and Frankfurter was not, however, absolute. On the one hand, although Brandeis proved fierce in his opposition to big business, he also feared the birth of a strong state, which would be 'big' in its turn and would risk limiting democratic expression and the fullness of local life; he feared Leviathan in all its forms and found himself to be a confirmed adversary of 'Big Government'—even though its creation was the condition *sine qua non* for implementation of the Second New Deal, a more determined and interventionist economic policy based on solid public institutions. On the other hand, Frankfurter, equally attached to local democracy, did not fear the arrival of 'Big Government' on condition that it was based on the activity of competent senior officials who were loyal and united. This no doubt was why

Frankfurter rather than Brandeis became the most directly pivotal figure in the New Deal. In Oxford, he had discovered the existence of the British civil service and the role of high public servants who remained at their post whatever the political majority, the need for a public service operated by professionals, the technicians of public law on which the State could depend.[28] Frankfurter ignored the specificity of the French-style high administration with its institutionalised *Grand Corps*, but through the example of the British civil service, he expected to bring into the United States the concept of State institutions served by their own administrative staff within the framework of the New Deal. For him, it was a matter of privileging 'the growth of "public service" as a permanent career for the best minds of the nation'.[29] Having refused the important position of Advocate General, which defended the government in the Supreme Court, Frankfurter expected to operate actively from his Harvard base in supporting this exceptional process of state-building nationalisation. In his eyes, it reflected that 'there was a great expansion of governmental activity and the need for lawyers and there was nothing more natural that they should turn to the institution that turned out the best lawyers'.[30]

Similarly, Frankfurter introduced Roosevelt to the interventionist thinking of John Maynard Keynes, whom he had met at Oxford, and sent the President a long analysis of the British economy which criticised the initial measures of his administration and, in particular, the NIRA, the monetary policy and the abandonment of the gold standard. In return, Roosevelt wrote to Frankfurter, 'You can tell the professor [Keynes] that in regard to public work we shall spend in the next fiscal years nearly twice the amount we are spending in this fiscal year, but there is a practical limit to what the Government can do.'[31] Meanwhile, Frankfurter addressed one memorandum after another to Roosevelt and drew up a platform plan for the Democrat Party for the 1936 election. This would be carefully annotated by the President in which he stressed that

> Modern government involves not merely the enactment of wise and honest laws but effective, skilled and unbiased administration. To perfect such administration the Democratic Party pledges itself to the progressive improvement and extension of the permanent civil service compatible with the maintenance of free government.[32]

Frankfurter was to show himself consistently as a firm partisan of the strengthening of the Federal State particularly because, as he wrote in

1944, 'court justice belongs to the State'.[33] From this point of view, his stance brought him close to Benjamin Cardozo, who, in 1934, in the *Blaisdell* decision, did not hesitate to propose that contractual relations kept between individuals 'were not to paralyze the state in its endeavour in times of direful crisis to keep its life-blood flowing'; Cardozo unreservedly took into consideration 'the rights and interests of the State in itself' to the extent that faced with the 'selfishness of individuals or classes' the state acted on the economic superstructure 'on which the good of all depends'.[34] American Jews working in the State administration thus showed their partisan support for this form of state regulation.

Frankfurter advised the President to encourage public works in the sectors of roads and ports, and to act with 'determination' through government action. Inspiration came from the particularly convincing example of the Tennessee Valley Authority (TVA). Under the leadership of David Lilienthal—the representative whose nomination was favoured by Frankfurter himself as a convinced 'Brandeisian', the TVA showed impressive results in agriculture; indeed it would later be seen as the most significant example of successful state interventionism alien to American tradition.[35] In this sense, the New Deal enabled 'the reconstruction of the American State' particularly because the administrative process demonstrated great convergence with the philosophy of the New Deal.[36] Certainly, the consolidation of federal bureaucracy desired by Roosevelt clashed with resistance in Congress where parties covering every form of conservatism were fearful of centralisation that appeared to run contrary to the nature of the American state.[37]

This fundamental shift of approach by the New Deal was however accompanied by measures which stressed the State's new grasp, for example, in the law on Social Security, the Wagner Act which modified labour relations in favour of the working world, the Banking Act which installed a strong State control over banking activity, the plan which established strong measures of taxation, or the Emergency Relief Appropriation Act which gave birth to vast public works financed by the State and which benefited even artists and writers. This time, the 'war' with the business world, so strongly desired by Frankfurter and his mentor Brandeis, was declared. But its success depended largely on the role of the Supreme Court, which, dominated by a conservative majority, handed down a majority rejection of all the measures of the New Deal. Roosevelt could depend on the liberal minority composed of Brandeis, Cardozo and Stone, but they were a minority. Following 'Black Monday', when the Court unanimously rejected a whole raft of measures that he saw as indispensable, the president's anger knew no limits. To break the Court's resistance, and without referring the matter to Frankfurter, Roosevelt decided to augment the Supreme Court by six members who would outweigh its conservative majority. But before proposing the project officially, Roosevelt showed it discreetly to Brandeis, who was shocked and told him that he was making a serious mistake. This incident was to tarnish relations between Brandeis and Frankfurter. The latter, although hostile to the presidential project and held in ignorance of its preparation, nonetheless rallied loyally to Roosevelt's strategy. To the great dismay of his friends and at the cost of suffering Brandeis' anger, Frankfurter undertook to help the President in bringing his quasi-revolutionary project to fruition. The conflict grew steadily, the Court resisted with all its powers, various pressures increased, the Chambers were constrained: finally, the dust settled and matters were calmed as if miraculously when the Court approved several measures proposed by the President and even managed to declare itself in favour of the National Labour Relations Act.[38] Roosevelt was more willing to abandon his plans for retaliation when very opportunely two Conservative judges of the Court, Willis Van Devanter and George Sutherland, retired in May 1937 and January 1938. This gave Roosevelt the opportunity to nominate individuals who favoured his ideas. In his turn, after the death of Cardozo, Frankfurter finally relented, and despite vigorous antisemitic attacks, joined the Supreme Court on 4 January 1939.

Frankfurter occupied a central place during these years of the New Deal. The three 'State Jews' sat together, briefly, or, as in the case of Cardozo and Frankfurter, succeeded each other in the Supreme Court during this dramatic period. Even more than Cardozo, who was very favourable to federalism and the autonomous action of administrations,[39] Frankfurter was the most strongly sympathetic to the policy set in train by Roosevelt. He became its *eminence grise*, the man for all work, the adviser, the supplier of young talents determined to throw all their strength into the fray. He selected many brilliant lawyers, generally in agreement with Brandeis, and according to the task under consideration. Even though he failed in some of his proposals—Dean Acheson did not, as he wished, get the Department of Justice—the cohort that he managed to place in key positions of the administration is impressive. With the approval of Brandeis, he favoured the nomination of Frances Perkins as Secretary of Labour, a crucial position in this period and one of the first women to reach the Cabinet. When she sought Frankfurter's help in choosing in turn an

Advocate General for the Department of Labour, together with Brandeis, he proposed Charles Wyzanski and counted on Thomas Corcoran, one of his loyal followers, to obtain his nomination by the Senate.

Brandeis and Frankfurter had very little influence on the Treasury Department under the leadership of Henry Morgenthau (whose nomination by Roosevelt as Secretary of State was regretted by both), an important individual who, according to a letter from Frankfurter to Brandeis, was determined above all not to see his name associated with 'liberal Jews' like themselves.[40] Other key figures in the administration were hostile to them, not least the members of the Brains Trust who feared the spread of their ideas—but their influence nonetheless often prevailed. While they were entirely isolated from the Department of State, which was fiercely hostile to Zionism, on several occasions, they nonetheless served as philosophical mentors in the eyes of the President to whom they had direct access and who consulted them frequently. Above all, they were successful in placing several of their loyal followers in various administrations. The best known were undoubtedly Thomas Corcoran and Jonathan Cohen; others were David Lilienthal, Jerome Frank, Dean Acheson, James Landis, Alger Hiss, James McCurdy, Nathan Margold, James Nicely, among others. Frankfurter considered that he simply made practical demands the more legitimate because they matched his own competence in his role at Harvard, the nursery of judicial elites whom he trained in person over many years and to whom he was very close. Over many years, for example, he advised several judges in the Supreme Court in their choice of colleagues. This did not, he thought, have any ideological significance—even if the press, in its need for drama and the wish to 'personalise', thought it could waste its time on discussing a 'great plot', the existence of a 'some cunning, conspiratorial, sinister, extremely exotic explanation' which simply showed 'what the psychologists call "projections"'.[41] Frankfurter employed few magisterial words to address such accusations, which increasingly spread and which in a period of socio-economic turmoil served to mobilise the radical masses in search of a scapegoat. Again, as he wrote to one of his friends,

> Through circumstances in the making of which I have had no share, I have become a myth, a symbol and promoter not of reason but of passion; I am the symbol of the Jew, the 'red', the 'alien'. I would be heard and interpreted [...] not as the man who by virtue of his long years of service in the government and his special attention to scholarship of constitutional law

and the work of the [Supreme] Court spoke with the authority of scholarship but as the Jew, the 'red' and the 'alien'.[42]

Frankfurter had favoured the career of Jews as of non-Jews based on aptitude alone, the confidence that he and Brandeis had in them for the effective fulfilment of those tasks essential to the New Deal. No matter, in the imagination of extremist thinkers and leaders—and also in the eyes of the 'common man' or in the popular press—he was the mastermind of a vast plot constructed by the Jews to take over the State. Even learned publications attributed to him and to Brandeis a fundamental degree of shadowy power. Their influence is undoubted, but was nonetheless 'exaggerated'.[43] But the myths persisted and their pernicious effects could be felt. A sort of obsession developed at the very heart of the administration, shared by the Jewish lawyers who feared being seen as too numerous. Independently, they rejected any new candidature from Jewish jurists. Nathan Margold, now (thanks to Frankfurter) Advocate General for the Interior, admitted that he was disturbed by matters of race and religion and explicitly rejected the candidature of Jewish protégés sponsored by Frankfurter.[44] The same applied to Jerome Franck, in the Agricultural Adjustment Administration and another of Frankfurter's protégés, who feared the presence of Jewish colleagues and openly admitted this to Frankfurter. He took care to limit their presence; on facing the arrival of one new outstanding lawyer, he barked out his displeasure. In this sense, we may consider that Franck, as an assimilated German Jew, did his best to avoid the burden of the 'Jewish lawyer' stereotype.[45] Adlai Stevenson, who was connected to Franck through family, did not disguise his WASP ('white Anglo-Saxon Protestants') antisemitism when he wrote of Franck that he fortunately showed none of the racial features of some other Jewish lawyers.[46]

As in the French Third Republic, the presence of a number of senior functionaries in the political-administrative staff of the state who were of Jewish background unleashed a violent antisemitic campaign; no matter that they constituted a minority. The State came increasingly to be seen as an overarching instrument through which the Jews managed to establish their own power, thus threatening the Christian values of society. The myth of the 'Jewish Republic', popularised in France in the second half of the nineteenth century by the likes of Edouard Drumont, and which accompanied the emergence of a strong state and the secularisation of society, was transplanted to the heart of an American society but one with a weak state which was nevertheless undergoing a certain growth in administrative power.[47] But Drumont's form of antisemitism appeared incongruous, dysfunctional and incomprehensible to a society with a weak state. Thus, antisemitism initially remained social, cultural or corresponding to economic prejudice; in particular, the fear of the Other triggered by the immigrants who arrived *en masse* in the second half of the nineteenth century. Thus, in a state lacking strong central institutions, political antisemitism remained absent. Yet Drumont's antisemitic *La France juive* (1884) found some admirers across the Atlantic. Telemachus Thomas Timayenis, for example, launched a series of violently antisemitic publications. In 1888, he published *The Original Mr Jacobs*, a full-scale synthesis of Drumont's ideas. Ignoring the French writer's attacks on American society and Protestants, which he considered 'puerile', Timayenis adopted the dichotomy between the valorous and rational Aryan and the sombre, pessimistic and oriental Jew, lacking creativity, conspiratorial, exploiting the poor, spreading disease and even committing ritual murder. He raised anxieties over an 'invasion' of the Jews who, after Germany, France and England, were travelling *en masse* to the United States. Here, they were manoeuvring to take over New York, where one 'will find Jewish names plenty as the locusts of Egypt'[48] and expressed the personal wish that Jews should be forbidden to live in Manhattan.[49] On the other hand, Timayenis passed over in silence the supposed conquest of the French state described by Drumont which was unlikely to find an echo in American society. But he ended with a warning: did the reader want what the Jews had accomplished in France to be repeated in the United States? In *The American Jew*, also published in 1888, Timayenis described the physical features of American Jews, denounced their power in Wall Street, their attitude in hotels, their criminal activities and their role in politics, even taking took care to provide convincing examples—having to content himself with assertions, without naming anyone who had been elected in the various State legislatures. Timayenis launched a dark warning:

> The Jew is an enemy of our country, of our laws, of our habits, of our institutions—in a word, of everything founded upon Christian doctrines and principles […] let one take pains to study the Talmud, that book of Jewish blasphemy and vituperation […] let him look into their past and he will, far from casting his vote to elect a Jew, even to the humblest public position, join the movement to have special laws passed prohibiting any candidate known to have a drop of Jewish blood in his veins from filling any public office.[50]

And in a further small publication, *Iscariot: An Old Type in a New Form*, he repeated the undesirability of Jews as citizens since they had no business with the American nation or laws.[51]

The tide of political antisemitism which was to emerge during the years of the New Deal built on this earlier wave from the last decades of the nineteenth century that also continued into the early twentieth century, as we shall see below. In the United States, a fundamentalist blend of messianism and patriotism, defence of the Bible, rejection of rationalism, reason and modernity, as represented by 'the city', revealed the unchallenged triumph of Protestant evangelism. The fundamentalist awakening which swept through the country during the later nineteenth century expressed the belief that was present in virtually all the virtues of a Christian (that is, Protestant) society. Yet antisemitism was in no way consistent with the Protestant fundamentalism which claimed the authority of biblical Israel.[52] This would not be understood until the coming of the New Deal when Drumont's and Timayenis' ideas were reinvigorated by the antisemitism from the pens of certain populist thinkers such as William Riley and, above all, Gerald Winrod. These figures based their violent anti-communist and pro-Nazi diatribes on a millenarianist interpretation of the notorious forgery, *The Protocols of the Elders of Zion*.

The *Protocols* had been already widely distributed by Henry Ford in 1920, establishing the climate in which these theories could re-emerge more strongly 15 years later. Ford also alleged there was a Jewish power hidden behind Presidents Taft and Wilson. His main target was Bernard Baruch, the chairman of the War Industries Board, who Ford claimed was a man of such influence that he could nominate his Jewish friends to various levels of power, for the greater benefit of the international Jewish plotters. According to Ford, 'Politically, while the rest of the country is entertained with the fiction that Tammany Hall rules the politics of New York, the fact is rarely published that Jews rule Tammany'.[53] According to him, just as in France, a Jew was at the head of government in the United States. 'In our country', he claimed, 'we have just had a four-year term of Jewish rule, almost as absolute as that which exists *in Russia*' under the rule of Bernard Baruch, the 'Disraeli of the United States', whose hold over President Wilson was absolute.[54] He alleged that the Christian character of American society would find itself endangered: the style of government clearly formed '*an attack on Christianity*' undertaken in the name of secularisation. Ford believed that 'the Jew [was] determined to wipe out of public life every sign of the predominant Christian Democrat of the United States'.[55] Thanks to his weekly publication, the *Dearborn Independent*, which returned repeatedly to the themes of the *Protocols*, Ford reached a very large audience; around 1925, his paper was achieving sales of 700,000 copies, hammering out the same message: 'There is a super-government which is allied to no government [...] and yet which has a hand in them all'.[56]

A signature campaign brought together leading Christian personalities, including President Wilson (Taft, like Harding, refused to sign, as did the presidents of Harvard and Yale), who protested against what they saw as 'a form of hatred that was incompatible with the concept of a loyal and intelligent American citizenship'; they called for unity and the destruction of an 'anti-Christian and anti-American agitation'. During the presidential election of 1924, the jurist Louis Marshall insisted that this campaign which risked leading, potentially, to Jewish extermination, must be brought to an end.[57] Finally, in 1927, faced with the resolute opposition of Marshall at the head of the American Jewish Committee, Ford suddenly apologised in the context of a libel suit brought by Aaron Sapiro and contacted Louis Marshall to put an end to the business; he claimed to regret his propaganda and stopped it.[58] Despite its wide diffusion and its extreme aggression, the antisemitic press campaign led by Ford thus ended in setback in the USA.[59]

In their classic study *The Politics of Unreason*, Seymour Lipset and Earl Raab depicted the 1930s as the decade of considerable change in Protestant fundamentalism. Transformed into Christian fundamentalism with a strong nationalist dimension, the 'nativism' which underpinned this took as its target not so much specific ethnic groups (e.g. the Irish, Italians, or blacks, or even the Jews), but their transformation into abstract threats which could be generalised and thus could all the more arouse a radical mobilisation. The 'Jew' as an abstract figure perfectly fulfilled this function, provoking an unprecedented reaction that matched the scale of power allotted to this mysterious figure.

The New Deal opened the door to new fears and fantasies already familiar in European societies with a strong state and where fascism was already on the rise. Thus the 1930s extended and amplified Ford's conspiratorial rhetoric and therefore as Lipset and Raab point out, 'marks the full entry of anti-Semitism in the political discourse of extremist American'.[60] The explosion of this political antisemitism in North America was unprecedented in its scale, and it shocked its main target, Felix Frankfurter, who had been identified by its exponents as the secret and designated tool for all Jewish plots. Responding to these attacks, Frankfurter wrote to Roosevelt, 'We live moments of madness, hatred and lies that are spreading every day, we have therefore more than ever to maintain our serenity, our sense of humor, our wisdom and our patience'.[61]

As under the Third Republic in France, Jews rallied to state power: during the American Civil War, they preferred the Republican camp and venerated Lincoln; later they equally supported the Republican Theodore Roosevelt, who in 1906 was the first president in American history to nominate a Jew, Oscar Straus, to the Cabinet as Secretary for Trade and Labor. In 1932, they switched overwhelmingly to the Democratic camp in favour of the 'protection of the State'.[62] At the time of the President's inauguration, Rabbi William Rosenblum addressed the faithful in his sermon in New York City Temple Israel: 'No President, not excepting Washington, Lincoln and Wilson, has assumed the office with so universal and genuine hope to be a Messiah [...] the Messiah of America's tomorrow'. In the same vein, at the annual conference of the United Synagogue of America which brought together all the branches of American Judaism, Henry Braude declared that the Jews should 'sustain with patriotic devotion the Administration's plan for a better social order', and a little later, Samuel Untermeyer addressed the Jewish Communitarian Centre of Yonkers, stressing that all men of faith were praying for the success of the NIRA.[63]

We can see here an echo of the enthusiasm of French Jews for the Third Republic which broke the grip on power of the old Catholic elites; the Episcopalian Franklin Roosevelt attacked the traditional domination of the superior class of WASPs. Thus in his first Cabinet, he nominated two Catholics, with other Irish or Italian Catholics, traditionally despised by the Protestant elites, who occupied places in different tribunals. If African Americans were kept out of the administration to avoid upsetting the Democrats of the south, black employees were taken on by various authorities in far greater numbers than previously. As we have noted, the impulse to include Jews in the administration often came from of Felix Frankfurter, but he was not the sole source. Roosevelt nominated his own *chef de cabinet*, in the shape of one of Frankfurter's enemies, namely Henry Morgenthau, Jr., who thus became the second Jew to join the Cabinet (the precedent being Oscar Straus). Morgenthau, whose father had been Ambassador to Turkey, became a key figure in the establishment of the New Deal after his appointment to the crucial post of Secretary to the Treasury in January 1934, thus coinciding with the beginnings of the welfare state. He was to remain *en poste* throughout the entire Roosevelt administration, dealing with tax, unemployment support and monetary reform policies before devising a plan for the dismembering of conquered Germany.[64] Others became ambassadors, such as Jessie Straus in France, and Laurence Steinhardt in Russia; Jerome Franck played an essential role as head of the Agricultural Adjustment Administration and then as head of the Securities and Exchange Commission; meanwhile, David Lilienthal was directing the TVA and yet others were nominated as federal judges. However, the scale of appointments should not be exaggerated: only a single Jew joined the Cabinet, none of them became Under-Secretary, the State Department like the Department of Trade remained closed to them and none of them reached the highest levels of the army. In all, fewer than 30 Jews can be counted at the heart of the highest executive staff.

The appointment of Henry Morgenthau Jr. to the Treasury was a matter of pride in the Jewish world. The *Jewish Morning Journal* guessed at Hitler's rage 'that a Jew is placed at the head of the most important ministry at such a time as this', while there were many who saw this measure as 'a tribute to the Jewish people'. But there was also caution. As in France when Léon Blum was appointed President of the Council at a time when many Jews feared the consequences of a Jew in a position of political power, fears were expressed in the United States that 'any misstep of his [viz Morgenthau] will be used by all professional anti-Semites in their Jew-baiting propaganda'.[65] In these same years of crisis and political tension and of growing State intervention, on either side of the Atlantic the American New Deal and the French *Front Populaire* offered access for some Jews to politico-administrative power. In return, they aroused fears of a counter-*coup* in the form of an aggressive and unprecedented wave of antisemitism. Although at the end of the nineteenth century Drumont's detestable proposals largely fell on deaf ears in American society, this was no longer the case in the 1930s.

The situation did not, however, become serious until 1933, with the opening onslaught of events which reached their paroxysm in 1940. Franklin Thompson's book *America's Ju-Deal*, published in 1935, may be taken as an example.

The New Deal when shorn of its disguise reveals us nothing short of a Ju-Deal [...] the Jewish minority has overthrown the Christian influence which has since the founding of our country guided and imbued the spirit of our institutions in their true administration [...] we object to the Jewish minority of the country on the grounds that they are inassimilable, opposed to the existing form of government and antagonistic to the interests of the people as a whole [...] the people of this nation believe that the United States of American is the land of Americans and so it shall remain.[66]

The accusation then became more precise:

> The present Administration in Washington is predominantly Jewish [...] Justices Benjamin Cardozo and Louis Brandeis, the Jewish members of the Court, have played a significant part in the Ju-Deal [...] the appointment of Felix Frankfurter to the Supreme Court would seal the doom of democracy in America. Frankfurter has been instrumental in Judaizing the Administration [...] with Bernard Baruch, they rule America.[67]

Through the law, which they allegedly dominated, the Jews were able to control the political parties and consequently the administration. Coming from the East, retaining their Mongol features, and being part of a Jewish 'international alliance of bankers', Thompson claimed

> That their race is planning the next holocaust for the purpose of subjecting the Gentile governments of the world to their dominance [...] that by refusing to be assimilated they have created a State of their own within the United States [...] that the oath of the land, a Christian institution is not tenable in the eyes of the Jewish people.[68]

Thompson was full of admiration for the measures undertaken by Hitler in Nazi Germany to break 'Jewish domination', and he espoused a Jewish state for the Jews of the world, returning thus to Drumont's infamous war cry, 'France for the French', but attuned to an American register.

Franklin Thompson's nasty pamphlet illustrates the explosion of political antisemitism, French style, plunging into an ancient Christian tradition of which he follows the full two-pronged logic in order to clamour for the expulsion of the Jews from the State and from society itself. His followers were legion. William Pelley, for example, spoke out passionately; in his pamphlet *Toward Armageddon* published by the Militant Christians Association of Charleston, Howland Spencer wrote in apocalyptic terms about Frankfurter as 'the Iago of this Government'. Colonel Eugene Nelson Sanctuary went further and supported the view that Roosevelt's accession to power was the first stage in the establishment of a worldwide Jewish state, while Robert Edmondson denounced this present Jewish

Administration, these international Frankfurters [...] who in the past four years have turned the Christian United States into a vast synagogue [...] the cabal of Morgenthau, Lehman, Frankfurter and Cohen which surrounds the wheel chair.[69]

Edmondson specialised in this kind of accusation, writing innumerable pamphlets *Invisible Government Brandeis* and similarly *Felix Frankfurter Unfit* among them. During a case brought against him, his partisans defended him through anonymous letters which alleged that Léon Blum in France was in the hands of Jews and Negroes.[70] These views were shared by the members of more than a hundred antisemitic groups and movements which were founded from 1933, from the Silver Shirts to the White, Blue and Khaki Shirts of Order 76, the American White Guard, the Christian Defenders, the German Nazi Party which became the German-American Bund, and so forth, reflecting, in the words of the magazine *Fortune*, '*Jew-baiting hysteria*'.[71] This massive propaganda proved effective: in 1938, according to a survey, 41 per cent of Americans saw the Jews in the United States as having too much power, with 31 per cent of them considering them to be less patriotic than other citizens.[72] Hence, this conclusion of a long report drawn up by Donald Strong, in 1941, for the American Council on Public Affairs:

> The greater the number of Jews in political positions, the more convincing will the antisemitic propaganda appear—the more probably will Jews be used as scapegoats for whatever difficulties the country encounters.[73]

From then on, in various social *milieux* of Anglo-Saxon origin, the great majority of those joining the many antisemitic groups were Protestant, with the exception of the militant Catholics of Father Coughlin. Around 120 radical antisemitic organisations were set up; some of them tried on several occasions to unite their efforts in order to constitute a powerful movement. During the summer of 1934, 11 antisemite leaders met in Chicago to plan such collaboration; in August 1936, in Northern Carolina, then in August 1937, in Kansas City, further attempts took place. These antisemitic personalities persisted in their efforts at coordination. Indeed, a collaboration was set up between the movements led by William Dudley Pelley (more of whom below), head of the Grey Shirts; Art Smith, leader of the Khaki Shirts of America; Fritz Gissibl, leader of the Bund modelled on its big German brother, Robert Edmondson; Gerald Winrod, head of the group Defenders of the Christian Faith; James True and Colonel

E. M. Hadley, at the head of The Paul Revere movement. They combined their efforts to publish at the lowest cost, took part in shared meetings and helped each other financially.[74]

These various movements gathered thousands of militants and together were capable of attracting crowds of nearly a million people at public meetings. But they could not compete with the antisemitic leagues which in the 1890s and again in the 1930s attracted a much greater number of disciplined and combative militants to their vast and crowded meetings. Matters were not hindered by the fact that the sermons of Father Coughlin, expressing unfettered antisemitism were heard by several million people, with two-thirds of his hearers explicitly approving his words.[75] Similarly, Coughlin's weekly publication *Social Justice*, in which he promoted the bogus *Protocols of the Elders of Zion*, was bought by up to a million readers, which made it the most widely read antisemitic journal in the United States. Nevertheless, at its peak in April 1938, 32 per cent of people questioned in a Gallup survey disapproved of Coughlin's ideas and 41 per cent expressed no opinion, while 27 per cent approved his ideas; the survey showed a positive correlation between confession and hostility towards Jews: Catholics and Lutherans among the most approving of Coughlin's ideas and Episcopalians the most hostile. Father Coughlin found support above all among the middle classes who were receptive to his hostility to cosmopolitan bankers and the elites of Washington. In a blend of 'nativism' and plot theories, the abstract Jew figure was designated as the enemy; it was no longer a case of disliking one minority or another but of constructing an abstract explanation of the threat hanging over the population.[76]

Coughlin was not alone. The journal *Defender*, the review of the Defenders of the Christian Faith led by Gerald Winrod whose programme consisted of 'To keep Christian America Christian', with his pro-Hitler tirades was equally well received by a hundred thousand readers. Admittedly, this was far behind the print runs of the popular or militant press in France with its violently antisemitic content which on several occasions achieved daily sales of several million papers. Less powerful than their French equivalents, these American movements were nonetheless remarkable—particularly because they modelled themselves on the 'big brother' figure of Hitler who had managed to create an abstract Jewish enemy and were more redoubtable in constantly and openly seeking his support. 'All of this coincided with the rise of influence wielded by Brandeis and Frankfurter'.[77]

In 1935, through the creation of the Christian Party, the pastor's son William Dudley Pelley sought to rally the nation behind him in order to prevent Roosevelt's re-election in 1936. Pelley failed miserably, but his stinging defeat did not halt the spread of his ideas. Two years before, in January 1933, at the precise moment of the birth of the New Deal, Pelley had created his Legion of the Grey Shirts of America, a centralised and disciplined organisation based on the German model. Its 15,000 members (to which were added 75,000 supporters who were not registered members) had to swear allegiance both to the 'Christian ideal' and to 'pride in the race' in order to promote the introduction of a theocracy in the form of a 'Christian democracy' which would abolish the 'Ju-Deal', thus eliminating a state which was alien to the culture of the American nation.[78] The new Christianity presupposed the rejection of atheist Jews, their expulsion from the now reclaimed Christian state, their concentration in a single city in each federal state directed by a Secretary for the Jews guaranteeing their security in a new form of ghetto which excluded them from the Christian public arena. In Pelley's eyes, the Jews did not deserve American citizenship because as inveterate Orientals they perverted its quality and threatened the very life of Americans. From that moment, commitment was required to engage in another even more radical path. Speaking as a fervent admirer of Hitler, 'the man of destiny', Pelley hoped to imitate Hitler's example in order to save America. He wrote that if any of 'The Sons of Jacob' attempted to seize the government, the consequence would be a 'violent tempest'.[79]

Pelley was not the only antisemitic leader to propose such drastic solutions. In New York, for example, the head of the local Bund exhorted:

> American Christian! Your country is sick! Its wholesome bloodstream has been polluted by a people diseased [...] Jewry is working for the emasculation and vassalage of the United States [...] this entire scheme is one leading up to the wholesale inoculation of gentiles with syphilitic germ vaccine.
>
> Now, if ever, the Sons of Jacob must take a last desperate gamble and find out if they can actually seize the government of the country before the vigilante storm breaks and a major part of the 7,000,000 Yiddishers who have managed to get into this country over the past ten years are slated for deportation or worse.
>
> The Jews are grabbing control of everything in this country. This is exactly what took place in Germany [...] we must be prepared to fight for the right kind of government. We must win the masses, the good people to

our side. There will likely be bloodshed and fighting. We shall have to do our part.[80]

Nor did Art Smith show any hesitation when it came to inciting violence against Jews. Following the example of the Italian Fascists March on Rome, his Khaki Shirts also aimed to eject the 'illegitimate' occupants on Capitol Hill. His proposition was simple: 'Kill all the Jews in the United States'.[81] Similarly, in 1936, James True, another antisemitic leader, warned that 'hundreds of Jews have reached the Administration' and were expecting great profits from it and their 'long planned crucifixion' of the nation.[82] According to True, 'more than [...] religion', the person responsible for this was 'Professor Karl Marx, Professor Frankfurter and his kikes'. For True as for Smith or for Pelley, or Fritz Gissibl, the leader of the Bund, the solution was self-evident. Brandishing a revolver, True announced, 'For a first-class massacre more than a truncheon is needed [...] we are not going to drive the Jews out of the country, we are going to bury them right here.' Finally, there is the declaration from Olov Tietzow, who led the American Guard, that 'our country will witness an uprising of unprecedented proportions and at the end of the civil war that probably would ensue there would hardly be one Jew or New Dealer left alive in the United States'.

Less virulent, Father Coughlin still called for nothing less than the removal of Roosevelt, who personified 'the anti-Christ' and the immediate end of the New Deal. Addressing more than 20,000 people in Madison Square Garden in New York, he raised the crowd's enthusiasm to fever pitch when he sarcastically pronounced the name of Frankfurter.[83] In September 1941, in his journal, *Social Justice*, he commented that '[t]he Jew should retire from the field of politics and government. He has no more business in that sphere than has a pig in a china shop'.[84] The impact of Father Coughlin deserves further study.[85] As we have shown, he enthralled several million people with his sermons and poured out a torrent of antisemitic literature. Before 1938, he generally held back from open antisemitism and even declared himself in favour of Roosevelt's New Deal.[86] Probably influenced by Father Denis Fahey among others,[87] his radical turn was all the more spectacular when in November 1938 he denounced it as foreign to the American people, whose America 'is the America of Christ'.[88]

In his sermons, Coughlin picked up almost word for word but without direct quotation, anti-Jewish statements made by Hitler's propaganda minister Joseph Goebbels at the National Congress of the Nazi Party in September 1935.[89] The objective of Coughlin's virulence went beyond the Jews to target the American political system. Thus, when many of these antisemitic leaders explicitly claimed Hitler's authority, they formed the Trojan horse that threatened American democracy from within. Starting in 1934, Roosevelt wanted the Federal Bureau of Investigation (FBI) to undertake an enquiry into these subversive movements which were accused of acting in the name of a Nazi conspiracy. It was an immense case that was still continuing in January 1944 in the Supreme Court, where Edmondson, Pelley, True and Winrod appeared as well as other radical antisemitic leaders. The Court found their guilt unproven. In a later trial, however, some of them, including Pelley, were convicted and sent to prison.[90]

Father Coughlin, like other antisemitic leaders, denounced Roosevelt as a crypto-Jew. Pelley had been one of the first to accuse Roosevelt of being of distant Jewish descent, originally called Rosenvelt, claiming he was 'the first Jewish president'.[91] The 'kosher President', as he called Roosevelt, was denaturing the American State.[92] Similarly, Reverend Gerald Winrod, head of the Defenders of the Christian Faith, was also among the first to strike such a chord in order to aim a blow at Roosevelt as 'not one of us'. On 15 October 1936, he published a strange and apparently scientific family tree in his widely read journal *The Revealer*. It purported to show that Franklin Roosevelt came from a long line of Netherlands Jews called Rosenvelt through his father, while on his mother's side, Sarah Delano was the descendant of Spanish or Italian Jews who had immigrated to northern Brazil. Like the French antisemites in the Drumont mould, this document cited the *Schulcran Aruch* in which Jewish law defined genealogical heredity through the mother's line.[93] The claim spread, as evidenced by the fact that in March 1935, it was already being questioned by the *Jewish Chronicle*. Roosevelt replied in a candid manner which revealed his own profound indifference to this kind of process: 'In the distant past they [Roosevelt's ancestors] may have been Jews. All I know about the origins of the Roosevelt family is that they are apparently descended from Claes Martenssen van Roosevelt'. The rumour sprouted wings unintentionally when his response was taken up by *The New York Times* as well as by many national newspapers. Further, and provocatively, during a meeting at the White House in which the Secretary of State showed him a declaration by Joseph Kennedy (the American ambassador in London who asserted that American politics was being led by Jews), Roosevelt was not disconcerted and merely retorted: 'It is true'.[94] Thus the claim acquired the force of truth, reviving other strands of antisemitism. Robert Edmondson, for example, took time to disseminate a vast body of antisemitic material which persistently repeated the same theme; he invented a medal which was supposedly awarded to Roosevelt in March 1936; on one side it read: 'Good luck and wisdom to F. Roosevelt, our modern Moses, leading the Jewish people in the Promised Land', while the flip side bore a Star of David.

Two years before in March 1933, Louis McFadden, who was close to Father Coughlin, stood up in the House of Representatives to attack the alleged Jewish power symbolised by Roosevelt's administration in a manner anticipating Xavier Vallat's speech to the city council in Paris in 1936 against Léon Blum.[95] McFadden's tirade was met with protest, with one Representative accusing him of infecting the House with Hitlerism, while another suggested that he should consult a 'Jewish psychologist'. These protests did not deter McFadden, for a few months later, in the manner of the *Protocols of the Elders of Zion*, he continued his crusade against the 'Administration controlled by the Jews'—with Frankfurter, Baruch and Morgenthau in his sights.[96]

In France as in the United States, such violent political antisemitic outbursts were always in the name of the defence of a Christianity which, through the advent of leaders who were Jewish or considered as such, would find itself stripped of its control over political power. Henry Ford, who saw himself as a defender of Christianity against the Jews, gave financial support to Father Coughlin, who like Charles Lindbergh, became a hero in Hitler's Germany.[97] In March 1942, three months after Nazi Germany had declared war against the United States, Coughlin declared himself a faithful reader of *Der Sturmer* and spoke out against 'this war willed by the Jewish race'.[98] Lindbergh posed the question more pointedly: instead of acting in support of the war, he proposed that American Jews would do better to oppose it because they would be the first to suffer its consequences. The greatest danger to the country, he claimed, came not from Nazi Germany but from Jewish influence over the press, radio and government.[99] The myth of the 'Jewish war' stirred up by Jews in favour of other Jews put American Jews in an uncomfortable position; some had no hesitation in speaking out openly against Hitler, accepting the risk of being portrayed as warmongers motivated by interest, while others preferred to maintain a low profile for fear of intensifying antisemitic propaganda.

Conclusion

In spite of the smears against him as a 'Jew in disguise' and the campaign against his closest advisers, Roosevelt was re-elected in 1936. We should therefore view the surge of political antisemitism, even in the later 1930s, with caution; it remained far behind that of France and Germany. Indeed, the 1936 election proved that political antisemitism was still a weak force in the United States. The same applies to 1940: despite all the diatribes from antisemitic leaders, their influence was slight and their forces remained meagre, while their propaganda was unable to mobilise the electorate in their favour. As such, they never posed the same threat to the state as their counterparts in France had to the Third Republic or Hitler's supporters to the Weimar Republic. Far from the theatre of war, and thus sheltered from the German invader, the New Deal state was spared the 'divine surprise' celebrated by the French antisemite and co-founder of the Action Française Charles Maurras, who in 1940, after the fall of France, celebrated the fulfilment of Drumont's sinister prediction: the long-awaited end of the 'Jewish Republic'. The 'state Jews' of the New Deal were thus spared the deadly antisemitism of Hitler and his acolytes in Europe.

Notes

1. Pierre Birnbaum. *The antisemitic moment. A Tour of France in 1898* (Chicago, 2011). Originally published as: *Le moment antisémite. Un tour de la france en 1898* (Paris, Fayard, 1998).
2. Shulamit Volkov. *Walter Rathenau* (New Haven, CT, 2014). On political antisemitism, see Peter Pulzer, *The Rise of Political Anti-Semitism in Germany and Austria* (New York, 1964); and on Jews in state-building, idem, 'Jews and Nation-Building in Germany 1815–1918', in: *Year Book of the Leo Baeck Institute*, 41 (1996), pp. 199–124.
3. Jeffry Herff. *The Jewish enemy* (Cambridge, Mass., 2008).
4. Ernst Fraenkel, *The Dual State* (New York, 1969). Originally published in 1941. See also William Ebenstein, *The Nazi State* (New York, 1943).
5. Hans Buchheim, *Totalitarian rule* (Connecticut, 1968), p. 91. It is of course a paradox that the Nazi state too centralized powers, albeit with chaotic results, see Martin Broszat, *The Hitler State* (London, 1981).

6. These two statements appear in Max Freedman, *Roosevelt and Frankfurter. Their Correspondence, 1928–1945* (Boston, 1967), pp. 93–94.
7. Pierre Birnbaum, *Prier pour l'Etat: les uifs, l'alliance royale et la démocratie* (Paris, 2005).
8. Freedman, *Roosevelt and Frankfurter,* op.cit., p. 27.
9. Harlan Phillips (ed.), *Felix Frankfurter Reminiscences* (Westport, Conn., 1978), p. 241.
10. Idem, p. 248.
11. Alphaeus Mason, *Brandeis, a Free Man's Life* (New York, 1946), p. 615.
12. . Quoted by Liva Baker, *Felix Frankfurter* (New York, 1969), pp. 195–6.
13. Quoted in Freedman, *Roosevelt and Frankfurter,* op.cit., pp. 303–10.
14. Nelson Lloyd Dawson, *Louis Brandeis, Felix Frankfurter and the New Deal,* (Hamden, Conn., 1980), p. 26.
15. Alan Brinkley, 'The New Deal and the Idea of the State', in Steve Frazer and Gary Gerstle (eds.), *The Rise and Fall of the New Deal Order,* 1989 (Princeton, 1989), p. 86.
16. Barry Karl, *The Uneasy State: the United States from 1915 to 1945* (Chicago, 1983), p. 181.
17. Laura Kalman, *Abe Fortas, A Biography.* (New Haven, Conn., 1990), p. 3. It will be recalled that Abe Fortas then joined the Department of Agriculture before becoming Undersecretary for the Interior. Kalman underlines Fortas' fear not to recruit only Jews to the administration, p. 69.
18. According to H. N. Hirsch, *The Enigma of Felix Frankfurter* (New York, 1981), p. 232: 'Frankfurter was, from many points of view, in his relations with Roosevelt, a perfect example of a Court Jew'. Citing Judith Sklar, Hirsch also describes Frankfurter as a being with above all the shame of self and of his origins in wishing to see himself more like the Brahmins of Boston. In the same sense, it seems difficult to use this concept of the 'Court Jew' in the case of Louis Marshall as was done by Morton Rosenstock. 'Louis Marshall and the of Jewish Rights in the United States', PhD, Columbia University, 1963, p. 94.
19. Alphaeus Mason, *Brandeis, A Free Man's Life* (New York, 1956), p. 614.

20. Lewis Paper, *Brandeis, An Intimate Biography of one of America's truly Great Supreme Court Justices* (New Jersey, 1983), p. 344.
21. Melvin Urofsky and David Levy (eds.), *Half Brother, Half Son, The Letters of Louis Brandeis to Felix Frankfurter,* (Oklahoma, 1991).
22. Thomas McCraw, *Prophets of Regulation* (Cambridge, Mass., 1984), pp. 108–9 and 140–41.
23. Melvin Urofsky, *Louis D. Brandeis. A Life* (New York, 2009), p. 149. Emphasis in original.
24. Dawson, *Louis Brandeis, Felix Frankfurter and the New Deal,* op.cit., p. 40.
25. Ibid. Emphasis in original.
26. Quoted by Peter Irons, *The New Deal Lawyers* (Princeton, NJ, 1982), pp. 20–1.
27. Quoted in Urofsky, *Louis D. Brandeis,* op.cit., p. 691.
28. Felix Frankfurter, *The Public and Its Government* (New Haven, CT, 1930), pp. 136 and 163–4. On the action of Frankfurter during the New Deal, Baker, *Felix Frankfurter,* op.cit., p. 165 *et seq.*
29. Philips (ed.), *Felix Frankfurter Reminisces,* op.cit., p. 377.
30. Freedman, *Roosevelt and Frankfurter,* op.cit., pp. 178–83.
31. Idem, p. 353.
32. *Flournoy v. Wiener,* 321 US 25.
33. Quoted by Stanley Brubaker, *Benjamin Cardozo. An Intellectual Biography* (University Microfilms, 1979), pp. 324–5.
34. Theda Skocpol and Kenneth Finegold, 'State Capacity and Economic Intervention in the Early New Deal', in: *Political Science Quarterly,* Vol. 97, No. 2 (Summer, 1982), pp. 255–278.
35. Ibid.
36. Ira Katznelson and Bruce Pietrykowski, l 'Rebuilding the American State: Evidence from the 1940s', in: *Studies in American Political Development,* Vol. 5, Issue 2 (Fall, 1991), pp. 301–339, here: p. 339. See also Theodore J. Lowi, 'The Roosevelt Administration and the New American State,' in Peter Katzenstein, Theodore Lowi and Sidney Tarrow (eds.), *Comparative Theory and Political Experience: Mario Einaudi and the Liberal Tradition* (Ithaca, NY, 1990).
37. Theda Skocpol, 'Political Responses to Capitalist Crisis: Neo-Marxists Theories of the State and the Case of the New Deal', in: *Politics and Society,* Vol. 10, No. 2 (Mar., 1980), pp. 155–201, here: p. 194.

38. For an account of this turn, Irons, *The New Deal Lawyers,* op.cit., chap.13 and conclusion.
39. See Dean Acheson, 'Mr Justice Cardozo and Problems of Government', *Michigan Law Review* Vol. 34, No. 4 (February 1939), pp. 513–539, here: pp. 524 *et seq.*
40. Quoted in Dawson, *Louis Frandeis, Felix Frankfurter and the New Deal,* op.cit., p. 57; to the extent that Frankfurter admitted to Brandeis, 'The Treasury, I can do nothing with', ibid., p. 59.
41. Phillips (ed.), *Felix Frankfurter Reminiscences,* op.cit., pp. 248–250.
42. H. N. Hirsch, *The Enigma of Felix Frankfurter* (New York, 1981), p. 122.
43. Leonard Baker, 'The Franklin Roosevelt Presidency, Louis Brandeis and Felix Frankfurter,' in Herbert Rosenbaum and Elisabeth Bartelme (eds.), *Franklin Roosevelt. The Man, the Myth, the Era, 1882–1945* (New York, 1987), p. 226. The author considers that, in their scientific works, Nelson Dawson as well as H. N. Hirsch give too much importance to the role of Frankfurter and Brandeis, p. 226.
44. Irons, *The New Deal Lawyers,* op.cit., p. 60.
45. Ibid., p. 128.
46. Ibid.
47. Pierre Birnbaum *Un mythe politique, 'La République juive'* (Paris, 1992). For the impact of Edouard Drumont's *La france juive* on French society under the Third Republic, see Birnbaum, *The anti-semitic moment* op.cit.
48. Telemachus Thomas Timayenis, *The Original Mr Jacobs,* reprint by the University of Michigan Library, 1889, p. 6. Reproducing, page after page, *La France juive,* he committed the same blunders, identifying Gambetta or Lockroy and many others as Jewish. His reading of Drumont was so faithful that he even quoted at length the Raphaël Levy Affair, pp. 244–258. We should note that Henry Adams also admired Drumont and the anti-Dreyfusards, and spread a similar kind of antisemitism. He wrote, for example, 'We are in the hands of the Jews. They can do what they please with our values'. Quoted in Michael Dobkowski, *The Tarnished Dream. The Basis of American Anti-Semitism* (Westport, CT., 1979), p. 124.
49. Timayenis, *The Original Mr Jacobs,* p. 86.

50. Telemachus Thomas Timayenis, *The American Jew: An Exposé of his Career* (New York, 1888), p. 167.
51. Telemachus Thomas Timayenis, *Judas Iscariot: an Old Type in a New Form* (New York 1889), pp. 15, 49.
52. See George Marsden, *Fundamentalism and American Culture. The Shaping of Twentieth-Century Evangelism: 1870–1925* (Oxford, 1980). In this classic book, Marsden devotes less than a page to the question of anti-Semitism, see p. 210.
53. Henry Ford, *The International Jew*, Article of 13 November 1920, reprinted by Liberty Bell Publications (York, 2004), p. 32.
54. Idem, speech of 20 November 1920, ibid., pp. 55–56. He added: 'It was not a Council Americans that ran the war, it was an autocracy headed by a Jew with Jews at every strategic point down the line', ibid., p. 63. He described Bernard Baruch again as 'the Jewish governor of the United States' whose power supplanted that of the President, ibid., p. 67.
55. Idem, speech of 12 March 1921, ibid., pp. 162–169.
56. Dobkowski, *The Tarnished Dream*, op.cit., p.198 *et seq.*
57. These two quotations are given by Morton Rosenstock, 'Louis Marshall and the Defense of Jewish Rights in the United States' (PhD, Columbia University, 1963), pp. 262 and 305. See also Robert Rifkind, 'Confronting Antisemitism in America: Louis Marshall and Henry Ford', in: *American Jewish History*, Vol. 94, nos.1–2 (March–June, 2009), pp. 71–90.
58. Victoria Woeste, *Henry Ford's War on Jews and the Legal Battle Against Hate Speech* (Stanford, CA., 2012).
59. Victoria Woeste, 'Ford, Henry (1863–1947)', in: Richard S. Levy (ed.), *Antisemitism : Historical Encyclopedia of Prejudice and Persecution*, 2 Vols., (Santa Barbara, CA., 2005), vol. 1, pp. 233–36.
60. Seymour Lipset and Earl Raab, *The Politics of Unreason. Right-Wing Extremism in America, 1790–1970* (New York, 1970), pp. 138, 165.
61. Freedman (ed.), *Roosevelt and Frankfurter*, op.cit., p. 343. This remark appears in a letter from Frankfurter dated 29 May 1936.
62. William Leuchtenburg, *Franklin D. Roosevelt and the New Deal* 1932–1940 (New York, 1963), p.331. See: Lawrence Fuchs, *The Political Behavior of American Jews* (New York, 1956), pp. 71 *et seq.*

63. These last declarations are quoted by Myron Scholnick, *The New Deal and Anti-Semitism in America* (University Microfilms, 1971), pp. 4, 20.
64. John Morton Blum, *Roosevelt and Morgenthau* (Boston, 1970).
65. All quotes here are taken from Scholnick, *The New Deal and Anti-Semitism in America*, op.cit., pp. 27–8.
66. Franklin Thompson, *America's Ju-Dea* (Woodhaven, NYC, 1935), pp. 2–3, 25–6.
67. Ibid., pp. 31–3, 38.
68. Ibid., pp. 12, pp. 196–7, 207–8.
69. These four last quotations are given in: George Wolfskill and John Hudson, *All But the People. Franklin Roosevelt and His Critics, 1933–1939* (London, 1969), pp. 70–78.
70. Dov Fisch, 'The Libel Trial of Robert Edward Edmondson: 1936–1938', *American Jewish History,* Vol. 71, No. 1 (September 1981), pp. 79–102, here: p. 93.
71. *Fortune* (December 1935).
72. Charles Herbert Stember, 'The Recent History of Public Attitudes: Reactions to Anti-Semites Appeals before and during the War', in Charles Stember et al., (eds.), *Jews in the Mind of America* (New York, 1966), pp. 124–8.
73. Donald Strong, *Organized Anti-Semitism in America. The Rise of Group Prejudice During the Decade 1930–40*, American Council on Public Affairs, Washington, 1941, p. 179.
74. *Idem,* chap. XII.
75. Some writers estimate that his sermons held the attention of forty million listeners. See Albert Fried, *FDR and his Enemies* (New York, 1999), p. 41. See also Donald Warren, *Radio Priest: Charles Coughlin, the Father of Hate Radio,* (New York, 1996).
76. Lipset and Raab, *The Politics of Unreason*, op.cit., p. 180.
77. Paper, *Brandeis, An Intimate Biography*, op.cit., p. 354.
78. See Geoffrey Smith, *To Save a Nation: 'Extremism', the New Deal and the Coming of World War II* (Chicago, 1992) and Scott Beekman, *William Dudley Pelley. A Life in Right-Wing Extremism and the Occult*, (Syracuse, NY, 2005), chapter 6.
79. Quoted by Leo Ribufo, *The Old Christian Right. The Protestant Far Right from the Great depression to the Cold Wear*, (Philadelphia, 1983), p. 60.

80. These last three citations are in Strong, *Organized Anti-Semitism in America,* op.cit., pp. 156, 158 and 160.
81. David Bennett, *The Party of Fear From Nativist Movements to the New Right in American History,* (Chapel Hill, 1988) p.244 The Party of Fear: The American Far Right from Nativism to the Militia Movement rev. (Vintage 1995).
82. Quoted by Scholnick, *The New Deal and Anti-Semitism in America,* op.cit., p. 84.
83. Wolfskill and Hudson, *All But the People.* op.cit., pp. 69–70 and 83.
84. Quoted by Charles Tull, *Father Coughlin and the New Deal* (Syracuse, NY, 1965), p. 229.
85. See the contribution by Mark Weitzman in this book.
86. See Alan Brinkley, *Voices of Protest. Huey Long, Father Coughlin and the Great Depression* (New York, 1982).
87. See Mary Christine Athans, *The Coughlin-Fahey Connection. Father Charles Coughlin, Father Denis Fahey and Religious Anti-Semitism in the United States, 1928–1954* (New York, 1991), pp. 15–23 and 157, *et seq.* Coughlin claimed that Bernard Baruch second given name was Menassah, 'A prince of Israel'. Baruch retorted that his second given name was Mannes. See Fried, *FDR and His Enemies,* op.cit., p. 111.
88. Father E. Coughlin, 'Am I an Anti-Semite?' Quoted in *Anti-Semitism in America, 1878–1939* (New York, 1977), p. 29.
89. Ronald Carpenter, *Father Charles Coughlin, Surrogate Spokesman for the Disaffected* (Westport, CT., 1998), p. 122.
90. Leo Ribuffo, 'United States v. McWilliams: The Roosevelt Administration and the Far Right,' in: Michal Belknap (ed.), *Americn Political Trials* (Westport, CT, 1994).
91. William Pelley, *New Dealers in Office,* undated, no publisher shown, p. 3.
92. Bennett, *The Party of Fear*, op.cit., p. 246.
93. *The Revealer*, 15 October 1936, Columbia Library, Rare Books section B 973.82 R67756.
94. Quoted by Scholnick, *The New Deal and Anti-Semitism in America,* op.cit., p. 1.
95. See Birnbaum, *Un mythe politique*, op.cit.
96. Scholnick, *The New Deal and Anti-Semitism in America,* op.cit., pp. 101–102.

97. Neil Baldwin, *Henry Ford and the Jews* (New York, 2001), chaps. 18 and 19.
98. Quoted in Tully, *Father Coughlin and the New Deal*, op.cit., p. 233.
99. Quoted in Fried, *FDR and His Enemies*, op.cit., p. 202.

CHAPTER 8

Nazi Propaganda to the Arab World During World War II and the Holocaust: and Its Aftereffects

Jeffrey Herf

As a result of research in the United States, Germany and Israel in recent years, historians have been able to offer extensive evidence about an important but brief chapter in the long history of Islamist anti-Semitism. That chapter took place during World War II in Berlin when a number of prominent radical Arab nationalist and Islamist leaders collaborated with the Nazi regime in efforts to spread its propaganda and policies to North Africa and the Middle East.[1] Cultural fusion between European forms of radical anti-Semitism and Islamist forms drawing on a selective reading of the Koran and the commentaries about it was at its core. Islamism, a hybrid of European and Islamist ideology, began in the Middle East in the 1920s, found refuge in Nazi Berlin during World War II, persisted in the postwar decades in the Muslim Brotherhood, shaped parts of Palestinian nationalism and, in recent decades, has inspired the terrorism of Islamist jihadism in Al Qaeda, Hamas, Hezbollah as well as the government of Iran.

Robert Wistrich wrote about a shift in the center of gravity of anti-Semitism from Europe to the Middle East.[2] Nazi Germany's propaganda

J. Herf (✉)
Department of History, University of Maryland, College Park, MD, USA

A. McElligott, J. Herf (eds.), *Antisemitism Before and Since the Holocaust*, DOI 10.1007/978-3-319-48866-0_8

aimed at the Arab world, and the cultural fusion that made it possible was an important chapter of this shift. It was produced by Nazi leaders who favored Arab nationalism and interpreted the religion of Islam as one compatible with National Socialism and some Arab nationalists and Islamist ideologues who looked with favor on the Nazi's attack on the Jews and on Zionism.[3] This cultural fusion between the radicalization of European, German and Christian forms of anti-Semitism, and those resting on a selective reading of the traditions of Islam and Arab nationalism, took place primarily in the propaganda offices of Joachim von Ribbentrop's Foreign Ministry but also in the think tanks of Heinrich Himmler's Reich Security Main Office, propaganda units in Nazi Germany's armies in North Africa and Joseph Goebbels' Propaganda Ministry. Its primary medium was shortwave radio broadcasts beamed from Germany to North Africa and the Middle East (as well as Persian-language programs aimed at Iran). From fall 1939 to March 1945, the Nazi regime was on the air, each evening with Arabic-language broadcasts sent from Rome, Bari, Athens and especially from very powerful transmitters in the town of Zeesen near Berlin. As the literacy rate of the societies of the Middle East and North Africa during the war was about 20% (and in some cases less for Muslims and still less for Muslim women), radio was by far the most effective means of reaching the politically engaged minorities of the region. American intelligence agencies estimated that there were about 50,000 radios in Egypt, 10,000 in Palestine and 15,000 in Lebanon and Syria. Radios were often heard by groups of listeners in cafés. Information about audience reception and size is scarce. The broadcasts were aimed at a relatively small audience that had access to shortwave radios and was already inclined to favor the Axis powers.

The connection between the secular and religious components of the Arabic-language propaganda was powerful and enduring. In the same texts and broadcasts, the Nazis spoke the secular language of attack on American, British and "Jewish" imperialism while also appealing to what they depicted as the ancient traditions of hatred of the Jews which they insisted were inherent in Islam itself. Nazi Germany presented itself both as an ally of Arab anti-imperialism as well as a soulmate of the religion of Islam. From the beginning to the end of the war, Nazism's Arabic-language propaganda attacked Zionism as an inseparable aspect of its attack on the Jews. Indeed, Nazi officials and diplomats understood before the war began that the Third Reich's hostility to Zionism was one of its major political advantages in the effort to secure support among Arabs and Muslims. Conversely, despite Britain's White Paper and Roosevelt's wartime refusal to clearly support the establishment of a Jewish state in Palestine, the Nazis—as well as leading American and British officials—believed that the association of the Allies with the Jews and with Zionism was a hindrance to Allied efforts to gain support for their war effort in the region. No aspect of Nazi propaganda fused its secular and religious dimensions more effectively than did its persistent and vehement attack on Zionist ideology and policy.

As I noted, the resulting Arabic-language propaganda was a joint effort that produced an intellectual and political fusion of very different anti-Semitic traditions with European and Islamic roots. The Germans lacked native Arabic speakers and the familiarity with the details of local politics in the Middle East. The Arab exiles provided both. In Berlin, the Arabs learned the finer points of anti-Semitic conspiracy theories emerging from Europe and the Nazi regime and adapted them to the local politics of the Middle East. As I mentioned above, the result was a consequential cultural fusion or, to use fashionable language, a hybridity resulting from a mixture and ferment between, in this case, fascist and Nazi ideologists from Europe, and radical Arabs and Islamists who found refuge from their Allied pursuers in wartime Rome and Berlin. Theirs was a meeting of hearts and minds, not a clash of civilizations.

The Koran, or rather the Nazi and radical Islamist reading of that work, became the key text in these labors of cultural fusion. Arabic translations of *Mein Kampf* and the *Protocols of the Elders of Zion* were circulating in the Middle East before 1939. Although the *Protocols* did have wide circulation during and even more after World War II in the region, neither of these texts nor major speeches by Hitler or Goebbels played a significant role in Nazi radio and print propaganda during the war. Indeed, by the mid-1930s, German diplomats were aware that Hitler's racist views of Arabs expressed in *Mein Kampf* posed a problem for German efforts to find allies and collaborators among non-Jewish, that is, Arab and Muslim "Semites." Rather, the propaganda displayed an integration of Nazi ideology with a selective reading of the already existent anti-Jewish themes in the Koran and Islamic commentaries about it and with the anti-Zionist currents of Arab nationalism. Leading officials in the "Orient" offices of the German Foreign Ministry such as Erwin Ettel and Kurt Munzel as well as Nazi Orientalists working with Heinrich Himmler's Reich Security Main Office of the SS concluded that it was the Koran, and the traditions of Islam as they selectively understood them, not *Mein Kampf* or the

Protocols, that offered the key point of cultural and political entry into a very hard to ascertain number of Arab and Muslim hearts and minds. Just as Nazism radicalized Europe's and Germany's preexisting traditions of anti-Semitism, so too did it appeal, lend support to and help to radicalize the anti-Jewish and anti-Zionist elements of Arab nationalism and Islamic radicalism.

Haj Amin el-Husseini's pro-Nazi sympathies in the 1930s have been known for many years. In fact, recent research offers abundant evidence of the enthusiasm with which Husseini and his colleagues tried to help Nazi Germany win World War II and to fan the flames of Jew-hatred. The German political scientist and contemporary historian Matthias Küntzel has found additional evidence that Husseini had produced one of Islamism's founding texts before he came to Berlin in November 1941.[4] While avoiding arrest by British authorities, Husseini organized an all-Arab conference of 400 delegates, held on September 8–9, 1937, in Bludan, Syria.[5] In Husseini's absence, one of his texts was read to those in attendance. The following year, a text by Husseini entitled "Islam and the Jews" was published in German in Berlin in a work entitled *Islam-Jewry-Bolshevism* in series on "the idea and form of National Socialism." The German text of Husseini's piece had the subtitle "The Grand Mufti's Appeal to the Islamic World in 1937."[6] It is almost certainly the same text delivered to the delegates in Bludan in September 1937 (See Note 3). "Islam and the Jews" offered a reading of the Koran that placed Jew-hatred into a millennial time span and applied it to modern times as well. Its publication in a German edition in 1938 in Berlin meant that Husseini's distinctively Islamist Jew-hatred could be known by those in German government and academic circles who followed developments in the Arab world:

> The battle between Jews and Islam began when Mohammed fled from Mecca to Medina ... Therefore they were seized by a deep hatred against Islam. This hatred intensified the stronger and more powerful Islam became ... In those days, the Jewish methods were exactly the same as they are today. Then as now, slander was their weapon. They said Mohammed was a swindler ... They tried to undermine his honor ... They began to pose senseless and unanswerable questions to Mohammed .... and then they tried to annihilate the Muslims. Just as the Jews were able to betray Mohammed, so they will betray the Muslims today ... The verses of the Koran and the Hadith assert that the Jews were Islam's most bitter enemy and moreover try to destroy it (See Note 4).

Husseini saw in his depiction of Jewish supposed Jewish hostility to Mohammed an early version of Zionism's designs on Palestine. Bassam Tibi has referred to Islamism as an invented tradition (See Note 6). Husseini's text from the Bludan conference in 1937 was one of its founding moments.

Husseini's enthusiasm for Nazism and Hitler was evident in the 1930s. The Nazi regime reciprocated with assistance to him between 1936 and 1939 in the violent campaign he waged against the Jews and the British in Palestine as well as the military assistance it offered to him and Kilani and others in their short-lived pro-Axis coup in Bagdad in spring 1941.[7] Yet the highpoint of their political and ideological collaboration with the Nazi regime took place between 1941 and 1945 in Berlin. Then and there they worked closely and regularly with the area specialists in German Foreign to produce shortwave radio broadcasts in Arabic to North Africa and the Middle East; intelligence operatives embedded in Rommel's North Africa Corps in writing Arabic-language printed materials, and with Himmler's Reich Security Main Office in both its propaganda efforts and in constituting an SS division composed of Bosnian Muslims. While the broad outlines of this active collaboration with the Nazi regime became public knowledge in the months following World War II, the full extent of the Arabic-language propaganda campaign has first entered historical scholarship with the recent publication of my book *Nazi Propaganda for the Arab World*. During the war, American diplomats in Cairo transcribed and translated what they called "Axis Broadcasts in Arabic." The resulting several thousand pages of verbatim transcripts were declassified in the US National Archives in 1977. These files and others, which I found in 2007, together research in German and British archives and recent scholarship by German historians deepen our understanding of the Nazi-Islamist collaboration in matters of propaganda and policy.

Before Husseini and Rashid ali-Kilani arrived in Berlin in November 1941, the German broadcasts drew primarily on the expertise of German Orientalists of Arabic and Islamic literature and poetry, the local knowledge gained by German diplomats in the prewar years and an impossible to ascertain contribution by pro-Axis Arabs living in Berlin when the war began. These early broadcasts sent a clear message that the Nazi regime, rather than celebrate the superiority of Aryans over inferior Middle Eastern Semites, was a friend to both Arab nationalists and Muslims. For example, on December 3, 1940, Munzel's Orient Office VII broadcast "a paper about the English occupation of Egypt."[8] With the incantation "*Oh Mohammedaner*" (Oh Muslims!), the broadcast made a direct appeal to Muslims and not only to Arab nationalists opposed to British rule in Egypt. It did so in the repetitive incantations of a religious sermon that evoked the authority of the "holy Koran" and past days of piety:

> Oh, God's servants! Above all of the other commandments, none is more important to the Muslims (*Mohammedaner*) than piety for piety is the core of all virtues and the bond of all honorable human characteristics. Muslims you are now backward because you have not shown God the proper piety and do not fear him. You do things that are not commanded and you leave to the side things that are. God's word has proven to be true and you are now the humiliated ones in your own country. This has come about because you don't have the piety and fear of God as your pious forefathers did. Of them, one can say that they 'are strong against the unbelievers and merciful amongst themselves.' Oh Muslims! (*Oh Mohammedaner!*) Direct your gaze to the holy Koran and the tradition of the prophets. Then you will see that Islamic law is driven by piety toward God and fear of his punishment. The Koran inscribed piety as above all other commandments. Read, for example, the words: 'Oh, believers, be pious and do not die without being a Muslim. Stand by God and don't be divided.'[9]

Nazi broadcasts repeated that the values of Islam, such as piety, obedience, community, unity rather than skepticism, individualism and division were similar to those of Nazi Germany. That such a melange of assault on modern political values was conveyed via the most modern means of electronic communication in 1940 was another example of what I've previously called the "reactionary modernist" character of aspects of Nazi ideology and policy.[10] This and other broadcasts conveyed the message that a revival of fundamentalist Islam was a parallel project to National Socialism's political and ideological revolt against Western political modernity. The message of this broadcast was that a return to a literal reading of the Koran and its application to contemporary events was not only or primarily a relic of a backward culture but part of the great movement now in power in Nazi Germany and Fascist Italy. On the same day that Radio Berlin broadcast the above message, it also sent out "A Government Statement for the Arabs."[11] It spoke of strong connections between the Germans and Arabs because they shared "many qualities and virtues," such as "courage in war … heroism and manly character." They "both shared in the suffering and injustices after the end of the [First] World War. Both of these great peoples had their honor insulted, their rights were denied and trampled underfoot. Both bled from the same wounds and both also had the same enemy: namely the Allies who divided them and allowed them no claim to honor. Now Germany has succeeded in getting out from under this disgrace and regaining all of its old rights so that Germany's voice is now heard everywhere and has again taken its old place."[12] Nazi Germany was a model to emulate of nation that had been humiliated yet had recovered its independence and unity.

These early broadcasts displayed both the talent and the limits of German Nazi Orientalism. They lacked a certain political punch and grasp of local idioms and politics. The arrival in November 1941 of Husseini, Khilani and their entourage ended this shortcoming.[13] They both met Hitler and Ribbentrop.[14] In his well-publicized but only meeting with Husseini in Berlin on November 28, 1941, Hitler heard Husseini's lavish praise on him and Nazi Germany and request that Germany and Italy issue a strong declaration in support of Arab independence from Britain. Though Hitler replied that the time had not yet arrived for issuing such a declaration, he told Husseini that when the German armies on the Eastern Front reached "the southern exit" form the Caucasus, Hitler would "give the Arab world the assurance that its hour of liberation had arrived. Germany's objective would then be solely the destruction of the Jewish element residing in the Arab sphere under the protection of British power."[15] In other words, in the same period in which Hitler had taken the decisions to launch the Final Solution of the Jewish Question *in Europe*, he also told Husseini that he intended to extend it as well *outside Europe*, that is, at least to the Jews living in Egypt, Palestine, Trans-Jordan and Iraq and possibly to all of the 700,000 Jews living in the North Africa, the Middle East and Iran.

Although German industry invented the tape recorder in the 1930s and used it to record a vast amount of its German-language radio broadcasts, its Arabic-language programs were both not taped and transcribed or, if they were, the documents were destroyed, lost or stolen. Although there is a great deal of important material in the files of the German Foreign Ministry about these matters, the most extensive and set of files about Nazi propaganda to the Arab world are those from the American Embassy in wartime Cairo. For it was there, under the direction of Ambassador Alexander Kirk, that a team he assembled transcribed and translated Nazi Germany's Arabic-language radio broadcasts. Kirk and his successor Pinkney Tuck sent the verbatim, English-language transcripts of "Axis Broadcasts in Arabic" each week to the Office of the Secretary of State in Washington. As far as I know, the several thousand pages of "Axis Broadcasts in Arabic" are the most complete record available anywhere in any language of Nazi Germany's Arabic-language propaganda aimed at Arabs and Muslims during World War II and the Holocaust.

Kirk sent the first of his Cairo dispatches about Nazi radio broadcasts in Arabic to the Office of Secretary of State Cordell Hull Washington on September 13, 1941.[16] The summaries continued and expanded in length and detail until April 1942, when Kirk's staff began to produce verbatim English-language transcripts. Kirk sent the texts to Washington every week until March 1944, when Tuck continued to do so until spring 1945. Kirk's dispatch of April 18, 1942, summarized German Arabic broadcasts of the preceding six months which now were evidence of the Nazi-Arab exile collaboration taking place in Berlin.[17] German propaganda, Kirk wrote, sought to convince the Arabs that the Axis countries had "a natural sympathy with the Arabs and their great civilization, the only one comparable with the civilization introduced by the New Order in Europe, which is now being suppressed by 'British Imperialism,' 'Bolshevik barbarity,' and 'Jewish greed' and more recently 'American materialism.'" The Arabs could "never be the friends of Britain because her promises are false. German Arabic radio denounced the Jews "ad nauseum." It asserted that the Jews, "backed by Britain and the U.S.A." were "the arch-enemies of Islam." They controlled American finance and had "forced Roosevelt to purse a policy of aggression." Roosevelt and Churchill were "playthings in the hands of the Jewish fiends who are destroying civilization."[18] Throughout World War II, Nazi radio propaganda attacked Britain and the United States in particular for the support they supposedly gave to the establishment of a Jewish state in Palestine. Every statement by any public figure in Britain or the United States expressing anger over the persecution of Jews in Europe or support for a Jewish state in Palestine was taken as further proof of the truth that the Jews were in control of the governments of Britain and the United States and also of "Jewish Bolshevism" in Moscow. As was the case in Nazi propaganda in Europe, Roosevelt and Churchill were the main culprits and stooges. As I stated above, anti-Zionism was central to the Nazi propaganda.

In the spring, summer and fall 1942, as General Erwin Rommel's North Africa Corps advanced to within 60 miles of Alexandria, Egypt, Nazi Germany's Arabic-language radio broadcasts envisaged imminent victory. On July 3, 1942, "Berlin in Arabic" announced that Germany and Italy resolved that "the troops of the Axis powers are victoriously advancing into Egyptian territory [...] to guarantee Egypt's independence and sovereignty." The Axis forces were entering Egypt "to dismiss the

British from Egyptian territory ... and to liberate the whole of the Near East from the British yoke. The policy of the Axis powers is inspired by the principle 'Egypt for the Egyptians.' The emancipation of Egypt from the chains which have linked her with Britain, and her security from the risks of war, will enable her to assume her position among the independent sovereign states."[19] The radio then broadcast the following statement by the Grand Mufti of Palestine, Haj Amin el-Husseini: "The Glorious victory secured by the Axis troops in North Africa, has encouraged the Arabs and the whole East, and filled their hearts with admiration for Marshall Rommel's genius, and the bravery of the Axis soldiers. This is because the Arabs believe that the Axis Powers are fighting against the common enemy, namely the British and the Jews, and in order to remove the danger of communism spreading, following the [Allied, JH] aggression on Iran. These victories, generally speaking, will have far reaching repercussions on Egypt, because the loss of the Nile Valley and of the Suez Canal, and the collapse of the British mastery over the Mediterranean and the Red Sea, will bring nearer the defeat of Britain and the end of the British Empire."[20] The German and Italian declaration in favor of Arab independence from Britain was one that Husseini and Khilani had been seeking ever since they arrived in Rome and Berlin and expressed their support for the Axis powers. Given that neither Vichy France nor Fascist Italy had gone to war in order to guarantee independence and sovereignty to the Arabs, Hitler and Mussolini had postponed making any such statement. Now that an uprising in Egypt might undermine British armed forces, the dictators agreed to do so.

At 8:15 p.m. Cairo time on July 7, 1942, the Nazi station "The Voice of Free Arabism," (hereafter VFA) the Americans in Cairo recorded one of the most remarkable Nazi broadcasts of the war, one which illustrated the links between the general propaganda line in Europe and its adaptation to the Middle East context. The text was entitled "KILL THE JEWS BEFORE THEY KILL YOU." It was a statement that equaled Hitler and Goebbels' genocidal anti-Semitism. The broadcast began with a lie, namely that "a large number of Jews residing in Egypt and a number of Poles, Greeks, Armenians and Free French, have been issued with revolvers and ammunition" in order to "help them against the Egyptians at the last moment, when Britain is forced to evacuate Egypt."[21] The statement continued:

> In the face of this barbaric procedure by the British we think it best, if the life of the Egyptian nation is to be saved, that the Egyptians rise as one

> man to kill the Jews before they have a chance of betraying the Egyptian people. It is the duty of the Egyptians to annihilate the Jews and to destroy their property. Egypt can never forget that it is the Jews who are carrying out Britain's imperialist policy in the Arab countries and that they are the source of all the disasters, which have befallen the countries of the East. The Jews aim at extending their domination throughout the Arab countries, but their future depends on a British victory. That is why they are trying to save Britain from her fate and why Britain is arming them to kill the Arabs and save the British Empire.
>
> You must kill the Jews, before they open fire on you. Kill the Jews, who have appropriated your wealth and who are plotting against your security. Arabs of Syria, Iraq and Palestine, what are you waiting for? The Jews are planning to violate your women, to kill your children and to destroy you. According to the Moslem religion, the defense of your life is a duty which can only be fulfilled by annihilating the Jews. This is your best opportunity to get rid of this dirty race, which has usurped your rights and brought misfortune and destruction on your countries. Kill the Jews, burn their property, destroy their stores, annihilate these base supporters of British imperialism. Your sole hope of salvation lies in annihilating the Jews before they annihilate you.[22]

Here, applied to the Arab and Muslim context, was the same logic of projection and paranoia that was a defining feature of Nazism's radical antisemitism in Europe. Incitement to mass murder was presented as a justifiable act of self-defense. The tirade combined the political and racial hatreds of Nazism with evocation of supposed religious demands of Islam. In its propaganda for domestic consumption, the Nazis asserted in blunt and shocking terms that the Nazi regime was in the process of "exterminating" the Jews of Europe.[23] In its radio propaganda to Arabs and Muslims, it was even more frank. The major difference was that it openly called for audience participation, that is, it urged listeners to take matters into their own hands.

In their important recent work, *Halbmond und Hakenkruez: Das Dritte Reich, die Araber und Palästina* [Crescent and Swastika: The Third Reich, the Arabs and the Palestinians], the German historians, Michael Mallmann and Martin Cuppers revealed an *Einsatzgruppe* of SS troops led by Walter Rauff in Athens was prepared to depart to Palestine to murder the Jewish population if Rommel won the battle of Al Alamein. German officials expected as much support for that endeavor from the local Arab population as Ukranians had given to SS units on the Eastern Front.[24] Nazi propaganda had the dual purpose of drawing Arabs and Muslims to the side of the Axis as well as inciting them to support Nazi plans to extend the Final Solution beyond Europe's geographical limits.

The question of the impact and reception of the propaganda among listeners was one that preoccupied German, British and American officials. An adequate assessment awaits further work by scholars who read Arabic (and Persian) who will now have the benefit of a much greater knowledge of what these listeners were actually hearing during the war. Some of the most detailed Allied reports about the Egyptian response to Axis policy and propaganda were those of Miles Lampson, the British Ambassador to Egypt. Lampson was probably the most experienced and well-informed Western diplomat observing developments in Egypt and the Arab world. Lampson's reports to London, far from expressing Orientalist generalizations about all Arabs, Muslims or Egyptians, were noteworthy for their remarkable detail and differentiation.[25] His concern about "fifth column activities" applied to specific groups and individuals such as Hassan al-Banna, head of the Muslim Brotherhood; the activities of the "Young Egypt" organization led by Ahmed Hussein; faculty and students at Al Azhar University; and Egypt's King Farouk and the advisers around him.[26] Far from generalizing about Arabs or Muslims in general, Lampson focused on specific individuals and organizations who were supporting the Axis and distinguished them from those Egyptians, mostly in the Wafd Party, who were supporting the Allies.[27]

Both Lampson and Kirk believed that the defeat of Rommel's Africa Corps in 1943 diminished the popularity of Nazi Germany and Fascist Italy in the region. Just as Nazi propaganda in Germany responded to the defeat in Stalingrad with dire warnings of the disaster that awaited the Germans should the Allies be victorious in Europe, so Axis defeat in North Africa led to equally dire warnings of the consequences of Allied victory in North Africa and the Middle East for Arabs and Muslims. From 1943 to spring 1945, the Nazi radio stations using the names "Berlin in Arabic," "Radio Berlin" and "VFA" presented graphic warnings of the catastrophe that would befall Arabs and Muslims if the Allies were to win the war. For example, on September 8, 1943, in a broadcast on "The Ambitions of the Jews," Berlin in Arabic asserted that the Jews would not be satisfied until they made "every territory between the Tigris and the Nile Jewish."[28] Their goal was to "remove the Cross and the Crescent form all Arab countries." If they succeeded, "there will remain not a single Arab Moslem or

Christian in the Arab world. Arabs! Imagine Egypt, Iraq and all the Arab countries becoming Jewish with no Christianity or Islam there."[29]

A month later, on November 3, 1943, the V FA discussed "Palestine between the Bolsheviks and the Jews."[30] It mirrored the incitement to murder of Nazi propaganda in Germany:

> Should we not curse the time that has allowed this low race to realize their desires from such countries as Britain, America and Russia? The Jews kindled this war in the interests of Zionism. The Jews are responsible for the blood that has been shed. Despite this, Jewish impudence has increased to such an extent that they claim that they alone are the sacrifice of this war and that they alone are tasting bitterness. The world will never be at peace until the Jewish race is exterminated, otherwise wars will always exist. The Jews are the germs which have caused all the trouble in the world.[31]

The broadcast presented the Jews' desire to realize the Zionist goal as the cause of World War II. Like the paranoia and projection that characterized Nazi propaganda in Germany, it combined this accusation with incitement to "exterminate" the Jews. During the Cold War, the claim that Nazi Germany worked closely with Zionists became a standard element of the propaganda campaign waged against Israel in the decades following World War II. In fact, in propaganda and policy, the Nazi regime despised Zionism, made no distinction between Zionists and Jews or Zionism and Judaism, and was convinced that its fierce opposition to Zionism was of decisive importance in forging and deepening ties to Arab and Muslim collaborators.

After the war, Husseini and his apologists argued that support for Nazi Germany was strictly an instrumental alliance of convenience. Yet their wartime collaboration was not primarily or only a chapter of Machiavellian political calculation. Evidence of deep ideological affinity was abundant. As I noted earlier, one of Husseini's distinctive contributions to the diffusion of European anti-Semitism to Arab and Islamic societies and to the political tradition of Islamism lay in his ability to combine Nazi ideology with references to the Koran. On November 5, 1943, VFA reported that Husseini had spoken at the Central Islamic Institute in Berlin to protest the Balfour Declaration.[32] The Institute then published a German text of Husseini's speech, and the German Foreign Ministry distributed thousands of Arabic editions of the text through its clandestine courier network in the Middle East and to soldiers in the Bosnian SS division. In the text, Husseini made clear that his hatred of the Jews lay both in ancient, that is, religious, as well as in modern secular sources. The Jews, he said, were egoistic. They had the "contemptible belief that they were God's chosen people," and that "other men are animals which could be used for their own purposes."[33] They could not be loyal citizens of any nation. Rather, "they live like a sponge among peoples, suck their blood, seize their property, undermine their morals yet still demand the rights of local inhabitants. They want every advantage but they won't assume any obligations! All of this brought the hostility of the world down on them and nourished the Jew's hatred against all the peoples that had been burning for two thousand years ... God's anger and the curse on the Jews mentioned in the Holy Koran" was due to these Jewish characteristics. The Jews, he continued, had "tormented the world for ages." They had been the enemy of the Arabs and of Islam since its emergence. The Holy Koran expressed this old enmity in the following words: "You will find that those who are most hostile to the believers are the Jews." They tried to poison the great and noble prophets. They resisted them, were hostile to them and intrigued against them. This was the case for 1300 years. For all that time, they have not stopped spinning intrigues against the Arabs and Muslims.[34]

In Husseini's view, Islam was an inherently anti-Jewish doctrine. He placed the Zionist effort to establish a Jewish home in Palestine into a longer continuity of supposed Jewish attacks on Islam and Muslims. Indeed, he called the Jews "the driving forces of the destruction of the regime of the Islamic Caliphate" in the Middle East. The Arabs and Muslims all knew of "Jewish desire" to seize the Islamic holy sites, such as the Al Aksa Mosque, and "to build a temple on its ruins."

In the spring of 1944, in response to reports of the persecution and murder of Europe's Jews, resolutions were introduced in the United States Senate and the House of Representatives to lift restrictions on Jewish emigration to Palestine and to support creation of a Jewish state there. Nazi broadcasts focused on the issue for in their view such sympathy for the Jews confirmed their assertion that World War II was a Jewish war. Husseini was the most prominent but not by any means the only voice in this chorus. On Berlin in Arabic on March 1, 1944, he stated that the "wicked American intentions toward the Arabs are now clearer, and there remain no doubts that they are endeavoring to establish a Jewish empire in the Arab world. More than 400,000.000 Arabs oppose this criminal American movement ... Arabs! Rise as one and fight for your sacred rights. Kill the Jews wherever you find them. This pleases God, history and religion. This serves your honor. God is with you"(emphasis in original, JH).[35] These and other similar assertions constituted a clear example of incitement to mass murder which was declared a crime against humanity in the United Nations postwar genocide convention. No one associated with Nazi Germany's Arabic-language broadcasts was ever indicted for violating this clause of the genocide convention.

As his collaboration with Erwin Ettel in the Foreign Ministry had demonstrated, Husseini's strongest supporters in the Nazi regime were among its truest believers, including the head of the SS, Heinrich Himmler. The connection produced a remarkable chapter in the history of the Nazi propaganda offensive. On May 14, 1943, Himmler requested that the *Reichssicherheitshauptamt* (RSHA) examine "themes in the Koran that lead the Moslems to the view that the Koran predicts and assigns to the Führer the mission of completing the prophet's work." The RSHA should examine the issue because "we can very probably use this idea in the Moslem population, above all among our own Moslem troops."[36] A series of memos from the RSHA in Berlin to the *Forschungsstelle Orient* at the University of Tübingen explored that possibility.[37] Their conclusion was that it might be possible to depict Hitler as Jesus in the form of an "Arab knight."[38] The resulting text of spring 1944 documents the efforts of the Research Division of Himmler's RSHA, the Arabic-language propaganda divisions Foreign Ministry and Propaganda Ministry to connect Hitler to Islamic traditions.[39] The translation of Arabic text read in part as follows:

> We know that the anti-Christ will appear at the end of days and he will enter and deceive … and this time will be a time of great oppression for the believers. Oh Arabs, have you seen that the time of the Anti-Christ has come? Do you know him? This the fat Jew that deceives the whole world and who lords over the whole world and steals the land of the Arabs. He is the ally of the devil. We know that the kingdom of the Anti-Christ is not eternal. … Oh Arabs, do you know the servant of God? He has appeared in the world and turned his spear against the Anti-Christ and his allies, and has injured them deeply, and he will kill the Anti-Christ as it is written and will fight his palaces and his allies will fall into hell.[40]

In addition to the above effort to identify Hitler as God's servant on earth to kill the anti-Christ, the Reich Security Main Office also intended to distribute a series of photos showing Husseini with the Bosnian Muslim soldiers in the SS Prinze Eugen Division through its network of agents in Syria, Iraq and Palestine.[41]

In the immediate postwar months and years, American and British officials explored the issue of the aftereffects of the Nazi propaganda campaign. In Washington, in preparation for the Nuremberg War Crimes Trials, the Office of Strategic Services (OSS) issued a report on June 23, 1945, about how the political actors in the countries of the Middle East would react to possible war crimes trials against the pro-Nazi Arabs.[42] The authors of the comprehensive report "The Near East and the War Crimes Problem" wrote that "in the Near East the popular attitude toward the trial of [Nazi, JH] war criminals is one of apathy. As a result of the general Near Eastern feeling of hostility to the imperialism of certain of the Allied powers, [i.e. Britain, JH] there is a tendency to sympathize with rather than condemn those who have aided the Axis."[43]

A year later, Husseini returned to a hero's welcome in Egypt. The reaction offered an example of what the OSS analysts had in mind. On June 11, 1946, Hassan Al-Banna, the leader of the Muslim Brotherhood, sent a statement to officials of the Arab League:

> Al-Ikhwan Al-Muslimin [the Muslim Brotherhood] and all Arabs request the Arab League on which Arab hopes are pinned, to declare that the Mufti is welcome to stay in any Arab country he may choose and that great welcome should be extended to im wherever he goes, as a sign of appreciation for his great services for the glory of Islam and the Arabs...The hearts of the Arabs palpitated with joy at hearing that the Mufti has succeeded in reaching as Arab country ... What a hero, what a miracle of a man ... *Yes, this hero who challenged an empire and fought Zionism, with the help of Hitler and Germany. Germany and Hitler are gone, but Amin Al-Husseini will continue the struggle*...God entrusted him with a mission and he must succeed ... The Lord Almighty did not preserve Amin for nothing. There must be a divine purpose behind the preservation of the life of this man, namely the defeat of Zionism. Amin! March on! God is with you! We are behind you! We are willing to sacrifice our necks for the cause. To death! Forward March.[44]

For Al-Banna to write that Germany and Hitler were gone, but that Husseini would "continue the struggle" the struggle against "the criminal British and against Zionism" gave the impression that it was the *same* "struggle" as before. If this was the same struggle, then who better to play a leading role than a political and religious leader with experience in fighting the enemy. Far from criticizing Husseini for having sided with "Germany and Hitler," al-Banna expressed admiration for his wartime activities. Living in wartime Egypt, al-Banna and the members of the

Muslim Brotherhood would have been able to hear what Husseini and others on Axis radio had to say about the Jews and the Allies. It was these words and actions that he found so admirable. Moreover, Husseini's survival, "escape" and arrival in Cairo were proof that God approved as well.

In 1950, Sayyid Qutb, the leading ideological figure of the Muslim Brotherhood and one whose writings have inspired radical Islamists, wrote an essay entitled "Our Struggle with the Jews."[45] It was republished in Saudi Arabia in 1970. Qutb attacked the Jews for their presumably ancient hatred of Islam, evident again in the formation of the state of Israel. The Jews, he wrote, had disobeyed Allah for centuries. Allah had punished them but they refused to listen. Finally, Allah sent Hitler to punish the Jews. Qutb did not deny the extermination of Europe's Jews. On the contrary, he justified an extermination which had taken place. We don't know if Qutb had read the leaflet produced by the SS. In any case, the idea that Hitler was a messenger from Allah sent to earth to do battle with the Jews that emerged from SS think tanks in 1944 (and which German diplomats in Iran had observed in Mosques there by 1941) was repeated in Qutb's postwar pamphlet.

Following his return to the Middle East, Husseini became the titular leader of the Palestinian national movement. In 1948, the Palestine National Council, meeting in Gaza, unanimously chose Husseini to be its president, putting him at the head of the leading organization of Palestinian nationalism and the precursor to the Palestinian Liberation Organization, which was founded in 1964.[46] Husseini rejected all efforts to reach a compromise with the Jews in Palestine and played a central role in organizing armed units to engage in what he called the "holy jihad," his term for the Arab war on the new state of Israel in 1948.[47] Husseini's political preeminence and his ascendency over moderate Palestinians constitute powerful evidence that at very least his partisanship for Nazism and his broadcast hatred for the Jews and Zionism during World War II did not disqualify him from continued participation in political life. The ideological fusion between Nazism and Islamism, an ideology that he helped to fashion in wartime Berlin, thus had an afterlife in the Middle East.

The scholarship of recent years has two implications that bear mention in conclusion. First, it has deepened our understanding of Nazi Germany's efforts to extend the Final Solution to the Jews of North Africa and the Middle East, and of the Nazi regime's willingness and ability to find collaborators among some radical Arab nationalists and Islamists. One important chapter in the history of the Islamist terror of our own time was written in Nazi Berlin. Second, this recent scholarship has also shown that Islamist hatred of the Jews existed before the foundation of the state of Israel in 1948. It not only was or even primarily the result of its foundation but was, instead, a major cause of the ensuing conflict. The selective readings of the traditions of Islam and their fusion with Europe's twentieth-century ideologies of fascism and Nazism offered by the twentieth century's Islamists and their successors such as Haj Amin el-Husseini and al-Banna played a key role in this history. Collaboration in the service of Nazi propaganda during World War II and the Holocaust constituted an important chapter in the longer and larger history of the global shift in the center of anti-Semitism from Europe to the Middle East.

Notes

1. This chapter draws on Jeffrey Herf, *Nazi Propaganda for the Arab World* (New Haven: Yale University Press, 2009; pb. 2010). Also see Jeffrey Herf, "Nazi Germany's Propaganda Aimed at Arabs and Muslims During World War II and the Holocaust: Old Themes, New Archival Findings," in *Central European History*, Volume 42, Issue 04, December 2009, pp. 709–736.
2. See Robert Wistrich, *A Lethal Obsession: Anti-Semitism from Antiquity to the Global Jihad* (New York: Random House, 2010).
3. On Hitler's Nazi Germany's enthusiasm for Islam as he and his government understood it, see the valuable study by David Motadel, *Islam and Nazi Germany's War* (Cambridge, MA.: Harvard University Press, 2014.
4. See Matthias Küntzel, "Das Erbe des Mufti," in *Tribune: Zeitschrift zum Verständnis des Judentums,* 46, No. 184, December 2007), pp. 151–158; also at: http://www.matthiaskuentzel.de/contents/das-erbe-des-mufti
5. On Husseini and the Baludan conference see Zvi Elpeleg, *The Grand Mufti: Haj Amin al-Hussaini, Founder of the Palestinian National Movement*, trans. David Harvey, ed. Shmuel Himelstein (London: Frank Cass, 1993), pp. 47–48.
6. Haj Amin el-Husseini, "Islam-Judentum. Aufruf des Großmufti an die islamische Welt im Jahre 1937," in Mohamed Sabry, *Islam-Judentum-Bolschewismus* (Berlin: Junker and Düunnhaupt, 1938), pp. 22–32. Husseini gave a similar version of the speech to members of the Bosnian SS division in 1943. For an English translation,

see Zeni Lebl, *Haj Amin el-Husseini and National Socialism* (Belgrade: Cigoya Stampa, 2007).

7. See Zvi Elpeleg, *The Grand Mufti: Haj Amin al-Hussaini, Founder of the Palestinian National Movement*, trans. David Harvey (London: Frank Cass, 1993); and Klaus Gensicke, *Der Mufti von Jerusalem und die Nationalsozialisten: Eine politische Biographie Amin el-Husseinis* (Darmstadt: Wissenschaftliche Buchgesellschaft, 2007); Lukasz Hirszowicz, *The Third Reich and the Arab East* (London: Routledge and Kegan Paul, 1966); Philip Mattar, *The Mufti of Jerusalem: Al-Hajj Amīn al- usaynī and the Palestinian national movement* (New York: Columbia University Press, 1988); Joseph Schechtman, *The Mufti and the Führer: The Rise and Fall of Haj Amin el-Husseini* (New York, T. Yoseloff, 1965).
8. Kult.R.Ref. VIII (VII) (Orient) Mn/P/B *Kultureller Talk vom 3. Dezember 1940, "Ein Blatt über die Besetzung der Englander in Ägypten,"* Berlin (December 3, 1940), *BAB R901 Auswärtiges Amt, R73039 Rundfunkabteilung, Ref. VIII Arabische und Iranische Sendungen, vorl. 39, Dez. 1940–Jan. 1941,* p, 2.
9. Kult.R.Ref. VIII (VII) (Orient) Mn/P/B *Kultureller Talk vom 3. Dezember 1940, "Ein Blatt über die Besetzung der Englander in Ägypten,"* Berlin (December 3, 1940), *BAB R901 Auswärtiges Amt, R73039 Rundfunkabteilung, Ref. VIII Arabische und Iranische Sendungen, vorl. 39, Dez. 1940–Jan. 1941,* p. 2.
10. Jeffrey Herf, *Reactionary Modernism: Technology, Culture and Politics in Weimar and the Third Reich* (New York: Cambridge University Press, 1984).
11. "Zur Regierungserklärung für die Araber," Talk vom 12. Dezember 1940 (arabisch), BAB) R901 Auswärtiges Amt, R73039 Rundfunkabteilung, Ref. VIII Arabische und Iranische Sendungen, vorl. 39, Dez. 1940–Jan. 1941, Kult.R, Ref. VIII (Orient), Mu/Scha, pp. 11–13.
12. Ibid.
13. On Haj Amin al-Husseini and Rashid Ali el Khilani in Berlin, see Elpeleg, *The Grand Mufti;* Gensicke, *Der Mufti von Jerusalem und die Nationalsozialisten;* Michael Mallmann and Martin Cuppers, *Halbmond und Hakenkreuz: Das Dritte Reich, die Araber und Palästina* (Darmstadt: Wissenschaftliche Buchgesellschaft, 2006), 105–120; and Hirszowicz, *The Third Reich and the Arab East*, 211–228.

14. On this, see Peter Longerich, *Propagandisten im Krieg: die Presseabteilung des Auswärtigen Amtes unter Ribbentrop,* (Munich: R. Oldenbourg, 1987).
15. "No. 515, Memorandum by an Official of the Foreign Minister's Secretariat, Record of the Conversation between the Führer and the Grand Mufti of Jerusalem on November 28, 1941, in the Presence of Reich Foreign Minister and Minster Grobba in Berlin," Berlin (November 30, 1941), *DGFP Series D (1937–1945) Volume XIII, The War Years,* June 23–December 11, 1941, pp. 881–882, p. 884.
16. Alexander Kirk, "Telegram Sent, September 13, 8 p.m., 1941 to Department of State form Cairo Legation, Number 1361," pp. 1–3, NARA RG84, Cairo Legation and Embassy, Secret and Confidential General Records, 1939, 1941–1947, 1941, 820.02–830, Entry 2412, 350/55/6/5, Box 4, Folder 820.02 1941.
17. Alexander Kirk to Secretary of State, "Telegram 340, General Summary of Tendencies in Axis Broadcasts in Arabic," Cairo (April 18, 1942), NARA, RG659, United States Department of State, Central Decimal File, 1940–1944, 740.0011/European War 1939, Microfilm Records M982, Roll 114, p. 21414.
18. Alexander Kirk to Secretary of State, "Telegram 340, General Summary of Tendencies in Axis Broadcasts in Arabic," Cairo (April 18, 1942), pp. 1–2.
19. "Despatch No. 502 from the American Legation at Cairo, Egypt, Axis Broadcasts in Arabic for the Period July 3 to 9, 1942, Cairo, July 21, 1942," NARA, RG 84 Foreign Service Posts of the Department of State, General Records, Cairo Embassy, 1942, 815.4–820.02, Box 77, p. 1.
20. Ibid., pp. 1–2.
21. "KILL THE JEWS BEFORE THEY KILL YOU," Ibid., p. 13.
22. Ibid, pp. 13–14.
23. On the blunt nature of Nazi Germany's German-language propaganda, see Jeffrey Herf, *The Jewish Enemy: Nazi Propaganda during World War II and the Holocaust* (Cambridge, MA: Harvard University Press, 2006).
24. Mallmann and Cuppers, *Halbmond und Hakenkreuz,* chs. 7–9.
25. Lampson, "From Cairo to Foreign Office, No. 1115," Cairo (April 26, 1941), NA, FO 371/27430 18, J1158. Also see Miles

Lampson Killearn, *The Killearn Diaries, 1934–1946: The Diplomatic and Personal Record of Lord Killearn* (London: Sidwick and Jackson, 1972); and M.E. Yapp, ed. *Politics and diplomacy in Egypt: the diaries of Sir Miles Lampson, 1935–1937* (Oxford: by Oxford University Press, 1997). Also see Lampson to Mr. [Anthony] Eden, "No. 156, General Review of Political Developments in Egypt ... 1941," Cairo (February 12, 1942), NA, FO 371/31569, Egypt and Sudan File No. 18, J111/38/16, 34, 35, 36; also see Herf, *Nazi Propaganda for the Arab World*, 94–95.

26. Ibid., 82.
27. In *Confronting Fascism in Egypt: Dictatorship versus Democracy in the 1930s* (Stanford, CA: Stanford University Press, 2010) Israel Gershoni and James Jankowski examine Egyptian opposition to fascism and Nazism.
28. Berlin in Arabic, September 8, 1943, "Talk: The Ambitions of the Jews," Alexander Kirk to Secretary of State, Cairo (September 23, 1943), "No. 1313, Axis Broadcasts in Arabic for the period September 2 to 8, 1943," NARA, RG 84, Foreign Service Posts of the Department of State, Egypt: Cairo Embassy General Records, 1933–1955, 820.00–822.00, 1943, Entry 2410, 350/55/1-6/2-5, Box 93. For my discussion of Goebbels "Do You Want Total War?" speech see Jeffrey Herf, *The Jewish Enemy,* op. cit., pp. 192–196.
29. Ibid.
30. Voice of Free Arabism, November 3, 1943, 8:15 P.M., "Palestine between the Bolsheviks and the Jews," Alexander Kirk to Secretary of State, Cairo (November 19, 1943), pp. 6–7, "No. 1410, Axis Broadcasts in Arabic for the period November 3 to 9, 1943," pp. 1–2, NARA, RG 84, Foreign Service Posts of the Department of State, Egypt: Cairo Embassy General Records, 1933–1955, 820.00–822.00, 1943, Entry 2410, 350/55/1-6/2-5, Box 93.
31. Ibid.
32. Voice of Free Arabism, November 5, 1943, 6:30 P.M., "The protests of the Moslems of Europe against the Balfour Declaration," Alexander Kirk to Secretary of State, Cairo (November 19, 1943), "No. 1410, Axis Broadcasts in Arabic for the period November 3 to 9, 1943," pp. 3–4, NARA, RG 84, Foreign Service Posts of the Department of State, Egypt: Cairo Embassy General Records,

1933–1955, 820.00–822.00, 1943, Entry 2410, 350/55/1-6/2-5, Box 93.

33. Ibid., 297878–879.
34. Ibid., 297880.
35. "Weekly Review of Foreign Broadcasts, F.C.C., No. 118, 3/4/44, Near and Middle East," NARA, RG165 Records of the War Department General and Special Staff, Military Intelligence Division, "Regional File." 1922–1944 Palestine, Entry 77, 390/33/07/6-7, Box 2719, Folder 2930.
36. Heinrich Himmler "An das Reichssicherheitshauptamt, Berlin" (May 14, 1943), *Bundesarchiv Berlin* (BAB) (microfiche) NS19/3544, p. 29. On this effort see Herf, *Nazi Propaganda for the Arab World*, 194–204.
37. Members of the "Orient Research Office" in Tübingen included SS Sturmbannführer Wilhelm Beisner and experts "Dr. Otto Rössler" and "Dr. Lorch." On Beisner, see "Beisner, Wilhelm," in Klee, *Das Personenlexikon zum Dritten Reich,* op. cit., p. 37. Also see Horst Junginger, *Von der philologischen zur voelkischen Religionswissenschaft* (Tuebingen: Steiner Verlag, 1999. On Amt VI seeMi chael Fahlbusch, "Reichssicherheitshauptamt Abteilung VI G (Reichssitftung fuer Laenderkunde)": in Michael Fahlbusch and Ingo Haar, eds., *Handbuch der voelkischen Wissenschaften,* Munich: Saur, 2008, pp. 545–555.
38. Ibid.
39. Zeischka, *"Druck und Verbreitung von Flugblättern in arabischen Ländern, Anlage 2, Übersetzung aus dem Arabischen,"* Berlin (January 26, 1944).
40. Ibid. Translation by Andrew Masloski.
41. Zeischka, *RSHA, Amt VI, "Propaganda in arabischen Ländern,"* Berlin (January 27, 1944), *BAB*) R55/20712, *RMVP.*
42. "'The Near East and the War Crimes Problem': Office of Strategic Services, Research and Analysis Branch, R and A, No. 1090.116, 23 June 1945, Situation Report: Near East, Analysis of Current Intelligence for the Use of OSS," pp. 1–28, in NARA, RG84, Foreign Service Posts of the Department of State, Syria: Damascus Legation, Confidential File, 1945: Vol. 1–2, 030-800B, Classified General Records, Entry 3248A, 350/69/5/6-7, Box 4, Vol. II, 711-800B.
43. Ibid., "Summary."

44. "Hassan Al-Banna and the Mufti of Palestine" in "Contents of Secret Bulletin of Al Ikhwan al-Muslimin dated 11 June 1946," Cairo (July 23, 1946). NARA RG 226 (Office of Strategic Services) Washington Registry SI Intelligence, Field Files, Entry 108A, 190/16/28/3-7, Box 15, Folder 2.
45. For the English translation, see Ronald Nettler, *Past Trials and Present Tribulations: A Muslim Fundamentalist's View of the Jews* (Oxford: Pergamon Press, 1987).
46. Herf, *Nazi Propaganda for the Arab World*, xi–xv; and Elpeleg, *The Grand Mufti*, 79–118.
47. On the use of the term "Jihad," during the war of 1948 see Benny Morris, *1948: The First Arab-Israeli War* (New Haven: Yale University Press, 2008). On Arab rejectionism in the years preceding the war of 1948, see the discussion of the Anglo-American Committee of Inquiry Regarding the Problem of European Jewry and Palestine" in Norman Goda, ed. et al., *To the Gates of Jerusalem: The Diaries and Papers of James G McDonald, 1945–1947* (Bloomington, IN.: Indiana University Press, 2014).

CHAPTER 9

Iranian Antisemitism and the Holocaust

Meir Litvak

Until very recently, the Islamic Republic of Iran was the only country whose leadership, official media, and a plethora of semi-academic institutions employed an unambiguous antisemitic discourse culminating in the denial and justification of the Holocaust. Iranian spokesmen as well as Western apologists of the Islamic regime often claimed that Iran distinguishes between Zionism and Judaism, and that this rhetoric is merely anti-Zionist, and therefore perfectly legitimate. Others contend that it is primarily a foreign policy tool intended to rally the support of the frustrated Arab masses behind Iran's regional policies. However, as I will show, Iranian discourse is thoroughly antisemitic in seeking to demonize the Jews as a whole, not just Zionists, often conflating both. In addition, while it serves Iran's regional aspirations, antisemitism constituted and continues to do so albeit in a toned down fashion, an important component of the Islamic Republic's official ideology directed at both Iranian and foreign audiences. In the past, the denial and occasional justification of the Holocaust represented the height of this antisemitism and had the purpose not only of demonizing the Jews but also of legitimating calls for the destruction of the state of Israel.

M. Litvak (✉)
Tel Aviv University, Tel Aviv, Israel

A. McElligott, J. Herf (eds.), *Antisemitism Before and Since the Holocaust*, DOI 10.1007/978-3-319-48866-0_9

Historically, Iran's record on tolerance of the Jews ever since it became a Shi'i state following its unification by the Safavid dynasty in 1501 is a poor one. In addition to imposing social and economic restrictions on the Jews, it was the only Muslim country to experience at the time mass forced conversions of Jews.[1] These anti-Jewish traits continued well into the nineteenth century under the Qajar dynasty. The root cause for the precarious situation of Iranian Jews was Shi'i religious intolerance, which greatly exceeded the common practice toward "protected minorities" (*ahl al-dhimma*) in Sunni countries. Most conspicuous was the doctrine of Jewish ritual impurity (*nejasat*), which perceived that anything touched by Jews to be ritually unclean and, therefore, untouchable by Muslims.[2]

A new element that appeared in the late nineteenth century was the influence of European racism and the myths of Aryan racial superiority on various Westernized Iranians. Such ideas retained a certain influence during the reign of Reza Shah (1925–1941), who was allegedly an admirer of Nazi Germany.[3] Conversely, the reign of his son Mohammad Reza Shah (1941–1979) was the "Golden era" of Iranian Jewry, which reached unprecedented achievements both intellectually and materially. It was also a period of extensive Iranian–Israeli economic, military, and strategic cooperation. Concurrently, various clerics and pro-Islamist intellectuals voiced and disseminated strong anti-Zionist and anti-Jewish attacks.[4]

The 1960s marked a turning point in the rise of antisemitism in Iran due to the growing rift between the Shah and the Islamic opposition which exacerbated Iranian Islamic animosity toward Israel for its alliance with the Shah. A shift took place in Iranian intellectual discourse from the perception of Western institutions and ideas as the solution to Iran's problems to open animosity toward the West as the source and cause of these problems. This change had important ramifications for attitudes toward Zionism and Judaism, which were now perceived by the Shah's opponents as offshoots of Western imperialism set up in order to oppress the Muslims.[5] Yet, it was Ayatollah Ruhallah Khomeini, who emerged in 1963 as the leader of the Islamist opposition to the shah, who incorporated antisemitism as an important component of his overall religious and political doctrine.[6] Therefore, following the 1979 Revolution and the emergence of the clergy under Khomeini's leadership, as the new rulers of Iran, antisemitism became an integral component of the regime's ideology and political discourse, even if Iran's Jewish population per se, as "people of the book," were not targeted for discrimination.[7]

Contemporary Iranian antisemitism contains several modern features, which distinguish it from the traditional anti-Jewish attitudes. In the past, anti-Judaism in Iran was led by a powerful and confident clerical establishment against the small and defenseless Jewish minority with the intention of eventually converting them to Islam. It was manifested by various legal and social restrictions against the Jews and was disseminated through anti-Jewish statements and commentaries on Islamic legal writings as well as in religious polemics against Judaism. The content carried a distinct Shi'i mark, manifested in the emphasis if not obsession with the impurity (*nejasat*) of the Jew.

The content of the antisemitic discourse in the Islamic Republic is similar to that of all other Islamist movements in the region and is influenced by Sunni movements and by Arab countries. Unlike the past, Iranian Jews are not the target. In fact they enjoy tolerance, though not full equality, under the Islamic regime in order to show that under the benevolent rule of Islam Jews can live in peace as a protected subordinated minority, and therefore, there is no justification for the aspiration of Jewish sovereignty, that is, Zionism. The targets of Iranian antisemitism today are the Jewish people as a group as well as Jewish culture and history, and in particular the political manifestation of Judaism, that is Zionism. Thus, the issue of Jewish *Nejasat* or impurity, which had been so important in the past, has been dropped completely as current Supreme Leader Ayatollah Ali Khamene'i has stated.[8] The uniquely Iranian elements of this discourse are the central role of the government, the extent of the antisemitic written production and the broad effort to endow it with a mantle of scholarly respectability.[9] For example, a search in the semi-official website Hawzah.net produces over 1200 references to Jews in periodical articles and over 3000 references in newspaper articles published since 2005 alone.[10] The seeming contradiction between Iranian treatment of its own Jewish community and the anti-Jewish discourse may be the outcome of several factors. First, antisemitism has always contained contradictions being based on prejudice and not on rational reasons, and on various occasions antisemites had their own "favorite Jew" which they differentiated from the Jewish whole. In addition, various Iranians appear to distinguish between the local Jewish community, which "behaves well" and knows its place as a subordinated minority. Conversely, the Jews as a group, as a concept, or as an abstract are associated with the perceived threats and challenges facing Islam and the Muslims in the modern age. As in other cases of anti-Westernism or Occidentalism, the Jews and the West are perceived as intertwined and the Jews are viewed as epitomizing the West.[11] David Nirenberg's term "anti-Judaism," which does not denote "simply an attitude toward Jews and their religion," but "a powerful theoretical framework for making sense of the world" perhaps best explains the Iranian situation. Accordingly, anti-Judaism puts old ideas about Judaism to new kinds of work in thinking about the world, it engaged the past and transformed it, and reshaped the possibilities for thought in the future."[12]

While the Iranian government since the 1979 Revolution, like most if not all Islamist movements, usually rejected Western cultural influence as an anathema to authentic Islamic culture, it did not hesitate from borrowing anti-Jewish themes from the same West in the service of its cause. Thus, the new approach fuses anti-Jewish elements from the Koran and early Islamic traditions together with modern Western antisemitic themes. It rests on the belief that Jews and Judaism have been hostile toward Islam from its inception and Jews and Zionism are a part of the Western cultural challenge and threat to Islam as a religion, identity, and culture. In other words, it reflects the anger of the Muslim world vis-à-vis the West and the crisis of Islam in the modern period. It thus stems from a widespread feeling of a threatened Islam, which is subject to Western economic and political domination and whose identity and culture are under attack by Western civilization.

Islamic fundamentalism at large requires the existence of a foreign conspiracy in order to find some external reason for Muslim weakness and dependence. Thus, Khomeini, who had set the basic contours of modern Iranian antisemitism, charges in the first page of his major political book *Velayat-e Faqih: Hukumat-e Eslami* (The governance of the jurist: Islamic government) that "from the very beginning," Islam "was afflicted by the Jews, for it was they who established anti-Islamic propaganda and engaged in various stratagems," against the Muslims.[13] In recent years, following Khomeini's model, Iranian religious and scholarly journals have published numerous articles which discuss various aspects of supposed Jewish animosity and activities against the Prophet Muhammad[14] or elaborate the evil traits of the Jews as described in the Koran.[15] The frequent references to the early Islamic period, particularly to Muslim military victories over the Jews and their expulsion from the Arabian Peninsula are also designed to serve as a model for resolving the current conflict and as a source of encouragement for the inevitable outcome of the struggle.[16]

Moreover, Khomeini charged that in the modern period, the Jews joined with other groups that were "even more satanic than they" in order to facilitate the imperialist penetration of the Muslim countries. Their main goal was the "extirpation of Islam" since "Islam and its ordinances" were the "main obstacle in the path of their materialistic ambitions." In addition, the West, consisting of Jewish and Christian elements, resisted the righteous cause of Islam to expand to the "four corners of the globe."[17] The Jews "may God curse them," Khomeini wrote, "are opposed to the very foundations of Islam and wish to establish Jewish domination throughout the world." Like other Islamic thinkers, Khomeini sometimes described the Jews as fifth columnists in the world of Islam and as agents of the West, and at other times, as the real power behind the West in its offensive against Islam.[18]

While claiming to distinguish between Judaism and Zionism, in fact Iranian leaders frequently conflated the two. Thus, Khomeini maintained that the clearest manifestation of the Jewish–Christian conspiracy against Islam was the establishment of Israel by Western imperialism in order to oppress the Muslims. Moreover, he claimed that as the Jews are burdened with the wrath of God and are condemned to eternal humiliation and subordination to Muslims because of their evil deeds, their very claim for statehood was and is considered to be a direct affront to Islam and to the natural historical order. Thus, whoever advances this claim must be corrupt and evil.[19] Such views were reiterated by Iran's former president Mahmud Ahmadinejad (2005–2013), who stated in August 2012 that "It has now been some 400 years that a horrendous Zionist clan has been ruling the major world affairs, and behind the scenes of the major power circles, in political, media, monetary and banking organizations in the world, they have been the decision makers." Since the Zionist movement only emerged in the late nineteenth century, Ahmadinejad conflated Judaism and Zionism in his polemic. Similarly, Ayatollah Ahmad Khatami, Tehran's deputy Friday preacher, lashed out at the "Zionists, whose crimes against the Muslims date back to the early days of Islam," while not explicitly including the Jewish minority in his tirade.[20] Such charges that link the past and the present typify Islamic polemics in general.[21] Thus, Grand Ayatollah Hossein Nuri-Hamadani referred to the Jews of Medina at the time of the Prophet as "the center of Zionists." He further described the massacre of 700 of the Jews of Medina in a single day as a "step toward strengthening Islam, in order to crush the bastion of the global arrogance." In so doing, he too linked the Jews of the seventh century with the present-day West or "global arrogance" in Iranian terminology.[22]

Another expression of the fusion between past and present, apparently under inspiration from Arab countries, is the resort to Iranian or even pre-Islamic Persian history. Dr. Hasan 'Abbasi, who served as a representative of Supreme Leader Khamenei's office in the Revolutionary Guards, modified the Biblical story of Esther, which states that the Jews killed 70,000 of their enemies throughout the Achaemenid Empire following the fall of Haman by claiming that the Jews had massacred more than 70,000 Persians. He presented this alleged episode as an example of Jewish brutality and enmity toward Iran, which continues to the present day. Under the title "Iranian Holocaust" other semi-official Iranian websites disseminated this tale of the Jewish massacre of Persians.[23] Since the beginning of the millennium, Abdollah Shahbazi, a former head of the state-run Political Studies and Research Institute (PSRI) and a well-known historian in Iran, has pursued the theme of Jewish conspiracy against Iran in a five-volume study titled *The Jew and Parsi Plutocrats, British Imperialism and Iran*, which contains conspiratorial anti-Jewish themes related to modern Iranian history, and which has been uploaded to his website.[24] In other articles, Shahbazi elaborated on the supposed role of "Zionist networks" and of the role of Jews, as Jews, in the secretive British efforts to elevate Reza Shah Pahlavi, the ultimate arch-villain in modern Iranian history, to power in 1921.[25]

In a TV debate, devoted to Jewish conspiracies, the participants explained how Iran has become "a target for the plans of Jewish societies in all of Europe," and spoke of the role of wealthy Jews in bringing about the 1921 Pahlavi coup d'etat. Dr. Sayyid Hamid Rouhani, of the Islamic Revolution university, asserted that the Jews "wanted Iran to be ruled by somebody who would implement and promote their anti-Islamic conspiracy, so that later, they would be able to bring the filthy Bahai party to power." Shams al-Din Rahmani former deputy director of the Institute for the Intellectual Development of Children and Young Adults, concluded that "[t]he sole reason the Reza Shah and the Pahlavi dynasty were brought to power was to enable the Jews and the Freemasons to take control of Iran."[26] In other words, these scholars turned the Jews into the direct enemy of Iran, not just of the Muslim world, probably in an attempt to appeal to those Iranians who were more attuned to Iranian nationalism than to Islamist ideology.

One of the most notorious manifestations of the theme of Jewish conspiracies, which also reflects the borrowing of antisemitic themes from the West, is the publication of the *Protocols of the Elders of Zion*, in translated installments by the establishment newspapers *Ettela'at* and *Jomhuri-ye Eslami* and in at least four book editions. Meanwhile, Iran's Islamic Propaganda Organization exhibited its edition at the Iranian pavilion at the 2005 Frankfurt book fair, with an additional large selection of English-language antisemitic books published in Iran sold at the same booth without interference from the German authorities. Iranian TV regularly broadcasts documentaries and drama shows based on the Protocols.[27] The appearance of the Protocols in various nongovernmental Persian-language websites may be another indication of their dissemination in Iran.[28] Another prominent borrowed theme is the blood libel, which had originated in Europe. Iranian academics have appeared on state TV to offer detailed explanations about how Jewish rabbis in Europe used to kill Christian children and take their blood for use during the Passover holidays.[29] Bringing together all the anti-Jewish motifs, Iran's vice-president Mohammad-Reza Rahimi accused the Zionists at an international antidrug conference cosponsored by Iran and the United Nations (UN) on June 26, 2012, of controlling the global drug trade based on the teachings of the Talmud. He further told stories of gynecologists killing black babies on the orders of the Zionists and claimed that the Bolshevik Revolution in 1917 was started by Jews, adding that mysteriously no Jews died in that uprising.[30]

The logical conclusion from these charges was that the Jews were, in the words of a former scholar, Professor Heshmatollah Qanbari "satanic" and "anti-human," as well as the source of "all corrupt traits in humanity." Moreover, Jewish corruption was a threat to humanity at large. Ayatollah Mohammad Taqi Mesbah Yazdi, the man widely regarded as the gray eminence behind the ultraconservative faction in Iranian politics stated that "the majority of centers of corruption in the world belong to Jews and Zionists." They try to corrupt the others and thus rule the world and added that "the Jews are the most corrupt in the world. You don't find such a tribe in any other nation, country or region." And "Jews are the most seditious group among all human beings and they will not leave Muslims alone until they destroy Islam."[31] Similarly, Mohammad-Ali Ramin, official advisor to President Ahmadinejad, declared that "[t]hroughout history, this religious group [i.e. the Jews] has inflicted the most damage on the human race, while some groups within it engaged in plotting against other nations and ethnic groups to cause cruelty, malice and wickedness."[32] It should be noted that the term "corruption in earth" (*fasad fi alarz*) has been coined by Khomeini to refer to anti-regime opposition and has entered the Iranian penal code as a crime deserving the death sentence.[33] Thus, Khomeini explained that since the Jews of Bani Qurayza were "causing corruption in Muslim society and harming Islam and the Islamic state," the Prophet "eliminated them." The modern goal behind these depictions of the Jews as corrupting all human societies may be inferred by one of Shahbazi's new books, which is called *The Beginnings and End of the Children of Israel*.[34]

Alongside the wide-ranging attacks on Judaism and Zionism, quite a few writers reject the charges of antisemitism. They describe this allegation as a malicious ploy in the psychological warfare which the Zionists wage against their enemies to deflect criticism from their hideous actions.[35] One writer, for instance, who denies the existence of antisemitism as a historical phenomenon, explains that "Jewishness" (*yahudiyat*) in itself is the problem. Being Jewish is essentially embracing both a sense of superiority over other people and deep fears and paranoia from them. Or in his words, Judaism is neither race nor religion, but in fact a "mental disease" (*bimar-e ravani*). The only solution for the Jews to cure this disease is to reject and deny Judaism.[36]

The various antisemitic arguments and portrayals of the Jews, mentioned above, culminated in the Iranian preoccupation with the Holocaust. Iran's former president Mahmud Ahmadinejad earned notoriety during his presidency for his repeated denial of the Holocaust. However, Holocaust denial did not start with him. Rather, it began among senior members of Iran's political and clerical elites, first and foremost Supreme Leader Khamene'i. However, it certainly underwent a qualitative leap under Ahmadinejad.

The first point to make is that Iranian Holocaust denial is not a consequence of ignorance of historical facts. The great effort to provide denial a pseudo-scientific basis reflects a certain awareness of the enormity of the valid evidence on the Holocaust. In addition, the widespread reliance on Western Holocaust deniers is a product of selective and manipulative reading and borrowing of material published in the West and of a conscious disregard for the vast scholarly output dealing with the Holocaust that does not suit ideological convictions. It also reflects the broader phenomenon of the narrow and superficial cultural borrowing from the West, which is typical of Islamist movements in general. However, whereas in Europe Holocaust deniers represent fringe elements that are rejected by members of mainstream intellectual and academic circles, in Iran, senior government officials and state or quasi-state media play the leading role in

Holocaust denial, frequently endorsing the Western deniers. Consequently, they prevent the Iranian public from exposure to serious historical scholarship about the Holocaust.

The Iranian discourse attributes the "Holocaust myth" (*afsaneh*) or "fabrication" (*dorugh*), to a Zionist–American alliance which exploited the common goal of the struggle against the Nazis during the war for the malevolent political goals of both parties. The advocates of this discourse assert that Zionism lacks any moral or historical justification and rests on a series of unfounded historical myths and outright distortions. They view the Holocaust as one of the major myths that Zionism invented in order to gain Western political and financial support. They label the murder of millions of Jews in Europe by Nazi Germany to be a falsehood and a "ridiculous pretext through which the Zionists, by fabricating and propagating it, managed to convince public opinion of the need to establish a Jewish state" in the midst of Muslim lands. The Zionists used this "myth" in order to fight anti-Zionism, which was rife throughout Europe before the war, seeking to "make the Jews look oppressed so they could achieve their murderous goals in other parts of the world." Concurrently, they claim that the United States used the Holocaust myth as a means for expanding its influence as a superpower "searching for colonies in the world and in Europe."[37] Like other Islamist movements, the Iranian government has turned the United States, rather than Nazi Germany into the real criminal-state during the Second World War, since it views Western (i.e. American) culture as the greatest threat to Islamic civilization. Supreme Leader Khamene'i established the contours of the denial theme line in a speech made in April 2001 maintaining that the "Zionists had exaggerated Nazi crimes against European Jewry in order to solicit international support for the establishment of the Zionist entity in 1948."[38]

Meanwhile, Mohammad Ali Ramin found additional reasons for the fabrication of the Holocaust myth, which combined antisemitism with Iran's ideological enmity to the West. In a conspiracy theory of gargantuan proportions, he first asserted that Britain and the United States wanted to prevent Germany from emerging as a major European power by presenting it as "a human-burning nation." Second, he postulated the existence of an American–British plot in cooperation with Zionism to create the state of Israel in the midst of the Islamic world in order to control it using the pretext of the Holocaust. Third, referring to the traditional animosity between Christians and Jews, he claimed that the United States and Britain, with the cooperation of France, Russia and Germany came up with the idea of the Holocaust after the Second World War in order to scare off the Jews and send them to what is now Israel in order to get rid of them in Europe and America. The state of Israel would, in turn, provoke the Muslims to rise up, confront the Jews, and massacre them. "This [conspiracy]" he said, "conducted by Europe and America, would lead to the total annihilation of global Jewry."[39]

The use of Holocaust denial as a means to delegitimize Israel was also evident in the frequent comparisons between Zionism and Nazism, and between the "Gestapo-like" policies of Israel and those of Hitler, by Iranian spokesmen and the official media. Thus Ali Akbar Rafsanjani, formerly second highest ranking person in the Iranian hierarchy, equated Zionist ideology, which considered the Jews "to be a unique and superior race," with Hitler's identical belief regarding the German nation.[40] While vilifying Israel, such comparisons served to belittle the scope of Nazi crimes and atrocities. In his sermon on Qods (Jerusalem) day on 23 January 1998, Rafsanjani "denounced Israel as 'much worse than Hitler,'" stating that the Zionists "killed more than one million Palestinians and made millions vagrant," an action that "is much worse than what Adolph (sic) Hitler did during World War II with the Jews." Priding himself as being "an expert in this field," Rafsanjani calculated that the number of Jews in Europe prior to the Second World War had been less than six million. He conceded that Hitler had "committed injustice against the Jews and other groups," and that he had "oppressed and persecuted Muslims, Christians, atheists [and] Marxists," but insisted that he had killed only 200,000 Jews. The figure of six million Jewish victims was therefore "only a propaganda act by the Zionists."[41]

While the numerous expressions of Holocaust denial reflect, in my view, the genuine convictions of their propagators, they also serve Iranian foreign policy aims. The instrumentalist premise behind Holocaust denial is that refutation of the "lie" would totally undermine Israel's international status and legitimacy and would facilitate its eventual destruction. Or in Ramin's words of "the resolution" of the Holocaust issue would end in the "destruction of Israel."[42] Thus, Iran was the only country to vote against UN Resolution 61/255 concerning Holocaust denial, which was passed on the eve of International Holocaust Memorial Day, January 26, 2007, by a vote of 103 countries in favor. Hoseyn Shari'atmadari, editor of the *Kayhan* daily, which is published by the Supreme Leader's office, denounced the Resolution as "preparing the U.N.'s corpse for burial in the graveyard of history," since it was "opposed to the most basic recognized principles of human rights." He reiterated Iran's position that the Holocaust was a "myth and a contrived story" which had been refuted by "many well-known European and American historians." He complained that the United States and European powers failed to provide "documents and records to prove the Holocaust," and they "threaten those who deny this myth with condemnation."[43]

Iran went further than any Arab country in hosting and officially endorsing Holocaust deniers who faced difficulties in their home countries. Ahmad Rami, a Moroccan exile in Sweden who propagated Holocaust denial on his Radio Islam and was sentenced in 1990 to six months in prison and three years on parole for racial incitement, became a guest of Iran immediately after his release. Rami boasted that his case was discussed in high-governing circles. The Iranian parliament (*Majlis*) held a special session in his honor. Upon his return to Europe, he set up an Internet website in ten languages, named Radio Islam, which was reportedly supported financially by Iran and which engaged in Holocaust denial and antisemitic propaganda.[44] The Swiss neo-Nazi activist Jürgen Graff, who had been sentenced in 1998 to 15 months in jail, fled his homeland and took up political asylum in Iran. He subsequently set out with the assistance of his hosts to organize an international conference for the denial of the Holocaust in Beirut in March 2001.[45]

The most celebrated recipient of Iran's largesse was Holocaust denier Roger Garaudy, author of *The Founding Myths of Israeli Politics.* Garaudy was tried in France in January 1998 and fined according to the Gayssot law adopted in 1990, which bans denial of the Holocaust. As a former Marxist convert to Islam, Garaudy also represented for Iranians and other Middle Eastern Islamists an additional angle, namely the superiority of Islam over the West. The Iranians viewed Western attacks on him as part of the West's attack on Islam. The Iranian media heaped praise on Garaudy's "scholarship" and courage in exposing the Holocaust "big lie" and "myths," and associated his claims and trial with Iran's own animosity toward Jews, Zionism, and the West. It also used the case to expose the alleged fallacy of the Western democratic and liberal systems and ideology.[46] Iran's political elite mobilized to offer its support for Garaudy. Even the reformist president Khatami, who purported to distinguish between anti-Zionism and anti-Judaism, chose Garaudy's trial to contrast the flawed nature of Western democracies, which "do not tolerate what they consider to be opposed to their own interests," with Islamic democracy that "tolerates opposition." Following his conviction, Garaudy was invited to Iran, where he was received by Supreme Leader Khamene'i and then President Khatami. Iran also helped him pay the FR120,000 fine imposed upon him.[47]

Under Ahmadinejad, Iran went further both in sponsoring official Holocaust denial and in its efforts to endow denial with scholarly respectability. As Ahmadinejad has sought to restore the regime's revolutionary goals and ideals, which had suffered a weakening in recent years and to advance Iran's popularity among its Middle Eastern neighbors, he adopted anti-Zionism and Holocaust denial as the two principal pillars of policy. As part of this new momentum, Iran convened on December, 11–12, 2006, an international conference titled "Review of the Holocaust: Global Vision" ostensibly to examine the historical veracity of the Holocaust. Rasoul Mousavi, head of the Foreign Ministry's Institute for Political and International Studies (IPIS), which organized the event, explained the need for the conference as an opportunity for scholars to discuss the subject "away from Western taboos and the restriction imposed on them in Europe."[48] Thus, the alleged lack of academic freedom of inquiry in the West regarding the Holocaust became the premise for holding such a conference. However, the attendance of notorious Holocaust deniers such as ex-Ku Klux Klan leader David Duke, as well as Frederick Toben and Robert Faurisson, revealed the conference's true aim, which was to serve as a public platform for Holocaust denial. The conference announced the establishment of a "world foundation for Holocaust studies" and unanimously appointed Presidential Advisor Ramin as its secretary-general.[49]

Alongside the conference, and officially in response to the cartoons published on the Prophet Muhammad in Denmark, Iran's biggest-selling newspaper *Hamshahri* launched the first International Holocaust Cartoon contest. The Iranian media explained that the contest was also intended to test the limits of freedom of speech in the West and examine whether it was reserved only to "crimes committed by the United States and Israel." Using traditional antisemitic stereotypes, the cartoons portrayed Israel's alleged exploitation of the Holocaust in order to justify its brutality in the Middle East and oppression of Palestinians.[50] Additionally, a 108-page book containing 52 caricatures from the exhibition plus satirical writings was published by the Islamic student movement of the Science and Industry University in 2008. The English translation was published on 27 January 2009, the same day as the international Holocaust Memorial Day marking the liberation of Auschwitz. The cartoons were also uploaded to a special website thus ensuring their wide circulation.[51]

Establishing pseudo scholarly respectability became an important feature of Iranian antisemitism in general and of Holocaust denial in particular. It has been evident in the growing participation of Iranian academics in Holocaust denial and in their adoption of the pseudo-scholarly arguments of Western deniers. Thus, political analyst Hossein Rouyvaran reiterated the lie that gas chambers and crematoria in the Nazi camps of Auschwitz, Mauthausen and Majdanek were used for "disinfecting the clothes and the possessions of the prisoners." Moreover, citing unnamed "researchers" he insisted that "of the several millions who died in the detention facilities, only 150,000 to 250,000 were Jews." While minimizing Nazi crimes, he stated that the real war crime during the Second World War was the American nuclear bombing of Hiroshima and Nagasaki.[52]

Anticipating the Teheran conference, the *Historical Studies Quarterly* (*Faslnamah-e Motale'at-e Ta'rikhi*) published by the Iranian Institute for Contemporary Historical Studies (IICHS) devoted an entire issue (No. 14, Fall 2006) to Holocaust denial, including articles such as "Did 6 Million Really Die?" "Truth Burning Furnaces," and "The School of True History," as well as favorable book reviews on publications of leading Western Holocaust deniers. In the five years since 2007, more than ten books have been published in Iran engaging in Holocaust denial, while other pseudo-scholarly books, articles, and studies continuously "uncover" and analyze the history of Jews and Zionism in antisemitic fashion.[53]

Some Iranian writers in scholarly journals sought to explain the political, financial psychological reasons that stood behind the "production" of the "Holocaust myth." These explanations ranged from Zionist efforts to produce justification and support for the illegitimate state of Israel; Zionist efforts to extort billions of dollars from Germany, Austria, and other countries; and finally to Jewish psychological needs. Accordingly, presenting the Jews as victims and as an oppressed minority throughout history not only prevented criticism against Israeli crimes but also enabled Western Jews to acquire excessive control over the economy and media.[54] Some commentators expressed understanding for the reasons that drove the Nazis to persecute (but not necessarily exterminate) the Jews. Professor Hasa Bokhari, a cultural adviser to the Iranian Education Ministry stated that "if you study European history you will see who the main power to hoard money and wealth, in the 19th century was. In most cases, it is the

Jews. Perhaps that was one of the reasons which caused Hitler to begin the anti-Semitic trend." He recommended that his listeners read the history of the Jews in Europe. It was their history that "ultimately led to Hitler's hatred and resentment."[55]

Rafsanjani found other reasons to rationalize Hitler's policy against the Jews. In a speech commemorating Jerusalem Day in October 2007, Rafsanjani stated that the Nazis' "first objective was to free Europe from the evils of Zionism," and that this was justifiable because "the Zionists who constituted a strong political party in Europe, caused much disorder there. Since the Zionists had a lot of property and controlled an empire of propaganda, they made European governments helpless." What Hitler and the German Nazis did to the Jews of Europe at that time, he added, "was partly due to these circumstances with the Jews. They wanted to expel the Zionists from Europe because they always were a great irritant to the governments there. This is how this calamity fell upon the Muslims, especially the Palestinians." "The first goal was to save Europe from the evil of Zionism, and in this, they have been relatively successful," he concluded.[56]

In a flight of imagination that recycled an old myth, Presidential Advisor Mohammad-Ali Ramin stated in an interview with the Iranian website *Baztab* held in December 2006 that Hitler himself was Jewish, as both his grandmother and mother had been Jewish prostitutes. Ramin then concluded that Hitler simultaneously developed feelings of solidarity with Judaism and hatred toward it, and this emotional ambivalence shaped his behavior toward the Jews. On the one hand, his entire family, the people who shared his views and his associates who brought him into power and stood by him to the last—including his lovers and his personal doctor—were [all] Jewish. Concurrently, he favored the expulsion of the Jews from Central Europe in order to facilitate the establishment of a Jewish government in Palestine and because "exiling the Jews from Europe and Germany was a general and historical demand of the Western Christian nations." Thus, in one interview, Ramin managed to deny the Holocaust, charge Hitler with Judaism and with collaboration with Zionism, thereby implicitly associating Judaism and Zionism with Nazism.[57]

Others too adopted the contradictory claim of denial together with a supposed Nazi-Zionist alliance in killing the Jews; sometimes even reversing the victim/perpetrator roles in the Holocaust.[58] Former *Majlis* (Parliament) Speaker Mehdi Karrubi, often regarded as a moderate reformist in Iranian domestic politics, denied the Holocaust, yet stated in an anti-Zionist rally in October 2000 that "Hitler's massacre of innocent

Jews in Germany was a conspiracy of the Zionists." "The first premier and the founder of the regime, which occupied Palestine," he added, was himself involved in these activities as he handed over 40,000 Jews to Hitler in order to carry out that plan.[59] Similarly, "historian" Abdollah Shahbazi contended that a joint effort by the British intelligence and Jewish capitalists played an important role in bringing Hitler to power in 1933.[60]

The phenomenon of raising contradictory charges against the Jews regarding the Holocaust, which also appears in the Arab Holocaust discourse, can be attributed to several factors. Charges of Zionist-Nazi collaboration alongside denial may stem from the [un]conscious realization of the writers that the Holocaust actually took place and had the dimensions confirmed by all serious historians, numerous judicial proceedings, thousands of eyewitness testimonies and ample documentary evidence in the Nazi regime's own archives. Hence, they seek to downplay its moral and historical significance by laying the blame for it on the Zionists.[61] In addition, these charges further demonize Zionists and Jews, who allegedly carried out such hideous actions as killing their own brethren for the sake of their worldly ambitions. The same is true with the rationalization of Nazi policy and denial. The writers hate the Jews, so they justify their extermination, but at the same time, they cannot admit that the Jews are victims, and therefore they deny the Holocaust. By presenting Hitler as a Jew, the various writers either seek to further humiliate the Jews not only by presenting their worst enemy as one of them but also by attributing his evil to the Jews themselves. Concurrently, this charge reveals latent racism among the Iranian writers themselves, who see Hitler as a Jew by blood if not by upbringing. Conceivably, these writers may be aware of a certain sympathy among their readers toward Hitler and knowing his true character, portraying him as a Jew will diminish these sympathies. Alternatively, this phenomenon may simply reflect deep irrational animosity which prompts those who harbor it to hurl every possible accusation at their object hatred, simply as a way to express or relieve their feelings regardless of its logical consistency or lack thereof.

Finally, I wish to briefly touch on the question of reception. Studies of intellectual history or public discourse in the Middle East face a serious methodological problem of ascertaining reception due to the difficulty of acquiring data on public opinion particularly among the "silent classes." As Iran is not a democracy and does not have freedom of the press, the government's official view of the Holocaust cannot be openly challenged. Hence the Iranian public is not exposed to the long established facts about the Holocaust that are present in both scholarship and public discussion in the West and indeed around the world. Thus, Mir Hossein Mousavi, the reformist candidate during the 2009 presidential campaign was careful not to explicitly acknowledge the Holocaust's existence, although asked twice about it by foreign journalists. He merely stated that Islam was "against killing of anyone, even one person, and considers it genocide," and that he did not understand "why the Palestinians should pay for it now."[62] Alternatively, it could be argued that the growing disenchantment of Iranians from their government may undermine their readiness to accept the official position on the Holocaust. Still, two phenomena may indicate that the official Holocaust discourse, primarily the theme of Holocaust denial has acquired more than a foothold in Iranian society.

One such indication is the dissemination of articles or essays denying the Holocaust or propound the blood libel in Iranian Internet blogs and websites.[63] There is no way of knowing whether these blogs are genuine personal enterprises reflecting the ideas and views of educated Iranians, or whether they are in fact government-sponsored blogs used as a means to disseminate the government's views through this popular medium to social groups that may incline more to the opposition. Be that as it may, these blogs further promote the theme of Holocaust denial.

More importantly, Hasan Da'i, a member of the opposition Green Movement, and himself a sharp critic of Israel, pointed to the endorsement of Holocaust denial even by prominent members of the opposition. Thus, the Iranian writer Dr. Majid Sharif, who was murdered in December 1998 as part of the "serial killings" of opposition intellectuals by Iranian security agents, translated into Persian Roger Garaudy's book which denies the Holocaust. Sharif's personal friend Rangin Keman, himself an opposition figure, highlighted this fact in his moving obituary.[64] More importantly, the publisher of the translation was none other than Ezatollah Sahabi, one of the leaders of the reformist-liberal Iranian Freedom Movement (*Nahzat-e Azadi-ye Iran*). In the introduction to the book, Sahabi praised Garaudy as a "learned statesman, a free thinker and a truth-seeker Frenchman," whose book shed light on Israel's true essence. As for the Holocaust, Sahabi minimized it to simple pressures exerted on the Jews to emigrate, while he accused the Zionist movement of opportunistic collaboration with the Nazis in pushing the Jews to emigrate from Europe to Palestine, while inventing the story of the Holocaust after the war in order to gain international support and justification for their "terrorist and inhumane measures in Palestine."[65] It is plausible to assume that if renowned reformist opposition figures in Iran share the regime's Holocaust discourse, there is no reason why ordinary Iranians should not do so as well. A 2014 survey carried out by the US-based Anti-Defamation League concluded that 56% of adult Iranians harbor antisemitic attitudes. While a high figure in itself, optimists could argue that this figure is lower than those surveyed in Arab countries and that it shows that a somewhat larger segment of society is immune to the anti-Jewish discourse.[66]

In conclusion, Holocaust denial not to mention its rationalization is a clear manifestation of antisemitism. In using the pretext of Zionist fabrication of the Holocaust, the Iranian discourse distorts and denies Jewish history and deprives the Jews of their human dignity by presenting their worst tragedy as a hoax. The claim that the Holocaust is a Zionist invention appeals both European and Middle Eastern antisemitism that emphasizes unscrupulous Jewish machinations in achieving illegitimate and immoral goals, mainly financial extortion at any price. According to this narration, only Jews could fabricate such an enormous lie as the Holocaust.

While Iran professes to be anti-Nazi, both Holocaust denial and the equation of Zionism with the Nazis minimizes the extent and depth of Nazi evil and brutality, thereby serving the cause of Western neo-Nazis and other antisemites. In a similar vein, the vilification of Zionists as Nazis serves to humiliate Jews at their most sensitive and painful point by equating them with their worst tormentors. Moreover, it seeks to deprive Jews of their dignity and to transform the victims into perpetrators of crimes. Most ominously, it threatens them with the same fate that the Nazis inflicted on the Jews, namely, their destruction. For it is one of the aims, if not the principal aim, of Holocaust deniers to destroy the legitimacy of the Jewish state, which they claim is based on the Holocaust myth. As such it is in tune with anti-Jewish and anti-Zionist sentiments in Europe, which argue that the Jews forfeited their status as victims by victimizing the Palestinians and that Israel does not have the right to exist, because the human price it requires is too high.

Since his assumption of office in August 2013, President Hasan Rouhani has toned down Holocaust denial and vulgar antisemitism by his government. He also made few public gestures toward Iran's Jewish community.[67] Speaking to the Western media in September 2013, Rouhani stated that "the crime that Nazis committed towards the Jews as well as non-Jews is reprehensible and condemnable," and that he "fully condemned any kind of crime committed against humanity throughout history, including the crime committed by the Nazis both against the Jews and non-Jews." Yet, he cautioned that since he was not a historian, he could not speak about the dimensions of those crimes. In other words, he tacitly equated Nazi policy of total extermination of the Jews with vicious and brutal terrorizing and murder of other groups, which were not genocidal. Likewise, his equivocation on the "dimension" implied refusal to acknowledge the true scope of the Holocaust. Significantly, after the interview, the Fars news agency denied that he acknowledges the Holocaust, claiming CNN had mistranslated his statement.[68] Iran's foreign minister Javad Zarif went further saying in Munich the Holocaust was "tragically cruel and should not happen again." In response, he was summoned to the Iranian Parliament on May 5, 2014, to answer for his "reactionary stance" toward the illegitimate Zionist regime and "the lie of the Holocaust."[69] More importantly, Supreme Leader Khamenei continued to deny the Holocaust's veracity.[70] While Khamenei stated that his calls for the elimination of Israel did not mean the extermination of its Jewish population, his insistence that most Jews living in Israel would have to go back to the places whence they had come, still carries a strong anti-Jewish undertone.

To conclude, the Islamic Republic's official discourse is strongly anti-Jewish in addition to being anti-Zionist. The demonization of the Jews as an inherently corrupt people, as enemies of Islam seems more ominous than a rhetorical devise to delegitimize Israel but of actually threatening the Jews with demise as this is the punishment, according to Islamic belief, which befits such offenders.

Notes

1. Vera Moreen, "The Problems of Conversion among Iranian Jews in the Seventeenth and Eighteenth Centuries," *Iranian Studies*, Vol. 19 Nos. 3–4 (Summer 1986), pp. 215–228; Roger M. Savory, "Relations between the Safavid State and its Non-Muslim Minorities," *Islam and Christian-Muslim Relations*, Vol. 14, Nos 4 (October 2003), pp. 435–458. Rula Jurdi Abisaab, *Converting Persia: Religion and power in the Safavid Empire* (London: I. B. Tauris, 2011), pp. 63, 103, 104, 127; Mehrdad Amanat, *Jewish Identities in Iran: Resistance and Conversion to Islam and the Baha'i Faith* (London: I. B. Tauris, 2011), pp. 37–60.
2. Daniel Tsadik, *Between Foreigners and Shi'is: Nineteenth-Century Iran and its Jewish Minority* (Stanford, Calif.: Stanford University Press, 2007); "Judeo-Persian Communities of Iran, v. Qajar Period

(1786–1925), *Encyclopedia Iranica*, Electronic Edition; The Jewish community of Mashad was forced to convert to Islam in 1839 under the threat of massacre. They remained crypto-Jews until the 1930s, see Hilda Nissimi, "Memory, Community, and the Mashhadi Jews During the Underground Period," *Jewish Social Studies* 9.3 (2003) 76–106.

3. Amnon Netzer, "Antisemitism in Iran, 1925–1950," *Peamim* No. 29 (1987, Hebrew), pp. 6–8. During the 1930s, Germany became Iran's number one trade partner. The Junkers firm, which built aircrafts for the Nazi airforce built a flying school in Iran, and Krup AG manufactured ammunition. Several other German firms were also active in the arms business, see Matthias Küntzel, *Germany and Iran: From the Aryan Axisto the Nuclear Threshold* (Candor, NY: Telos Press, 2014), pp. 27–28. While Iran declared nuetrality at the outbreak of World War II, trade with Germany increased. See also the report of Hans Smend, the German Ambassador in Tehran "The popular mood is overwhelmingly for us and rather blatantly against England," Politiches Archiv des Auswätogem Amts, "Iran und die internationale Lage," DG Teheran an AA v.27, Oktober 1939, R 28 866, Büro RAM Iran, 5/39–6/43 cited in *ibid*, p. 8.
4. David Menashri, "The Jews of Iran: Between the Shah and Khomeini," in Sander Gilman and Steven Katz (eds.), *Anti-Semitism in Times of Crisis* (New York University Press, 1991), pp. 353–71; Mahdi Ahouie, "Iranian Anti-Zionism and the Holocaust: A Long Discourse Dismissed," *Radical History Review* No. 105 (2009), pp. 58–78.
5. Ahouie, "Iranian Anti-Zionism," pp. 60–63.
6. For Khomeini's attitude toward the Jews, see Khumayni, *Islam and Revolution, Writings and Declarations of Imam Khomeini*. Translated and annotated by Hamid Algar (Berkeley: Mizan Press, 1981), pp. 27, 47, 109, 127.
7. Meir Litvak, "The Islamic Republic of Iran and the Holocaust: Anti-Semitism and Anti-Zionism," *The Journal of Israeli History* Vol. 25, No. 1 (March 2006), pp. 267–284; Ray Takeyh, "Iran, Israel and the Politics of Terrorism," *Survival*, Winter 2006 (Electronic edition).
8. "9320–3: Physical contact with non-Muslims," in http://www.khamenei.de/fatwas/12quesions.htm

9. See the Center for Research and Studies on Awakening (Kanun-e pezhuash va-tahqiqat bidari—Ettela'at dar baraye hulukast va-yahud be-zeban-e farsi), http://h-l.persianblog.ir/page/list, and Yahud-shenakht—http://www.jew.blogfa.com/
10. http://hawzah.net/hawzah/Default.aspx
11. For the concept of Occidentalism, see Ian Buruma and Avishai Margalit, *Occidentalism: The West in the Eyes of its Enemies* (New York: Penguin Press, 2004).
12. David Nirenberg, *Anti-Judaism: the Western Tradition* (New York: W.W. Norton, 2013), pp. 3, 5, 464.
13. Ayatollah Ruhallah Khumayni. *Al-hukuma al-islamiyya* (Beirut: Dar al-Tali'a, 1979), p. 7.
14. See for instance, Sayyid Mohammad Hossein Tabataba`i, "Piyambar Islam va-Yahud," *Mizan*, No. 9—http://www.hawzah.net/Hawzah/Articles/Articles.aspx?id=4992&LanguageID=1&SearchTextدوهی=; Mustafa Sadeqi, "Barkhurdha-ye musalamat-amiz piambar sala Allah alayhi wa-alihi wasalam ba yahud," *Tarikh-e Islam* No. 2—http://www.hawzah.net/Hawzah/Articles/Articles.aspx?id=78246&LanguageID=1&SearchTextدوهی=; Tabataba'i "Taghyir qibla va-atharat an, va-i'tiraz mushrikin va-yahud," al-Mizan, No. 1 — http://www.hawzah.net/Hawzah/Articles/Articles.aspx?id=3572&LanguageID=1&SearchTextدوهی= The Andishe-ye Qom website, which belongs to the Center for Information and Responses to Accusations (Markaz Motale'at va-pasokh be shabahat), has a special section on Judaism, which contains twelve categories of polemics and criticism on Judaism and Jews, http://www.andisheqom.com/Files/faq.php?level=2&id=99
15. See for instance the five-part essay by 'Alama Tabataba'i, "Dastan Hazrat Musa ('A) va-Qwum Yahud dar Koran," Mizan (n.d.), http://www.hawzah.net/Hawzah/Articles/Articles.aspx?id=5925&LanguageID=1&SearchTextدوهی=
16. MEMRI [The Middle East Media Research Institute] Special Dispatch Series, no. 897, 22 April 2005; http://www.yahoodi.com/peace/antizionism.html. For more references to this period, see Memri, Inquiry & Analysis Series Report No.922, January 27, 2013—http://www.memri.org/report/en/0/0/0/0/0/51/6956.htm

17. Khomeini, *al-Hukuma al-Islamiyya*, p. 7; Khomeini, *Islam and Revolution*, 27, 47, 89, 109, 127; Hamid Dabashi, *Theology of Discontent: The Ideological Formation of the Islamic Revolution in Iran* (New York: New York University Press, 1993), p. 426.
18. Khomeini, *Islam and Revolution*, p. 127.
19. Reuters, 22 December 2000; Islamic Republic News Agency (IRNA), 24 April 2001.
20. Mehr News Agency, 17 August 2012.
21. For this phenomenon, see Jacob Lassner, *The Middle East Remembered: Forged Identities, Competing Narratives, Contested Spaces* (Ann Arbor, 2000), p. 28.
22. MEMRI Special Dispatch Series, no. 897, 22 April 2005; http://www.yahoodi.com/peace/antizionism.html. For more references to this period, see MEMRI, Inquiry & Analysis Series Report No.922, January 27, 2013—http://www.memri.org/report/en/0/0/0/0/0/51/6956.htm
23. Cited in http://yahood-mir.blogfa.com/post-10.aspx (accessed August 2010); http://www.bachehayeghalam.ir/articles/cat_05/009070.php, and http://h-l.persianblog.ir/post/94/. See a popular version of the story titled "The Purim Festival: Jewish Dancing on the Iranian Holocaust," which contains gruesome pictures of Jews and Israelis with blood, in http://www.fetan.ir/home/6587
24. http://www.shahbazi.org/Plutocracy/index.htm
25. Shahbazi, "Kanunha-ye este'mari, kudeta-ye 1299 va-su'u saltanat Pahlavi," http://www.shahbazi.org/Articles/Coup.pdf; and "Penhanikari Inglisi va-asrar do kudeta," http://www.shahbazi.org/Articles/Secrets.pdf
26. "The Secret of Armageddon", www.memritv.org—Clip No. 1802, May–June, 2008.
27. Menashri, "Iran," in *Anti-Semitism World Wide 1995/6*, 198; "The Protocols of the Elders of Zion: An Iranian Perspective," MEMRI. *Special Dispatch Series*, no. 98 (7 June 2000), Memri, Special Dispatch No.855, 28 January 2005; Memri Special Dispatch No.1975, July 2, 2008. "The Iranian Vice President's Anti-Semitic Speech," 3, July 2012—http://www.terrorism-info.org.il/en/article/20361
28. MEMRI, Special Dispatch No.735 29 June 2004.
29. MEMRI, Special Dispatch No.1053, 22 December 2005.
30. *New York Times*, 26 June 2012.

31. MEMRI, Special Dispatch No.855, 28 January 2005; http://www.terrorism-info.org.il/en/article/18156
32. www.memri.org—Special Dispatch—No. 1397, 15 December 2006.
33. Geoffrey Cameron-May, "On Mofsed fel-Arz—Spreading Corruption on Earth," http://www.iranpresswatch.org/post/2737; http://www.guardian.co.uk/commentisfree/2010/jan/08/iran-judiciary-military-colour
34. Khomeini, *Islam and Revolution*, p. 89.
35. Ibrahim Rajablu, "Jang Revani sahyunism, mafahim va-mazamin," *Hawzah*, no. 189 28 Mordad, 1385; "Tuhmat-e yahudsitizi be mathabat-e yek silah-e siyasi manfa'at talabane," http://www.farsnews.net/newstext.php?nn=8901141028
36. The article originally appeared in the website of the semi-official Iranian news agency, Farsnews in http://www.farsnews.net/newstext.php?nn=8901211582, but was disseminated in other blogs and websites dedicated to fight Zionism. The "Zionist Regime" blog or site carries on its banner the Koranic passage: "Verily, you will find the strongest among men in enmity to the believers (Muslims) the Jews," (Surat al-Ma'ida verse 82), http://zionistregime.blogfa.com/post-43.aspx. Another website, "For Palestine," is dedicated to "Palestine, Zionism and the Holocaust," http://4palestine.blogfa.com/post-65.aspx
37. *Jomhuri-ye Eslami*, 14 January 1999; *Kayhan International*, 19 January 1998; *Kayhan*, 13 June 2002; Mahdi 'Alikhani, "Afsaneh-ye shu'a va-san'at-e Hulukast," http://www.tebyan.net/index.aspx?pid=102832&ParentID=295987&Language=1; "Hulukast: dorugh-e moqaddas-e gharb," Interview with Mohammad Taqi Taqipur, http://www.tebyan.net/index.aspx?pid=102832&ParentID=295987&Language=1; Mohammad Tayib, "Hulukast: marg-e takhm-e talayi-ye sahyunistha," http://www.rahpouyan.com/article/showsub.asp?sid=713
38. IRNA, 6 March 2000; 24 April 2001 (text of Khamene'i's speech). See similar assertions by *Jomhuri-ye Eslami*, 14 January 1999.
39. www.memri.org—Special Dispatch—No. 1397, 15 December 2006.
40. Radio Iran, 23 January 1998 (BBC-Summary of World Broadcast, SWB). Elsewhere he described Israel as being "imprisoned by its own Hitler-like policy in Palestine." Iran TV, 23 February 2002 (BBC-SWB).

41. *Iran*, 27 April 2003.
42. www.memri.org—Special Dispatch—No. 1397, 15 December 2006. Each of the eleven articles dedicated to Holocaust denial in the website of the Rahpuyan Cultural center (Kanun-e farhangi Rahpuyan) ends with the statement "Israel must be wiped of the map," http://www.rahpouyan.com/article/showsub.asp?sid=713
43. *Kayhan*, 28 January 2007, cited in Memri—Special Dispatch—No. 1443, 30 January 2007.
44. *Ma'ariv*, 22 November 1997; Rami to *Maroc Hebdo International* (no date), http://abbc.com/mh/mh-eng.htm; Esther Webman and Sara Rembiszewski, "The Unholy Alliance between Muslim Fundamentalists and Holocaust Deniers," *Occasional Paper*, Tel Aviv University, October 1993.
45. Another Holocoust denier who found refuge in Iran was Wolfgang Fröhlich in 2000—Anti-Defamation League, "Western Deniers in the Middle East," http://www.adl.org/holocaust/Denial_ME/western_deniers.asp; http://www.radioislam.org/revisionism/confer-beiru/010303asshafir.html; http://www.us-israel.org/jsource/anti-semitism/trend2001.html
46. *Resalat*, 13 January 1998; *Jomhuri-ye Eslami*, 14 January; *Kayhan International*, 17 February, 20 April 1998.
47. IRNA, Iran TV, 20 April 1998 (BBC-SWB); Iran Press Service, 17 March 1998; AFP, 22 April 1998.
48. *International Herald Tribune*, 11 December 2006, cited in David Menashri, "Iran, the Jews and the Holocaust," http://www.tau.ac.il/Anti-Semitism/asw2005/menashri.html. See also the contribution from Elhanan Yakira in the present volume.
49. Menashri, "Iran, the Jews and the Holocaust,"
50. *Hamshahri*, 6 February 2006; "Afsaneh-ye Hulukast Pashene Ashil Isra'il ast," http://www.mehrnews.com/fa/NewsDetail.aspx?NewsID=292791; AP, 2 November 2006; http://www.msnbc.msn.com/id/15525133/
51. Reuters, 18 January 2009; Jerusalem Post, 8 August 2010; http://www.irancartoon.com/120/holocaust
52. Iranian TV, Channel (IRINN), December 27, 2005—www.memritv.org—Clip No. 982, 27 December 2005; www.memri.org—Special Dispatch—No. 1072, January 18, 2006; See also, "Baznegari Hulukast," psri.com/Show.php?Page=ViewArticle&A

rticleID=305&SP=Farsi; 'Ali Reza Mohammadi, "Naqd dalayil Hulukast," *http://bmf.parsi*blog.com/-1529398.htm

53. Among such books, were Hasan Halaq, *Naqsh-e yahud va-qodratha-ye beyne-melali dar khal' sultan 'Abd al-Hamid az saltanat (1909–1909)*, (Tehran: PSRI, 1380); which attributes to the Jews a key role in toppling the Ottoman Sultan Abd al-Hamid II (r. 1876–1909), and Antony Alferi, *Edwar haftom va-darbar-e yahudi-ye U*, (Tehran, PSRI, 1381),which speaks on the "Jewish court" of King Edward VII.
54. See for example, 'Ali Reza Mohammadi, "Sahyunism, Hulukast, Israi'l," *Shamim Yas* No. 38 (Farvardin 1385); (electronic edition); "Hulukast: buzurgtarin-e durugh-e ta'rikhi," *Porsemanm,* No. 41 (Bahman, 1384) (electronic edition); Mohammad Tayyib, "Hulukast: marg-e takhm-e talayi-ye sahyunistha;" 'Adhra Khatibi, "Hulukast: Mo'mala penhani," http://www.iichs.org/index.asp?id=112&doc_cat=1
55. www.memritv.org—Clip No. 1049, 19 February 2006.
56. Iranian TV Channel 1, October 5, 2007—memritv.org clip. No 1575, 5 October 2007.
57. MEMRI—Special Dispatch—No. 1408, 3 January 2007.
58. Khatibi, "Hulukast: Mo'mala penhani."
59. Iran TV Network 1, 5 October 2000 (http://gulf2000.columbia.edu/); *TT*, 7 May 2000; IRNA, 24 April 2001; *Kayhan*, 13 June 2002. *MEMRI Special Dispatch Series*, No.855, 28 January 2005. IRNA gladly endorsed the accusation by ultra-Orthodox Jewish spokesmen that the "Zionists sacrificed religious Jews in the holocaust," whose occurrence it denied, 14 August 2000.
60. Abdollah Shahbazi, "Razha-ye penhan su'ud Nazism,"—http://www.shahbazi.org/Articles/Nazism.pdf. The allegation of Hitler's Jewish origins also appeared in internet blogs, see "Hitler va-madarebozurgesh yahudi budand," http://www.tebyan.net/index.aspx?PID=102832&PageSize=10&PARENTID=295987&PageIndex=1&LANGUAGE=1
61. See for instance the symposium which opens the volume on Holocaust denial, where some of the speakers expressed their concern that the ordinary Iranians may not know of the true facts, "regarding the Holocaust, hence the need for its scholarly refutation," "GofteGu," *Faslnamah-e Motale' at-e Ta'rikhi* Vol. 14.
62. *New York Times*, 7 April 2009.

63. See, Mehdi Khalaji, "The Classic Blood Libel Against Jews Goes Mainstream in Iran," Washington Institute for Near Eastern Policy, Policy Watch 2411, April 21, 2015—http://www.washingtoninstitute.org/policy-analysis/view/the-classic-blood-libel-against-jews-goes-mainstream-in-iran; see also March 6, 2013 Inquiry & Analysis Series Report No.944 http://www.memri.org/report/en/0/0/0/0/0/51/7050.htm
64. http://asre-nou.net/1381/aban/25/m-sharif.html
65. Da'i, "Ma Iranian, Isra'il va-yahudsitizi." http://hambastegi-ran.org/spip.php?article255
66. ADL Global100: An Index of Anti-Semitism 2015—http://global100.adl.org/#country/iran
67. Nada Garrett, "Khamenei vs. Rouhani on Non-Muslims," Iran Primer, January 8, 2015—http://iranprimer.usip.org/blog/2015/jan/08/khamenei-vs-rouhani-non-muslims
68. Arash Karami, "Rouhani's Holocaust Comments on CNN Spark Controversy," September 26, 2013—http://iranpulse.al-monitor.com/index.php/2013/09/2894/rouhanis-holocaust-comments-on-cnn-spark-controversy/; http://english.farsnews.com/newstext.aspx?nn=13920703001316
69. http://www.reuters.com/article/2014/05/06/us-iran-politics-idUSBREA450Q320140506; http://www.timesofisrael.com/iranian-hawks-grill-foreign-minister-on-holocaust/
70. See his speech on March 16, 2014, in which he stated that the *"Holocaust is an event whose reality is uncertain and if it has happened, it's uncertain how it has happened,"* http://iranprimer.usip.org/blog/2014/mar/21/khamenei-nowruz-questions-holocaust

CHAPTER 10

Antisemitism in Contemporary Germany

Werner Bergmann

Since the start of the third millennium, new developments in the manifestation of antisemitism and its public discussion have been observable in Germany, while the same can be said to apply to the political efforts to monitor and combat it. In my view, there are contradictory trends. How the situation is assessed depends in essence on which dimension of antisemitism we focus on. In this chapter, we will discuss, using quantitative data, the trends that emerged in Germany since the German reunification in 1990.

Antisemitic Attitudes

Let us first look at the dimension of antisemitic attitudes. As we do not have a "clinical thermometer" to measure antisemitism, the percentage of antisemitic attitudes measured by surveys varies according to the questions asked and the respective scales used. The range spans from 8% to 23% in recent years; it is generally assumed that the proportion of persons with a coherent antisemitic prejudice is around 15%. Approval of an individual antisemitic item can be significantly more common, especially those which

W. Bergmann (✉)
Technical University of Berlin, Berlin, Germany

A. McElligott, J. Herf (eds.), *Antisemitism Before and Since the Holocaust*, DOI 10.1007/978-3-319-48866-0_10

are connected to Israeli politics in the Middle East conflict. Grading on a scale is based on approval to several items, whereby the demarcation between antisemites and non-antisemites is naturally arbitrary and has to be undertaken within a continuum. As far as the quantitative development is concerned, long-term studies reveal a mixed picture. Covering the years from 2002 to 2014, the diachronic study on "group-focused enmity" (GFE) employed a short scale comprising two items ("Jews have too much influence in Germany" and "Jews are complicit in their persecution due to their behaviour") and has registered, with minor fluctuations, a decline to levels beneath the data of 2002 (Table 10.1).[1]

Overall, we can characterize this development of attitudes as stable; according to GFE data, it reveals a slight downward trend, but we also see the period effect which is triggered by the Gaza conflict in the summer of 2014 leading to a considerably, but normally short lived increase of negative answers. The same short-lived period effect has been observed already during the Gaza conflict in 2006. In spite of this short-lived effect, the negative attitude in the German population towards Israel's Middle East politics decreased from 2004 to September 2014, although the Gaza campaign fostered antisemitic attitudes in general ("Israel makes a war of annihilation upon the Palestinians": 2004: 67.5% agree strongly or mostly; in 2014: 39.9%; "My antipathy toward Jews is growing stronger and stronger due to Israel`s politics": 2004: 31% agree strongly/mostly, in 2014: 20.1%).[2] In 2014, almost two-thirds of the German population (62%) harbour negative attitudes towards Israel's government, while 42% show a negative attitude towards Israel in general (46% have a positive attitude). While the negative attitude remains

Table 10.1 Antisemitic attitudes among Germans 2002–2014 (in %)

Item	*2002*	*2003*	*2004*	*2005*	*2006*	*2007*	*2009*	*2010*	*2011*	*2014 June*	*2014 Sept.*
Jews have too much influence in Germany	21.6	23.4	21.5	20.9	14.1	15.6	17.1	16.4	13.0	13.7	15.3
Jews themselves are partly to blame that they were persecuted	16.6	17.9	17.3	12.9	10.0	17.3	10.5	12.5	10.0	10.4	18.0

Source: Heitmeyer, 2002–2011, Zick and Klein 2014—Answers: Strongly agree/mostly agree: in %

almost the same since 2008 (44%), there has been an increase of positive answers from 35% to 46%.[3]

Those collated data in another series of studies by Oliver Decker et al. covering the same period as the GFE studies show a downward trend for West Germans and an upward trend for East Germans for the last ten years—adding up to a stable total amount.[4] This change is due to a different development in the younger generations in East and West Germany. While among West Germans, in the age group of those older than 60 years antisemitic attitudes are more widespread than among East Germans (14.5% and 9.7%), it is the other way round in the younger age groups (18–30: 5.5% and 6.5%; 30–60: 5.5% and 12%).[5] The results of 2014 are quite surprising, because we do not only observe a strong decrease in antisemitic attitudes but, for the first time, there are more widespread among East Germans. Since we find a quite strong decrease of xenophobic, chauvinist and other right-wing attitudes too, these deviating findings may be due to different survey methodologies (Table 10.2).[6]

A different picture emerges when comparisons are drawn extending beyond a period of ten years. The ALLBUS collected data on attitudes towards Jews in two dimensions in 1996 and 2006. The first focussed on anti-Jewish prejudice. The second dimension revolved around the question of social distance and the legal–cultural integration of Jews (and other groups).[7]

Attitudes towards Jews reveal a negative trend between 1996 and 2006: in 1996, 18% were classified as antisemitic; in 2006, this had risen to 22.6%. The trend is registered to the same degree among West and East Germans. While in the Decker et al. studies, the East–West difference had diminished almost completely (1.2%), the gap on the ALLBUS scale had narrowed only slightly. The proportion of persons with anti-Semitic attitudes remained significantly higher in the West (West, 1996: 21.3%, 2006: 25.1%; East, 1996: 11.3%, 2006: 17%). Here the anti-fascist orientation

Table 10.2 Antisemitic attitudes among Germans 2002–2014 (%)

Year	*2002*	*2004*	*2006*	*2008*	*2010*	*2012*	*2014*
Germany (total)	9.3	10.0	8.4	9.0	8.7	8.6	3.2
East	4.8	7.0	4.2	7.9	7.7	7.7	4.3
West	13.8	10.9	9.5	9.3	8.9	9.0	2.9

Source: Decker et al., 2002–2012, Zick and Klein 2014

of the GDR obviously had an impact, which, however, in the younger cohorts born after 1989, is gradually losing its influence. In 2006, the percentage of antisemites amongst East Germans between 18 and 29 years of age is meanwhile 5 percentage points higher than the same aged persons from West German (15.5% in relation to 10.6%); for all other cohorts, the gap between West and East Germans increases as age rises, and for over 60s was 16 percentage points.

Observing the dimension of social distance to Jews in the decade between 1996 and 2006, we can see that hardly anything changed; the trend is only slightly negative. In both years from amongst the selected reference group for comparison (Italians, Turks, ethnic German emigrants, asylum-seekers), following the Italians, German Jews were least prejudiced against in terms of keeping social distance (Table 10.3).

Antisemitic attitudes vary in the intensity of their distribution, depending on the respective age group, education level and political orientation. All empirical studies come to the conclusion that antisemitic attitudes decrease the higher the education level; in contrast, they increase as the age group gets older. In 2010, for instance, the figure was 5.0% amongst the 14–30-year-olds, and 13% amongst the over 60s. As far as the influence played by political orientation is concerned, in 2006 the approval of antisemitic items rose only slightly in the spectrum from the left to the centre, while to the right of centre it rose clearly, before shooting up again amongst the extreme right (scaled values 8–10 amongst West Germans, 9–10 amongst East Germans) (Figs. 10.1 and 10.2).

When compared to 1996, it becomes clear that antisemitic attitudes grew in the right of centre spectrum (scale grade 6). This led some observ-

Table 10.3 Social distance—West and East Germans in 1996 and 2006 (in %)[a]

Group	*Jews*		*Italians*		*Ethnic Germans from Eastern Europe*		*Turks*		*Asylum-seekers*	
Year	*1996*	*2006*	*1996*	*2006*	*1996*	*2006*	*1996*	*2006*	*1996*	*2006*
Germans (total)	11.9	*12.6*	8.9	*5.4*	12.1	*19.1*	33.6	*36.5*	47.3	*44.6*
West Germans	11.2	*12.2*	6.9	*3.7*	11.2	*19.6*	32.7	*35.4*	41.9	*47.2*
East Germans	13.4	*13.3*	12.4	*8.5*	13.5	*18.2*	35.4	*38.6*	44.2	*39.8*

Source: Allbus 1996 and 2006

[a]The distance was measured through the following items: acceptance as neighbours, marriage of a member of the group into the family, and legally anchored equal treatment for the respective minority.

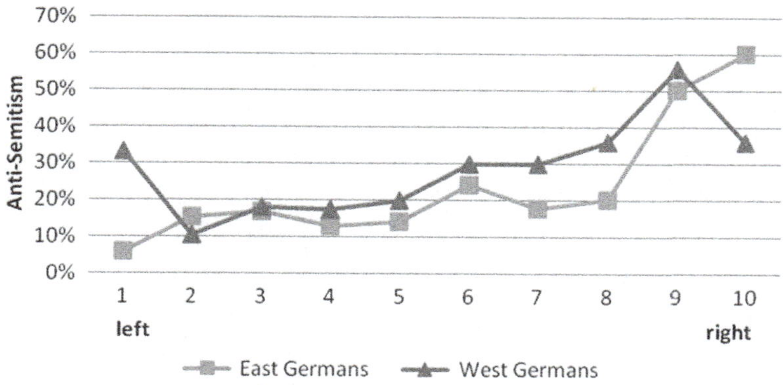

Fig. 10.1 Antisemitic by political orientation (left-right scale) (Data from: ALLBUS 2006)

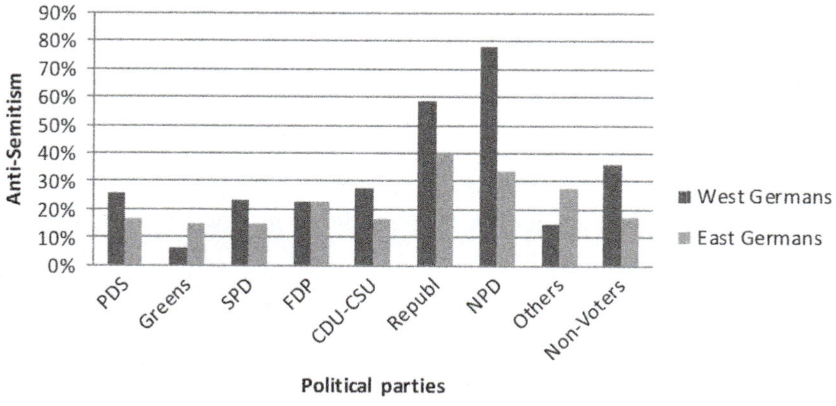

Fig. 10.2 Antisemitism by party preference (Data from: ALLBUS 2006; PDS = Party of Democratic Socialism (left-wing party); Bündnis 90/Die Grünen = Greens; SPD = Social Democratic Party; FDP = Liberal Party; CDU/CSU = Christian Democrats; NPD = National Democratic Party (extreme right-wing party); Republikaner (right-wing party))

ers (like Decker et al.; Heitmeyer) to formulate the thesis that there is a "crisis of the middle class", who are becoming more intolerant towards out-groups in general. What is just as striking is that for extreme leftist positions, the ratio of persons expressing antisemitic attitudes amongst West Germans reached a similarly high level as the extreme right; in contrast, the lowest scores were registered amongst East Germans on the extreme left. It may be assumed that it is the markedly negative attitude towards the state of Israel which has so significantly raised the acceptance of antisemitic opinions amongst West Germans of the extreme left. This is also revealed by the party preferences, where those West Germans who express a preference for the *PDS/Die Linke* (The Left) now lie—unlike 1996—above the average of the overall population. Despite the official anti-Zionism of the GDR, East German voters of *Die Linke* or persons who consider themselves to be of the extreme left do not appear to transfer their probable Israel-critical opinions to attitudes towards Jews. Here it is possible that an earlier anti-fascist position continues to reverberate, namely a strict distinction between anti-Zionism and antisemitism. Apart from the extreme rightist position, there is no identifiable connection between party preference and antisemitic attitudes amongst East Germans: from the *PDS/The Left* through to the *Christian Democrats* (CDU/CSU) and *non-voters,* there are hardly any recognizable differences. In general, the attitude towards Jews has no significant influence on voting behaviour except—among other factors—for the extreme right-wing parties.

A major topic in the public debates during the period under review is the question of how widespread antisemitic attitudes are in immigrant minorities, especially among those from Arab countries and Turkey.[8] Opinions as to the extent of antisemitic attitudes in the Muslim communities differ widely. Whereas some scholars consider claims that there is a high ratio of antisemitic attitudes amongst Muslims in Germany to be nothing more than an attempt to divert attention from the antisemitism in German society,[9] others come to the conclusion, based in part on qualitative empirical studies, that such attitudes are more widespread in the Muslim communities than in the German population. These qualitative studies have shown that many young migrants consider it to be the "normal stance" of a Muslim to be an enemy of Israel and the Jews.[10] The results of some non-representative studies point in the same direction: Two studies on high school students show that Muslims of migrant background more often agree to items on antisemitism than Muslims with a German background and with a non-Muslim background.[11] The second study also reveals that antisemitic attitudes related to Israel, religious anti-Judaism, classic antisemitism were more widespread among Muslim students, particular among Arab students, that among other students, who, on the other hand, show a higher degree of "secondary" antisemitism connected with the memory of the Holocaust than the Muslim students.[12]

Criticism of the prevalence of antisemitic attitudes is meanwhile being expressed from within these ethnic groups. Cem Özdemir from Alliance 90/The Greens, who is of Turkish extraction, has recently pointed out that antisemitism is on the rise in particular amongst young males of Turkish, Kurdish and Arab background. Özdemir assumes that this stems from an "over identification with the conflict in the Middle East", which he in turn interprets as a reaction to their marginalization in German society.[13] As the journalist Ahmad Mansour sees it, antisemitism has developed, inconspicuously, into a phenomenon of everyday life amongst the Arab, Turkish and Muslim population.[14] This phenomenon cannot be considered in isolation from the social context of migrant communities; instead, we need to approach it as an expression of antisemitic attitudes and hostility towards Israel which ferments and develops in interaction with experiences (of exclusion) in these societies.[15] Here we need to not just focus on Muslim migrants but also take into account other migrant groups, in Germany for instance migrants from Eastern Europe and their interaction with the German host society, while avoiding a "culturalizing displacement of antisemitism to a group of migrants separated from the imagined majority society". Unfortunately, studies dealing with this topic are still quite rare in Germany.

In a European perspective, Germany ranges right in the middle between countries like the UK, the Netherlands and the Scandinavian countries, where antisemitic attitudes are less widespread, and eastern and south European countries like Poland, Hungary, Spain or Greece, where these attitudes are more widespread than in Germany (Table 10.4).

Antisemitic Offences

While studies into attitudes reveal a rather stable picture, if not a slight decline in antisemitic attitudes since 2002, the dimension of individual behaviour covered by criminal offences shows an entirely different story (Figs. 10.3 and 10.4).

Table 10.4 Attitudes towards Jews in ten European countries[a]

Country	*Antisemitic attitudes (in %)*
Austria	28
France	24
Germany	21
Italy	35
Hungary	63
Poland	48
Spain	53
United Kingdom	17
The Netherlands	10
Norway	15

Source: ADL 2012

[a]Percentage of those surveyed who answered "true and probably true" to at least three out of the four following questions: (1) Jews are more loyal to Israel than to this country; (2) Jews have too much power in the business world; Jews have too much power in international financial markets; Jews still talk too much about what happened to them in the Holocaust, in: ADL, Attitudes Towards Jews in Ten European Countries, March 2012; the same pattern we find the more recent ADL-Global Study. An Index of Antisemitism, July 2013–February 2014

Parallel to the number of politically motivated criminal acts from the right in general, which in the last decade stood at between 16,000 and 20,000 a year, the number of antisemitic criminal offences has risen considerably over the past 25 years since 1990. From just a few hundred at the beginning of the 1990s and interrupted by the odd deviation, the number meanwhile rose to an average of about 1500 cases annually. As it is the case in the surveys on antisemitic attitudes, we can observe an increase in the number of offenses from 1275 in 2013 to 1596 in times of escalations in the Middle East conflict, as it was the case during the Gaza conflict in the summer of 2014 (and also in 2006 and 2009). Most of these offences are committed by persons of right-wing political orientation. In comparison to the Netherlands and France, the proportion of migrants (especially from Arab countries) involved in antisemitic crimes is low, and yet below the level of reported criminal offences verbal attacks upon Jews committed by this group increased in the later years of the decade.[16] But in 2014, due to the Gaza conflict, we can observe a considerable increase in antisemitic offenses by foreigners and of those, who cannot be counted as

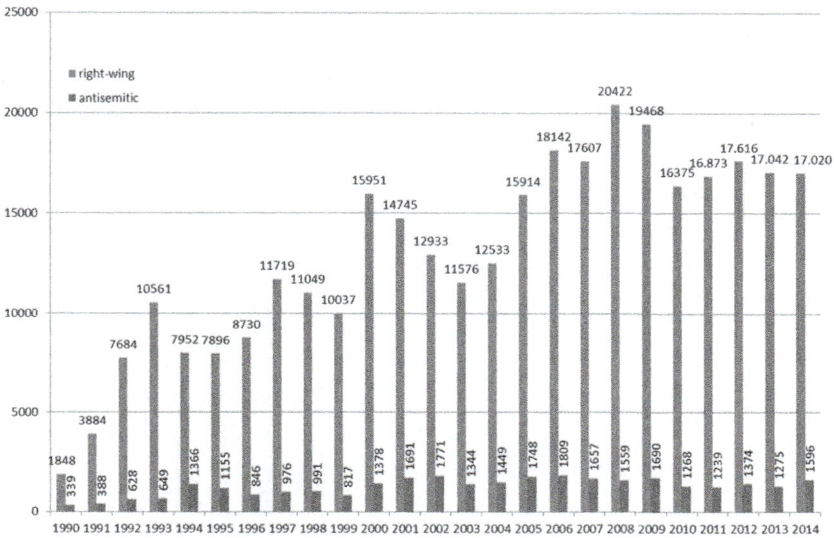

Fig. 10.3 Right-wing extremist and antisemitic offences 1990–2014 (*Source*: Federal Republic of Germany, *Verfassungsschutzberichte 1990–2014* (Reports of the Office for the Protection of the Constitution))

politically right- or left-wing motivated. This was also the case during the escalations of the Middle East conflict in 2006 and 2009. Compared to the antisemitic offenses by right-wingers and foreigners the proportion of anti-Semitic offences from the extreme left is minimal. They have committed almost no violent acts in recent years (Table 10.5).

The overwhelming majority of antisemitic offences during this period were propaganda and hate crimes; violent crimes (murder, grievous bodily harm, arson, extortion, disturbing the peace, resisting arrest etc.) made up about 3%. These figures represent only reported cases however; most of the insulting letters and telephone calls directed at Jewish communities and verbal abuse of individuals are not covered by the data, similar to how much of what is published and circulated on the internet by right-wing extremists and radical Islamists, this defies quantification. The Federal Office for the Protection of the Constitution estimates that fewer than 5% of genuinely right-wing extremist home pages contain criminally relevant material.[17]

A number of incidents that took place over a few weeks in 2012 in Berlin triggered a wave of concern: a rabbi was assaulted and a group of Jewish school pupils was subject to antisemitic verbal abuse by young men

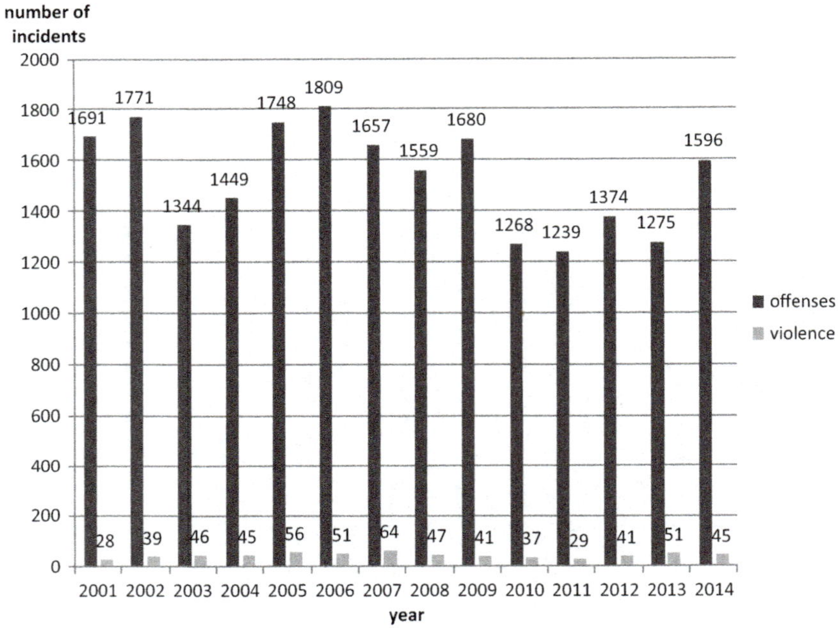

Fig. 10.4 Antisemitic offenses and acts of violence 2001–2014 (*Source*: Federal Republic of Germany, *Verfassungsschutzberichte 2001–2014* (Reports of the Office for the Protection of the Constitution))

presumably of Arab background, the General Secretary of the Central Council of Jews in Germany was verbally abused by an individual, and a taxi driver refused to take some Jewish women to the synagogue. On the one hand, a wave of outrage among the population was evident, resulting in a willingness to help and support Jews; on the other hand, these incidents also prompted a public debate on the safety of Jews in Germany, many of whom no longer felt safe, especially in quarters with a strong Muslim population, above all when they are readily identifiable as Jews by wearing the kippah.[18] These complaints flared up in the months following the anti-Israeli demonstrations in the summer of 2014 during the Gaza conflict, in which antisemitic slogans were shouted and banners shown by the mostly Arab demonstrators. In some cities, they were left-wing groups, who notified the authority of these demonstrations.

Moreover, this anxiety was compounded when the German political establishment and the general public were confronted with the revela-

Table 10.5 Antisemitic offences 2001–2014

Year	*2001*	*2002*	*2003*	*2004*	*2005*	*2006*	*2007*	*2008*	*2009*	*2010*	*2011*	*2012*	*2013*	*2014*
Antisemitic crimes														
Politically motivated right wing	1629	1594	1226	1346	1682	1662	1561	1496	1520	1192	1188	1314	1218	1342
Politically motivated left wing	2	6	6	4	7	4	1	5	4	1	6	3	0	7
Politically motivated foreigners	31	89	53	46	33	89	59	41	101	53	24	38	31	176
Politically motivated other	29	82	59	53	26	54	36	17	65	22	21	19	26	71
Politically motivated total	1691	1771	1344	1449	1748	1809	1657	1559	1690	1268	1239	1374	1275	1596
Anti-semitic violent acts														
Politically motivated right wing	27	30	38	40	50	44	61	44	31	31	26	37	46	32
Politically motivated left wing	0	1	0	1	1	0	0	2	0	0	1	0	0	1
Politically motivated foreigners	1	7	7	3	3	7	3	1	9	6	2	4	4	12
Politically motivated other	0	1	1	1	2	0	0	0	1	0	0	0	1	0
Politically motivated total	28	39	46	45	56	51	64	47	41	37	29	41	51	45

Source: Federal Republic of Germany, *Verfassungsschutzberichte 2001–2014* (Reports of the Office for the Protection of the Constitution)

tion that from 2000 to 2007 a small right-wing extremist terror cell, the National Socialist Underground (NSU), could commit numerous murders, killing nine migrants from Turkey and Greece as well as a policewoman, carry out two bomb attacks injuring scores as well as numerous bank holdups, without the police authorities or the Protection of the Constitution agency able to pick up their trail. Subsequent investigations revealed that the authorities had followed completely false leads (blaming "mafia-like" structures amongst the migrants, most of them owners of small businesses) and then failed to follow up the evidence pointing to right-wing terrorism. This contributed to a massive sense of insecurity amongst Jewish and other citizens with a foreign background. This case is still on trial.

Organized Antisemitism

In terms of the size of those organizations whose members count antisemitism amongst their political convictions, in 2013 the main right-wing extremist party, the National Democratic Party of Germany (NPD) is still losing members, and in 2013 there were 5500 members left (2011: 6300), while the other main party, the German Peoples Union (DVU) broke up in 2012. In addition, there were about 7400 right-wing extremists prepared to use violence who are active in the subcultural scene, whereby membership is in slight decline (from 9000 in 2009), and some 5800 neo-Nazis, whose number slightly decreased since 2012 from 6000. Altogether, the number of right-wing extremists dropped from 23,400 in 2011 to 21,700 in 2013.[19]

These political parties generally avoid expressing antisemitic views all too openly; instead, they employ allusions or thinly veiled references relativizing the Holocaust (for instance, the Allied aerial bombings on Dresden in 1945 are labelled the "bomb Holocaust"), and hold up to ridicule remembrance of the Holocaust by calling the Holocaust Memorial in Berlin a "wreath-dropping site". At the 2011 elections to the Mecklenburg-Lower Pomerania state parliament, the NPD not only used a campaign poster with the slogan "Gas geben!" ("step on the gas!"), which in German means simply to accelerate when driving, but also openly draws on the allusion to the use of gas in the Holocaust. The provocation fulfilled a double function; it triggered outrage amongst opponents while at the same time generating a positive resonance amongst supporters. Time and again, the NPD uses the Holocaust to denounce the imminent "genocide of the German people". The NPD party manifesto of 2010 virulently opposed migration to Germany, claiming that "integration is genocide", while in summer 2011 the homepage of the NPD group in the Berlin suburb of Neukölln, where around a third of the population is from a migration background, pronounced that "multicultural society is genocide in instalments".[20] For this immigration and "foreign infiltration" ("Überfremdung"), the Jews are held responsible, who also "try to drive Europe into war against the Islam for the benefit of Zion".[21] Classical antisemitic stereotypes like Jewish financial domination and world conspiracy plans are repeatedly communicated in updated and oblique forms. It is argued that the Jews ("das Machtjudentum") uses "antisemitism" as a weapon to divert the attention away from their subjugation of the world by means of wealth they have sucked of the world.[22] The former local NPD politician Rigolf Hennig for instance claimed that the revolutions in Arab countries were uprisings against "parasitic globalism and International Zionism"[23]; while in general, it is believed that the current finance and bank crisis is in fact an intricate Jewish plot. Rigolf today is active in the "Europäische Aktion" (EA), a revisionist and antisemitic organization seated in Switzerland. In Germany, the revisionist scene has largely been broken up through bans and depriving organizations of their financial basis. In contrast, amongst neo-Nazis and in the right-wing subculture antisemitic and racist ideas are being expressed openly and brutally, for instance in the racist lyrics of right-wing extremist rock bands.

As far as the supporter basis of these parties is concerned, the NPD still managed to achieve between 2.2% and 6.0% of the vote for the state assemblies in the East German states, and were especially successful in Mecklenburg-Lower Pomerania (6% in 2011) and Saxony 4.9 in 2014), while the party gained far fewer votes in West German states (0.6–2.2%). At the federal elections of 2013, the NPD only gained 1.3% of the votes, with the overall trend in clear decline. Nevertheless, the National Democrats were successful in establishing strongholds in some remote regions of the former GDR close to the border with Poland, where they made an effort to influence not only less-educated young people but also local politics.[24]

Studies also found an anti-capitalist/anti-imperialist antisemitism often related to the USA and the "Zionists" in a few of the smaller left-wing extremist groups and smaller Islamic organizations like Hizb Allah (950 members), which contests Israel's right to exist, Hamas (300 members), and Hizb ut-Tahrir, banned in 2003. These organizations are however hardly present in the public realm on a continual basis, only becoming active for anti-Israeli demonstrations, for instance in response to the Gaza conflict and the Al-Quds Day, an event with a permanently decreasing number of participants (2012: 1100; 2013: 800).[25] Similarly, the Turkish organization with the most members (31,000), Milli Görös, takes a strongly "antizionist" position ("the malignant tomour of Zionism") and became active with demonstrations against Israeli forces entering the Gaza Strip in 2009.[26]

The Al-Aqsa intifada and the events of September 11—one can also add the Iraq War—have on the one hand directed extreme left-wing currents back onto the old anti-Zionist line, while on the other hand have spawned a radical counter movement.[27] One camp is made up of the "anti-German friends of Israel", who consider themselves to be part of the radical left while, however, uncompromisingly adopting the position of Israel; they are pro-American, consider the Palestinians to be an "aggressive antisemitic collective" and speak of "Islamic fascism" as a rebirth of National Socialism. Accordingly, they criticize the traditional understanding of anti-fascism, based on a reductionist socio-economic model of capitalism, which blends out the racial ideology of Nazism, as well as the internationalism/anti-imperialism of the left, both of which they believe have misled the left to denounce Israel as fascist–imperialist and call its right of existence into question while proclaiming the Palestinians and Islamists to be "objectively anti-imperialists". The other camp is made up of the "anti-imperialist enemies of Israel", drawn from the communist and Trotskyite factions of the party *Die Linke* (The Left) and dogmatic traditional leftists affiliated with the West German Communist Party. For these groups, the "anti-Germans" are reactionary "leftist warmongers". Amongst these "traditional leftists", the link between capitalism and world Jewry or Zionism, forged by the SED as early as the 1950s, plays a key role. As the West German left, motivated by the Vietnam War, identified fascism with the USA in the late 1960s ("USA-SA-SS!"), it would now seem that a later generation, disappointed at the actions of the paradigmatic Nazi victim, equated with Israelis, is repeating such an identification: Israel is accused of employing Nazi methods and conducting a "war of annihilation". Left-wing papers like the Communist Party's *Unsere Zeit* speak of Israelis as a "master race" unleashing "pogroms" against Palestinians, while others see Israel as pursuing a "völkish" agenda aiming to achieve a "final settlement of the Palestinian question". Similar Nazi comparisons are also to be found in sections of the anti-globalization and the peace movements. Heated debate rages amongst the extreme left about the lessons to be drawn from the Holocaust: while one side deduces a pro-Israeli position, the other warns that remembering Auschwitz should not be exploited as way of ignoring or banalizing "Israeli politics of oppression".

Public Debates

In the German public realm, it is above all how the Nazi past is approached and dealt with: commemoration of the Holocaust and the Middle East conflict, which give rise to antisemitic breaches of taboos every now and then. A shift in emphasis over the last few years is discernible. Since the last public scandals in 2002–2003, the Nazi past and problems of "coming to terms with the Nazi past" ("Vergangenheitsbewältigung") has receded somewhat as a prominent trigger, with Israeli policy, in particular during the Israeli military campaigns of 2002, 2006, 2009 and 2014, becoming the overriding issue. Although 45% of the German population in 2009 felt sympathy for Israel, it is also seen by many Germans (about 50%) as an "aggressive country", which pursues its interests irrespective of the interests of other countries.[28] This issue once again came to the fore in April 2012 after the German Nobel laureate for literature, Günter Grass, published the poem "Was gesagt werden muss" ("What must be said").[29] While Grass considers himself to be a friend of Israel, he criticized the state as a nuclear power of "endangering fragile world peace" by exercising its "claimed right to a preventive strike" and exterminating the "Iranian people". In the poem, he goes on to criticize the politics of the West and the delivery of a German submarine to Israel. Public opinion was divided: while there was almost unanimous condemnation of the writer among some sections of the educated and political elites and the mass media, with a number of critics even going so far as to accuse him of antisemitism, there emerged at the same time a groundswell of support for Grass among the population in general, particularly in letters to the editor applauding his stance.[30]

In the media and amongst members of the elite, the comparison between Israel's policy and that of the Third Reich is put forth now and then, for instance when parallels are drawn between Palestinian suicide bombers and the insurgents of the Warsaw Ghetto, or when Israel is criticized for conducting a war of annihilation against the Palestinians. Secondary antisemitism, which, amongst others, employs the argument that the Holocaust is exploited for political purposes, comes to bear more in respect of the German stance towards Israeli policy, considered to be far too accommodating, or the evoking of an "Israel lobby" in the USA, rather than in activating a defence mechanism against the past, or, for example, in the question of restitution demands (e.g. in the cases of restitution of "Aryanized art"). At times, we can even find "potential antisemitic set pieces" in the coverage of national newspapers on the Middle East, often using the inversion of Holocaust denial by describing Israeli politics in comparison to the National Socialist persecution of the Jews. At the same time though, in comparison to the coverage presented elsewhere in Europe, in particular the Scandinavian countries and Spain, it is—similar to the line taken by the German federal government—balanced, if not pro-Israel. But the main topic of heated public debates in recent years is of course the question of integration of migrant minorities, especially Muslim minorities, and the "danger" that political Islam may pose for a German or European culture which is seen as a Jewish–Christian tradition and into which Jews are now included. In this way, a veil is drawn over the repeated repudiation of Jews and Judaism throughout European history.

Besides the problems of "coming to terms with the past" and the Middle East conflict, in recent years other sensitive points of contention have emerged impacting on the coexistence between Germans and Jews, creating contexts in which antisemitism can be articulated. A verdict passed by a Cologne district court in May 2012 is a case in point. The court classified the circumcision of a Muslim boy which had unfortunately led to severe complications as "bodily harm", triggering a public debate in June on ritual circumcision. Politicians and the media generally discussed the issue in a sober and understanding tone, whereby criticism of the Cologne verdict was almost universal.[31] Politicians responded very quickly to find and implement a satisfactory legal solution. The whole episode provided antisemites however with a prime opportunity to express their resentments in the internet and the letters section of the press.

Monitoring Antisemitism

For decades now, monitoring antisemitism in Germany is in the hands of the Office for the Protection of the Constitution, and the task is accorded a great deal of attention politically. In the wake of the escalation of the Middle East conflict and the wave of antisemitic attacks in Europe during 2002, the problem was addressed on the European level for the first time—by the European Monitoring Center on Racism and Xenophobia (today: European Union Agency for Fundamental Rights). At two large conferences held in 2003 and 2004 in Vienna and Berlin, respectively—

with a series of follow-up conferences, Organization for Security and Cooperation in Europe (OSCE) member states committed themselves to monitoring antisemitism.

Over the last few years, the problem of antisemitism has been placed high on the agenda of federal politics in Germany, presumably due to the continuing high number of criminal offences, sporadic anti-Israeli demonstrations and the issue, empirically underexposed, of how widespread antisemitic attitudes are amongst Muslim (and other) migrants. At the beginning of 2008, a hearing of the Bundestag home affairs select committee was held on "Antisemitism in Germany", where experts debated the current state of knowledge. All parliamentary factions issued a declaration in November 2008 entitled "Supporting the fight against antisemitism, promoting Jewish life in Germany".[32] In the document, antisemitism was characterized as a serious social problem in Germany and solidarity with Israel as an inalienable part of German raison d'état. Since then, antisemitism is seen as a phenomenon not limited to political extremism that has to be combated across the board by both the state and civil society. Excluded by the other parties, *Die Linke* formulated an almost identical declaration. So as to bolster and better coordinate these efforts, an expert committee was set up by the German Parliament (Bundestag) in the Interior Ministry which is obligated to present a report on antisemitism in Germany. State-supported projects not only deal generally with fighting right-wing extremism but also explore questions of prevention and educational intervention in relationship to antisemitism, as well as how to deal with the history of the Holocaust in a migrant society. The first report was published in 2011.[33] In 2015, a new expert committee started its work on a follow-up report on antisemitism in Germany today. In November 2014, Berlin hosted a high-level conference on the 10th Anniversary of the OSCE's Berlin Conference on Anti-Semitism dealing with questions of countering contemporary antisemitism.

Besides these preventive efforts, the problem is also being tackled by a strict prohibition policy and criminal prosecution. Since the 1990s, numerous organizations of the extreme right have been banned, most recently an association calling itself the "rehabilitation of those persecuted for disputing the Holocaust" and another called "Heimattreue Deutsche Jugend". Following the failed attempt from 2003 to ban the NPD, the German Bundesrat submitted a new petition to the Federal Constitutional Court to have the party classified as anti-constitutional. The case is still pending. In addition, several Muslim organizations and bodies have been banned in recent years for denying the Holocaust or spreading antisemitic propaganda (e.g. Hizb ut-Tahrir, al-Manar-TV).

All things considered, a mixed picture of the situation in Germany as it entered its second decade of the new millennium emerges, with stability at the attitudinal level, a high number of hate crimes, small pockets of zealous antisemitic groups, not very successful right-wing extremist parties and a state and society trying to monitor and combat antisemitism as best it can.

Notes

1. Wilhelm Heitmeyer (ed.), *Deutsche Zustände*, Folge 1–10, Frankfurt a. M. 2002–2011; Andreas Zick, Anna Klein, Fragile Mitte. Feindselige Zustände. Rechtsextremismus in Deutschland 2014, Bonn 2014.
2. Klein/Zick, Fragile Mitte, Table 4.2.1.
3. Steffen Hagemann and Roby Natanson, Deutschland und Israel. Verbindende Vergangenheit, trennende Gegenwart, Gütersloh 2015, p. 35 and 37.
4. Oliver Decker/Marliese Weißmann/Johannes Kiess/Elmar Brähler, *Rechtsextreme Einstellungen in Deutschland 2010*, Berlin 2010; Decker et al. 2002. 2004, 2006, 2008, 2012.
5. Oliver Decker, Johannes Kiess, Elmar Brähler, Die Mitte im Umbruch. Rechtextreme Einstellungen in Deutschland 2012, Bonn 2012, p. 43.
6. Until 2012, these series of studies on right-wing extremist attitudes in Germany, sponsored by the Friedrich-Ebert-Foundation was conducted by Decker et al., who used face-to-face interviews; in 2014, it was for the first time conducted by Zick and Klein, Fragile Mitte, 2014, who used the telephone interviews (CATI).
7. ALLBUS (the German General Social Survey) collects up-to-date data on attitudes, behaviour and social structure in Germany. Every two years since 1980, a representative cross section of the population is surveyed using both constant and variable questions. The ALLBUS data become available to interested parties for research and teaching as soon as they are processed and documented. Werner Bergmann/Rainer Erb, Antisemitismus in der Bundesrepublik Deutschland 1996, in: Richard Alba/Peter

Schmidt/Martina Wasmer (eds.), *Deutsche und Ausländer: Freunde, Fremde oder Feinde? Empirische Befunde und theoretische Erklärungen*, Opladen 2000, p. 401–438; Werner Bergmann/Verena Münch, Antisemitismus in Deutschland 1996 und 2006—ein Vergleich, in: *Jahrbuch für Antisemitismusforschung*, vol. 21, 2012, p. 325–369.

8. For an overview, see Juliane Wetzel, Moderner Antisemitismus unter Muslimen in Deutschland, in: Thorsten Gerald Schneiders (ed.), *Islamverherrlichung. Wenn die Kritik zum Tabu wird*, Wiesbaden 2010, p. 379–391.
9. Wolfram Stender, Der Antisemitismusverdacht. Zur Diskussion über einen "migrantischen Antisemitismus" in Deutschland, in: *Migration und soziale Arbeit* 30 (2008), no. 3/4, p. 284–291, p. 289; also Wolfram Stender/Guido Follert/Mihri Özdogan (eds.), *Konstellationen des Antisemitismus: Antisemitismusforschung und sozialpädagogische Praxis*, Wiesbaden 2010.
10. The first qualitative studies for Germany have been published: Sina Arnold/Günther Jikeli, Judenhass und Gruppendruck. Zwölf Gespräche mit jungen Berlinern palästinensischen und libanesischen Hintergrunds, in: Jahrbuch für Antisemitismusforschung 17 (2008), p. 105–128; Günther Jikeli, "Jude" als Schimpfwort im Deutschen und Französischen. Eine Fallstudie unter jungen Berliner und Pariser Muslimen, in: Jahrbuch für Antisemitismusforschung 18 (2009), p. 43–66; see also the recently published English translation of his Ph.D. dissertation Günther Jikeli, European Muslim Antisemitism. Why Young Urban Males Say They Don't Like Jews (= Studies in Antisemitism), Bloomington 2015.
11. Muslim youths agreed to a far greater degree than German youths (15 % in comparison to 5.4 %) to the statement: "People of the Jewish faith are arrogant and greedy". Katrin Brettfeld/Peter Wetzels, Muslime in Deutschland—Integration, Integrationsbarrieren, Religion und Einstellungen zu Demokratie, Rechtsstaat und politisch-religiös motivierter Gewalt. Ergebnisse von Befragungen im Rahmen einer multizentrischen Studie in städtischen Lebensräumen (ed. BMI), Hamburg 2007, p. 275; http://www.bmi.bund.de/cln_183/SharedDocs/Downloads/DE/Broschueren/DE/2007/Muslime%20in%20Deutschland.html (retrieved 13.9.2010).

12. Jürgen Mansel and Viktoria Speiser, Abschlussbericht Forschungsprojekt: Soziale Beziehungen, Konfliktpotentiale und Vorurteile im Kontext von Erfahrungen verweigerte Teilhabe und Anerkennung von Jugendlichen mit und ohne Migrationshintergrund, Universität Bielefeld 2010.
13. Cem Özdemir, quoted in: "Warnung vor antijüdischen Tendenzen unter Migranten. Studie: Zahl antisemitischer Straftaten steigt", in: Berliner Zeitung 24th of February 2009. The mood amongst Turkish youths has changed since the Israeli attack on the Turkish ship "Mavi Marmara" that was part of the Gaza flotilla, which claimed the lives of several activists, and the shift of Turkey's foreign policy onto an anti-Israeli line.
14. "So tief sitzt der Hass. Antisemitismus in muslimischen Communities", in: Der Tagesspiegel 9th of September 2012.
15. Stender/Follert/Özdogan (eds.), Konstellationen des Antisemitismus.
16. Wetzel, Moderner Antisemitismus unter Muslimen, p. 381.
17. Verfassungsschutz Report 2011, p. 104.
18. See: Juden ohne Angst, in: taz.de, 5th of September 2012.
19. Report of the Office for the Protection of the Constitution 2011, 2012, 2013, published by the Federal Ministry of the Interior, Berlin.
20. Homepage NPD-Neukölln, 26th of July 2011, in: Verfassungsschutz Report 2011, p. 64.
21. Internet domain: Altermedia Deutschland, 6th of January 2013, cited in the Report of the Office for the Protection of the Constitution 2013, p. 125.
22. Homepage "National Journal", 1st of June 2013; cited in: Report of the Office for the Protection of the Constitution 2013, p. 128.
23. Deutsche Stimme 5/2011, p. 10 (party organ of the NPD).
24. Report of the Office for the Protection of the Constitution 2011, p. 66ff.
25. Report of the Office for the Protection of the Constitution 2013, p. 228f.
26. Report of the Office for the Protection of the Constitution 2011, p. 233ff.; Report 2013, p. 250.
27. Thomas Haury, Der neue Antisemitismusstreit der deutschen Linken, in: Neuer Antisemitismus? Eine globale Debatte, ed. Doron Rabinovici et al., Frankfurt a. M. 2004.

28. Result of a public opinion survey in: Der Stern, No. 4, 2009, p. 23.
29. Günter Grass, Was gesagt werden muss, in: Süddeutsche Zeitung, 4th of April 2012, p. 11.
30. Examples of the criticism levelled at Grass: Thomas Steinfeld, Dichten und meinen, in: Süddeutsche Zeitung, 81, 5./6. of April 2012, p. 13; here other reactions to Grass are given, namely from the Israeli ambassador in Berlin, the president of the Central Council of Jews in Germany, foreign minister Westerwelle, and several members of federal parliament; Jens Jessen, Das Opfer des Dichters, in: Die Zeit, 16, 12th of April 2012, p. 47.
31. Beschneidungs-Urteil des Landgerichts Köln. Vierjähriger Junge war mehrfach in Narkose, Süddeutsche Zeitung, 14th of July 2012; Streit über Beschneidungsurteil "Du bist beschnitten, du bist ein Mann", Spiegel-online, 13th of July 2012.
32. "Den Kampf gegen Antisemitismus zu verstärken, jüdisches Leben in Deutschland weiter zu fördern". Antrag der Fraktionen CDU/CSU, SPD, FDP und Bündnis90/Die Grünen, Den Kampf gegen Antisemitismus zu verstärken, jüdisches Leben in Deutschland weiter zu fördern, in: Deutscher Bundestag 16. Wahlperiode, Drucksache 16 (10775), 4th of November 2008.
33. *Antisemitismus in Deutschland. Erscheinungsformen, Bedingungen, Präventionsansätze. Bericht des unabhängigen Expertenkreises Antisemitismus*, Federal Ministry of the Interior, 2011.

CHAPTER 11

Antisemitism in Britain: Continuity and the Absence of a Resurgence?

Tony Kushner

Introduction

In 1969, at the end of a remarkable career, the Christian scholar, the Reverend James Parkes, remained convinced about the origins of antisemitism. It was, he believed, the Christian church which 'turned a normal xenophobia and normal good and bad communal relations between human societies into the unique evil of antisemitism'. In an article entitled 'Anti-Semitism from Caesar to Luther' published in 1938, Parkes elaborated the point further. Jews, he argued, had been involved in conflict that was not antisemitic. In their long history, there had been 'quarrels with their neighbours, in some of which they were wrong, and in some of which it was six of one and half a dozen of the other'. It would be absurd, Parkes continued, 'to call the Philistines or Assyrians "anti-Semites"'. Parkes believed conflict in antiquity between groups such as the Jews and Philistines were part of *normal* relations within human societies. In contrast, he underlined that 'Anti-Semitism is essentially an *abnormal* hostility'. Parkes was a modernist within the Anglican Church and it was within

T. Kushner (✉)
University of Southampton, Southampton, England

A. McElligott, J. Herf (eds.), *Antisemitism Before and Since the Holocaust*, DOI 10.1007/978-3-319-48866-0_11

that intellectual context that he examined various responses towards the Jews across the ages:

> [hostility] to the Jews can only be called anti-Semitic when it is abnormal in the sense that there is no adequate explanation for the form or the severity of its manifestation in the actual contemporary conduct of the Jews against whom it is directed. Its roots will be found at the point where something abnormal enters into the ideas of non-Jews about their Jewish neighbours.[1]

Parkes was, in many respects, decades ahead of his contemporaries and bravely so. First, he had, by the very early 1930s, moved beyond racialised thinking. Even many contemporary and progressive anti-racists in Britain and America, whilst rejecting the politicised use of racism in Nazi Germany and elsewhere, were still prone to think of groups such as Jews and blacks as essentially different. Not until the late 1940s was there a beginning of consensus, as reflected in the work of UNESCO in this field, that 'race' as a scientific method of classifying people, was utterly flawed.[2] Second, he was willing to acknowledge the role of his own Christian faith in what his contemporary Jules Isaac called the 'teaching of contempt'.[3]

***

Since 1945, most continental European countries to a greater or lesser extent have been in some form of denial about their past treatment of the Jews, especially those involved directly or indirectly with the deportation and destruction of the Jews during the Nazi era. Outside the western world, that difficult confrontation prompted by the Holocaust has hardly begun. Yet in spite of this incomplete acceptance of past responsibility, there is a danger in using the Nazi era as the starting point of analysis. If the Holocaust acts as a warning signal about the dangers of antisemitism, a careful perspective is required to ensure that every manifestation of intolerance towards Jews is not labelled as 'the new antisemitism' or as foregrounding mass destruction. More generally, in spite of all the work, historical and otherwise, on antisemitism in the wake of the Holocaust, we are still at an early stage in building up a sociology of knowledge of the subject. Certainly much of the analysis, especially of those arguing for a 'new antisemitism', has been journalistic and poorly and inaccurately researched. And if the Holocaust has been a stimulation to sober academic study of past antisemitism, it has also, perhaps inevitably, proved to be a distorting lens with which to view later manifestations of hatred with balance and proportion.

A Longer View of the 'Resurgence' of Antisemitism

Three decades after his death, James Parkes bequeaths to us a challenging and insightful analysis of attitudes towards Jews; one that is relevant and pertinent when confronting the alleged 'resurgence of antisemitism'[4] and *other* forms of prejudice. In Parkes' account there is, first, the issue of rationality and what Parkes regarded as 'normal' relations between majority and minority groups. Parkes was right to emphasise that if Jews have been involved in a conflictual situation, it is not necessarily antisemitic. Nevertheless, the limitations of his rationalistic approach were exposed in the 1930s. Reviewing the situation in Europe as a whole, for example, he argued that the Nazis had led to the 'creation of a Jewish problem where, in fact, none exists'.[5] This contrasted to the situation in Eastern Europe, especially Poland, where Parkes believed there was a 'genuine' Jewish problem. During the war, Parkes was an active campaigner on behalf of European Jewry and wrote that if measures of rescue led to three million Jews arriving in Britain then the numbers involved were no reason not to take them. It might lead to a 'Jewish problem', but one that was manageable. In less sympathetic hands, including that of the British government at the time, the fear of antisemitism being created by the sheer presence of a large Jewish influx became an insurmountable obstacle to action.[6]

Indeed, the basis of immigration control in much of the western world through the twentieth and now into the twenty-first centuries has been the desire to avoid creating such a 'problem' by refusing entry to a perceived 'alien wedge'. Parkes believed and continuously emphasised that antisemitism was a 'problem for non-Jews', by which he meant that its roots were with the majority and not the minority. It was thus a problem that could only be solved by actions of the former. Even so, reflecting the tense atmosphere of the Nazi era in which much of his writing and activism was concentrated, Parkes still placed much emphasis on Jewish difference and the problems this caused, in spite of his belief in the *irrationality* of most of the charges levelled at the Jew. Post 9/11, much attention is now being focussed on the need for minority groups, especially Muslims, to conform, to be good British, French and Dutch citizens and so on. Intriguingly, multi-culturalism is under question not just from its traditional opponents—those on the right, including the then British Prime

Minister, David Cameron, in an international speech given in February 2011—but also from those in the left-liberal world, exemplified by the interventions of Trevor Phillips, head of the (British) Equality Commission and through the columns of the progressive journal *Prospect* at the same point.[7] In Britain, since the 1960s especially, good 'race relations' have been seen as being dependent on the need for tolerance on behalf of the majority but with more emphasis placed on some form of integration on behalf of the minority.

As Robert Miles has pointed out, the concept of 'race relations', in part at least, tends to blame the minority for the existence of racism.[8] Parkes' concept of 'normal' relations involving Jews and non-Jews has its value, but it fails to take into account both the role of power in such relations and also more mundane prisms through which 'the Jew', or other minorities, might have been viewed. Equally, it assumes that hostility between one group and another is 'normal'—the philosophy of the 'new right' across the west. Whilst the language may have slipped from biology to culture (though we must not assume that the idea of scientific race thinking is dead—indeed it has revived recently with genetic research), it is assumed by politicians and philosophers of the right, and now increasingly of the centre and centre left, that ethnic difference, especially in the form of immigration, itself causes problems. One of the main themes I want to emphasise in this chapter is that it is dangerously misleading, from both a theoretical or practical perspective, to regard antisemitism or any form of racism as normal or natural.

The second issue with Parkes is that of his emphasis on the 'unique' nature of antisemitism. Working for various student bodies during the 1920s, Parkes confronted nationalist and racialist antisemitism in the continental European universities where it was particularly rife and violent. He became aware of the menace faced by the Jews much earlier and more profoundly than most in the western world. Aside from his practical efforts to help, Parkes devoted his life thereafter to seeking for the roots of this antisemitism. Having discovered to his own satisfaction that these originated with the church, he then, in some 400+ publications, outlined the history of antisemitism over the millennia. Others have subsequently followed Parkes, including Leon Poliakov, who was much influenced by him, in the French Jew's multi-volume history of antisemitism which started in antiquity and ended in 1933.[9] Similarly, Coudenhove-Kalergi's *Anti-Semitism throughout the Ages*,[10] Shmuel Almog's similarly entitled volume, *Antisemitism Through the Ages*,[11] Robert Wistrich's *Antisemitism:*

The Longest Hatred and similarly his *A Lethal Obsession*,[12] and Fineberg, Samuel and Weitzmann's *Antisemitism: The Generic Hatred*,[13] whilst, as with Parkes, allowing for changes in accusations and of emphasis, also place, as their titles suggest, greater stress on continuity. This is also true within a specifically British context of Anthony Julius' *Trials of the Diaspora*, which covers the period from the medieval period through to the late twentieth century.[14]

Since antiquity, Jews *have* been subject to various forms of hostility, including collective violence, expulsion, discrimination and mass murder. As early as the 1920s, however, major Jewish historians on both sides of the Atlantic, Salo Baron and Cecil Roth, warned against the 'lachrymose' version of the Jewish experience focusing on persecution. Since the Holocaust, which has stimulated much further investigation of past hatred of Jews, the justification for writing a beginning to end history of antisemitism has, not surprisingly, intensified. It remains that the very best work on the subject tends to be both specific both in time, space or theme, and the least convincing that which spans different eras and all subjects in an attempt to provide a narrative revealing a continuous history of hatred.

Given the enormity of the Holocaust and the irreparable damage done to Jewish culture in much of Europe, it is not surprising that antisemitism has become regarded as natural and even inevitable. This is ahistorical in that it ignores large chunks of Jewish history in which hostility was not predominant as Baron and Roth emphasised. Even the medieval period, in which hostility was formalised and became in places state sponsored, was, in reality, complex and multi-layered. Nevertheless, as Patricia Skinner has highlighted, 'medieval' has become a label of abuse—in the twentieth century, contemporary violence against the Jews was often given that label, especially in relation to Tsarist Russia and Nazi Germany. Skinner concludes that almost by definition, '"medieval" for early twentieth-century historians functioned as shorthand for barbaric, cruel and irrational'.[15] Such distancing fails to get to grips with the ambivalence and sometimes positive responses towards the Jew in the Middle Ages. It also reveals a reluctance to accept that antisemitism could be a feature of the modern world.

What then are the implications of the critique provided so far of studying antisemitism in general when confronting its existence today? Perhaps the most significant feature is the tendency to portray antisemitism as a natural feature. This may be in the form of a monster, one that has devoured millions of Jews and might do so again. In quieter times, antisemitism is often described as being 'dormant', or, to quote the title of a Runnymede Trust study carried out into antisemitism in Britain during the early 1990s, as a 'very light sleeper'.[16] Such a monster in the past required a Jewish equivalent, the Golem, or, in the American Jewish version in mid-twentieth century, various forms of extra-terrestrial 'supermen' to rescue its helpless victims. Brian Klug has pointed out a similar metaphorical tendency amongst commentators which views antisemitism as a '"virus" that "mutates"'.[17]

An alternative, unfabricated metaphor for antisemitism has been to link it to natural and especially water-driven disaster. In April 2002, Jonathan Sacks, then Chief Rabbi of Britain and the Commonwealth, stated that in the 'past 12 months the floodgates have opened to everything we have fought against for the past 57 years. A wave of hate has filled the world.'[18] On 1 January 2006, in a radio broadcast marking the 350th anniversary of the readmission of the Jews to England, Sacks took this further and cautioned that there was a 'tsunami of antisemitism' spreading globally.[19] Sacks emphasised that it was not a word he used lightly. Indeed, in December 2004, he called the devastation caused by the tsunamis in Asia 'the worst humanitarian disaster in 40 years' and a 'tragedy of biblical proportions'.[20] In his January 2006 broadcast, Sacks, in giving his warning, stated that he was scared by the rise of antisemitism, and also 'very scared that more protests have not been delivered against it'. If there is a practical parallel in Jonathan Sacks' metaphor—early warning systems might protect against the potential destruction of both a tsunami and a global wave of antisemitism, there is a much greater implication that antisemitism can erupt, very quickly, at any time, and, like a virus out of control, wreak devastation.

This is not to argue necessarily that antisemitism has not risen or changed in its focus. It is simply to highlight the fundamental ahistorical nature of the argument that antisemitism is somehow out there, needing only to be awakened out of slumber or mutate in some massively infectious airborne disease, or, alternatively, to re-emerge from the bowels of the earth as the result of random volcanic eruptions. Human agency is in danger of being downplayed in Sacks' tsunami metaphor. Yet that both Jews and non-Jews have used such ocean-inspired warnings about the danger of antisemitism suggests the existence of wider anxieties at work, of a world out of control and dangerous, and to which antisemitism is an acute danger signal. It is, as Sacks added, 'that kind of feeling that you don't know what's going to happen next' which was so frightening.[21] It must be suggested that such sensitivity is absent when other forms of racism and prejudice in the contemporary world are considered, or more often than not, not considered. It suggests that post-Holocaust, antisemitism has become a symbol of a world that went mad, and can go mad again, regardless of there being perhaps far more obvious signals of human rights abuse and other catastrophic disasters.

What then of Sacks' thesis that antisemitism is on the rise across the world, including Europe? Whilst his use of the tsunami metaphor was unique, Sacks' overall analysis is part of an overall consensus today that there is the biggest growth of antisemitism internationally since the Second World War. The All-Party Parliamentary Inquiry into Antisemitism, for example, set up in 2005, 'has been launched in response to evidence that British Jews are living in a state of fear and discomfort as a result of a perceptible rise in antisemitism'.[22] By using the example of Britain, it will be possible to examine whether this analysis is correct, and, more fundamentally, whether the right questions are being asked.

Choosing Britain as a case study raises its own issues and dilemmas. Internally and externally, and inside and outside the Jewish world, there is a myth of British, more frequently, English, exceptionalism: that of all European nations, England has, post-readmission, been most free of antisemitism. In Anglo-Jewish historiography, at least until the 1970s, antisemitism was dismissed as being of little significance, and when it did manifest itself, as with Hilaire Belloc at the turn of the twentieth century, or Oswald Mosley in the 1930s, it was foreign inspired—French in the former case and German in the latter.[23] From the 1980s onwards, a so-called new school of Anglo-Jewish historians and literary scholars, including David Cesarani, Bryan Cheyette, Tony Kushner, Nadia Valman and Bill Williams, emerged to provide a more critical perspective allowing for tendencies within British culture that were less welcoming of the Jew, or Jewish difference. More recently, however, their work has been parodied, especially by American academics. Bill Rubinstein, for instance, has suggested that 'the younger school seems to be engaged in a kind of Dutch auction to determine who can discover the most insidious examples of British antisemitism, reminiscent of the "Four Yorkshiremen" in the famous Monty Python skit who outdo one another to depict the exaggerated horrors of their youth'.[24] Another American historian has labelled this group as a 'new and very pessimistic generation of scholars'.[25]

What is missing in these critiques of this historiographical shift in Anglo-Jewish historiography is that it was not about seeing antisemitism everywhere. Rubinstein uses the example of Bill Williams' seminal article 'The Antisemitism of Tolerance' to make his point. In fact, Williams was showing, within the liberal city par excellence, Manchester, how there was pressure placed on elite Jews to wipe out any form of difference amongst their poorer, foreign brethren. It led, Williams concludes, to the rapid destruction of Yiddish culture that the immigrants brought with them. If the elite Jews were part of middle-class Manchester, then their acceptance was conditional on 'good' behaviour and controlling the behaviour of poorer, foreign Jews.[26]

If there is an underlying theme to the new school's work, it is summarised by the word *ambivalence*. Those who hated or campaigned against all Jews were rare and generally marginal in British society and culture. In contrast, ambivalence—supporting some Jews or their alleged activities and opposing others—was the norm. This was often in the form of praising westernised, assimilated Jews and rejecting those who were deemed foreign, especially those from the east of Europe—a bifurcation that was the basis, in practice, of British immigration control procedures from the 1900s to the 1940s. Alongside ambivalence, there has also been an emphasis in this new scholarship on culture and the place of the 'Jew' in constructing national identities and more specifically concepts of Englishness. The crude and alternative world made up of philosemites and antisemites is replaced by what Bryan Cheyette, a leading literary scholar, has termed 'semitic discourse' through which society was interpreted.[27] Indeed, rather than seeing antisemitism everywhere, the new school has largely abandoned the term as being too limiting and too provocative in the associations it draws to be of analytical value. Ironically, however, those opposed to it have produced a revisionist historiography that in many respects returns to the apologetic, defensive and ethnic cheerleading approaches that existed before the 1980s. Rubinstein's history of the Jews of Great Britain is largely dedicated to proving an absence of antisemitism. In total contrast, Anthony Julius in *Trials of the Diaspora*, part of the new mood of concern, emphasises that in England 'The anti-Semitism of no other country has this density of history. The anti-Semitism of no other country is so continuously innovative'.[28] Yet despite (or perhaps better because) of their polar extremes, neither Rubinstein nor Julius can get to grips with the concept of ambiguity towards the Jews that is at the heart of the more sophisticated scholarship.

There is a wider problem here. In spite of the new school's subtle and multi-layered approach to studying the place of Jews in British society, culture and politics, it is dismissed cheaply as pessimistic and negative. The debate, as with recent commemorations of the 350th anniversary of read-mission, has been literally simplified into either/or camps: answering the question: 'Britain—good or bad for the Jews?' In Britain, as, to a large extent, with the USA, there is a denial of any past intolerance as it runs counter to the narrative of a country typified in its own mythology by decency, tolerance and fair play. This is also the case with other forms of intolerance in Britain where a hostile tradition is denied or downplayed. Thus in summer 2005, when black teenager, Anthony Walker, was murdered with an axe by two local racist thugs in a Liverpool suburb, the Labour MP for the constituency refused to accept that there had been any previous racist intimidation in the area in spite of plentiful testimony to the contrary. Racism, including antisemitism, is regarded as somebody else's problem in Britain, and not 'our' own. The recent ease in which the Holocaust has been assimilated into the pedagogic and museum world in Britain is largely due to the emphasis that is placed on it happening elsewhere, especially as the perpetrators were German. Britain, in contrast, plays the heroic role as liberator or rescuer with the increasing attention given to the *Kindertransport* refugee movement in popular memory work.[29]

Even Jonathan Sacks, who has, as we have seen, played a key role in warning against the rise of antisemitism, largely exempted Britain from his analysis. Britain, when it is convenient to be so, can be regarded as outside Europe. In 2004, Sacks made this point explicit. 'Britain is not, and is not about to become, an anti-Semitic society. I do not say that about all European countries. In some places—France in particular—many Jews do live in fear'.[30] In a similar vein, the Runnymede Trust 1994 report *A Very Light Sleeper* projected the problem onto the continent: 'Whilst Britain has never experienced the virulent strains of antisemitism which have now appeared in continental Europe, there is always the fear that any increase in antisemitic activity in other European countries will find a ready echo in the UK. Given the pattern of antisemitic incidents in Britain over the last decade or so, it is clear that copy-cat incidents occur following highly publicised events on the continent'.[31]

Measuring Up

Several decades ago, the Jewish historian Lucy Dawidowitz pondered whether antisemitism could be measured.[32] Her question is even more pertinent today in an age of ubiquitous opinion polls and monitoring bodies. But how can we measure antisemitism? The sociologist of genocide, Helen Fein, created a model explaining why some Nazi occupied countries lost almost all their Jews and others hardly any. The relative strength of antisemitism in each of these countries was a major, in fact *the* major factor, she argued, in her bleak league table of deportation.[33] But comparing antisemitism nation against nation is a dangerous pursuit. Death tolls in the Holocaust might reflect locally based antisemitism, but, more than anything, they correlate to the level of Nazi control over countries and the specific animus against eastern as opposed to western Jews. The Jews of Denmark, for example, mattered less in the Nazi mentality than those of Poland—hence their markedly different survival rate.

Violence today, however, against Jews, has less of an immediate foreign influence than in times of total war and it thus may, on the surface, be easier to detect which national culture is the most/least antisemitic. It is only since the last decades of the twentieth century that statistics have been collected on racial attacks, and such data on antisemitism specifically has an even more recent history. At a blatant level, the totals obtained on a year-by-year basis have some use in 'measuring' racism or antisemitism. There are two major problems with this source. First, the range of racism or antisemitism included as harassment varies from name calling in the street and receiving hate letters through to serious assault and murder. Second, some increase in the figures is due to better reporting and dealing with such incidents. In the 1980s and beyond, it was argued that less than half incidents of racial harassment in Britain were reported, reflecting a distrust of police and authority in general on behalf of Afro-Caribbean and Asian minorities in Britain, as well as the fear of reprisals.[34] The police, especially after its failures after the murder of another black teenager, Stephen Lawrence, in 1993, have made much greater efforts to get racial crime reported and to deal with it. It seems likely that fewer incidents now go unrecorded. In this respect, there is a great sensitivity towards Jewish victims, and the state structure regard the Jewish Community Security Trust (CST) as a model for other minority groups to follow with regard to protecting against and reporting attacks. Whilst it is possible that sections of the very orthodox community might still feel uneasy with reporting antisemitic incidents, overall the Jewish community is probably much more likely and able to report such violence than other ethnic minorities in Britain, a pattern that is also largely the case across the western world. Authority and the state structure is trusted by British Jewry, whereas for many within Afro-Caribbean, and especially the Muslim communities, it is still regarded as a threat and a menace, as reflected in police stop and search practices on an everyday level.

What then do the statistics tell us? In 1999, there were 270 antisemitic incidents in Britain, according to the CST, rising to 405 in 2000, falling to 310 in 2001 and rising steadily to 375 in 2003 before expanding to 532 in 2004 and then falling to 450 in 2005. Within the peak year of 2004, the number included 83 violent assaults, up from 54 the year before. Whilst overall figures fell in 2005, violent assaults remained at the same level and included two rated as 'extreme'. Police figures for 2004 and 2005 actually showed a small increase for the latter year with a total of 390 offences for incidents involving antisemitism.[35] The year 2006 saw an increase in attacks monitored by the CST with close to 600 incidents, four involving extreme violence. Numbers slowly declined in 2007 and 2008 before reaching a new level of 926 (although with only three of extreme violence) in 2009 before falling to 639 incidents in 2010.[36]

The 1994 Runnymede Trust report, *A Very Light Sleeper*, started with the statement that 'In Britain between 1984 and 1992 there was an 85% increase in the reporting of antisemitic incidents'.[37] Almost all monitoring related analyses of antisemitism seem to start from the premise that the problem is increasing. This percolates through at even a popular level. A 1993 Gallup Poll in Britain found that one quarter of the sample expected antisemitism to rise and only 6 per cent for it to decline.[38] In a post-Holocaust world, to query such assumptions of the growth and future potential of antisemitism is to risk accusations of complacency, even appeasement, given the historical precedents of the 1930s and the warnings that were, with hindsight, ignored.

If we return to the contemporary statistics: the figures through the first decade of the twenty-first century do suggest a rise in antisemitic incidents—especially those involving physical assault. Again, two qualifications are in order. The first is historical, the second is putting the findings in a comparative framework. Racial violence in Britain was not statistically monitored before the 1970s. Only when there was collective violence, as against Jews in 1904 in Ireland and 1911 in South Wales, or in 1919 and 1958 against black groups, has there been acknowledgement of a wider problem of physical harassment.[39] Even then, these riots have been subject to collective amnesia. Yet from oral and written testimony, it would seem that minor physical assaults, especially on school children, were common in the period of mass immigration and into the interwar period, especially when Jews stepped outside the main areas of Jewish settlement. This was even more the case of black communities in Britain. During the 1930s, organised antisemitism in the form of the British Union of Fascists was at its strongest, and assaults on Jews were a regular occurrence. In 1947, the most widespread collective violence against Jews took place in Britain, although attacks on individuals—as opposed to property—were rare. Indeed, for the Jews of Britain, as elsewhere in Europe, the immediate post-war years were extremely difficult, with their loyalty called into question in the light of Zionist extremist activities in British Mandate Palestine. It is possible that the 1950s were a quieter time for the Jews though certainly not for the new Commonwealth migrants coming to Britain. The early 1960s, however, saw the return of violent neo-Nazi activities leading to the death of several Jews in an arson-related attack and a swastika epidemic that also affected the rest of Europe. In that temporal context, with our intense knowledge of the situation now compared to the past, it does not appear that there is anything unprecedented about the current situation taking the last hundred years as a whole. That is not to deny that there is a problem and one that may well be subject to a recent growth, albeit one that is not exceptional if a secular view is employed. Why there may be an upturn will be dealt with shortly, as will the impact of such attacks. Before then, however, a comparison with other forms of contemporary violence is in order.

To quote Tony Lerman, an alternative and sober voice on the nature of contemporary antisemitism:

> The emphasis placed by commentators on the rise in incidents in the UK makes it look as if Jews are in front line of racial attacks. But how true is it? Figures for London produced by [the police] and the Greater London Assembly suggest that if you're black, Arab or from the Indian subcontinent, you are 11-13 times more likely to be the victim of racial crime than a white European. If you are a Jew, three times as likely.[40]

Lerman concludes that whilst this is 'entirely unacceptable … seen in the large context, Jews are hardly in the front line'.[41] I would add to this that the differentiation between Jews and non-white groups is likely, in reality, to be even larger, due to under-reporting in the case of the latter. But rather than see this as a competitive list of victimhood, it would, it must be argued, be better to understand attacks on Jews and other ethnic minorities as part of the same problem—that of the impact of exclusive nationalism manifesting itself violently. In fact, those suffering the most day-to-day violence, often murderous, are asylum seekers, Gypsy and traveller groups and Muslims in Britain. There is surely a correlation that the most socially acceptable form of intolerance in Britain is against these groups which are prone to the greatest harassment. Conversely, Jews, as an ethno-religious minority are probably the least subject to violence, and antisemitism has the greatest social taboo against its articulation.

It is not immediately obvious why there is any underlying socio-economic reason for racial violence in contemporary Britain. It is amongst the top ten most prosperous nations in the world and until the economic downturn in the latter part of the first decade of the twentieth century had historically low unemployment. Underneath, however, there are tensions such as the strain being placed on the welfare state, especially the health service and pensions, job insecurity and the speed of change in work practice and life as a whole, and very high relative and absolute deprivation within some areas, especially in the north of England, which are suffering from de-industrialisation and the impact of global competition. Alongside these more specific factors are wider fears over war, climate and general international instability. We operate in what Frank Furedi has called the 'politics of fear'.[42] Within Britain, minorities—especially as emphasised asylum seekers, Muslims and Gypsies (and most recently East European migrants)—are those upon whom these anxieties are expressed. Jews have been subject, if on a less profound level, to these frustrations.

This is not to deny a specific dynamic at work with regard to antisemitism and antisemitic incidents. Roughly 20 per cent of the incidents in one of the peak years—2004—were connected to Israel or the Middle East, according to CST figures[43] and the sudden growth in incidents in 2009 was undoubtedly indirectly connected to the intense tension in that region. Whether such incidents should be included within the overall total is debatable, but even if they are it remains that the large majority in most years do not have that linkage. Moreover, in contrast to the views expressed by some commentators, it does not appear that Muslims are especially prominent in these attacks and nor are they particularly the work of right-wing extremists. They are, in short, part of 'everyday life' carried out by ordinary people and all the more worrying for their more random nature. Whilst a specific discourse is at work in these attacks (with explicit references made in such attacks to the Jewishness of the victims, often drawing upon long-held negative stereotypes), more generally they fit into a wider picture of societal intolerance of those deemed to be different.

Tony Lerman, whilst calling for calm, has acknowledged that 'if your synagogue is vandalized, the tombstones of your relatives are desecrated or you are subject to antisemitic abuse, the world will feel a nasty place'.[44]

Two examples from the south coast of England will reveal the motivation and impact of such attacks. In 1993, the Jewish cemetery in Southampton was desecrated. Almost every tombstone was daubed with antisemitic graffiti. The attack achieved international attention and condemnation.[45] Since then, with far less notice, the cemetery has been attacked several times. Whilst the antisemitic graffiti has been removed quickly, more recent attacks, as elsewhere in Britain, have left irreparable damage to many of the tombstones. The 1993 desecration caused distress to the small Jewish community but the speed with which it was cleaned up, the condemnation within Southampton, including a protest march, and outside of it, brought comfort and reassurance. The subsequent attacks have caused further heartache and also financial problems of repair. Alongside a minor attack on the synagogue by right-wing extremists, it has intensified the caution and unease felt by the community as a whole.

The second case relates to the brutal beating up of a Southampton teenager in 2003 by an 18-year-old that left the victim with a badly broken jaw and ongoing lasting trauma. The perpetrator was the leader of a gang with a Nazi obsession, but he was aided by his followers, male and female. The victim had a Jewish father who had told him to be proud of his heritage. The leader of the gang, after an antisemitic tirade, demanded to know if any of the innocent group of teenagers they had come across were Jewish, hence the attack. Subsequently the teenage victim has been frightened to go out on his own and has constant flashbacks. The perpetrator had offences for many other forms of racial violence.[46] This case, one of many thousands that take place in Britain every year, is an indication of the damage done by any form of racism. That perhaps only between one in 500 to 1000 Jews a year have been subject to its terror is not a measure of Britain's tolerance, but an indication of the depths of a much wider social malaise in which one in ten of those of colour have been affected.

Before turning attention away from the statistics and onto culture, a few final comparative perspectives will be helpful. It is likely that antisemitism still operates in some informal way in the employment and housing market and in social interaction through clubs and societies. Few cases, however, go to the Equality and Human Rights Commission (EHRC) and there is probably far less of this 'polite' discrimination than ever before. If there is economic discrimination, it makes only limited impact on Jewish well-being. According to data from the 2001 census and other sources, Jews, alongside Christians, have the lowest unemployment and best health and education of all religious groups in Britain. In contrast, Muslims had the highest unemployment and worst health and education.[47]

The data from antisemitic incidents, alongside the socio-economic profile of British Jewry when probed, produces a complex picture of different forms of integration. On one level, most, but not all Jews are comparatively middle class and relatively prosperous—they have the highest wealth level of all religious groups in the UK. Any antisemitism in the workplace that still lingers, in contrast to the interwar period, has not stopped their social mobility which is higher than that for the population as a whole. On another, antisemitic attacks, and their rise, shows an integration into the wider treatment of ethnic and minority groups in Britain, and reveals that the Jews, whilst not the major victims of such violence, are still not, for some, regarded as 'one of us'.

Contemporary Controversies

In the remainder of this chapter, I want to explore further the unacceptability of antisemitism, or otherwise, in British culture and politics, and whether there are developments that would merit the idea of a resurgence or even the label of a 'new antisemitism'. The first case study comes from the 2005 General Election and the treatment of the then Conservative leader, Michael Howard. In 1997, Howard failed to become leader of the Conservatives and there were widespread allegations of an antisemitic whispering campaign against him from the Conservative backbenchers and constituency workers.[48] Not all Conservative supporters were as happy as Margaret Thatcher in having more old Estonians than old Etonians in leading positions.[49] In 2004, rather appropriately given his vampire image, Howard came back from the dead and was chosen to be the new Conservative leader. It should be added that this was after several disastrous leaders and facing an almost unwinnable general election.[50]

Rather than downplay his Jewish immigrant origins and the impact of the Holocaust on his family as he had before, Howard put these to the forefront in an attempt to soften his previously prickly, nasty and untrustworthy image. It also allowed him to campaign on a blatantly anti-immigrant platform in 2005 claiming that his background as the son and grandson of Holocaust survivors meant that he could not possibly be racist.[51] In the end, this dubious campaign paid only minor dividends, but Howard did as well as any figure could have done to revive Conservative fortunes: it is unlikely that his Jewishness stopped people voting Conservative in all but a small number of cases. Indeed, the false legitimacy his immigrant origins provided for his assault on asylum seekers perhaps brought in, comparatively, far more support. Analysing the imagery associated with Michael Howard in 2005 is therefore not concerned directly with that election result, but relates more to the place of the Jew in the twenty-first-century British imagination.

In January 2005, posters depicting Howard as either a pickpocket or a hypnotist and he and his fellow Jewish conservative, Oliver Letwin, as flying pigs were used by the Labour Party. Much was made of these images then and throughout the election of whether they were, or were not, antisemitic. A year earlier, Labour propagandists had labelled Letwin as 'Fagin'.[52] On the surface, they were utilising antisemitic tropes from the medieval period through to the Victorian age as a way of packaging Conservative leaders and policies as dangerously Jewish. The *Judensau* particularly was a vicious medieval image of the diabolic Jew as was Dickens' portrayal of the fence, Fagin. Du Murier's Svengali was another sinister Jewish figure, powerful, subversive and a sexual menace. If this is added to the constant portrayal of Howard as a Transylvanian vampire, then representations of this leading Conservative have apparently managed to cover the history of antisemitism as might be drawn by Julius Streicher.

A closer reading of these images, however, reveals a more nuanced situation. In the case of the two little Jewish pigs, the direct connection to the *Judensau* is coincidental: if anything, the images managed to make Howard and Letwin endearing. Yet if the point that the Conservative figures on tax and spending simply did not add up—hence pigs might fly—it was insensitive of the Labour spin doctors not to show some awareness that to connect Jews to pork, the subject of past Christian fascination, crude humour and physical persecution, lacked an element of sensitivity. This was much more so with the indirect and direct references to Fagin and Svengali. It is conceivable that the Labour propagandists wanted to make these connections and play negatively on Howard's new found open Jewishness. More likely, they revealed that post-Holocaust, these images still play a role (perhaps subconscious) in British culture. It is revealing, in this respect, to explore the comments of a leading journalist coming out of this minor election scandal. Not known for his sensitivity towards the Jews, Richard Ingrams, late editor of the satirical weekly *Private Eye*, rejected all claims of antisemitism in the 'Howard as Fagin' poster, and bemoaned in his column in the British weekly newspaper *Observer*

(6 February 2005) that nowadays no film director would allow Fagin to be played as monster in the way portrayed by Alec Guinness in the late 1940s. Interestingly, in 2001, another commentator, John Mortimer, writing in the right-wing *Daily Mail*, had praised the representation in a BBC dramatisation of Augustus Melmotte in Anthony Trollope's *The Way We Live Now*, as a 'snoop-shouldered, swivel-eyed maniac' based on Robert Maxwell. Mortimer was delighted that it marked the return of such stereotypical portrayals free from what he alleged was the censorship of 'political correctness'. 'No such built-up nose has been seen since the death of Olivier and this potent mixture of Shylock and Disraeli', argued Mortimer, a prominent writer himself, 'is now a weekly treat for an audience starved of such performances'.[53] This semitic portrayal was ironic, as Bryan Cheyette has commented: whilst Trollope created many unpleasant Jews in his literature, Melmotte is not specifically Jewish. Referring to the dramatisation, Cheyette commented that it was a 'disturbing Jewish stereotype, bringing Shylock up to date. The BBC is circulating these Victorian stereotypes once again'.[54] It suggests that there is a cultural market for baser depictions of the Jews and that the cultural traditions they draw upon are deeply embedded.[55]

At a blunter level, 192,850 people voted for the neo-Nazi British National Party in the 2005 General Election a figure rising to 563,743 in 2010. They were attracted, I would argue, *not* to the BNP because under the surface its leadership maintains a core antisemitic ideology. Instead, anti-Muslim and anti-asylum seeker phobia (and more general xenophobia) were the more blatant reasons for its appeal. As with the National Front in the 1970s and 1980s, some of its supporters at the ballot box were essentially registering a protest vote. Nevertheless, the Nazi credentials of the BNP did not *stop* people voting for them. Indeed, the BNP had unprecedented success for a British far right party in local councils (maximising at 55 seats across the country in 2007 before declining rapidly thereafter) as well as having two MEPs elected in 2009, including its leader, Nick Griffin. But most of these gains were localised—largely in the north of England—and were short-lived. They cannot compare to the worrying success of equivalent parties and movements in many other European nations. The memory of the Second World War still stands as a major obstacle to the success in Britain of any party which could be directly or indirectly linked to Nazism. It does not follow, however, that all forms of intolerance and prejudice have disappeared in Britain since 1945, as the remaining sections of this article will explore.

The final example in the cultural–political realm concerns the long-standing left-liberal weekly the *New Statesman* and its now infamous cover illustration on 14 January 2002. It is important more generally as it, for many, typifies the 'new antisemitism' emerging in left-liberal circles. It also brings us back to why Britain is a significant case study in analysing 'the resurgence of antisemitism'. Britain is meant to be a major focal point of this new intellectual assault upon the Jews. Thus Paul Iganski and Barry Kosmin's *A New Antisemitism? Debating Judeophobia in 21st-Century Britain* devotes 14 pages out of 300 to that issue of the *New Statesman* and Bernard Harrison's *The Resurgence of Anti-Semitism* dedicates a whole chapter to it.[56]

The cover and the two related articles within the issue were widely criticised. Professor Stefan Reif of Cambridge University suggested that the illustration, 'depicting the Star of David piercing the heart of the Union Jack, was in the best traditions of Nazi Germany's *Der Sturmer*, as were the generalisations [in the articles] made about wealthy and powerful Jews' (*New Statesman*, 21 January 2002). David Triesman, then general secretary of the Labour Party, suggested that the cover 'must be one of the most offensive images I have seen. It gathers together a symbol of Jewishness (not of Israel), conspiracy, and wealth in ways candidly redolent of the extreme right'. Triesman concluded that he had read the *New Statesman* for 40 years: 'I never thought I would come to regard it as anti-Semitic. But I do today'.[57]

Three weeks later, the editor of the *New Statesman*, Peter Wilby, admitted that 'We got it wrong'. He added that 'The cover was not intended to be anti-Semitic; the New Statesman is vigorously opposed to racism in all its forms'. Such denial and proclamation of anti-racism is almost automatic in Britain. Nevertheless, it should not be dismissed lightly in this case—the *New Statesman* has an honourable tradition in this respect, especially in the Nazi era in confronting antisemitism at home and abroad. Why then did it get it so wrong and use, in its editor's own admission, 'images and words in such a way as to create unwittingly the impression that the New Statesman was following an anti-Semitic tradition that sees Jews as a conspiracy piercing the heart of the nation'?[58]

The blatant, 'new right', explanation is that the *New Statesman* was providing a classic example of this new, left-liberal version of antisemitism which used attacks on Israel and its supporters as a way to articulate an animus against Jews as a whole. The left-liberal world, then, is the new enemy of the Jews and what is most precious to their Jewish identity—the state of Israel. Taken to its extreme, all criticism of Israel is antisemitic and to query the legitimacy of the Jewish state is to continue the destruction wrought by the Third Reich. A far more convincing case is provided by reversing the causality. Those attacking the legitimacy of the state of Israel, or specific Israeli policies are not motivated in the first instance by a desire to inflict harm on the Jewish world. Rather, they sometimes, but far from always, write about Jews, especially as a collectivity, through a semitic discourse in which the idea of power is still powerful. This is far from new. As David Cesarani has illustrated, such language permeated right-wing critiques of the alleged pro-Zionist policies of British politicians during the 1920s.[59]

Generalising, the western world as a whole has a problem in dealing with Jews as weak and defenceless because the dominant discourse has demanded, in spite of all evidence to the contrary, that Jews be powerful and menacing. This discourse has cut across right and left, although in the twentieth century the latter has had much greater empathy with the Jews as downtrodden victims. When Jews are no longer so obviously victims, or where there is contradictory evidence, as in the Middle East today, confusion has emerged and there has been a tendency to use the tropes of Jewish victimhood, especially the Holocaust, to attack alleged instances of 'Jewish' abuse of power. Hence the Labour politician, Oona King, who is black and Jewish, likened a Gaza Palestinian refugee camp to the Warsaw ghetto.[60] The former mayor of London, Ken Livingstone, got into even deeper trouble by likening a Jewish journalist working for a right-wing newspaper chain to a concentration camp guard.[61] Translated into the fractured and paranoid world of Northern Ireland politics, Unionists have adopted the Israeli flag and Republicans the Palestinian, especially in street murals and banners in sectarian marches.

Overall, it remains that the left-liberal world's identification with the Palestinian cause is not motivated by an opportunity to be anti-Jewish but with a genuine, if sometimes naive, identification with another group who are seen as defenceless and powerless victims. In the context of the life chances of the Palestinian refugees in areas like Gaza, it is not an unreasonable perception. The legitimacy of this concern, however, is dangerously compromised when it is articulated through a semitic discourse which sees Jews as *naturally* powerful and dangerous.

What is ironic about the *New Statesman* issue is that whilst its main accompanying article by Dennis Sewell talked of the 'semi-public face of Britain's Zionist lobby', it ended by debunking the power of those who tried to influence the media into adopting a more sympathetic approach to Israel. It came to the conclusion that pro-Israel lobbying in Britain is largely ineffective but is equally open and transparent. In the most clumsy and stupid way, the cover of this issue and the early contents of Sewell's article set up an antisemitic trope only to largely knock it down.[62] It represented a very public coming to terms with the past that exposed, aside from its insensitivity, the power of past discourse. That many others still uncritically referred to the 'Jewish cabal' of advisers influencing Tony Blair, as did Labour MP, Tam Dalyell in 2003,[63] and, more frequently, see this power operating within American politics, is thus not a new phenomenon but a long standing inability to deal with 'the Jew' as a complex historical actor, operating beyond the categories of victim or secretive power broker.

We are, however, expecting too much of the impact of the Holocaust if we expect the deeply ingrained western discourse about Jewish power to have simply disappeared after 1945. This reassessment will be all the more difficult as this discourse has now been taken up within sections of the Arab and Muslim world, including diasporas within Europe. It has led to crude, politicised attacks on Israel and so-called Zionist politics. The almost farcical articulation of Holocaust denial as a form of de-legitimising Israel, most recently in Iran, is, somewhat bizarrely, an indication of how artificially constructed such borrowings from the west are. Once unleashed, however, the belief in Jewish power may not disappear so quickly. Nevertheless, progress or deterioration in the Middle East will be the most important factor determining the level of rhetoric in this respect. Returning to the west, what has *not* happened is a restraining influence of the Holocaust that has now worn off.

Conclusion

James Parkes was asked by his major funder in the 1930s how long education would take to eradicate antisemitism. Parkes responded that because thinking about the Jew was so integral to cultural, religious and national attitudes, it would take 'about three hundred years'.[64] If this sounds depressing, a sense of balance is still needed. In the early years of the twenty-first century, whilst antisemitic incidents may be on the rise, Britain and most western nations are still places where it is relatively safe to be a Jew. It is important to return to the point made earlier that the Jewish experience has not always been about persecution. Whilst a sense of history, especially recent history, may lead Jews to feel constantly anxious about their status and security, it can, if confronted carefully, also provide reassurance. And if a comparative approach is adopted, it can provide awareness that others may now be the major victims of local and global exclusivities that in the past, but only to a lesser extent today, marginalised the Jews from our world of moral obligation.

Notes

1. J. Parkes, 'Anti-Semitism from Caesar to Luther', *Query Books* no.2 (1938), p. 12.
2. E. Barkan, 1992; *The Retreat of Scientific Racism: Changing Concepts of Race in Britain and the United States Between the World Wars*, Cambridge, Cambridge University Press, 1992); G. Schaffer, *Racial Science and British Society 1930–62*, Basingstoke, Palgrave Macmillan, 2008).
3. J. Isaac, *The Teaching of Contempt: Christian roots of anti-Semitism*, (New York, Holt, Rinehart and Winston, 1964).
4. B. Harrison, *The Resurgence of Anti-Semitism: Jews, Israel and Liberal Opinion*, (Lanham, Rowman & Littlefield 2006).
5. J. Parkes, 'Post-War Anti-Semitism in the Light of Letter of Resignation of Mr James G. McDonald', *The Jewish Academy* vol.2 no.1 (March 1936), pp. 6–7.
6. T. Kushner, *The Holocaust and the Liberal Imagination: A Social and Cultural History*, (Oxford, Blackwell, 1994).
7. P. Gilroy, 'Melancholia or conviviality: the politics of belonging in Britain' in Sally Dawson (ed.), *Race, Identity and Belonging*, (London, Lawrence and Wishart, 2008), pp. 48–59.
8. R. Miles, *Racism and Migrant Labour*, (London, Routledge & Kegan Paul, 1982), pp. 32–3.
9. L. Poliakov, *The History of anti-Semitism* vol.1, London, Routledge, Kegan Paul, 1974a); idem, *The History of anti-Semitism* vol.2, London, Routledge, Kegan Paul, 1974b); idem, *The History of anti-Semitism* vol.3, (London, Routledge, Kegan Paul, 1975); idem, *The History of anti-Semitism* vol.4, (Oxford, Littman Library, 1985).
10. H. Coudenhove-Kalergi, *Anti-Semitism throughout the Ages*, (London, Hutchinson, 1935).
11. S. Almog, (ed.) *Antisemitism Through the Ages*, (Oxford, Pergamon, 1998).

12. R. Wistrich, *Antisemitism: The Longest Hatred*, (London, Methuen, 1991), idem, *A Lethal Obsession: Anti-Semitism from Antiquity to the Global Jihad*, (New York, Random House, 2010).
13. M. Fineberg, S. Samuels and M. Weitzmann (eds.), *Antisemitism: The Generic Hatred*, (London, Vallentine Mitchell, 2007).
14. A. Julius, *Trials of the Diaspora: A History of Anti-Semitism in England*, (Oxford, Oxford University Press, 2010).
15. P. Skinner, 'Confronting the "Medieval" in Medieval History: The Jewish Example', *Past and Present* vol.181 no.1 (2003), pp. 219–47, here, 233.
16. Runnymede Trust, *A Very Light Sleeper: the persistence and dangers of antisemitism*, (London, Runnymede Trust, 1994).
17. B. Klug, 'A Plea for Distinctions: Disentangling Anti-Americanism from Anti-Semitism', in Ivan Krastev and Alan McPherson (eds), *The Anti-American Century*, (New York, CEU Press, 2007), pp. 127–60, here, 140–41.
18. *Jewish Chronicle*, 19 April 2002.
19. BBC Radio 4, 1 January 2006.
20. *Jewish Chronicle*, 31 December 2004.
21. Radio 4, 1 January 2006.
22. All-Party Parliamentary Group Against Antisemitism, *Report of the All-Party Parliamentary Inquiry into Antisemitism*, (London, HMSO, 2006), p. 1.
23. C. Holmes, *Anti-Semitism in British Society, 1876–1939*, (London, Edward Arnold, 1979).
24. W. Rubinstein, *A History of the Jews in the English-Speaking World: Great Britain*, London, Macmillan, 1996), p. 32.
25. J. Warner, 'Violence Against and Amongst Jews in an Early Modern Town: Tolerance and Its Limits in Portsmouth, 1718–1781', *Albion* vol.35 (2003), pp. 428–52, here, 428.
26. B. Williams, 'The Anti-Semitism of Tolerance: Middle-Class Manchester and the Jews, 1870–1900', in A. Kidd and K. Roberts (eds), *City, Class and Culture*, Manchester, Manchester University Press, 1985), pp.74–102.
27. B. Cheyette, *Constructions of 'the Jew' in English literature and society: Racial representations, 1875–1945*, Cambridge, Cambridge University Press, 1993).
28. Julius, *Trials of the Diaspora*, p. xlii.

29. T. Kushner, *Remembering Refugees: Then and Now*, (Manchester, Manchester University Press, 2006).
30. J. Sacks, 'Dignified defiance is the only proper weapon', *Jewish Chronicle*, (2 July 2004), p. 31.
31. Runnymede Trust, *A Very Light Sleeper*, p. 51.
32. L. Davidowicz, 'Can Anti-Semitism be Measured?', *Commentary*, vol.50 (July 1970), pp. 36–43.
33. H. Fein, *Accounting for Genocide*, (Free Press, New York, 1980).
34. S. Virdee, *Racial Violence and Harassment*, (London, PSI, 1995).
35. T. Lerman, 'Anti-Semitism: cool heads needed', *Jewish Chronicle*, (27 January 2006), p. 28.
36. Community Security Trust, *Antisemitic Incidents Report 2010*, London, CST, 2011), p. 35.
37. Runnymede Trust, *A Very Light Sleeper*, p. 11.
38. Ibid., p. 50.
39. P. Panayi (ed.), *Racial Violence in Britain, 1840–1950*, (Leicester, Leicester University Press, 1993).
40. Lerman, 'Anti-Semitism', op cit.
41. Ibid.
42. F. Furedi, *Politics of Fear*, (London, Continuum, 2005).
43. Lerman, 'Anti-Semitism', op cit.
44. T. Lerman, 'Sense on antisemitism', *Prospect* no.77 (August 2002), pp. 34–8, here, 35.
45. *Southern Evening Echo*, 3 August 1993.
46. *Southern Daily Echo*, 21 August 2004.
47. *Guardian*, 12 October 2004 and 27 January 2010.
48. A. Palmer, 'The genteel art of Tory anti-semitism', *Sunday Telegraph*, (18 May 1997), p. 34.
49. This was a quip about the then Conservative leader preferring to appoint Jews of East European origin to her Cabinet rather than non-Jews from England's elite public schools.
50. M. Crick, *In Search of Michael Howard*, (London, Simon & Schuster, 2005).
51. *Sunday Telegraph*, 23 January 2005.
52. *Jewish Chronicle*, 5 March 2004 and 11 March 2005.
53. *Daily Mail*, 19 November 2001.
54. *Jewish Chronicle*, 23 November 2001.
55. Julius, *Trials of the Diaspora*, op. cit.

56. P. Iganski and B. Kosmin (eds.), *A New Antisemitism? Debating Judeophobia in 21st-Century Britain*, (London, Profile Books 2003); Harrison, *The Resurgence of Anti-Semitism*, chapter 2.
57. *New Statesman*, 21 January 2002.
58. *New Statesman*, 11 February 2002.
59. D. Cesarani, 'Anti-Zionist politics and political antisemitism in Britain, 1920–1924', *Patterns of Prejudice* vol. 23 no.1 (1989), pp. 28–45.
60. O. King, 'Israel can halt this now', *Guardian*, (12 June 2003), p. 21.
61. *Jewish Chronicle*, 18 February 2005.
62. *New Statesman*, 14 January 2002.
63. Harrison, *The Resurgence of Anti-Semitism*, p. 187.
64. J. Parkes, *Voyage of Discoveries*, (London: Gollancz, 1969), pp. 128–9.

PART IV

Metaphor and Discourse

CHAPTER 12

"Stealing the Holocaust from the Jews"? The Holocaust as Metaphor in Public Discourse

Esther Webman

The title of this chapter is taken from Edward Alexander's article "Stealing the Holocaust," published in November 1980 in the American quarterly *Midstream*. Alexander pointed to a process which "began with small acts of (usually innocent) distortion" in the American civil rights movement, "with its references to the curtailment of free lunch programs in Harlem as genocide, or its casual descriptions of Watts as a concentration camp, and of the ordinary black neighborhood anywhere as a ghetto." A campaign to steal the Holocaust from the Jews and invert the roles of the victim and the predator, he went on to say, was also carried out by the Arab and Soviet-inspired "Zionism is racism" United Nations (UN) resolution in 1975.[1] In the late 1980s, Elie Wiesel also expressed alarm that other victim groups are "stealing the Holocaust from us."[2]

The Holocaust and Holocaust metaphors, or to be more precise: Nazi era terminology, are invoked in various ways in human rights discourse, national identity narratives and the discussion of racism. In an interview to the London-based Saudi-owned daily *al-Sharq al-Awsat*, to mark the 15th anniversary of the Srebrenica massacre on July 11, 1995 during the war

E. Webman (✉)
Herzliya, Israel

A. McElligott, J. Herf (eds.), *Antisemitism Before and Since the Holocaust*, DOI 10.1007/978-3-319-48866-0_12

in Bosnia, the Grand Mufti of Bosnia and Herzegovina, Mustafa Tsirich, made an indirect comparison between it and the Holocaust, saying that "in World War II the whole world experienced the Holocaust in various ways, … and in the 1990s the extermination in Srebrenitsa occurred. Europe should take heed of these historical realities to avoid another Srebrenitsa."[3] Fidel Castro and others described the French crackdown in August 2010 on the Roma and their expulsion as a "racial holocaust."[4] Even the crackdown on the Syrian uprising by the regime during 2011, and previously in 1982 against the Muslim Brothers opposition in Hama, was defined as "the Syrian holocaust" by commentator Husayn Shubakshi in *al-Sharq al-Awsat* on October 27.[5] In a very different context, Mongolian radical right-wing groups [as their counterparts elsewhere] have adopted Nazi paraphernalia, including the swastika and the Nazi salute, as well as Nazi racist ideology.[6] Similarly, in view of security relaxation in Egypt in the wake of "the Arab spring," a group of Egyptians announced in May 2011 the formation of a Nazi party, aimed at achieving Egyptian and Arab supremacy based on the precepts of Islam, albeit rejecting Nazi ideology of Jewish extermination.[7]

In an article in the *Guardian*, Gilbert Achcar referred to a Palestinian demonstration held on January 9, 2009, in the West Bank village Bil'in during which protesters wore striped pyjamas with small yellow cutouts in the shape of Gaza with the word "Gaza." Achcar agreed that the message the Palestinian demonstrators conveyed was "exaggerated" but found it natural, and also an expression of identification with the Jewish victims of Nazism and of regarding the Holocaust as the highest standard of horror, rather than denying it. As one who criticizes Holocaust denial yet thinks its significance in Arab political culture has been exaggerated, he tried to prove in this article as well as in his study *The Arabs and the Holocaust,* published in 2010, that Holocaust denial fails to reflect "the many Arabs who believe the genocide bears lessons for all persecuted peoples."[8]

But these comparisons are not the only way the Holocaust is being invoked in political and intellectual discussion. The most common themes in the vilification of Israel in the reactions to Israel's military operation "Cast Lead" in Gaza (December 27, 2008–January 18, 2009) manifested in protesters' banners, graffiti, cartoons and articles in newspapers and web-blogs were based on Holocaust terminology, inverting the role of the Jews as victims and turning them into perpetrators, and equating Israel with Nazi Germany and the Swastika with the Star of David. During a pro-Palestinian, anti-Israel demonstration in Brussels on January 11, 2009, for example, protesters carried posters and banners stating: "Gaza Worse than Auschwitz," "Stop the Holocaust of Palestinian People," "No to the Final Solution," "Ghetto Warsaw = Gaza," "Gaza the new Shoah" and "Stop the Genocide in Gaza." As these slogans demonstrate, at least some Western intellectual circles and the media do not consider their anti-Zionist perceptions and their instrumentalization of the Holocaust in their political analogies as deriving from antisemitism but rather from a moral standpoint.[9]

I am not a scholar of the Holocaust, nor of the study of genocide or racism, but in examining Arab representations of the Holocaust, I face the dilemmas that preoccupy historians of these fields. The examples brought above present two sets of categories of the use and abuse of the Holocaust in the public discourse. One set pertains to the issue of the uniqueness of the Jewish experience versus its universal meaning and its relation to other persecutions or genocides; and the other to the manifestations of Holocaust inversion. The expanding Holocaust consciousness and learning around the globe enhance the integration of its concepts and symbols in the global contexts of racism, genocide and anti-imperialism. Yet, this process proved to have a double-edged result. On the one hand, the Holocaust turned into a yardstick of all evil and its memory and lessons are revered by the international community, but on the other hand, its symbols and terminology are increasingly inverted and used against the state of Israel. Moreover, Israel and the Jews are accused of instrumentalizing the Holocaust. Scholars, journalists, writers, bloggers, activists in the West and in the Arab and Muslim worlds raise several claims in their writings: that Holocaust memory has become exclusive; it is all about Jewish suffering and ignores the non-Jewish people who were also murdered by the Nazis; the Jews have become obsessed by their own suffering at the expense of others; no longer is any universal meaning drawn from collective memory; the Holocaust is used instrumentally to protect Israel from criticism and justify its crimes; what Israel does is "like" the Holocaust and the victims of the Holocaust have now become the victimizers of the Palestinians. In short, as sociologist Robert Fine wrote, the difficulty we all face is how to combine the specificity of the event with its universal resonance.[10] I would add another difficulty: How can we separate the benign use and comparison of the Holocaust from its intentional misuse and instrumentalization?

Leaving the question open for discussion, this chapter focuses on the Arab, particularly Palestinian public discourse which has incorporated the Holocaust into its own indigenous political vocabulary either for the reconstruction of Palestinian national identity, juxtaposing it with the *nakba*—the Palestinian catastrophe,[11] or for the demonization and delegitimization of Israel. Based mainly on Arab newspapers articles and literature on the Arab–Israeli conflict, Zionsim and Israel from the mid-1940s to the first decade of the twenty-first century, I will discuss the entrenchment of the comparison between the *nakba* and the Holocaust and the equation of Zionism and Israel with Nazism in the Arab discourse and the impact of the Holocaust Terminology on the Palestinian National Narrative. My argument is that in the Arab context, the result of the adoption of Holocaust metaphors distorted Arabs' perceptions of the Holocaust. The Arab political and intellectual adapters of the Holocaust created a moral equivalence between what happened to the Jews in Europe under Nazi domination and what is happening to the Palestinians at the hands of Israel. In so doing, they diminished the significance of the Holocaust and challenged its uniqueness.

Comparing the *Nakba* and the Holocaust, Equating Zionism and Israel with Nazism

The Palestinian national narrative considers the moment of the establishment of the state of Israel as the moment of defeat and displacement of the Palestinian people. Whereas the events of 1947 and 1948—The UN decision of November 29, 1947, on the partition of Palestine, the declaration of the state of Israel on May 15, 1948, and the defeat of the Arab armies that launched a war against the nascent state on the same day—are for Israelis a national rebirth after the Holocaust and a cause for national celebration, for Palestinians "the same events are seen as an unmitigated disaster and are the focus of national mourning," as Palestinian scholar Rashid Khalidi wrote.[12] "What has been a success for one party has been a failure for the other party," explained Ibrahim Dakkak, a leading Palestine Liberation Organization activist from Jerusalem.[13] As the result of the war, about 700,000 Palestinians fled the country and lost their homes. They found refuge in Arab countries, maintaining the refugee status even in Palestinian territory and cherishing aspirations for return. Although some of the refugees had been evicted and sporadic massacres did occur, the Israeli defense forces never conducted persecution policies or a war of annihilation against them.[14] Hence, there was no factual basis for any comparison between the Palestinian tragedy and the Holocaust which was a deliberate war of extermination against the Jews.

Yet, even before the occurrence of the actual events, the tragedy inflicted on the Jews by the Germans was compared to the tragedy which might be caused by the establishment of the Jewish state. Egyptian intellectual Muhammad 'Awad Muhammad wrote in April 1945 in the literary magazine *al-Thaqafa* that "the imposition of a Jewish state on Palestine is an act that supersedes the aggression of the worst crimes perpetrated by the Axis states."[15] Several months later, the major Egyptian newspaper, *al-Ahram* wrote that Zionist attempts to evict people from their homes, scatter them and ruin their lives "are the same catastrophe (*ma'asa*) that the Jews experienced."[16]

The analogy between what befell the Jews and Palestine's Arabs is a major motif in the Palestinian and Arab discourses on the Holocaust since then, minimizing or ignoring Arab wrongdoings toward the Jews, while magnifying the injustice toward the Palestinians.[17] Over the years, the use of this theme intensified and was manifested in growing sophistication especially in discussions either of the *nakba* or the Holocaust. These discussions demonstrated that the Arab and Palestinian discourses converged with evolving trends in Western academia and public opinion on the perceptions of the Holocaust. Most revealing was the debate of the UN commemoration of the 60th anniversary of the end of World War II (WWII) on January 27, 2005, the day of Auschwitz liberation, and its decision to designate this date as International Holocaust Remembrance Day.

The decision was met in the Arab world with reservations. The Egyptian Parliament, for instance, took a unanimous decision rejecting it, and the Muslim Council of Britain, the umbrella organization of British Muslim representative organizations, headed by Iqbal Sacaranie refused to take part in the British official Holocaust Remembrance Day. These reactions proved again that the Arab discourse on the Holocaust still fails to separate its human aspects from what is perceived as its political implications and disentangle the linkage they made between it and the Palestinian catastrophe. There is no doubt that the liberation of the concentration camps was an important historical event, wrote Lebanese journalist Ghida Fakhri in *al-Sharq al-Awsat* on January 21, 2005, but does it really represent the end of the war? Why did the UN General Assembly decide to commemorate only one aspect of the horrors of the war which caused millions of death in Europe, Asia and Africa? Why it did not commemorate a year ago ten years to the genocide in Rwanda?[18]

In an editorial on January 27, entitled "Auschwitz and Palestine," *al-Hayat* editor, 'Abd al-Wahhab Badrakhan, made a plain linkage between the two. It is natural that the UN takes interest in this memory which concerns all humanity as well as the Jews, he wrote, but its exploitation to exonerate Israel's "bloody record" is a different issue. Any confusion between Israel and the Holocaust is a manipulation of its memory and detrimental to its lessons. Israel considers the worldwide sympathy with the Jews in the remembrance of the Holocaust as sympathy with her crimes against the Palestinian people he contended, and complained that the event and Kofi Annan's failure in his speech to mention the Palestinians, who paid the price of Israel's rise from the ashes, were an organized denial of the Palestinian catastrophe.[19]

Another claim was Israel's alleged exploitation of Holocaust memory. Several Egyptian writers, who assessed that the UN decision reflects the change in the global balance of powers and a victory to Israel, accused Israel of slighting other persecutions, including African slavery and the persecution of non-Jews by the Nazis. The same UN which a few years before had denounced Zionism as a racist movement wrote Egyptian ambassador Sayyid Qasim al-Misri in the mainstream daily *al-Akhbar* on February 3, not only abolished its decision but also succumbed to Zionist pressures. Even leftist intellectual Muhammad Sid Ahmad, who fully supported the preservation of the memory of Hitler's death camps, viewed the anniversary celebrations as attesting "to Zionism's ability to mobilize public opinion at the global level." In an article in *al-Ahram Weekly* on February 3, he lamented that the message of the triumph of the values of humanity over the dark forces unleashed by the Nazi ideology did not come across and warned that Jews are not entitled to exploit their victimization by the Nazis to justify depriving the Palestinian people of their basic human and political rights.[20]

In his editorial "in the margins of Auschwitz' liberation," Liberal Lebanese writer Hazim Saghiya justified Arab writers who criticized Israel's exploitation of the Holocaust. Their agitation, he commented, is understandable in view of the disregard of the Palestinian sufferings, however, the linkage made by either Israel or the Arabs between the Holocaust and the conflict in the Middle East is unacceptable. Saghiya referred to another aspect raised in the discussion when he added that today's Europe desisted from seeing the Jew as "the other." "'The other' today is first of all the Muslim and then the non-European immigrants and minorities." The lessons of the Holocaust led to the unification of Europe, especially its human rights values and pluralism. Sanctification of the Holocaust in Europe was a spiritual need which transcended religion, he wrote, and its political and material exploitation should not cancel out the rich and valid findings about the Holocaust that were continually coming to light.[21] In a similar vein, Syrian Minister of Expatriates and columnist Buthayna Sha'ban in *Tishrin* contended that the slogan "never again" was important but the manifestations of discrimination, aggression and violation of human rights continued in the European continent against Muslims, now considered a security threat.[22]

Islamists, on the other hand, mostly denied the Holocaust in response. Hizballah's mouthpiece *al-'Ahd al-Intiqad*, argued on January 24, 2005 that the commemoration of the 60th anniversary of the end of WWII had no symbolic meaning. It referred to the "alleged" massacres of "large numbers" of Jews in gas chambers and crematoria in Auschwitz, and to the Western revisionist historians persecuted for trying to demonstrate that the so-called Holocaust was invented to perpetuate European feelings of guilt toward the Jews and to cover up "the unprecedented crimes" against the Arabs, particularly the Palestinians.[23] "Today the world celebrates the security of Israel," asserted Jordanian Islamist Ibrahim 'Allush in Islamist Jordanian weekly *al-Sabil* on February 1. Notorious for his ideational support of Holocaust denial, 'Allush defined the Holocaust as "an invented lie" and "a global ideology" of the Zionist movement. Jews died in WWII like the other 45 millions who died due to the war, hunger and diseases. If we accept that Jews were exterminated in gas chambers, as a result of a predetermined extermination policy that caused the annihilation of 6 million out of 15 million Jews, then we acknowledge the "amazing Holocaust story."[24]

A second wave of discussion of the Holocaust took place following the actual adoption of the UN resolution on November 1, reiterating similar motifs.[25] Most articles did not deny the occurrence of the Holocaust but rejected its uniqueness and compared it to other human tragedies and specifically the Palestinian one, accusing Israel and Zionism of manipulating its memory and of racism.[26] "Yes to humane commemoration, no to racism"[27] and to "the Holocaust industry,"[28] were typical titles and themes. Palestinian Islamic Jihad monthly *al-Mujahid* described the new resolution as "a new crime," which reflected the Zionist campaign to control the minds and Judaize the world,[29] whereas Egyptian permanent representative at the UN, ambassador Majid 'Abd al-Fattah demanded to designate another day for the commemoration of other genocides, such as in Rwanda, Bosnia and Cambodia, and called to "set up a comprehensive agenda for the combat of ideologies and extremist national movements as well as violence against foreigners and hatred of Islam and other religions."[30]

We do not oppose the UN decision "in principle," claimed Rashad Ibrahim Mahjub in Egyptian opposition paper *al-Wafd*, but because of the racist campaign which enforces the decision for the sake of the Jews and singles them out as victims. Moreover, it justifies and encourages the horrors done by Zionism and tyrant Jews, and prohibits any scientific research of the Holocaust. He concluded by questioning the international silence to the ongoing bloodshed and terrorism against the Palestinians and others in the prisons of Abu Ghrayb (in Iraq) and Guantanamo.[31] The Holocaust, explained Jordanian writer Nawaf al-Zaru, paved the way practically, politically and morally for the *nakba*, and therefore, the "Holocaust file" should always remain open and questioned. Thus, he introduced the doubts voiced by Holocaust deniers, referring specifically to American technician Fred Leuchter, who allegedly refuted the Jews' claims on collective extermination in the Nazi camps, and contended that the Zionist state established the Holocaust story as a means of extortion.[32] The Vienna-based Palestinian, on the other hand, acknowledged the Holocaust in pan-Arab London-based *al-Quds al-'Arabi*, and believed that recognition of the Holocaust would break the moral monopoly over it. Seeking a parallel recognition of the Palestinian tragedy, he asserted that there would be no recognition of the Holocaust victims without a genuine recognition of the Palestinian victims of "the second holocaust."[33]

The debate reflected a climate of opinion not only in the Arab world but also among various circles, mainly from the radical left including Jewish political activists in the West and Israeli post-Zionists, who promote boycott, disinvestment and sanctions (BDS) on Israel because of its alleged policies against the Palestinians. Although the Arab responses to the decision are authentic, it can be assumed that they draw encouragement from this kind of criticism and activity. The major themes consisted of the accusation of Israel of curtailing the universalization of the Holocaust lessons; of instrumentalizing it for stemming criticism of its policies; and of appropriating its memory and ignoring the sufferings of other victims of WWII as well as victims of other ethnic massacres and genocides.

The inversion of roles of victims and perpetrators, the equation of Israel and Zionism with Nazism and the usage of Holocaust metaphors, emerged as the most widespread motifs in the Arab and Muslim discourse in the wake of the military conflicts between Israel and the Palestinians since the first Lebanon War in 1982, and which also created for the first time a clear convergence between the Western Left and Arab and Islamist groups. The usage of these motifs for the demonization of Israel and Zionism is increasingly dominating the writing and the imagery in the Arab media. It intensified with the outbreak of the Second Intifada in September 2000, and especially during the Second Lebanon war in July–August 2006 and "Operation Cast Lead" in Gaza. It typified mainstream, nationalist as well as Islamist discourses, and paralleled similar trends in the West.

The expression "Israeli Nazism" is an oxymoron, admitted Lebanese columnist Jihad al-Khazin in London-Based daily *al-Hayat*, one of the most liberal papers in the Arab world, in his column of July 22, 2006, a few days into the Second Lebanon War. Describing Israel's actions as Nazi, and Israeli PM Ehud Olmert as "a small führer" and his generals as "SS generals," he wondered "Is it logical for the survivors of the Holocaust and their descendants to do what the Nazis had done to them?" Al-Khazin is not a Holocaust denier. On the contrary, he criticized Arab denial but he has been repeatedly equating Israel with Nazi Germany and the Gaza Strip with a concentration camp in his columns. The utilization of the Holocaust further intensified after the incident in the village of Qana—a hotbed of Hizballah's activities—on July 30, during which an Israeli air strike caused the death of 28 civilians of which 16 were children. Despite the fact that Hizballah used the civilian buildings as a shield for the launching of missiles on Israel, and an official Israeli apology was issued, the incident was presented in the media as a deliberate action and a "mass massacre." Thus "It was an Israeli-made holocaust"; "more than the Holocaust"; "Israeli terrorism is an integral part of Israel's nature and creation"; "the symbiotic relationship between Zionism and Nazism"; "the era of new Nazism"; were just a few of the phrases and titles in Arab papers. Israelis were defined as the disciples of Hitler, and as war criminals who should be brought to trial. A few articles contemplated when Arabs and Palestinians would inaugurate museums, such as Yad Vashem, to exhibit the Israeli atrocities and the "Arab holocaust."[34]

The military escalation in the Gaza Strip at the end of February 2008 in reaction to hundreds of rockets launched on Israeli towns, triggered a massive attack on Israel in the Arab media, which minced no words in portraying its alleged brutality, making extensive use of the term "Holocaust" and other related terms such as "massacre" and "annihilation" to describe it. Moreover, the statement of Deputy Defense Minister, Matan Vilnai, on February 29 using the Hebrew word "shoah" in threatening the catastrophe that will befall the Palestinians if they continue to launch rockets on Israel, gave the Arab media further legitimization to the comparison between the Holocaust and the Palestinian suffering and between Nazi and Israeli conduct. Palestinian Authority chairman Mahmud 'Abbas stated on March 1 that "what is actually going on [in Gaza] is more than a holocaust," while Khalid Mash'al, head of Hamas political bureau said that it is "the real holocaust."[35] Wittingly or unwittingly, such statements reflect the minimization and relativization of the Jewish Holocaust.

Operation "Cast Lead," launched at the end of December by Israel in response to the continuing rocket attacks on Israeli towns, marked yet another peak in the anti-Israeli discourse in the Arab media, laden with Nazi era terminology.[36] Commentators were unanimous in their depiction of the Israeli operation as "a crime against humanity," "a premeditated war of annihilation," "an ethnic cleansing project," and "a new holocaust." Seeking to find "the real aims" of the Israeli operation, Egyptian journalist Galal Nassar in *al-Ahram Weekly* presented it as a "Nazi-inspired onslaught" and "a re-enactment of the Holocaust."[37] Rasim al-Madhun in the Lebanese daily *al-Mustaqbal* defined the war "as a hysteria of collective killing," which can only be termed "a holocaust." In all their political arguments on their bloody history in Palestine, he wrote, the Israelis raise the Nazi Holocaust as "a moral justification" that provide them the right for a national home in Palestine. However, it is not difficult to notice that the old Holocaust repeats itself by the Jews themselves, in a more sadistic and barbaric way.[38]

Palestinian writer Nawaf al-Zaru called in Jordanian *al-Dustur*, May 12, 2008, to globalize "the Palestinian 'holocaust,'" which is still going on and bring it to the attention of the world as Israel managed to do with its so-called Holocaust, whereas Jihad al-Khazin in *al-Hayat*, May 15, reproached the Simon Wiesenthal Center for publishing on Israel's 60th anniversary a list of ten wanted Nazis. "Why is Wiesenthal looking for a 93 year old fugitive, who is probably not even alive, while Israel commits daily Nazi crimes" and "there are tens of others like him in the Israeli government and army command?," he asked. Calling the Gaza strip a "Nazi concentration camp," he added that the Wiesenthal's list was published just when "the new Nazis of Israel" killed a woman and four of her children.[39] Similarly, Shaykh Kamal Khatib, the deputy leader of the northern Islamic Movement in Israel, also linked the Holocaust to the *nakba* on its 60th commemoration. In an article in the Arab–Israeli daily *al-Sinara*, April 18, 2008, titled "On the sixtieth commemoration of the nakba: their Holocaust our nakba," he reiterated the claim that the Palestinians "paid the price" for the Nazi crime, though they had no connection to it. Khatib described Gaza as a big concentration camp that Israel threatens to annihilate, just like what the Nazis did to the Jews in the concentration camps before the gas chambers and after their starvation and humiliation.[40]

In the mid-1990s, with the collapse of the Soviet Union, the signing of the Israeli–Palestinian accords in 1993 and the 1994 Israeli–Jordanian peace agreement, liberal Arab intellectuals began to question the Arab perceptions of the Holocaust, which seemed no longer congruent with those processes. They called for the unequivocal recognition of the suffering of the Jewish people, which eventually would lead to the recognition of the Palestinian tragedy by the Israelis and facilitate reconciliation and coexistence between the two peoples. The gist of this new approach is the acknowledgment of the Holocaust as an undisputed historical fact, a crime against humanity, and the separation of its human aspects from its political repercussions. The propagators of this approach, Palestinian, Lebanese, Tunisian, Egyptian liberal scholars and journalists genuinely advocated a change in the Arab attitude toward the Holocaust and do not deny its uniqueness, but most of them failed to isolate the political dimension from their discourse and fell into the trap of instrumentalizing the Holocaust for achieving recognition of the Palestinian *nakba*.

Seeking a basis for coexistence, the late Palestinian professor for comparative English literature at Columbia University Edward Said claimed that a link exists between what happened to the Jews in WWII and the catastrophe of the Palestinian people, and unless this connection is recognized there would be no foundation for coexistence. He insisted that he does not attach conditions to the comprehension of and compassion for the Jewish tragedy, however, he believed that "such an advance in consciousness by Arabs ought to be met by an equal willingness for compassion and comprehension on the part of the Israelis and Israel's supporters."[41] Said, who accused Zionism and Israel of instrumentalizing the Holocaust for their ends connected the recognition of the two tragedies. "We must recognize the realities of the Holocaust not as a blank check for Israelis to abuse us, but as a sign of our humanity, our ability to understand history, our requirement that our suffering be mutually acknowledged." The Holocaust does not excuse Zionism for what it has done to Palestinians, he went on to say. Hence, "by recognizing the Holocaust for the genocidal madness that it was, we can then demand from Israelis and Jews the right to link the Holocaust to Zionist injustices towards the Palestinians, link and criticize the link for its hypocrisy and flawed moral logic."[42]

Another theme, which typifies this new approach, is the universalization of the Holocaust. The lessons from the Holocaust became universal moral values that serve as a bulwark for democracies against the threats of fundamentalism, extremism and racism, which target Jews and Muslims alike, argued Lebanese liberal intellectual and editor of *al-Hayat* daily Hazim Saghiya and Tunisian writer Salih Bashir in a joint article published in December 1997. In recent years, they claimed, the Jews, whose consciousness had been shaped by the Holocaust, are losing the "monopoly" they held on human suffering. The increasing recognition of the Holocaust's significance, the widening of the sphere of memory and the participation of other peoples in it, point to the expropriation of the Holocaust from the limited Jewish possession, and of its assuming a meaning and a message for all humanity. Only this broader perception of the Holocaust by the Jews accompanied by a similar recognition by the Arabs can lead to a real reconciliation in the Middle East, according to this approach. Defining the Holocaust as "the most complex and intractable knot in the Middle East conflict," Saghiya and Bashir insisted on the "dissociation between the acknowledgment of the Holocaust and what Israel is doing," for the development of a discourse which says that "the Holocaust does not free the Jewish state or the Jews of accountability" for the Palestinian tragedy. Any injustice perpetrated by Israel against the Palestinians, they added, or any denial of their rights "will be tantamount to an infringement of the sanctity of the Holocaust, which has become a yardstick for universalistic values." Moreover, "if the memory of the Holocaust" comes between the Jews and "their capacity to coexist with that other people at whose expense the 'Jewish question' was solved, it will be a victory for Hitlerism after its defeat."[43]

From an Arab, and particularly Palestinian, perspective, the comparison between the tragedies of the Jewish and Palestinian peoples seemed compelling. Palestinian activist Ata Qaymari, for example, acknowledged in a candid presentation at a seminar for Israeli and Palestinian scholars and journalists in 2004 that many Palestinians perceive the Holocaust through the prism of their *nakba*, "the counterpart of the Holocaust in Palestinian history, in which their whole social, economic and cultural fabric was destroyed and uprooted." Therefore, he continued, there were significant similarities in the ways in which both communities address their "catastrophe," in commemoration and historiography, and "the Palestinians are trying, just as the Jews did and are still doing, to gather a kind of collective memory that preserves their own social, cultural and historical fabric."[44]

The Impact of the Holocaust Terminology on the Palestinian National Narrative

The terminology and discourse of the Holocaust deeply affected the Palestinian discourse on the *nakba* from its early emergence. In the preface to the Arabic translation of the articles of French Holocaust denier Robert Faurisson, published in Beirut in 1988, the translator Majid Hillawi bitterly admitted that the Arabs and Palestinians accepted the Holocaust as a criterion for many of their political, cultural and artistic decisions and repeat "the Zionist lies in order to gain international sympathy" by describing the suffering of the Palestinian people in terms invented by the Jews such as "Holocaust," "massacre," "victimhood," "diaspora" and "memory."[45]

The *nakba* has become a sanctified identity symbol, and as a writer in the Palestinian Jerusalem-based daily *al-Quds* put it, is a unique and acute "unprecedented historical experience," that is "a scar on the forehead of the world and a calamity for humanity,"[46] and the "biggest crime history ever known."[47] In the process of its evolution, concepts associated with the Holocaust, such as redemption, victimhood, reparations, commemoration, memorialization, have been incorporated into the Palestinian discourse on the *nakba*. The official Palestinian People's Appeal, issued on May 14, 1998 by the Palestinian National Authority [PNA], commemorating the 50th anniversary of the *nakba* reflected the Palestinian self-perception as victims on the one hand, and the new hopes for embarking on nation building on the other hand, similar to the Jewish perception of redemption after the Holocaust. "We do not seek to be captives of history or victims of the past. The Palestinian people have launched a redemptive journey to the future. From ashes of our sorrow and loss, we are resurrecting a nation celebrating life and hope," it asserted.[48]

The issue of victimization and victimhood, which was crucial for the representation of Jewish experience and identity, became a major component of Palestinian narrative. The Palestinians considered themselves the victims of the victims, as Edward Said and Rashid Khalidi wrote, and they strove to gain a "status of victimhood" and recognition of their tragedy.[49] Hazim Saghiya contended in his book *Defending Peace* (*Difa'an 'an al-salam*), published in 1995, that the Palestinians were envious of the Jews who became the "model of victimhood" and of their "profitable" tragedy.[50] Saghiya voiced the harshest criticism of the traditional Arab approach to the Holocaust and particularly of the Palestinian indulgence in their victimhood and concentration on the adverse political dimensions of the Jewish tragedy. Since they failed to get recognition for their own tragedy, they were blinded and could not identify with its human aspects, he claimed and could not understand the meaning and significance of the Holocaust in European history and culture.[51]

Arab governments raised the issue of compensation already in the early 1950s, during the discussion of the German reparations to the Jews and the state of Israel. They appealed to the Western big powers and to the Germans, seeking to make a connection between reparations to the Jews and compensation for the Palestinians, and to bring about a decision that would either freeze the German reparations until Israel pays her dues to the Palestinians according to UN resolutions, or divert part of them to the Palestinian refugees, who were considered more entitled to compensation.[52] Contrasting the settlement of the Jews in Palestine and the deportation of the Arabs, the Palestinians felt that the Jews cry and complain about the cruelty and oppression against them and the world compensate them with money and sympathy while they receive neither a fair treatment nor compensation from the big powers and Israel which are considered responsible for the loss of Palestine to the Jews.[53]

The issue of compensation was raised again in the mid-1990s with the negotiations agreement on the restitution of Jewish property lost during the Nazi era, revealing deep-seated resentment toward the West for its alleged unfair treatment and exploitation of third world nations.[54] Several Palestinian writers focused on perceived similarities between Jewish and Palestinian claims for moral and financial restitution. Tamim Mansur of the nationalist Arab–Israeli party Balad criticized the Zionist policy of "wailing and crying," which instilled the memory of the Holocaust in the Western mind to such an extent that many other similar tragedies, which had subsequently occurred to other peoples, including the Palestinians, did not receive the same universal attention. Using the same term *karitha* (catastrophe) in reference to the Holocaust and the Palestinian tragedy, Mansur criticized the Israeli government for emphasizing the humanitarian and moral aspects in demanding financial remuneration for Jewish funds stored in Switzerland, while simultaneously refusing to return the property of the displaced Palestinians.[55] In a similar vein, London-based Palestinian scholar Ghada Karmi emphasized the "striking contrast" between the moral attitudes and practical steps taken toward resolving the issue of compensation for Jewish victims of Nazism and "those towards rectifying outstanding Palestinian losses from 1948 onward."[56]

While discussing this issue, Karmi raised another aspect—the denial of the *nakba*. "The essence of the Palestinian grievance," she wrote, "is not only that they lost their homeland, but that the perpetrators have consistently refused to make reparation or even to acknowledge their responsibility in the matter."[57] Rashid Khalidi also points to the "unremitting pressure from the Israeli side for more than 50 years to ignore, diminish and ideally to bury the whole question of the Palestinians made refugees in 1948," and that "the key requirement for a solution is not so much compensation (important as it is), as acceptance of responsibility and some form of atonement."[58] Thus the denial of the Palestinian tragedy is similar to denial of the Holocaust, "with all the allowances necessary when making comparisons between situations which are inherently dissimilar," he concluded.[59]

New York-based Palestinian scholar of modern Arab politics and intellectual history in the department of Middle Eastern, South Asian and African Studies at Columbia University, Joseph Massad, compared the "obscene number games on the part of holocaust [sic] deniers" to Zionist Jewish denial of the Palestinian *nakba* and to the continued Zionist position to play down the number of Palestinian refugees. "While the *nakba* and the holocaust are not equivalent in any sense," he contended, "the logic of denying them is indeed the same."[60]

In the public debate on the *nakba* in 1998, marking its 50th anniversary, it was argued that the motif of victimhood should turn into a call to the world to recognize its guilt toward the Palestinians, and a demand to be added "to the list of Holocaust victims" entitled to restitution. This recognition entails also the acknowledgment of the responsibility for the *nakba* by Israel and by the West, which was blamed of hastening to relieve its conscience after the Holocaust by granting a state to the Jews. The Palestinian People's Appeal called upon the world "to undertake not only recognition of guilt and admission of culpability in relation to the Palestinian people, but also to undertake an active and massive process of rectification to secure the implementation of Palestinian rights."[61] Moreover, there is an expectation for an explicit apology by Israel and Britain to the Palestinians, as the apologies made to the Jews by Spain, France and Portugal and by Pope John Paul II in his March 16, 1998 document "We Remember: Reflections on the Shoah."[62] More militant Palestinians called for the establishment of a special tribunal to sentence Israeli "war criminals" for crimes committed against Palestinians.[63]

The argument that the Palestinian *nakba* is being ignored by the international community whereas a great deal of attention is given to the

Holocaust was also dominant in the Arab debate over the UN decision to commemorate the liberation of Nazi concentration camps in January 2005 and the resolution to designate a Holocaust Memorial Day on January 27. Nawaf al-Zaru, for example, who denied the Holocaust in an article published in the Jordanian newspaper *al-Dustur*, on January 27, 2005, claimed that the Israeli governments in the last six decades "succeeded in exploiting 'the Holocaust' in a Shylockian racist and imperialist manner which exceeded any reason, logic and justice." Why had Annan decided to commemorate the so-called Holocaust when so many scholars and European researchers doubt it and when the Palestinian *nakba* was totally ignored, he asked.[64]

The commemoration of the *nakba* in 1998 seemed to provide an appropriate point of departure for the documentation and memorialization of the Palestinian story, for the scholarly accounts on the 1948 war as well as personal testimonies of survivors.[65] Although these efforts continued the historical documentation started immediately after 1948 by Palestinian historians,[66] there was a clear shift in the works of 1998 from the collective memory or high rhetoric to the personal memory and experience, which also typified the Israeli historiography of the Holocaust. The cinema also reflected the shift from national to private memory and from a male story to a feminine point of view.[67] Oral history was part of the campaign of history recording that included personal accounts especially of Palestinian refugees and of Palestinian camp women.[68] Palestinians became also aware that there is no museum or memorial which records their suffering. Attempts are being made to build up a national museum to restore the heritage and formulate the national ethos, both as a political tool for preserving the national entity and as an effective way to mobilize the people into a process of national struggle to gain their legitimate rights. "All this and other forms of identification recall the Israeli attempts to create a part of their national ethos out of the Holocaust," elaborated Ata Qaymari.[69]

A major effort was made by a group of Jews and non-Jews in 1995, who launched the "Deir Yassin Remembered" project, aiming at building a permanent memorial at the site of the former village within sight of Yad Vashem Holocaust memorial center.[70] Deir Yassin, which was constructed over 50 years as a symbol of the *nakba*,[71] became the focus of memorialization, but in fact the project did not materialize. Concurrently, some writers suggested erecting a Palestinian center for the commemoration of the Palestinian catastrophe and heroism or an Arab museum for "Zionist victims," as a suitable answer to all the Jewish memorials.[72] Such an effort was made in March 2008, when a Palestinian group called the "National Committee for Defense of Children from the Holocaust" unveiled in Gaza its premier exhibit, entitled "Gaza: An exhibit describing the suffering of the children of the Holocaust." The exhibit reportedly included a large oven and inside it small children are being burned. Meanwhile IslamonLine.net launched in the same month a virtual Palestinian Holocaust Memorial Museum (PHMM), featuring photos, names and stories of Palestinian children killed by Israeli forces "in the context of a new Holocaust," and highlighting the locations, weapons and impacts as well as testimonies of survivors.[73]

The commemoration of the *nakba*'s 60th anniversary in 2008 was not an occasion for self-examination as ten years earlier, but a return to old patterns of discourse, seeking to put the onus of past and present predicaments on external forces and amplifying the Zionist and Israeli wrongdoings. Whereas 1998 was still the heyday of the new discourse acknowledging the Jewish tragedy, the 2008 debate of the *nakba* comprehensively intertwined Nazi era terminology and Holocaust metaphors. Articles, as well as demonstrators and speakers at rallies, launched scathing attacks on Israel and Zionism. In contrast to the hopes for a better future expressed in the PA national appeal of 1998, the National Committee to Commemorate the Nakba at 60 pledged to "continue to remain steadfast and resist and resist and resist. ... For there is no right that is not granted without the sacrifices of struggle, and there is no oppressor that can continue to commit grave injustice for ever."[74]

Based on Israeli anti-Zionist academic Ilan Pappe's book *The Ethnic Cleansing of Palestine*, translated in 2008 into Arabic, the Palestinian Mustafa Barghouti in *al-Ahram Weekly*, May 15, and Egyptian 'Abd al-Wahhab al-Masiri, in UAE's *al-Ittihad*, May 17, suggested that the term "ethnic cleansing" was more accurate than "nakba" to describe what had happened and was still happening in Palestine.[75] Joseph Massad, an opponent of the link between the *nakba* and the Holocaust, nonetheless did not shun from using Holocaust terminology in his articles.[76] For example, he used the term *Judenrat* (Jewish Council) to describe the Palestinian Authority leadership, and the term *Arabrein* (*Judenrein*) denoting the alleged Zionists intention to ethnic cleanse Palestine, while continuing to portray the Palestinians as the victims of victims, and accusing Israel of exploiting the Holocaust for rehabilitating its tarnished reputation, or denying the existence of the victimized people and monopolizing its identity.[77]

Conclusion

The usage of Holocaust metaphors brings to the fore a crucial question in the discussion of the Holocaust as a Jewish unique experience versus its universalistic meaning. The controversy over this issue continues unabated as the corollary of the process of the universalization of its memory by the international community, which reached its peak with the Stockholm International Conference's resolution in January 2000 to develop Holocaust studies in schools[78] and the designation of January 27, as an international Holocaust Memorial Day. Why does this process elicit a counterreaction? Does universalization of the Holocaust necessarily mean undermining its uniqueness? Why is it difficult to combine the specificity of the event with its universal lessons? Is it possible to separate benign use of the Holocaust from its intentional misuse and instrumentalization?

Judging from Arab Holocaust discourses, which internalized the language of victimhood and Holocaust concepts, it seems that universalization contradicts, especially among the Palestinians, any kind of acceptance of the specificity of the Holocaust. The Palestinian national identity discourse suggests that they "aspire to become the 'David of the Holocaust with a stone in their hand,'" and wish to demonstrate "the mutation of the 'Jew as victim.' Being in exile has created the Palestinian collective consciousness, and they see themselves as the real Jews, the victims in exile."[79] Therefore, they preserved the refugee camps as the visible presentation of victimhood, and a living symbol of both Israeli oppression and universal injustice and aggression.[80]

The competition over victimhood status not only distorted Arabs' perceptions of the Holocaust but also drove them almost automatically to take a contentious stand over issues related to it. The comparison between the two tragedies implicitly recognizes the Holocaust as a benchmark for evil and unwittingly acknowledges that it took place, yet at the same time it seeks to deny it or minimize its dimensions. Moreover, it challenges its uniqueness and creates a moral equivalence between it and the Palestinian tragedy. When the issue of teaching the Holocaust was raised in April 2000 in a symposium on "How to strengthen Peace through Education," the Chairman of the Education Committee of the Palestinian Legislative Council (PLC), Musa al-Zu'but, rejected any possibility to include the history of the Holocaust in the Palestinian curriculum. Hatim 'Abd al-Qadir, a PLC member and Fatah leader clearly stated that teaching the

Holocaust constitutes "a great danger to the developing Palestinian mentality." If such a decision is made, he said, "it will undoubtedly ruin the Palestinian dream and aspirations. It will entirely obliterate the past, present and future of the Palestinians."[81]

Comparison of Israel to the Third Reich and Israel's policies to Nazi crimes causing a "holocaust disaster," or defining Gaza as a concentration camp, are not benign uses but intentional misuses of terms and metaphors. They are accompanied in many cases not only by relativization and minimization of the Holocaust but even by its denial. Leading Saudi dailies, *al-Watan*, *al-Riyadh* and the London-based *al-Sharq al-Awsat*, for example, reported in March 2008 after operation "Cast Lead" that Saudi Arabia views the acts allegedly perpetrated by Israel during the war as an "imitation of Nazi crimes," which recall "the false Holocaust in Germany, where it is claimed that a few Jews were cremated."[82] Even those who acknowledged the Holocaust, such as Ziyad bin 'Abdallah al-Daris, a Saudi who lives in France, and considers the Holocaust an inhuman crime, believed that it is legitimate to compare the "old Holocaust" with the "new holocaust" against the Palestinians, which has endured for over 60 years.[83]

Historians of genocides and political scientists, such as William Miles, Dirk Moses, David Moshman and Peter Novick, challenge the uniqueness of the Holocaust but cherish the universalization of its lessons. Miles explains that Eurocentric accounts of WWII and the Holocaust "generally ignore linkages to the non-western world whereas Third World perspectives underline the relevance of the Holocaust to their own condition,"[84] and Moses calls to "dispense with the vocabulary of uniqueness."[85] In many ways, their approach reflects the views of some Arab writers who do not deny the Holocaust but perceive it as a means for the recognition of the Palestinian tragedy. In his review of Achcar's book *The Arabs and the Holocaust,* Hazim Saghiya complained that Europeans developed a high level of sensitivity to the Holocaust but failed to export this sensitivity outside Europe, pointing to two impediments, the conflict in Palestine and the tendency of "some radical Zionists to keep it as a monopoly to prevent the dissolution of Jewish victimhood into a more comprehensive human victimhood."[86] Similarly, albeit from a different angle, Muhammad Na'ma, the publisher of the Paris-based "Western Orbits," warned Westerners and Israelis that "sinking in a routine of remembering the past" (i.e., the Holocaust) and reinforcing its universalization might lead to the obfuscation of the link between the memory and the event. There would be no remedy to the wounds, he asserted, if the West remains blind to all its crimes in the last century and as long as the Zionists continue to ignore their responsibility to their victims, the Palestinian people.[87]

Palestinian scholar, Khalid al-Hurub as well, in an article published in *al-Hayat* on February 10, 2008, accuses the discourse of the Holocaust of being too particularistic. Supporting the position of British historian Tony Judt, he claims that the discourse regarding the Holocaust is being exploited by Israel and that it must become a universal discourse that deals with racism and genocide in general. Al-Hurub believes that it is also necessary to recognize the Palestinians as victims of the Holocaust, since they are the victims of its consequences—the establishment of the state of Israel. Nonetheless, he emphasizes that the changing of the discourse would not lessen the uniqueness of the Jewish Holocaust and that the Arabs need to recognize it, in order to create a new discourse.[88]

As renowned Israeli Holocaust scholar Yehuda Bauer contends "the universal implications of this unique event are precisely in its uniqueness."[89] There is no contradiction in the acknowledgment of other tragedies and genocides and in drawing universal lessons from the Holocaust and the preservation of its memory and uniqueness. The competition over victimhood status, especially in the process of shaping collective memories, abuses the possibility of reaching an accommodation between the universal and the specific and leads to the distortion of both the universal implications and the unique memory of the Holocaust.

Notes

1. *Midstream*, November 1980, p. 48.
2. As quoted in A. Dirk Moses, "Conceptual blockages and definitional dilemmas in the 'racial century': genocides of indigenous peoples and the Holocaust," *Patterns and Prejudice*, Vol. 36, No. 4 (2002), p. 13, note 30.
3. *Al-Sharq al-Awsat*, July 13, 2010.
4. http://articles.cnn.com/2010-08-19/world/france.roma_1_roma-camps-romania-and-bulgaria-french-minister?_s=PM:WORLD; AFP, September 11, 2010; *Guardian*, September 13, 2010.
5. *Al-Sharq al-Awsat*, October 27, 2011. In Hama in 1982, various sources estimated that between 20,000–45,000 people had been killed by the military upon orders of president Hafiz al-Asad.

6. ubpost.mongolnews, December 4, 2008; *Time*, July 27, 2009; *Guardian*, August 2, 2010.
7. http://blog.foreignpolicy.com/posts/2011/05/25/springtime_for_the_egyptian_nazi_party; *Jerusalem Post*, May 26, 2011; *al-Masry al-Youm*, September 25, 2011; Memri video clip #3131, September 22, 2011.
8. *Guardian*, May 12, 2010. See Gilbert Achcar, *The Arabs and the Holocaust: The Arab-Israeli War of Narratives* trans. G.M. Goshgarian (New York: Metropolitan Books, 2009).
9. http://www.tau.ac.il/Anti-Semitism/asw2008/gen-analysis-08.pdf.
10. Robert Fine, "Legacy of Hope: Antisemitism, the Holocaust and Resistance Yesterday and Today," January 27, 2010—www.EngageOnline.org.uk.
11. *Nakba* is the term adopted by the Palestinians to denote their national disaster in the wake of the Arab military defeat in the war of 1948. For a discussion of the term, see, Esther Webman, "The Evolution of a Founding Myth—The Nakba and Its Fluctuating Meaning," in Meir Litvak (ed.), *Palestinian Collective Memory and National Identity* (New York: Palgrave Macmillan, 2009), pp. 27–46.
12. Rashid Khalidi, "Truth, Justice and Reconciliation: Elements of a Solution to the Palestinian Refugee Issue," in Ghada Karmi and Eugene Cotran (eds.), *The Palestinian Exodus 1948–1998* (Reading: Ithaca Press, 1999), p. 224.
13. "1948–1998 in the Eyes of Two Peoples: A Roundtable Discussion," *Palestine-Israel Journal of Politics, Economics and Culture*, Vol. V, No. 2 (1998), p. 24. See also Joseph Samaha, *salam 'abir. Nahwu madd 'arabi lil "mas'ala al-yahudiya"* [A Passing Peace: Toward an Arab Extension of "the Jewish Question"] (Beirut, 1993), p. 28; *al-Sharq al-Awsat,* April 7, 1998.
14. See Benny Morris, *1948 and After: Israel and the Palestinians* (Oxford: Clarendon Press, 1994); Idem, *The Birth of the Palestinian Refugee Problem, 1947–1949* (Cambridge: Cambridge University Press, 1987); Idem, *The Birth of the Palestinian Refugee Problem Revisited* (Cambridge: Cambridge University Press, 2004).
15. *Al-Thaqafa*, 10 April 1945, p. 391.
16. *Al-Ahram*, 4 November 1945, 11 January 1946.

17. For a discussion of the representation of the Holocaust in the Palestinian discourse, see Meir Litvak and Esther Webman, "Perceptions of the Holocaust in Palestinian Public Discourse," *Israel Studies*, Vol. 8, No. 3 (Fall 2003), pp. 123–141.
18. *Al-Sharq al-Awsat*, January 21, 2005.
19. *Al-Hayat*, January 27, 2005.
20. *Al-Akhbar*, *al-Ahram Weekly*, February 3, 2005.
21. *Al-Hayat*, January 29, 2005.
22. *Tishrin*, January 31, 2005.
23. *Al-'Ahd al-Intiqad*, January 24, 2005.
24. *Al-Sabil*, February 1, 2005. See also an interview with 'Allush aired on al-Jazira TV on 23 August: MEMRI Special Dispatch, No. 976, August 31, 2005; *al-Sabil*, November 8, 2005.
25. *Ha'aretz*, 2 November 2005.
26. See, for example, *al-Sabil*, November 8, *al-Dustur*, November 16, *Tishrin*, November 22, *al-Badil* (Jordanian bi-weekly), December 3, *al-Hayat al-Jadida*, December 18, *al-Mustaqbal*, December 19, 2005.
27. *Al-Sharq al-Awsat*, November 5, 2005.
28. *Al-Khalij*, November 7, 2005.
29. *Al-Mujahid*, December 2005.
30. *Al-Ahram al-'Arabi*, November 12, 2005. Commentaries in the same vein, see *al-Qabas*, January 30, *al-Ahali*, February 8, 2006.
31. *Al-Wafd*, April 1, 2006.
32. *Al-Dustur*, April 30, 2006. See also *al-Dustur*, May 3, 2006.
33. *Al-Quds al-'Arabi*, May 4, 2006.
34. http://www.tau.ac.il/Anti-Semitism/asw2008/gen-analysis-08.pdf.
35. *Jerusalem Post*, *Ha'aretz*, *al-Safir*, *al-Akhbar*, *al-Thawra*, 1 March 2008; Intelligence and Terrorism Information Center, March 12, 2008—www.terrorism-info.org.il/malam_multimedia/English/eng_n/htm/hi_090308e.htm.
36. For further details, see http://www.tau.ac.il/Anti-Semitism/asw2008/gen-analysis-08.pdf.
37. *Al-Ahram Weekly*, January 15, 2009. See also *al-Dustur*, December 28, 29, 2008; *al-Thawra*, January 1, *al-Quds al-'Arabi*, January 8, 12, *al-Ghadd*, January 13, 2009.
38. *Al-Mustaqbal*, January 11, 2009.
39. *Al-Hayat*, May 15, *al-Dustur*, May 12, 2008.

40. *Al-Sinara*, April 18, 2008.
41. *Al-Hayat*, November 5, *al-Ahram Weekly*, November 6, 1997; *Ha'aretz*, February 20, *Le Monde Diplomatique*, August–September 1998.
42. *Al-Ahram Weekly*, June 25, *al-Hayat*, June 30, 1998.
43. *Al-Hayat*, December 18, 1997. The article entitled "Universalizing the Holocaust or breaking the Jewish monopoly over it," gained them the "Common Ground Award for Journalism in the Middle East" in 1999 (*Ha'aretz*, February 21, 2000). See also Matthijs Kronemeijer, *An Arab Voice of Compromise. Hazem Saghieh's "In Defence of Peace" (1997)* (Ultrech University, 2005), pp.46–50—igitur-archive.library.uu.nl/student-theses/2006-0324-082630/UUindex.html.
44. Ata Qaymari, "The Holocaust in the Palestinian Perspective," in Paul Scham, Walid Salem and Benjamin Pogrund (eds.), *Shared Histories. A Palestinian-Israeli Dialogue* (Walnut Creek, Ca.: Left Coast Press, 2005), p. 149.
45. Robert Faurisson, *al-ukzuba al-tarikhiya: hal fi`lan qutila sitta malayin yahudi?* (The Historical Lie: Were Six Million Jews Killed?) (Beirut: 1988), p. 18; Hazim Saghiya, *difa'an 'an al-salam* (*Defending Peace*) (Beirut: Dar al-Nahar lil-Nashr, 1997), p. 69.
46. *Al-Quds*, May 15, 1998.
47. See, for instance, Muhammad Fayiz al-Qasri, *harb filastin, 'am 1948. al-sira' al-siyasi bayna al-sahyuniya wal-'arab* (The War in Palestine. The Political Conflict between Zionism and the Arabs) (Cairo: Dar al-Ma'arifa, 1961), p. 41.
48. The Palestinian People's Appeal on the 50th Anniversary of the Catastrophe "Al-Nakba,"—www.pna.org/mininfo/nakba.
49. Rashid Khalidi, "A Universal Jubilee? Palestinians 50 Years after 1948," *Tikkun*, Vol. 13, No. 2 (March/April 1998), pp. 54–6; Edward Said, *The Politics of Dispossession* (New York: Vintage Books, 1994), p. 121; *al-Ahram Weekly*, May 14, 1998.
50. Saghiya, *Defending Peace*, pp. 67–8. A similar argument was introduced by Ata Qaymari, "The Holocaust," pp. 150–1, 159.
51. Saghiya, *Defending Peace*, pp. 63–9. Faysal Jalul, a Lebanese journalist living in Paris agreed with this criticism in his review of Saghiya's book, *al-Nahar*, December 29, 1997.
52. *Al-Ahram*, September 12, 1951, November, 16, 15 December 1952.

53. For a discussion of the Arab reactions to the reparations agreement, see Meir Litvak and Esther Webman, *From Empathy to Denial*, pp. 59–91.
54. Ibid., pp. 350–56.
55. *Fasl al-Maqal*, November 8, 1996. Similar themes appeared in: *al-Watan*, March 6, *al-'Ahd*, April 11, *al-Ahram*, May 5, *al-Majd*, May 5, December 15, 1997.
56. Ghada Karmi, "The Question of Compensation and Reparations," in Ghada Karmi and Eugene Cotran (eds.), *The Palestinian Exodus 1948–1998* (Reading: Ithaca Press, 1999), pp. 197, 201. See also her article in *al-Hayat*, July 31, 1998, which describes the Holocaust as a fabricated Israeli myth.
57. Ibid., p. 201.
58. Ibid., pp. 221–222.
59. Ibid., pp. 225–6.
60. *Al-Ahram Weekly*, December 9, 2004.
61. *The Palestinian People's Appeal*; see also *Al-Hayat*, January 20, 21, May 15, *al-Ahram Weekly*, May 14, *Jordan Times*, May 9, *al-Sharq al-Awsat*, May, 11, 18, 25, *al-Quds*, February 16, May 15, 1998; "1948–1998 in the Eyes of Two Peoples," pp. 24, 31, 33.
62. *Al-Ahram*, March 22, *Al-Quds*, April 24, 1998.
63. *Al-Hayat*, April 28, *al-Hayat al-Jadida*, May 11, 1998.
64. *Al-Dustur*, January 27, 2005. See also: *al-Dustur*, January 30, *al-Hayat*, January 24, *al-Babil*, December 3, 2005.
65. *Al-Ahram Weekly*, February 19, 1998; Rosemary Sayigh, "Dis/Solving the Refugee Problem," *Middle East Report*, No. 207 (summer 1998), pp. 19–23; Walid Khalidi (ed.), *All That Remains: The Palestinian Villages Occupied and Depopulated by Israel in 1948* (Washington, DC: Institute for Palestine Studies, 1992).
66. On the early Palestinian historiography, see Beshara B. Doumani, "Rediscovering Ottoman Palestine: Writing Palestinians into History," *Journal of Palestine Studies*, Vol. XXI, No. 2 (Winter 1992), pp. 13–17.
67. Nurit Gertz and George Khleifi, *Landscape* in Mist: Space and Memory in Palestinian Cinema (Tel Aviv: Ofakim, 2006, in Hebrew), pp. 69–76. See also: Qaymari, "The Holocaust," in pp. 150–159.
68. Rosemary Sayigh, "Palestinian Camp Women as Tellers of History," *Journal of Palestine Studies*, Vol. XXVII, No. 2 (winter 1998),

pp. 42–58; "Reflections on al-Nakba," *Journal of Palestine Studies*, Vol. XXVIII, No. 1 (autumn 1998), pp. 5–35; *Palestine Times*, No. 84, June 1998; *Jordan Times*, April 20, *Ha`aretz*, November 16, 1999.

69. Qaymari, "The Holocaust," pp. 151, 159.
70. Daniel A. McGowan and Marc H. Ellis (eds.), *Remembering Deir Yassin. The Future of Israel and Palestine* (New York: Olive Branch Press, 1998).
71. Kimmerling and Migdal, *Palestinians*, p. 152; Walid Khalidi, "Deir Yassine: Autopsie d'un massacre," *Revue d'études Palestiniennes*, Vol. 17, No. 69 (automne 1998), pp. 20–58.
72. *Al-Hayat*, February 4, *al-Ahram*, May 27, 1998; Khalidi, "A Universal Jubilee," p. 56.
73. *Jerusalem Post*, March 25, 2008; http://www.palestinianholocaust.net/index.shtml. See also www.palestineremembered.com.
74. See, http://www.tau.ac.il/Anti-Semitism/asw2008/gen-analysis-08.pdf.
75. *Al-Ahram Weekly*, May 15, *al-Ittihad*, May 17, 2008.
76. Joseph Massad, "Palestinian and Jewish History: Recognition or Submission?," *Journal of Palestine Studies*, Vol. XXX, No. 1 (Autumn 2000), p. 63.
77. *Al-Ahram Weekly*, May 15, 2008.
78. Litvak and Webman, *From Empathy to Denial*, pp. 169, 184–86.
79. Ruth Linn and Ilan Gur-Ze'ev, "Holocaust as a Metaphor: Arab and Isareli Use of the Same Symbol," *Metaphor and Symbolic Activity*, Vol. 11, No. 3 (1996), p. 195. See also Ilan Gur-Ze'ev, *Philosophy, Politics and Education in Israel* (Haifa: Haifa University Press, 1999, in Hebrew), p. 105.
80. Linn and Gur Ze'ev, ibid., p. 203; Qaymari, "The Holocaust," pp. 151–2.
81. *Al-Risala*, April 13, *al-Istiqlal*, April 20, 2000. For an extensive report on the controversy around this issue, see: *Al-Quds al-'Arabi*, 11 April, *al-'Arabi*, 20 April 2000; Memri, Dispatch No. 187, February 21, 2000.
82. *Al-Watan*, *al-Riyadh*, *al-Sharq al-Awsat*, March 3, 2008.
83. *Al-Hayat*, March 19, 2008.
84. William Miles, "Third World views of the Holocaust," *Journal of Genocide Research*, Vol. 6, No. 3 (2004), p. 379. The article pre-

sented the gist of deliberations of a conference under this title held in Northeastern University in April 2001.

85. Moses, "Conceptual blockages and definitional dilemmas," pp. 18–19.
86. http://www.alarabiya.net/views/2010/06/22/111977.html.
87. *Al-Quds al-'Arabi*, February 3, 2006.
88. *Al-Hayat*, February 10, 2008.
89. Yehuda Bauer, "Whose Holocaust?," *Midstream*, Vol. XXVI, No. 9 (November 1980), p. 45.

CHAPTER 13

Soft Denial in Different Political and Social Areas on the Web

Juliane Wetzel

Introduction

This chapter is concerned not so much with Holocaust denial in those European countries where it is an offense, but rather examines the various and different forms of trivialization of the Nazi genocide of Europe's Jews during the Second World War. This trivialization of the Nazi genocide does not always occur with the intention of diminishing it but rather with the intention of using the Holocaust to draw attention to political or social issues, such as abortion, mass animal transports and so on or, indeed, simply to serve as an advertising ploy. Those who use such a clearly loaded historical term in order to dramatically publicize their concerns usually do so not to defame or discredit Jews. This is different to what is often referred to as 'Holocaust distortion' in which a reversal of perpetrator-victim depicts Israel as the 'new Nazis' and puts 'the Jews' in general under general suspicion for all the evil in the world and in particular for the conflict in the Middle East. In this instance, the conduct of the Israeli military in the Gaza Strip and the Israeli government's policy is equated with Nazi persecution. The terms 'Holocaust inversion' and 'Holocaust equivalence' thus describe a situation in which Israel is delegitimized

J. Wetzel (✉)
Berlin, Germany

A. McElligott, J. Herf (eds.), *Antisemitism Before and Since the Holocaust*, DOI 10.1007/978-3-319-48866-0_13

because the government or the military are accused of behaving toward the Palestinians in the same way as the Nazis had against the Jews, leading to the 'annihilation' of the Palestinians.

***

In countries that were directly involved in the Holocaust, guilt is projected onto Israel in the form of a perpetrator-victim reversal in which ultimately 'the Jews' are collectively vilified. In Germany and Austria, such guilt-relief strategies dominate the discourse. In 2012, a member of the German 'Pirate Party' tweeted: 'Ah, now I know why millions had to die in concentration camps: so that Israel can wage its war of aggression with … complete impunity WTF?' And: 'The Israelis are the root of all evil'.[1] Similar patterns of expression can be observed in many other European countries, even when—at least in Western Europe—the question of guilt and shame is not the dominant feature. Nonetheless, content and objectives are similar. In the Arab world as well as in Iran, whose former president Ahmadinejad constantly made headlines with Holocaust denial, European patterns of demonizing Israel are used.[2] Forms of belittling and trivializing the Holocaust, indeed even Holocaust denial itself, are used in this part of the world to suggest that Israel's right to exist was deviously acquired by the 'Holocaust lie'/'Auschwitz lie'.

In the countries of Central, Eastern and Southeastern Europe, such displacement strategies are en vogue in which the Jews are blamed for the fact that the memory of the Holocaust is omnipresent, thus overshadowing one's own victimhood. The Polish Bishop Tadeusz Pieronek, a former Chairman of the Polish Bishops' Conference, in an interview in January 2010 with an Italian Catholic website on the occasion of Holocaust Memorial Day, called for the introduction of observance for the 'victims of communism, for Catholics, for persecuted Christians and so forth' and accused 'the Jews' at the same time of using the Holocaust as a propaganda weapon, 'in order to reap benefits that are often unjustified'. Pieronek's thinking is obviously conditioned by conspiracy theories as can be seen when he further stated: 'The Jews receive a good press because powerful financial resources are behind them; a huge power and the unconditional backing of the United States, and that promotes a certain arrogance that I find unbearable'.[3] All of this is mixed with current political issues: in the end, the Bishop felt he had to supplement his comments with the observation that the Palestinians are treated like animals. Pieronek had in the past explicitly challenged the antisemitic Polish broadcaster 'Radio Marija', but his remarks in the interview show that he is socialized in an environment where over generations traditional antisemitism played a central role and is now mixed with forms of secondary antisemitism. The equation of Stalinist and Nazi terror, as represented by Pieronek, is today commonly found in Central and Eastern European countries and is referred to by some historians as 'soft denial'/'soft core denial'.

Such equivocation of Nazi and Stalinist crimes can also be found in Timothy Snyder's book *Bloodlands*.[4] Snyder's basic thesis is that the similarities between both regimes lie in the fact that they both murdered on one and the same territory—the 'Bloodlands', and that the famine as well as the Great Terror initiated by Stalin had genocidal intentions based on a policy of ethnic persecution. His claim that 'the hundreds of thousands of executed Soviet peasants and workers during the Great Terror 1937/38 were victims of Stalin's explicit commands like those at between 1941 and 1945 gassed and shot millions of Jews of an explicit policy of Hitler's victim to fall'[5] lacks a necessary differentiation between the two regimes.[6] Symptomatic for this leveling of the terror of the two regimes is the introduction a few years ago in a number of countries of 23rd August, the date of the signing of the Molotov-Ribbentrop Pact, as a day of commemoration.[7]

Following the historian Deborah Lipstadt, one can also speak of 'soft core denial' when, for example, the Muslim Council of Britain refuses to take part in Holocaust Memorial Day unless also discrimination against Muslims is mentioned.[8] Lipstadt had already minted the term 'soft core denial' in an interview in 2003 when she criticized the German historian Ernst Nolte for his equation of fascism, National Socialism and Bolshevism and noted:

> Historians such as the German Ernst Nolte are, in some ways, even more dangerous than the deniers. Nolte is an anti-Semite of the first order, who attempts to rehabilitate Hitler by saying that he was no worse than Stalin; but he is careful not to deny the Holocaust. Holocaust deniers make Nolte's life more comfortable. They have, with their radical argumentation, pulled the center a little more to their side. Consequently, a less radical extremist, such as Nolte finds himself closer to the middle ground, which makes him more dangerous.[9]

Nolte had put Nazism and Bolshevism on the same level in his book *The European Civil War of 1917–1945*, published in the 1980s.[10] Ultimately, his thesis calls into question the unprecedented, indeed the singular, nature of the Holocaust by reducing the years 1917 to 1945 to a mere civil war. Nolte's book met with more than a little resonance and went to the heart of society, influencing the public discourse in Germany in the late 1980s and early 1990s. In a later book published in 2009 and titled *The Third Radical Resistance Movement: Militant Islam*, he referred to the Grand Mufti of Jerusalem as a 'valiant champion of the Palestinians, who one should not refuse to honour'.[11] Nolte repeatedly cited statements that equated Zionism and the 'Living Space' (*Lebensraum*) ideology of the Nazis without distancing himself from them and disparaged Israel as a 'fascist state'. Finally, in his concluding chapter, Nolte asked whether it is not understandable that there should be a 'reasonable' antisemitism among the population in the Palestinian territories, which had been expelled by Israel.[12] The eminent Israeli Holocaust historian Yehuda Bauer, like Deborah Lipstadt, also refers to those forms that trivialize the genocide of the European Jews as 'soft denial': 'I think that outright denial in the West is marginal, though it continues to exist. But there is "soft" denial—comparisons between Nazis and Israelis, questioning the figures, arguing for a non-difference between the genocide of the Jews and other genocides, etc.'[13]

Despite the legitimate arguments that lead not just Lipstadt and Bauer to use the term 'soft denial', I would argue for the use of the term 'Holocaust trivialization' because it better captures the complexity of the wide spectrum of minimization strategies, including those forms that do not follow any historical political objectives. Comparisons with Holocaust do not use the genocide of European Jewry as a frame of reference to displace responsibility from oneself, nor are they intended to blame Jews for the fact that 'the past cannot be forgotten', for example, in the form of a perpetrator-victim reversal in order to stigmatize Israel or Israelis as the 'new perpetrators'; instead, the term 'Holocaust' is employed to draw attention for sensitive issues in public discourse. Here there is no indication that the intention is to discredit Jews, but rather the aim is solely to shock the public and draw attention, for example, by using drastic images from the concentration camps to equate these with those of mass animal transports, and thus to stir publicity for one's own campaign. That the victims of the Holocaust could be insulted as a consequence, or that the genocide of the Jews is as a result trivialized, does not even feature in the calculations of the initiators of such campaigns.

In the context of the entire scala of Holocaust trivialization, those of animal rights movements and anti-abortion campaigns are peripheral. Without a doubt, much more widespread in relativizing the Holocaust or distorting the past are those strategies connected with the Middle East conflict. Here, Jews and Israelis are equally depicted as the 'new perpetrators', the 'new

Nazis'. The 2011 study of 'group focused enmity' (Gruppenbezogene Menschenfeindlichkeit) in several European countries by a team of investigators at the University of Bielefeld, led by Andreas Zick, showed that 47.7% of Germans, 42.4% of the British, 38.7% of the Dutch, 37.6% of Italians, 48.8% of Portuguese, 63.3% of Poles and 41.0% of Hungarians fully or partially agreed to the assertion: 'Israel is conducting a war of extermination against the Palestinians'.[14] The phrase 'war of extermination' is clearly a term associated with Nazi ideology and is acknowledged as such. In this respect it becomes clear how widespread such equivalence patterns are in many European countries and not just in those countries where it is an articulation of the attempt to exculpate one's own direct involvement in the Holocaust. Similar high scores were seen with the statement 'Jews try to take advantage of having been victims during the Nazi area'. In Germany, 48% responded approvingly to this statement. The highest values were again found in Poland (72.2%) and Hungary (68.1%), but that in Portugal (52.2%) was also quite high. The Netherlands (17.2%), followed by Britain (21.8%), stood at the lower end of the scale.[15]

Here, it is certainly possible to conclude that a projection of blame on 'the Jews', as those who continuously remind 'us' of the Holocaust, has now mutated into a European phenomenon. A considerable part in this is played by the media, which has focused broadly on the persecution of the Jews in recent years—especially in the context of anniversaries—and thus for some has triggered a feeling of saturation, or even the fanciful idea that the intense coverage is due to the alleged influence of the Jews plays a not insignificant role. In the final analysis 'The Jews' are made responsible for the fact that the past cannot be consigned to history, and thus the desired normalization in the relationship between majority and minority is not possible.

The Misuse of the 'Holocaust' by Italian Fascists and the 'Bombing Holocaust' in Germany

A trivialization or belittling of the Holocaust also occurs when historical events such as the bombing of Dresden by the allies in February 1945, or the so-called Foibe massacres in Istria and Dalmatia where, in 1943–1949, Yugoslav Partisans murdered between 5000 and 10,000 fascists, or those they considered as such, by throwing them into the deep sinkholes of the Karst region, are equated with the Holocaust. In particular, such equations play a dominant role within right-wing extremism. For example, this approach is found in the narrative of the Italian right-wing splinter party 'Forza Nuova', whose Palermo branch celebrated on its website in February 2011, the torchlight procession of supporters that took place on 10 February on the occasion of the commemoration day of the Foibe introduced by the former Prime Minister Silvio Berlusconi. The protesters had carried placards with the words 'We will not forget the Holocaust of the Istrian people'.[16] In the same month, a student group 'Lotta Studentesca' (Student Combat), also linked to 'Forza Nuova', attached a banner with a similar inscription to the Holocaust Memorial 'Binario 21', the rail track in Milan Central station from which the deportation trains departed with Jews from the area.[17]

The 'Bombing Holocaust', as right-wing extremists in Germany call the firebombing of Dresden from 13 to 15 February 1945, is a widespread slogan in the Internet that equates the victims of the Holocaust with the fatalities of the Allied bombardment of Dresden. Not only are such notorious associations circulating in the cyber world, but also the numbers of victims of the air strikes are completely exaggerated, with over 500,000 alleged dead; serious historiography today gives approximately 25,000 dead. Internet platforms such as YouTube present a range of videos on the 'Bombing Holocaust' of which the following are illustrative: the German-language 'Bombing Holocaust of Dresden: vigil in Aulendorf 2007', with more than 2400 hits[18]; 'Bombing Holocaust of Dresden: Remembrance in Sweden 2007', which, however, on the German-based YouTube platform is age-restricted and can only be viewed by registering[19]; or 'Dresden a real Holocaust'.[20] On 'YouRepeat', a website linked to YouTube, the supposedly serious three-part 'documentary about the Bombing Holocaust of the allies on 13th and 14th February 1945' can be viewed.[21] It was uploaded on the far-right 'Globalfire.TV' platform, which also hosts the extreme right-wing 'National Journal'. Finally, in February 2012, an 'Action Alliance Against Forgetting' was launched on the North Rhine-Westphalian Web page of the extreme right-wing National Democratic Party of Germany (NPD) exhorting its viewers: 'On to Dresden: "In memory of the victims of the Allied bombing Holocaust!"'[22]

23 August: A Trivializing Memorial Day to Nazi and Stalinist Terror

In recent years, there has been a tendency in the public discourse of many countries to equate Nazi violence with the terror of Stalinism at the expense of differentiation, thus abandoning legitimate scholarly comparisons (but not necessarily that provided by Snyder, as mentioned above). From the point of view of the victims, it was relatively irrelevant what political background the persecution had, especially since the extent of terror in its entirety could be detected only retrospectively. For the historical narrative and the confrontation with Stalinism and National Socialism in the following generations however, an equation of the two dictatorships is not permissible. Such an approach ultimately ends in a belittling of the Holocaust. The 'Holodomor', the Stalinist starvation of not only the Ukrainian peasantry but also of Kazakhstan and of the North Caucasus, Stalin's purges and the Gulag resulted in several million deaths, but they were not aimed against a certain racially biologically defined population group, which, solely because they were Jews, were to be entirely eliminated with the help of an industrially driven mass murder.

This upsurge, or *Konjunktur* as it is referred to by the Munich historian Jürgen Zarusky, in equivocation of the two regimes, is not only common in the historical community; it dominates public discourse in those countries which suffered under the Stalinist dictatorship, from the Baltic States, Poland, the Ukraine and so on. However, the fact that in many of these regions the collaboration of the local populations facilitated the Holocaust is frequently overlooked. Quite a few were not only victims of Stalinism but also perpetrators who supported the Nazi regime in its policy to get rid of the 'Judeo Bolsheviks'. These dispositions are today largely effaced when politicians publicly equate both dictatorships and thus ultimately reflect public discourse.[23] A similar conclusion can be reached for a number of museums that have appeared in recent years, such as the 'House of Terror' in Budapest or the 'Museum to the Victims of Genocide' in Vilnius in which the Lithuanian collaboration in the Holocaust is not addressed but instead where the 'victims of genocide' refer only or mainly to those of Stalinist terror.

It is not surprising, therefore, that such leveling tendencies in comparing the two dictatorships are influential at the European political level since the accession of Eastern European countries to the European Union (EU). Following an International Conference in Prague on the theme of 'European Conscience and Communism', prominent former prisoners, Eastern European politicians and historians signed the 'Prague Declaration on European Conscience and Communism' on 3 June 2008, according to which communist crimes were condemned and a European Day of Remembrance introduced, which would at the same time commemorate the victims of Stalinism and those of National Socialism.[24] On 2

April 2009, the European Parliament adopted a resolution on 'European conscience and totalitarianism' with 553 votes in favor, 44 against and 33 abstentions which demanded a 'proclamation of 23 August as a Europe-wide day of remembrance for the victims of all totalitarian and authoritarian regimes, to be commemorated with dignity and impartiality'.[25] Although the 'uniqueness of the Holocaust' was referred to, this new pan-European day for the victims of Nazism and Stalinism adopted by the EU Parliament, and subsequently by the Organization for Security and Co-operation in Europe, nevertheless threatened to thrust the Holocaust into the background. The Day of Remembrance was to be held in future on 23 August, the same date as the signing of the German-Soviet Non-Aggression Pact in 1939. As is well known, this Pact, signed by Foreign Ministers Molotov and Ribbentrop, included a secret supplementary protocol to divide the Baltic States, Poland and parts of Romania and Finland between Nazi Germany and the Soviet Union. In the Baltic States, in whose collective memory the Soviet occupation has left much deeper marks than that by Nazi Germany, dissidents have demonstrated publicly—under strict conditions—since 1987 on 23 August against the Soviet regime.

Unimpressed by the critical comments of former concentration camp prisoners, by historians and the directors of sites of memorial, advocates for the Day of Remembrance on 23 August pushed ahead undeterred. In October 2011, the 'platform of European Memory and Conscience', which is particularly active in the Internet, was established in the presence of some Eastern European prime ministers.[26] It has its headquarters in Prague. Its president is the former conservative member of Swedish parliament, Lars Göran Axel Lindblad, who in 2006 initiated a Council of Europe resolution which urged an international condemnation of crimes of totalitarian communist regimes.[27] Membership of the Platform is confined almost exclusively to those institutions and organizations dealing with communist terror. The agreement establishing the Platform and written in English points explicitly to the Holocaust—'noting [its] exceptionality and uniqueness'—[28]but it also leaves the impression that the real purpose of its members, as too its substantive orientation, is focused only on the victims of Stalinism.

On 23 August 2012, the online newspaper 'The Baltic Course', under the banner title 'Baltic States commemorate the victims of crimes of Communism Nazism', reported the upcoming celebration of 23 August in Tallinn, where the Estonian foreign minister delivered a speech.[29] In 2012, Hungary played host of the central event of the 'European

Memorial Day of the Victims of Totalitarian Regimes', as announced on the Hungarian government's website on 21 August. At the center of the events of Memorial Day was a Conference on the theme 'Facing the Past' held in the Hungarian parliament in Budapest, at which the justice ministers of different countries were in attendance and which was initiated with a ceremony in front of the 'House of Terror'. The announcement on the government's website points out that 'the Hungarian House of Terror Museum is one of the most dramatic in Europe' and as such, a 'symbolic' place.[30] During the Conference, the representatives of Hungary, Lithuania, Latvia, the Czech Republic, Croatia, Poland and Slovakia (with the exception of Czech Republic, all with blemished wartime records vis-à-vis the persecution of the Jews), as well as the president of the 'Platform of European Memory and Conscience', Lindblad, signed an agreement on the creation of a 'European Museum of Totalitarianism'.[31] The document, according to the Platform's Web page, expressed the will of all the institutions active in the field, dedicated to the study of totalitarian regimes, to establish a museum, which at the same time would serve as a memorial to the victims.[32]

Unanswered in all of this is the question why the Europe-wide introduction of 23 August as a Day of Remembrance for the victims of both regimes was accepted uncritically by EU politicians and most of the European press. The result is that representatives of these states and victims' organizations, whose main concern is only the fate of those who suffered under Stalinist terror, seek to establish the primacy of communist state terror during the twentieth century as a whole, thus threatening to drive the annihilation of European Jews into the background and consequently, relegating it to a secondary place.

The Handling of Information in the Net

International websites which promote 23 August as a Joint-Remembrance Day of the terror of Stalinism and National Socialism are ubiquitous in the Internet, today the central information medium for youth. The complex historical issues and the dangers that a comparison of the two dictatorships bring if there is not extensive knowledge about the respective contexts open up a wide field in which teachers and thus also their students are rarely equipped to negotiate their way. The lack of competence in dealing with the new media in schools and non-formal education is similarly problematic. Nonetheless for German versions of search engines or YouTube, or Google video, the hazards that users will encounter right-wing extremist content are at least reduced because in recent years operators and providers have tried to make sure that access to extremist content is getting more complicated or even not possible or the sites are provided with an appropriate warning.

That not only the providers of such sites of Generation Web 2.0, but also German online newsrooms, now act more responsibly is evident also in the policy of regularly preventing comments on films and contributions being uploaded to these sites. Either such contributions on the Web inciting hatred are present briefly before being taken down or they are barred from the outset because providers fear that criminal content will get them into trouble with the law.[33] Where comments are allowed, the forum moderators of reputable newspapers ensure that inflammatory content is deleted. Nonetheless, the comments on the Web in response to serious online newspaper articles in response to the recent controversy on whether or not circumcision in Germany should be treated as assault against a child reveal how widespread anti-Jewish stereotyping (this applies also to Islam) is and how it can find a foothold in such forums. An example of this form of secondary antisemitism is illustrated by the online comment to an article 'Survey—many Germans against circumcision' in the *Kölner Stadt Anzeiger* of 19 July 2012 from 'Friedrich T' who wrote: 'The judgment in the circumcision case will be revised! The corresponding law whipped quickly through the parliament (Bundestag) and Upper Chamber (Bundesrat)! And as penance a U-boat will be given to Israel! The Cologne judges will be [...] chased from office with a Nazi cudgel! Lovely democratic WorlD!!'[34]

In recent years, the distribution of antisemitic content by right-wing extremist groups on the Internet appears to have receded into the background of media attention. Instead more in focus are young people with an immigration background, who take advantage of the possibility of exchanging data online as an agitatory platform to distribute antisemitic content but without reaching the same level of impact as right-wing smear campaigns. The weekly newspaper, *Die Zeit* in an article in June 2010 titled 'Jew-hatred on Facebook', reported on right-wing extremist content and pointed out that many Holocaust deniers had joined the Facebook group 'We respect you Hitler'. However, detailed information on the contents of the NPD-Community found on Facebook is difficult to verify. It is remarkable, nonetheless, that a search with specific terms such as 'Jew' on 'Openbook', which for a while provided a search function for 'Facebook', showed that the authors of posts in German were given foreign-sounding names. The authors of these posts assumed that German neo-Nazis could encrypt their entries and spread the content on pages that were not easily accessible so that until July 2012, when 'Openbook' was closed down for legal reasons, it was difficult to trace such content.[35]

Dangerous Camouflage—Right-Wing Online News Portals

Kreuz.net

The antisemitic, anti-Islam and homophobic Internet platform *Kreuz.net* (Crucifix-net), which portrayed itself as a serious Catholic online news portal but from which the German Bishops Conference, as well as Vatican Radio, clearly distanced themselves, has been active since 2004 as an anonymous blog and was shut down in December 2012. It provided a variety of information about the 'Society of Saint Pius X (SSPX)' and at least has given the impression of a close connection with this sectarian offshoot of the Catholic Church. The points of convergence between *Kreuz.net* and SSPX are obvious, for example, in relation to the rejection of the Second Vatican Council with its distancing from antisemitic aspects of the Catholic Liturgy or *Kreuz.net*'s favorable attitude toward the Holocaust denier Bishop Richard Williamson, whom it labeled the 'Hero Bishop'. Even after his expulsion from the fraternity of SSPX in October 2012, *Kreuz.net* published on its site a text by Williamson justifying his position.[36] Another Holocaust denier, Father Florian Abrahamowicz, added his voice of support for Williamson: 'Monsignor Fellay under pressure from the Zionist world first forced him to sacrifice me in 2009 as Holocaust [*sic!*] and now Bishop Williamson. How shameful!'[37]

According to its imprint, '*Kreuz.net* was an initiative of an international private group of Catholics in Europe and overseas, which was professionally engaged in ecclesiastical service'. The blog was run by the California-based, anonymous 'Sodalicium for "Religion and Information"', which has been registered in Hong Kong since April 2012. From August 2012, *Kreuz.net* was delivered via a server in San Francisco and then via a server in a suburb of Los Angeles. The itinerant nature of the server was a defense mechanism and meant that the Web page could be moved to a different location, making it difficult so far for hackers to shut down the site. Around the same time as the Bishop Williamson affair, the Berlin-based

Office for the Protection of the Constitution and the Austrian Federal Office for the Protection of the Constitution initiated an investigation into the operator after it had unleashed a vicious homophobic campaign in the wake of the death of a homosexual German actor.[38]

Kreuz.net served a wide variety of topics, occupying the gray area between arch-Catholicism and right-wing extremist content. Thus abortion was put on par with the Holocaust; indeed, it was even claimed that to compare the two is to trivialize abortion—'the slaughter of the innocents'—which is worse than the Holocaust (2 October 2009). Holocaust survivor Elie Wiesel was called a 'Holocaust denier' because he allegedly does not speak out against 'the Jewish atrocities against the Palestinians', and the Holocaust still does a 'roaring trade' financially and politically (30 October 2009). In another article in *Kreuz.net* on 22 March 2011 titled 'The Jew-State again kills children', one could read: 'The world finds itself in the *rigor mortis* of antisemitism and watches impassively as Israel organizes a new Holocaust in occupied Palestine [sic]'. Under the heading 'Holocaust 2.0', *Kreuz.net* claimed at the end of August 2012: 'Terrorists supported by the United States and Israel massacre Christian families in Syria'. Shortly before the ostensible news website reported under the title 'The antisemitism over which nobody cries. Tens of thousands living in the shadow of Jewish Terror': 'The hand behind these attacks belongs to Israeli Jews who are violating international law by living in the West Bank' (14 August 2012). Unsurprisingly, readers' comments about Jewish dominance of the German press and the malice of 'Jewish leaders and their henchmen' abound. *Kreuz-net* obviously had few fears about contact with the otherwise negatively portrayed Muslims when it came to the common enemy Israel. In October 2011, a report appeared about Ayatollah Khomeini's original call in 1979 for Al-Quds day (Jerusalem day), which has been the occasion for propaganda events among radical Islamists in European cities since. For the article, *Kreuz-net* interviewed the operator of the German Islamist website 'Muslim Market' and organizer of the annual Al-Quds anti-Zionist demonstration in Berlin, who was allowed to repeat the hate speeches of the then Iranian President Ahmadinejad, who used to deliver these on the occasion of Al-Quds day in Tehran.

Kreuz-net for a longer time stood under observation by German State authorities. The German Federal Department for Media Harmful to Young Persons has listed parts of the website on its index of banned sites because of Holocaust denial. But the site was nevertheless available in its entirety, although it could not be advertised or provided to minors. On a popular level, the Facebook group 'Initiative against Kreuz.net' fought back against the antisemitic and racist content of its Weblogs, and 'Watch Kreuz.net' from January 2011 to January 2013 has been active against 'A website of reactionary and radical right-wing forces that hides behind the guise of the Catholic Church and the anonymity of the Internet, to preach hatred and homophobia', albeit using strongly polemical language.[39]

Altermedia

The right-wing news portal *Altermedia* (World Wide News For People of European Descent, Alter[native] Media), providing 'world wide news for people of European descent', which has been online since about 2002, presents itself as a supposedly reputable website that wants to convey the impression of a news agency, and is present in more than 20 countries in different languages. The American neo-Nazi David Duke seems to be responsible for the English-language, international version. In May 2011, a video was uploaded to YouTube showing Duke talking at the insignificant revisionist 'Danish Society for Free Historical Research', a forum which has referred to the Holocaust as a myth and which regularly invites Holocaust deniers to give lectures.

The German offshoot *Altermedia Germany/Störtebeker Network* provided for a long time daily articles on the net that to some extent were adapted from reputable media and reworded accordingly or commented on. Contributions from the NPD organ *German Voice* or *Kreuz.net* were met with praise. With approximately five million hits annually, *Altermedia* has long been probably the most popular website of the right-wing extremist scene. Advertising banners revealed the proximity to the extreme right-wing spectrum. It polemicizes against 'media witchhunts' and 're-education', which would lead to a wrong view of history. On the occasion of the commemoration of the liberation of Auschwitz, the deputy national chairman of the NPD, Karl Richter, on 28 January 2010, railed against a 'privileging of certain groups of victims'. 'The normal German population', he stated, 'need to take a stand against such exclusive demands (Alleinvertretungsansprüche) of a specific group of victims that are always insolently shoved in their faces'.[40] On 5 March 2010, the following quote appeared in an article on *Altermedia* that is entirely in keeping with extreme right-wing strategies to defame Jews using Israel as a surrogate:

> Israel has for years transformed itself from a victim of the Holocaust victims into a dangerous Monster. [...] Antisemitism is promoted by all means not

> only to maintain the talk of Jewish victim status, but also to promote first and foremost the cohesion of the Jews in the world. This makes them very strong, but also disliked everywhere. But their famous arrogance and hubris could soon crumble sharply.[41]

Finally, in September 2012, *Altermedia* was shut down after the online organization YouthProtection.net put pressure on the American host server.[42] Notwithstanding this, *Altermedia* resurfaced on the net to resume baiting. In addition, until late November 2012, there was also a Twitter platform that displayed almost 4500 tweets and nearly 600 followers, making it more up to date than its affiliate *Altermedia International*, which had no new entries after December 2011. *Altermedia* still exists; it now continues under the name 'Altermedia.info', and since 2014 it obviously uses a Russian provider.[43] In April 2015, it published an article by the Holocaust denier Ursula Haverbeck, who spoke about her experiences with an interview for a German TV channel under the title 'Does the "Lügenpresse" (lying media) now finally ask for the truth?' (Beginnt auch die "Lügenpresse" nach der Wahrheit zu fragen?).[44] The term 'Lügenpresse' (lying media) is well known as a key word used by the Nazis to blame an alleged Jewish press conspiracy.

From the foregoing, it is clear that the central agitation and recruitment platform for the right-wing extremist scene is the Internet nationally and internationally. In 2009, 107 right-wing blogs were accessible and 93 neo-Nazi social networks were available.[45] In 2011, 1,671 right-wing extremist websites could be identified. This is a small decline on the previous two years (2010:1,707; 2009:1,872, of which 67% was via a German Server), but is offset by a fourfold increase in right-wing extremist Twitter accounts. In 2012, with 1,519 websites, a further decrease could be noted, but in 2013 the numbers rose again to 1,628. Much more important is the raise in platforms of social media: in 2011, the German organization YouthProtection.net counted 3,715 Web offers; in 2012, 5,500; and in 2013, 3,879.[46] While the majority of the 1,628 extreme right-wing websites in 2013 were operated through local servers (58%), almost all of the 3,879 social media offers were hosted abroad (93%), mostly on US-hosted offers like Facebook, YouTube and Twitter (3,327, 86%). But also provider in Russia via the video platform Rutube and the Social Network VK gained increasing importance for the extreme right-wing scene in Germany.[47] Already in 2011, YouthProtection.net stated, 'Right-wing extremists are trying to recruit young people via the

Internet and use this Web 2.0'.[48] Corresponding messages are transported mainly via music and are available not only on right-wing sites but can be downloaded from 'iTunes' or YouTube, at least until the host server is made aware of the criminal content and removes them. In a press release in July 2012 referring to 'Online Rightwing Extremism', the operators of YouthProtection.net make the point that 'neo-Nazis try especially on Facebook and YouTube to use provocative events and subversive tactics as bait to reach their avowedly main target audience—namely youth. And thus rapidly reach an audience of millions'.[49]

Connecting to Left-Wing Discourses

An example of how content from the extreme right-wing spectrum can be quite adaptable to anti-globalization arguments of the most diverse political groups can be found in the case of the publisher Kopp. On the margins of the right, this publishing company repeatedly trivializes the Holocaust and supports the video 'Give me the world plus 5 percent: the history of the Goldsmith Fabian', which is distributed on the Internet. Based on a text written in 1971 by the Australian Larry Hannigan, Michael Kent (Hinz), an adherent of Scientology, through his production company Neue Impulse (New Impulses) e.V., created an animated movie that subtly transports antisemitic stereotypes about 'power junkies of financial dynasties', who gain 'power over the masses' and thus come to dominate the world. Obviously, teachers fall for this nonsense when they see this animation as useful teaching material, which supposedly explains the financial, monetary and interest rate system. At least, this is what we learn when looking at the postings on YouTube: 'so, in school we looked at Part 2. The rest was homework', or 'one can use this well as a school video… Our teacher spent a whole hour on it!!!'[50] Even if throughout the entire film the word 'Jew' or similar direct attributions do not appear once, one can deduce from the posting by 'Commander Black Pudding' ('Commanderblutwurst') that the movie is understood as antisemitic among the right-wing scene. As 'Black Pudding' writes: 'you have probably not understood, that fabian mayer symbolizes amschel bauer (rothschild)'.[51]

Since 2009 until recently, about 310,000[52] users have watched the film, available in six parts, on YouTube; it can be watched in its 50-minute-long entirety on Google Videos and is sought after by esoteric sites and on right-wing extremist networks.[53] As long as this was still possible, numerous Facebook entries via Openbook.org and the posting 'Fabian

Goldsmith' recommended the film in order to gain an insight into the financial and monetary policy. The anti-capitalist movement 'Occupy Frankfurt' refers to the film as an 'enlightening report' on the 'compound interest and money system'.[54] A now deleted posting on the website of 'Occupy Frankfurt' shows what sort of antisemitic stereotypes are circulating among the 'Occupy Wallstreet/99-Percent Movement': 'A small mafia-like organized group, whose members probably already over generations, pass between themselves positions [of power], abuse the Jewish faith for their goals'.[55] That within parts of the Occupy Movement antisemitic clichés are spread as a result of reference to hostile Jewish stereotypes such as the alleged dominance of 'the Jews' in the financial sector and the stock markets has been criticized repeatedly in recent years. Others in the anti-globalization spectrum faced similar accusations.

Examples of the links between left discourses about the financial world, which sometimes serve antisemitic sentiment, and debates on the Middle East conflict that trivialize the Holocaust by equating the two can be found time and again among the national variants of the globalization-critical platform *Indymedia*. Some regularly have antisemitic postings. Even Alfred Rosenberg's version of the antisemitic 'The protocols of the elders of Zion' can be found.[56] Other versions of *Indymedia* regularly publish caricatures by the Brazilian Carlos Latuff, who equates the conduct of the Israeli military or the Israeli Government with the Nazi persecution of the Jews in his cartoons; in 2006 he thus won the second prize of an Iranian State Holocaust cartoon contest for his depiction. Latuff, who not only presents analogies to the Holocaust but also employs classic antisemitic motifs in order to discredit Israel, circulates freely his countless cartoons on the Internet in order to serve the 'Palestinian cause'. Such content, however, does not go unchallenged. Readers repeatedly demand that such posts should be deleted or consigned to the 'censorship bucket' (Zensurkübel). However, *Indymedia* prefers not to respond citing freedom of expression.[57]

The Term Holocaust and Its Inflationary Use

In March 2004, PETA ('People for the ethical treatment of animals'), the international animal welfare organization founded in 1980 in the United States and representing 800,000 members according to its own figures, launched a campaign against factory farming under the title 'The Holocaust on your plate' in Germany, Austria and Switzerland. PETA used large-scale posters depicting the farming and transport of animals that drew directly from images of Nazi concentration and extermination camps. In March 2004, the regional court of Berlin (*Landgericht*) obtained an injunction against seven of the eight posters shown in the exhibition. On one of the giant posters was the main gate of Auschwitz-Birkenau over which two interwoven emblems rose like the sun above the gates. One was the blue EU flag with its ring of stars and the other a black swastika on a white circle with a red background. In the foreground to the left a cow was shown, hauled up by a cord tied to its leg. In the right half of the image a pig stood unsteadily. The slogan written in red simply states: 'Déjà vu?' and illustrates the intended coincidence of Holocaust and mass animal slaughter.

More posters from the exhibition included the iconic image of children under the title 'Child Slaughter' in striped prison uniforms on the day of their liberation from Auschwitz, and next to them pigs cooped up behind bars. In another poster, the well-known photograph from Buchenwald after its liberation in 1945 showing skeletal survivors lying in a vegetative state in their bunk beds was used, which was matched with another image depicting a battery farm crammed with chickens. A court in Berlin banned the campaign in May 2004, which had been accessible through the Internet on a website sponsored by PETA. In March 2009, the German Federal Constitutional Court upheld the verdict. PETA responded to the judgment as follows:

> The HOYP [Holocaust on Your Plate] display—which was also funded by a Jewish PETA member—traveled all over the U.S., where it sparked a tremendous amount of debate and discussion about both animal rights and human rights issues. Then across the pond, PETA Germany took the idea and ran with it. And that's where the trouble began. Yesterday, Germany's high court banned PETA Germany's Holocaust display, stating that it would have made 'the fate of the victims of the Holocaust appear banal and trivial.'[58]

In November 2012, a final ruling was made by the Lesser Chamber of the European Court in Strasbourg which upheld the decision of the German courts.[59] However, PETA Germany refused to accept even this judgment and appealed to the Grand Chamber in Strasbourg.

The outcome of the legal challenge to PETA's exhibition was quite different in Austria. Although the Supreme Court in Vienna stated in its verdict in October 2006: 'The collage consists undoubtedly of shocking images about the life and death of people who were incarcerated in concentration and extermination camps during the Nazi Holocaust. Without a doubt, it can easily be assumed that the people [depicted] were overwhelmingly Jews (left side of the posters). Also the documentary photos of farm animals (right side of the posters) when considered alone convey, at least for a major part of the viewing public a startling, shocking, or at least emotionally unpleasant impression', it nonetheless concluded that PETA's campaign was protected under freedom of expression and thus did not ban it. Nevertheless, the court also observed that it 'does not ignore the fact that the exhibition campaign for animal welfare is clearly impious, tasteless, exaggerated and can even be judged as immoral'.[60] Perhaps one should simply have called this campaign tasteless and referred to the ignorance of the makers as immoderate. This also applies to the work of rubric 'Animal Auschwitz' on the website of the animal protection organization 'Welfare for Animals Global'.[61]

A similar stunt was pulled by a young Dutch student, Dicky Thijssen, who created and distributed on the Internet a video 'Dance makes free—Housewitz'. Thijssen described the tasteless, inflammatory content as a joke, and later apologized for it. Using fast-moving images, edgy music and images of Auschwitz-Birkenau, its notorious ramp and piles of corpses, the viewer was invited to a dance party on 4 May, the Dutch day of commemoration for the victims of the war. In the video, the DJs are named as 'Michel the Heidi' and 'Adolf von Bauren'. A voice-over announces: 'seven million party people set their bodies on fire' and adds that the dress code is 'skinny Jew'. Images of gas chambers are shown and the voice announces 'hot showers, free of charge' and 'train stops at party ground'. The clip ends with 'Sieg Heil'. The video landed Thijssen in court. In May 2006, a Dutch court sentenced him to 40 hours of community work.[62] While German Myspace and YouTube have removed the video, it can be still downloaded on 'heretical.com', a website of the right-wing extremist Simon Sheppard, who has served a prison sentence in the United Kingdom for incitement to racial hatred. Access is also easy via Google where a search for 'Housewitz' leads directly to the video. On a positive note, it should be noted that Google is aware of the problematic searches in relation to Jews and Holocaust, providing users with the following explanation:

> If you recently used Google to search for the word 'Jew' you may have seen results that were very disturbing. We assure you that the views expressed by

> the sites in your results are not in any way endorsed by Google. We'd like to explain why you' re seeing these results when you conduct this search. [...] If you use Google to search for 'Judaism', 'Jewish' or 'Jewish people', the results are informative and relevant. So why is a search for 'Jew' different? One reason is that the word 'Jew' is often used in an anti-Semitic context. Jewish organizations are more likely to use the word 'Jewish' when talking about members of their faith.[63]

Conclusion

The trivialization and minimization of the Holocaust achieved a particularly high level in the cases we have been discussing. This is evident with PETA's campaign where animals and humans were presented on a single level. This is completely different to the equation of the Holocaust with 'Holodomor', the massacre of people through Stalin's famine policy in the Ukraine, in Kazakhstan and in the Northern Caucasus during 1932/1933 which we discussed above. For the people affected by 'Holodomor', which is acknowledged up to the present day as a catastrophe, that event continues to play a central role in their family narratives. Moreover, they use the term 'Holocaust' because, in this way, they believe they can better draw attention to their concerns.

However, when 'Holodomor' is depicted as having been 'committed by the Jewish mafia' and the number of victims in the Ukraine doubled from circa 3.5 million to 7 million, as claimed by the right-wing, fundamentalist Catholic and sectarian website 'Holywar.org', then this is done not to draw attention to the fate of people, but follows the strategy of 'Holywar.org' to attribute all the wrongs of the world to 'the Jews'.[64] The murder of the European Jews is described by 'Holywar.org' as the 'false Holocaust', whereas as a true Holocaust, one could call the lot of Black America or, referring to Russia, those '30 million Christian victims, who were slaughtered by Bolshevik Jews in the coup d'état in 1917'. These phrases are part of a text that 'Holywar.org' published on the occasion of Holocaust Memorial Day on 27 January 2009 under the heading 'MAI PIÙ' ('never again') in the Italian language. As with other fundamentalist Christian websites, 'Holywar.org' also describes abortion as murder and sees in this 'the only Holocaust of history'. Finally, using large lettering, 'Holywar.org' has issued a 'warning' of the 'Holocaust in Progress—Act now to Save Gaza'. The website thus combines a wide range of topics that trivialize the Holocaust, although Alfred Olsen, a Norwegian living in

Italy, who is behind this incendiary Internet platform, should be counted among the patent deniers of the Holocaust.

The dangers of antisemitic indoctrination today lie in the worldwide electronic exchange of information between politically different groups that have discovered antisemitism as a unifying theme and use the Internet for agitation and communication.[65] Here, one can also find in recent years fundamentalist Islamists who, since the mid of 1990s, increasingly use the so-called Auschwitz lie—that is, questioning the very substance of the Holocaust—as a political tool.[66] The conveyance of these prejudices is directed primarily against Israel, but also against Jews worldwide, and serves conspiracy fantasies and the trivialization, indeed, the negation, of the Holocaust. The World Wide Web as an easily accessible, anonymous communications and propaganda medium is used not only by radical Islamists to distribute such content but also by extremist right-wing networks which can connect to one another around the world on these issues. In recent years, it has become clear that groups from both camps are communicating with each via the Internet, newsgroups or chat forums and blogs and, despite their different political objectives, find common ground with the proliferation of the 'Auschwitz lie', also in order to attack Israel. The increase in antisemitic postings on the Web after the Israeli attack on the Gaza flotilla on 31 May 2010, in which expressions such as 'shit Jews, best to gas them all', posted on Facebook as well as on right-wing extremist and radical Islamist Web pages, occured, are an invitation to murder Jews.[67] The widespread anti-Israel sentiment is restricted neither to youth nor to right-wing extremists, nor to radical Islamist circles, but could be found in private discussions and in the media, with the latter's one-sided reporting only gradually giving way to a more balanced view of what was taking place, not least because the quality press made an effort to present a more differentiated picture and not let just the peace activists dominate.

Notes

1. (Israelische) Soldaten sind Mörder!, 15.11.2012, http://www.publikative.org/2012/11/15/israelische-soldaten-sind-morder/, accessed 27.11.2012.
2. See Kasra Naji, Ahmadinejad: the secret history of Iran's radical leader (Berkeley, 2008); Katajun Amirpur, 'Eine Antwort auf Matthias Küntzel', Network Fachjournalisten islamische Welt, 2010, http://www.netais.net/author/kamirpur/, accessed

26.11.2012; ‚Symathie für den Satan?', Frankfurter Allgemeine Zeitung (FAZ.net), 7.2.2006, http://www.faz.net/artikel/C30351/iran-und-israel-sympathie-fuer-den-satan-3033126.html, accessed 26.11.2012.

3. 'Polnischer Bischof nennt Holocaust 'Propaganda Waffe', in *Spiegel online*, 26.1.2010, http://www.spiegel.de/politik/ausland/0,1518,673999,00.htmil, accessed 5.6.2012.
4. Timothy Snyder, *Bloodlands. Europe between Hitler and Stalin* (New York, 2010).
5. Ibid., p. 12.
6. Ian Kershaw and Moshe Lewin (eds.), *Nazism and Stalinism. Dictatorship in Comparison* (Cambridge, 1997).
7. Juliane Wetzel, Eine Trivialisierung des Holocaust? Der 23. August als Gedenktag an die Opfer von Stalinismus und Nationalsozialismus, in: Wolfgang Benz (ed.), *Ein Kampf um Deutungshoheit. Politik, Opferinteressen und Historische Forschung. Die Auseinandersetzung um die Gedenk-und Begegnungsstätte Leistikowstrasse Potsdam*, (Berlin, 2013), pp. 250–263.
8. Holocaust scholar warns of new 'soft-core' denial, *Jerusalem Post*, 2.6.2007, http://www.jpost.com/JewishWorld/JewishNews/Article.aspx?id=50600, accessed 16.10.2012.
9. 'Denial of the Holocaust and Immoral Equivalence. An Interview with Deborah Lipstadt' in: *Post-Holocaust and Anti-Semitism*, No. 11, August 1, 2003, http://www.jcpa.org/phas/phas-11.htm, accessed 16.10.2012].
10. Ernst Nolte, *Der europäische Bürgerkrieg 1917–1945. Nationalsozialismus und Bolschewismus* 4th ed., (Frankfurt am Main, 1989).
11. Ernst Nolte, *Die dritte radikale Widerstandsbewegung: Der Islamismus* (Berlin, 2009), p. 347.
12. Ibid., p. 341.
13. See The Jewish Star, March 24, 2010, http://thejewishstar.wordpress.com/2010/03/24/q-and-a-with-yehuda-bauer/, accessed 23.4.2015.
14. Andreas Zick, Beate Küpper, Andreas Hövermann, *Intolerance, Prejudice and Discrimination. A European Report* (Berlin, 2011), p. 57 (see also: http://library.fes.de/pdf-files/do/07908-20110311.pdf, accessed 24.4.2015).
15. Ibid.

16. Forza Nuova Homepage, Palermo, 'Communicato Stampa del 13-02-2011', http://www.forzanuovapalermo.org/home.htm, accessed 29.9.2011. This website in April 2015 was not accessible anymore. Forza Nuova Palermo presents its ideas now on Facebook and Twitter. See http://www.milano.forzanuova.info/blog/2011/02/10/foibe-una-testimonianza-contro-loblio-blitz-davanti-al-binario-21, accessed 23.4.2015: 'We used "Binario 21" for remembering the wagons the expellies from Friaul-Dalmatia who have been forced to leave their territories and houses used for escaping the terrible persecution of the partisan hate'. (Abbiamo scelto il "Binario 21" per ricordare i carri merci con cui gli esuli giuliano-dalmati furono costretti ad abbandonare la loro terra e le loro case per sfuggire alle terribili persecuzioni dell'odio partigiano.)
17. Website of the right-wing extremist Roberto Fiore, http://robertofiore.net/communicatie/fiore-iniziativa-milano-sulle-foibe--una-testimonianza-contro-loblio, accessed 29.9.2011. This website in April 2015 also was not accessible anymore.
18. https://www.youtube.com/watch?v=Q49Q49WyZCc, accessed 24.4.2015.
19. https://www.youtube.com/watch?v=nShc_omnLZc, accessed 24.4.2015.
20. https://www.youtube.com/watch?v=RQGoV6wGH20, accessed 24.4.2015.
21. https://www.youtube.com/watch?v=A1cX0YBvotM; https://www.youtube.com/watch?v=yquk4peHIC8; https://www.youtube.com/watch?v=qysxELMS7fY; all accessed 24.4.20915; see also via globalecho "Crypto-Juden": http://www.globalecho.org/28759/dokumentation-uber-den-bombenholocaust-der--alliierten-am-13-und-14-februar-1945-teil-1/, accessed 24.4.2015.
22. http://www.npd-mv.de/index.php?com=news&view=article&id=808&mid=8, accessed 25.3.2015 (from end of March 2015 only accessible via cache).
23. For example, as the former Latvian Foreign Minister and EU commissioner Sandra Kalniete at the Leipzig Book Fair in 2004 equated both dictatorships and Salomon Korn as representatives of the Central Council of Jews in Germany left the room in protest. Kalniete: 'These [studies] prove that both totalitarian regimes—

Nazism and Communism—were equally criminal. There should never be a distinction between them, just because a site has been on the winning side." [http://www.die-union.de/reden/altes_neues_europa.htm, accessed 2.10.2012. In April 2015, the speech was not any more accessible via this link. There is a possibility to read the text via a right-wing newspaper; Die junge Freiheit.

24. Prague Declaration on European Conscience and Communism, 3 June 2008, http://www.praguedeclaration.eu, accessed 24.4.2015.
25. http://www.europarl.europa.eu/sides/getDoc.do?pubRef=-//EP//TEXT+TA+P6-TA-2009-0213+0+DOC+XML+V0//EN, accessed 24.4.2015.
26. For the Agreement and Statutes and signatories, see http://www.memoryandconscience.eu/wp-content/uploads/2011/12/Agreement-and-Statute-of-the-Platform.pdf, accessed 24.4.2015.
27. Platform of European Memory and Conscience, http://www.memoryandconscience.eu/, accessed 24.4.2015.
28. http://www.memoryandconscience.eu/wp-content/uploads/2011/12/Agreement-and-Statute-of-the-Platform.pdf, accessed 24.4.2015.
29. *The Baltic Course*, 23.8.2012, http://www.baltic-course.com/eng/baltic_news/?doc=9719&underline=victims+of+crimes+of+communism, accessed 20.9.2012.
30. 'Budapest to Host the European Memorial Day of the Victims of Totalitarian Regimes', http://www.kormany.hu/en/ministry-of-public-administration-and-justice/news/budapest-to-host-the-european-memorial-day-of-the-victims-of-totalitarian-regimes, accessed 10.10.2012.
31. Ibid.
32. European Day of Remembrance of Victims of Totalitarianism commemorated in Budapest, 23.8.2012, http://www.memoryandconscience.eu/2012/08/23/european-day-of-remembrance-of-victims-of-totalitarianism-commemorated-in-budapest/, accessed 11.10.2012.
33. For example, with the ARD-channel series 'Die jüdische Lobby-Spurensuche in Amerika' ('On the Search of the Jewish Lobby in America'), 30.6.2010, available on YouTube, http://www.youtube.com/watch?v=IDcVdaqEEAE&feature=related, accessed 24.4.2015.

34. http://www.ksta.de/politik/umfrage-viele-deutsche-gegen-beschneidung,15187246,16656034.html, accessed 19.9.2012.
35. *Die Zeit*, 'Judenhass auf Facebook', 4.6.2010, http://www.zeit.de/digital/internet/2010-06/antifa-antisemitismus-facebook, accessed 24.5.2014.
36. 'Ausschluß von Bischof Richard Williamson. Wo liegt das wirkliche Problem?', 26.10.2012, http://www.kreuz.net/article.16085.html, accessed 26.10.2012.
37. '"Wir bleiben katholisch". Zum Ausschluß von Bischof Richard Williamson aus der Piusbruderschaft.' By Pater Florian Abrahamowicz, 25.10.2012, http://www.kreuz.net/article.16083.html, accessed 26.10.2012.
38. See reports in *Süddeutsche Zeitung*, 17./18.11.2012, and *Süddeutsche Zeitung*, 23.11.2012.
39. See Der Spiegel, 5.10.2012 http://www.spiegel.de/panorama/gesellschaft/kreuz-net-hetzt-gegen-schwule-muslime-und-protestanten-a-859698.html, accessed 24.4.2015.
40. Cited in Bundesministerium des Innern (ed.), *Verfassungsschutzbericht* (Berlin, 2010), p. 113, available at http://www.verfassungsschutz.de/download/SHOW/vsbericht_2010.pdf, accessed 24.4.2015.
41. Ibid., p. 122.
42. *Süddeutsche Zeitung*, 12.9.2012.
43. http://www.altermedia-deutschland.info/content.php?s=f167d85c5fccd9a0773949070e46fdb6, accessed 24.4.2015.
44. http://www.altermedia-deutschland.info/content.php/9056-Beginnt-auch-die-Luegenpresse-nach-der-Wahrheit-zu-fragen, accessed 24.4.2015. Parts of the interview were transmitted in a TV program of the first German channel on 23 April 2015, ARD—Panorama, http://www.daserste.de/information/politik-weltgeschehen/panorama/videosextern/wohltaeter-hitler-besuch-bei-auschwitz-leugnern-100.html, accessed 24.4.2015.
45. Jugendschutz.net (ed.), *Rechtsextremismus online beobachten und effektiv bekämpfen. Bericht 2009 über Recherchen und Maßnahmen* (Mainz, 2010), p. 17f., available at http://www.hass-im-netz.info/fileadmin/dateien/PK_Berlin/Projektbericht_2009.pdf, accessed 26. 8.2010; Jugendschutz.net (ed.), *Jugendschutz im Internet. Ergebnisse der Recherchen und Kontrollen, Bericht 2010* (Mainz 2011), http://www.jugendschutz.net/pdf/bericht2010.pdf, accessed 2.8.2011.

46. Jugendschutz.net, Rechtsextremismus online—beobachten und nachhaltig bekämpfen (Mainz, 2014), p. 3 http://www.hass-im-netz.info/fileadmin/dateien/pk2014/bericht2013.pdf, accessed 24.4.2015.
47. Ibid., p. 4.
48. http://www.jugendschutz.net/pdf/bericht2011.pdf, accessed 26.11.2012. About 40% of 1607 reports from Internet users referred to contributions in Web 2.0. *Rechtsextremismus online—beobachten und effektiv bekämpfen. Bericht 2011 über Recherchen und Maßnahmen* (PDF) (Mainz, 2012), http://www.hass-im-netz.info/fileadmin/dateien/pk2012/bericht2011.pdf, accessed 26.11.2012.
49. 'Neonazis im Netz: subversiv, provokant, immer radikaler. Mehr strafbare Inhalte im Social Web. Emotionale Themen als Köder. Reichweite im Web 2.0 über Szene hinaus. Größeres Engagement von Plattformbetreibern gefordert.' Available at http://www.hass-im-netz.info/fileadmin/dateien/pk2012/pm2012.pdf, accessed 26.11.2012; 'Rechtsextremismus online—beobachten und effektiv bekämpfen. Bericht 2011 über Recherchen und Maßnahmen' (PDF) (Mainz 2012), http://www.hass-im-netz.info/fileadmin/dateien/pk2012/bericht2011.pdf, accessed 26.11.2012.
50. http://www.youtube.com/watch?v=XdlsQ02G25Y&feature=related, accessed 2.1.2012.
51. http://www.youtube.com/watch?v=69D1K7Q8Y9s&feature=related, accessed 2.1.2012.
52. https://www.youtube.com/watch?v=_h0ozLvUTb0, accessed 24.4.2015.
53. *Gegenrede. Informationsportal gegen Rechtsextremismus für Demokratie*, 13.11.2008, available at http://www.gegenrede.info/news/2008/lesen.php?datei=081113_01, accessed 3.1.2012.
54. http://www.occupyfrankfurt.org/camp-info/das-camp/, accessed 3.6.2015.
55. *Die Welt online*, 16.11.2011, http://www.welt.de/debatte/kommentare/article13719989/Neid-und-Antisemitismus-in-der--Occupy-Bewegung.html, accessed 3.6.2015.
56. Alfred Rosenberg, *Die Protokolle der Weisen von Zion und die Weltpolitik* (Munich, 1924), http://media.de.indymedia.org/

media/2010/02/272441.pdf, accessed 3.1.2012 [In 2015 no longer accessible].

57. See, for instance, 'Stellungnahme der Gruppe F.E.P.A. (Für einen progressiven Antikapitalismus), welche sich mit antisemitischen Postings bei Indymedia auseinandersetzt', 2001, http://www.conne-island.de/nf/85/28.html, accessed 3.6.2015.
58. http://www.peta.org/blog/peta-germanys-holocaust-display-banned/ (27.3.2009), accessed 3.6.2015.
59. *Stern.de*, 8.12.2012, http://www.stern.de/panorama/urteil-gegen-peta-werbekampagne-kein-holocaust-auf-ihrem-teller-1922947.htmll, accessed 3.6.2015.
60. OGH Urteil, 12.10.2006, http://www.ris.bka.gv.at/Dokumente/Justiz/JJT_20061012_OGH0002_0060OB00321_04F0000_000/JJT_20061012_OGH0002_0060OB00321_04F0000_000.html, accessed 3.6.2015.
61. http://www.wagny.org/holocaust, accessed 3.6.2015.
62. *Jewish World*, 24.5.2006, http://www.ynetnews.com/articles/0,7340,L-3254679,00.html, accessed 3.6.2015.
63. http://archive.adl.org/internet/google_explanation.html, accessed 3.6.2015.
64. Thus the poster on the portal of 'Holywar.org' with the title: 'Ukraina'—'7.000.000, 1932/1933 Genocide by Starvation committed by the jewish mafia (sic)!'. The website was accessed on 26.11.2012. The link to this website is not provided here because the author believes it is wrong to advertise it given the nature of the organization.
65. Cf, Juliane Wetzel, 'Antisemitismus im Internet. Die Vernetzung der rechtsextremen Szene', in: Bundesprüfstelle für jugendgefährdende Medien, BPjS Aktuell, Sonderheft Jahrestagung 1999, (Mönchengladbach, 2000), pp. 16–25; ide., 'Rechtsextreme Propaganda im Internet. Ideologietransport und Vernetzung', in: Wolfgang Benz (ed.), *Auf dem Weg zum Bürgerkrieg? Rechtsextremismus und Gewalt gegen Fremde in Deutschland* (Frankfurt a. M., 2001), pp. 134–150.
66. Juliane Wetzel, 'Die internationale Rechte und der arabische Antizionismus im World Wide Web', in: *Jahrbuch für Antisemitismusforschung* 12 (2003), S. 121–144; ide., 'Antisemitismus und Holocaustleugnung als Denkmuster radikaler

islamistischer Gruppierungen', in: Bundesministerium des Innern (ed.), *Extremismus in Deutschland. Erscheinungsformen und aktuelle Bestandsaufnahme* (Berlin, 2004), pp. 253–272.

67. Facebook entries 2010, e.g., Borak G.: 'shoot the Jews in the head' (Gib jeden Juden ein Kopfschuss) 1.6.2010 at 17:18 hours; Momo O.: 'simply exterminate the shit jews' (einfach nur ausrotten die scheiss juden) 2.6.2010 at 19:28 hours; Bülent B: 'shit jews, best to gas them all' (scheiss juden, am besten alle vergasen), 2.6.2010.

PART V

Two Further Observations

CHAPTER 14

Five Reflections on Holocaust Denial, Old and New Forms of Hatred of Jews and the Delegitimation of Israel

Elhanan Yakira

A Preliminary Reflection

Some five years have passed between the Dublin conference on antisemitism and Holocaust Denial and the final writing of this chapter. Many things have happened during that period in the Middle East, in Europe and in the USA: there have been fresh rounds of violence between Israel and the Palestinians, at least one of them particularly violent; the collapse of a few Arab states under the attacks of different Islamist, Jihadists and other forces; daily atrocities committed by ISIS or others and more. The Israeli-Palestinian peace process finds itself in a cul-de-sac, and each side blames the other for the stalemate. The last elections in Israel brought a right-wing government to power. The future is uncertain, and there are not too many reasons for optimism. The ambiguity and complexity of the situation is probably one of the reasons why the BDS[1] movement has gained a lot of ground on American and European campuses. In fact, many artists, scientists and others refuse to come to Israel, and in many places Israeli products are taken off supermarkets' shelves; meanwhile,

E. Yakira (✉)
Department of Philosophy, Hebrew University, Jerusalem, Israel

A. McElligott, J. Herf (eds.), *Antisemitism Before and Since the Holocaust*, DOI 10.1007/978-3-319-48866-0_14

Israel is frequently vehemently denounced in the public sphere, and this is only a partial list. In Israel itself the seriousness of the boycotting campaigns has been only lately fully understood. Although the actual damage to the country, to its academic institutions or to its economy seems to be, for the moment at least, rather limited, concern is growing.

Beyond the BDS's potential to harm Israel, what looms is an essentially symbolic issue. I believe it would be impossible to force Israel to do anything it does not want to do. The future of the occupation will be decided within Israel and by the Israelis. There are of course deep ideological and political rifts within the Israeli society. Many Israelis are against what is referred to as "the occupation", and others are against any withdrawal from the territories occupied since 1967; others still—a minority—believe the whole land belongs to the Jewish people by divine right; here and there, from both, right and left, extremities of the political spectrum, the idea of a so-called one-state solution is heard. Political pressure from the EU, the USA or the UN, political isolation and critical media may have some influence on the internal debates in Israel and affect the decision making but not, however, the BDS.

Why do I think the BDS, despite its potential to harm Israel, cannot affect its policies, certainly not in the direction of ending the occupation? The reason is simple. The deep differences between the American and European governments and the Israeli current government concern mostly one issue—the Jewish settlements in the West Bank, not the existence of Israel as a Jewish state, not the seriousness of Israel's security concerns, not even the "occupation" itself. Most informed and not unduly hostile observers and players understand very well that even if the "two states solution" principle is accepted, there are huge obstacles down the road and a full implementation of such a solution will take, if it is at all possible, much effort and time. The BDS is another matter. It is very hard to know what its supporters on the American campuses or on the streets of Dublin, London or Paris know about the Israeli-Arab conflict and what they think they advocate or march for. Those who chant "mort aux juifs" are what they are—antisemites; those who tolerate this obscenity—namely, most participants in the "Israel Apartheid weeks" and similar events—seem to know next to nothing, or very little, about what the real stakes of the BDS discourse are. But the leaders of the campaign are quite explicit. Omar Barghouty, for example, one of the central figures in the BDS global movement, has explained recently that it struggles for three fundamental rights (it is, he explains, a "civil rights" movement): the end of the Israeli occupation of Palestinian and other Arab lands taken by Israel in the 1967 war, including the dismantling of settlements and walls; the end of the "racial discrimination" regime against Palestinian citizens living in Israel itself; and respecting the right of the Palestinian refugees to return to their homes.[2] Some 720 million Europeans seem to be afraid of losing their identity if a couple of million non-European immigrants cross the frontiers of the EU; who could seriously think that 7.5 million Israeli Jews could accept the "return" of 2–3 million Palestinians? To take one more example, Judith Butler is an important BDS activist. On a number of occasions, she has spoken on transforming the Jewish State into something she describes as a Jewish-Arab "cohabitation". This is supposed to be a peaceful solution achieved peacefully to a situation that in truth has more elements of "cohabitation" than she admits (or knows about). One thing she does not consider worth respecting is the Jewish right of self-determination.[3] In both cases, what is advocated is a dejudaisation of the State of Israel. Leaving aside everything else, the insistence on the "right of return" is enough to show how absurd the whole thing is: the influx of millions of Palestinians, most of them hostile, into Israel would mean the end of the Jewish state.

Some, perhaps even many, might welcome such an eventuality. Given the overwhelming opposition among (at least) Israel's Jewish citizenship to the dejudaisation of the country, it is highly unlikely that such a dejudaisation of Israel can be accomplished without massive bloodshed. The advocates of changing the Jewish nature of Israel can masquerade it in many ways, but the stakes of the principled anti-Zionist discourse, of the BDS movement's leaders, for example, are the destruction of the State of Israel. The idea that this can happen by peaceful means is, in the best of cases, pious wishful thinking.

How can one envisage seriously the destruction of a state? Even if its existence creates trouble (and let's assume, for the sake of argument, that this is the case with Israel), the dismantling of a country is conceivable only if it is, in itself and, as it were, by its essence and not simply by its conduct, criminal and, in some sense, *illegitimate*. This is often implied, and sometimes explicitly claimed, by many of Israel's enemies and critics. And, indeed, much of the public discussion about the BDS and other anti-Israeli campaigns turn around the rather vague concepts of *illegitimacy*, *delegitimation* and the like. I have attempted to tackle this problem elsewhere, arguing that strictly speaking the juridical-political category of *legitimacy* is applicable only to the space existing between the government and citizens of a given state and that, consequently, a state can be "legitimized" or "delegitimized" only by its citizens.[4] Hence, by definition, a democratic state, as Israel is, cannot be "illegitimate". Therefore, what is the meaning of the delegitimizing discourse of the BDS advocates and other anti-Zionists? If it is indeed an alleged justification for the destruction of the state, and since this cannot be achieved by peaceful means, the delegitimizing discourse may very well be an implicit advocacy for killing Israel's Jewish citizens. The recent spate of attacks against Jews globally as well as the persisting and horrific attacks within Israel are themselves evidence of words turned into action *accompanying* the anti-Israel and anti-Jewish discourse. Moreover, I also argued that notwithstanding the oft-repeated claim/self-justification of BDS advocates that anti-Zionism or anti-Israelism are not forms of Judeophobia, there are good reasons to think the contrary. What subsumes these allegedly different—antisemitism and anti-Zionism—phenomena under one generic title is not the *content* of the affective or ideological attitudes they manifest but what can be referred to as their common *moral substance*. For in both cases, what is under attack is the legitimacy of a certain concrete form of life, of ways, more precisely, in which Jews have chosen to live their life.

Many Jews and some Israelis support the BDS movement. This in itself seems to be a good enough argument to support the claim that it is not antisemitic and that its ideological/affective content is not the hatred of Jews. Besides, anti-Zionist attitudes have always been very rife among Jews, and there is no reason to say that all of these anti-Zionist Jews suffered of what is often referred to (unjustly in most cases, I believe) as "self-hate". Moreover, there are good reasons to say that antisemitism is not just xenophobia or even hatred. What makes it into a rather sui generis phenomenon (or class of phenomena) is precisely its ideological content: since its very beginning, in the times when early Christianity was struggling to legitimize itself as the "New Israel" and to relegate the Hebrew Bible into the status of an "Old Testament", Christian anti-Jewishness has always been a project of delegitimation. More than once it has proven to be a license to kill.

In other words, there are some structural continuities between more traditional forms of Judeophobia and the current anti-Zionism. A paradigmatic case in question, where delegitimizing antisemitism and anti-Zionism are welded into one outrageous phenomenon is Holocaust Denial. In recent years, Holocaust Denial has gained much attention. Although important and interesting in many ways on its own account, it is also quite obvious that Holocaust Denial is part of the more general phenomenon of "antisemitism" or "Judeophobia". However, notwithstanding its recent resurgence, antisemitism as simple anti-Jewishness has been very largely discredited by the destruction of European Jewry it had led to. This, arguably, is one reason why anti-Zionism has become so widespread and why it is not explainable, in my view, by the conduct of Israel (even judged by the most severe standards) and why it is not an innocent "criticism" of its policies. One of the proofs for this claim is the centrality of Israel and of Zionism for the deniers.

Holocaust Denial

Holocaust Denial is as old as the facts and deeds it denies. The Nazis used subterfuge and metaphor while carrying out the crime of genocide. After the war, it was at first more or less ignored or considered as a marginal issue, before attracting serious attention in the 1970s and 1980s. Today, more than seven decades after the ending of the war and in spite of the work of dedicated researchers, the fact that there are people who would explicitly deny the Holocaust ever took place cannot be ignored any more. Indeed, the ever more blatant and impudent ways in which the Holocaust is denied makes this a desideratum.

In all respects, Holocaust Denial is a curious phenomenon. Thus, on the one hand, the individual deniers are all connected in different ways and form all kinds of networks; they have a number of media outlets, notably on the cyber space, and in the end a bizarre parallel universe of denial comes into being. Within these unholy alliances, there are many variants of denials and deniers. There are softer and more hard-core, primitive and more sophisticated forms of denials; there are all kinds of companions de route too. Denial in Europe or in North America is not exactly the same as denial in the Arab world; forms of denial differ in respect to the narratives they tell, the styles they employ, the public they address and so on. Born in Europe and North America, it seems that the main Holocaust Denial activity is to be found nowadays in the Arab and Islamic world. It is probably more widespread there than it has ever been in the Christian world.

There is one aspect of this multifarious phenomenon which seems not to occupy the place it deserves, especially in the English written literature: there is a left-wing and radical left-wing Holocaust Denial. Valérie Igounet, who has written a very comprehensive and interesting book on what is called in France *négationisme*, qualifies this brand of denial as a

French peculiarity,[5] although it seems that it has since migrated, usually under its softer variants, across the French borders and also across the Atlantic. Igounet conducted a series of interviews with a number of French Holocaust deniers, and it makes for disturbing reading.[6] It shows, among many things, how varied are the ideological paths leading to hard-core or somewhat softer denials, how different are the political agendas served by it, and indeed, how multifaceted is the phenomenon of Holocaust Denial. It also makes fascinating reading for anyone who is interested in what can be perhaps called psycho-politics: Who are the deniers? What kind of people are they? Igounet's study shows that there is no simple topos of "the denier". Instead, we find very different personal pathologies, including people who are not necessarily corrupt in their intention or who are simply politically naive and who even sometimes manifest some bizarre innocence.

One of the most striking observations to emerge from these interviews is perhaps not only how many of the persons interviewed are from the left but also the extent to which they still belong to it. In their brand of denial, with its self-proclaimed anti-fascism, it is not the defense of the Germans or their collaborators which is the purpose, nor is the main ideological foe the Jews or Judaism as such, but Zionism and the State of Israel, often as emblems of colonialism, world capitalism, fascism, genocidal criminality—you name it. It is often through the widespread use of the Holocaust in anti-Israeli and anti-Zionist discourses—not always in the form of explicit denial—that the irrational, malevolent, morally bankrupt, in short, antisemitic, nature of allegedly innocent and legitimate forms of "criticism" of Israel and of Zionism can be exposed. The overall presumption of these uses and abuses of the Holocaust in the service of ideological anti-Israelism is that the Holocaust is the cause and the only possible justification for the creation of the State of Israel. Hence—this is fully explicit in the cruder forms of denial coming from the ideological left—if we can show that the Holocaust is a lie, we can also pull the rug under the feet of the Zionists and expose in full light the "illegitimacy" of the entity they created on stolen Palestinian land.[7]

In subtler and seemingly more sophisticated uses of the Holocaust for anti-Israel purposes, it is not very different, only less explicit. Beside tactics in which the enormity of the crime is turned in different ways against its victims (e.g., the Jews do to their own victims what the Nazis did to them), there is a more-difficult-to-detect strategic aim, which cruder as well as the subtler forms of denial arguably share and which can perhaps be described as the silencing of Jewish memory. On the one hand, it is often said, there is a "Holocaust inflation"—too much discussion of the Holocaust, too many monuments, too many trips to Auschwitz—which is detrimental to the memory and taking into account of other mass murders and genocides. On the other hand, it is alleged that the insistence on the enormity and, in particular, the alleged uniqueness of the Holocaust serves to cover or belittle the crimes committed by Jews and Israelis. It is also theoretically harmful, as it prevents theorizing with the aid of the general category of "Genocide".[8] "You", the soft deniers seem to say, "Jewish educators or Zionist propagandists, speak so much of the Holocaust? We shall make it ever more difficult for you to do it." At a fundamental level, this amounts to an attempt to delegitimize all forms of specifically Jewish views of the Holocaust and of the different expressions these views assume. Given the importance of the Holocaust and of its memory for Jews in the post-1945 world, this is nothing less than a negation of the Jews' right to have their own identity (and few can argue against its centrality to post-1945 Jewish identity); it is, one might suggest, just another form of delegitimation. In the case of the left-wing deniers, the delegitimizing venture is directed mainly against the *political* expression of Jewish life, namely, the State of Israel and its supporters within the Jewish communities outside Israel. This is how Holocaust Denial serves anti-Zionism.

Holocaust Denial and the Delegitimation of Israel

Can one bring some order into the chaotic picture of Holocaust Denial? I suggest arranging the particular cases of Holocaust Denial according to two axes, scales or criteria. The one would be the axe of "hardness", intensity or straightforwardness. The other is the ideological or political agendas and ends which the denial anti-narrative (if I may call it so) serves. I assume that Holocaust Denial is never innocent, and it always originates in one kind or another of hatred—ideological, affective or other. When the motivations of the denier are purely psychopathological or personal frustration of one kind or another, this is a matter for the psychologist. But when there is an ideological background to the denial, it is of interest for the political scientist as well.

According to the first criterion, one can distinguish between more hard-core forms of Holocaust Denial and softer ones; between cases of outright denial at one end of the spectrum and at its other end, the "lighter" forms in which the systematic destruction of European Jewry or the existence of gas chambers are not denied straightforwardly, but their importance is downplayed in different ways or their uniqueness questioned. In these allegedly more sophisticated cases, doubts concerning, for example, the accuracy of the number of victims are raised, or, while admitting the fact of the killing of the Jews, one might question its outstanding brutality. A famous example of the hard-core denial is Robert Faurisson.[9] I mention him here because even in his case we witness an attempt, as awkward and as stupid as it is, to accord some semblance of sophistication and scientific dignity to the denial. I think, among other things, of his notorious "proof" that the extermination by gas could not have possibly taken place in the way it is described in the writings of the "official" historians; ergo—so goes the iron-clad logic of the literature professor from Lyon—the claim that Germans killed Jews (and others) en masse by gassing them was a lie; ergo, the Holocaust is a lie.

Alongside those who deny outright that Jews were exterminated during the Second World War are those who do not deny that the killing of the Jews took place but who repudiate that this was criminal in any exceptional way, and it is not altogether rare that one hears regret that the Germans did not "finish" the job. As Jeffrey Herf has remarked, some Arab intellectuals, like Sayyid Qutb, for example, celebrated the destruction of the Jews in Europe. But in the West, usually pronouncements of this kind are marginal and do not constitute much more than a venomous provocation, usually quite primitive and, I would add, not very interesting theoretically. The vocabulary on such occasions belongs to the language of violence and rather than a vehicle of meaning they should be considered as *acts*, expressions of *will* (a will to hurt, maybe to kill) or, as Jean-Paul Sartre once remarked, of *passion* or *affect* and not of *thought*. What is indeed lacking in these extreme cases of Holocaust Denial is anything that belongs to the *ideational* realm. One would usually not find in them anything which can be considered as much as an appearance of coherence.

By contrast, Faurisson's wretched "proofs" or his boast of offering a "textual interpretation" of the Shoah discourse is indeed a kind of gesture toward investing meaning in what is basically meaningless. Awkward as it may be, it manages to some degree to masquerade as a discourse. But one can advance along the axis of sophistication and arrive at cases where not only the straightforward denial of the extermination of the Jews has practically disappeared but where Holocaust Denial is indeed denounced in the strongest terms. And yet, one has sometimes the feeling that paradoxically, these denunciations of Holocaust Denial are still part of the phenomenon we are talking about. Sometimes the denunciation of the Holocaust is done with one hand, while the other opens the door to all kinds of antisemitic, and especially anti-Zionist, abominations. In such cases, the non-denial, even the anti-denial, is not much more than an alibi, and in some cases one can even talk of non-denying denial. This is less of an oxymoron than it may look,[10] since we sometimes witness that non-denial may serve as the basis or justification for precisely the same delegitimizing discourse the deniers justify by their denial.

This leads us to the second typological axis—namely that of the ideological aims and agendas served by Holocaust Denial. Holocaust Denial provides a curious meeting point for people of very diverse ideological leanings. In 2006, an assortment of right wingers and neo-fascists, Islamists, ultra-orthodox Jews (*Neturei-Karta*), scientifically trained scholars (like Faurisson) and leftist ideologues, among others, met with great conviviality in Tehran for a conference on the Holocaust. They were all united by their common wish to conduct an "open debate" (as they called it) on the subject.

The case of *Neturei-Karta* (the Guardians of the City) is particularly illuminating. *Neturei-Karta* is a Jewish fundamentalist sect known especially for its radical anti-Zionism, for its uncompromising opposition to the idea of Jewish political sovereignty and for its intense hatred of the State of Israel. Originally from Hungary, many of its members perished in the Holocaust. Thus there is no doubting that the Jewish delegates in Teheran knew very well what Auschwitz had been all about; some of them must have had relatives who died there. The official position of this sect is that the Holocaust took place as a terrible punishment for the terrible sin of Zionism. The handful of *Neturei-Karta* delegates in Teheran were severely denounced not only in the Jewish world in general but within their own communities as well, but their participation in that conference was all the same quite significant. Weird and morally corrupt as the members of this group may have been, they were certainly not stupid. They knew they would find in Teheran exactly what they were looking for, which had little to do with the question of the gas chambers but everything to do with hatred of Israel and the will to destroy it. This is true also of their hosts and the other deniers, some of whom anti-fascists, some radical Islamists and some outright antisemites, who nevertheless received these Jews (whose outward appearance conforms to stereotypical images of "the Jew") with great warmth. No need to look hard for a common cause. An uncompromising opposition to Israel and to Zionism united all these people, and the discourse about the Holocaust was completely contingent on the real ideological end: the wish to destroy Israel.

This common ground for ideological denial was conspicuous not only in Teheran. The small world of French left-wing Holocaust Denial has ideological allies in other European countries and also in the USA. Noam Chomsky is a case in question. His acerbic, and if I may add, mostly unfounded and sometimes malicious, criticism of Israel has been a kind of obsession for him for many years.[11] One of the most important intellectuals of our time, Chomsky thought, after meeting Faurisson, who was under attack for his views challenging the Holocaust, that the latter was a liberal scholar and not politically motivated. Consequently, Chomsky composed a petition, jointly signed by a group of intellectuals, in defense of Faurisson's freedom of expression. It was later added as a preface to one of Faurisson's books. The "Faurisson affair" created uproar, but it was also instrumental in catapulting Holocaust Denial into the center of French public opinion and in giving it the respectability of an issue which needs to be addressed.

Despite the obvious risks involved, I would venture to suggest that Chomsky's involvement in this affair was not an accident, no matter what he or his followers say. It is true that he stood up in defense of Faurisson's freedom of speech, but he was recruited to this by Pierre Guillaume and Serge Thion,[12] two of the leading French hard-core deniers. Guillaume is the founder of *La Vieille Taupe* (The Old Mole), a bookstore (long since defunct) and a publishing house which was the main outlet of the French deniers, among them Faurisson and Garaudi. Thion is a *tier mondist*, as it is called in France, ex-scholar and an anti-colonialist, who was the main link to Chomsky. Chomsky has a very sizeable following in the USA and elsewhere, including Israel, and as is the custom in rabbinical courts, the Rabbi is infallible. Since the last thing one can say of Chomsky is that he is easily duped or is naive, there must be something else which could have brought him together with these people. It was, of course, their common anti-colonialism, but one suspects that anti-Zionism was not altogether alien to it as well.

There is a network here, consisting of post-colonialists, third-world ideologues and people with other left-wing leanings of all sorts. The Holocaust Denial which thrives on its margins is of a specific nature. Anti-fascist not less than anti-anti-fascist, not even antisemitic in its more traditional sense (there had been even a few Jews involved with *La Vieille Taupe*), it is here that the political pathologies and ideological perversion beneath the denial discourse can be easily exposed. We know how anti-fascist anti-anti-fascism may lead to Holocaust Denial: Auschwitz is the one thing that makes the side-by-side rejection of fascism and Western anti-fascism impossible. What remains as a main testimony of Auschwitz, not just symbolic but fully real—too real indeed—is of course Israel.

Pierre Guillaume and his "Old Mole" have been at the center of the French small world of Holocaust deniers for very many years. He was first a revolutionary, close to Trotskyite circles, and his embracing of the cause of the non-existence of the gas chambers is posterior and completely dependent on his identity as a leftist ideologue. With a kind of irresistible inner logic, Holocaust Denial has become for him an end in itself. It has remained however a surface phenomenon. The real stakes of what has become the quintessence of his whole existence have never been the truth, or lack of truth, of the "narrative" of the extermination or the nature, whether criminal or not, of the conduct of the Germans during the Second World War or other such "historiographical" questions. No matter how thick are the layers of argumentation (if one may call it so) directed against the "official" or "hegemonic" history of Holocaust or how "scientific" are the proofs for the inexistence of the gas chambers, one does not have to dig deep to see that what looms behind it is the hatred of the American "empire of evil", a concern for its victims or for those of Western colonialism in general. The ultimate scandal for him, however, is Israel and Zionism. It is only the importance of this scandal which explains Guillaume's obsession with the Holocaust and his enduring attempt to prove that the existence of "homicidal Gas chambers" is a wicked Jewish-Zionist lie.[13]

Delegitimizing Israel (A Case Study)

Sometime before the Dublin conference took place, a British-Lebanese scholar by the name of Gilbert Achcar published a book which drew some attention.[14] The book is a historical study of Arab attitudes toward the Holocaust; it is very critical of many of their aspects, notably of the widespread Holocaust Denial in the Arab world, but is also very apologetic and, in particular, very critical toward Israel and Zionism. It received a fairly positive reception in respectable circles, but it also drew some criticism. Achcar is a competent scholar and his book is a sophisticated piece of academic work, and as Herf remarked in his review of the book, there is a lot to learn from it.[15] There is also no apparent reason to question the sincerity of either his rejection of Holocaust Denial generally, and in the Arab world in particular, or of his affirmation that the Holocaust was the most terrible crime ever.

Yet, already the book's subtitle—*The Arab-Israeli War of Narratives*—raises some puzzlement. For, in fact, what could be an Arab Holocaust "narrative"? Does the author suggest there is symmetry between the Israeli and Arab "narratives" of the Holocaust? Can these two narratives—assuming that there is such a thing as an Arab Holocaust narrative—be placed alongside one another?

One part of the analysis Achcar offers his reader is little more than systematic apologetics of the Arabs' attitude to the Holocaust. Central to this is his discussion of the Grand Mufti of Jerusalem whose exploits are often presented as a proof for the existence of a significant alliance between the Palestinian national movement and the Nazis and which perhaps explains to some degree, and at least according to some unsympathetic observers, the Palestinian national movement's ethos. Achcar does not question the basic facts known about the Mufti's conduct during the Second World War, and he even deplores the damage he caused to the Palestinian national struggle. But he criticizes severely the "Zionist narrative" of the matter and refuses to accept the conclusions of historians of the period such as Meir Litvak and Esther Webman or Matthias Küntzel, whose conclusions he dismisses as dictated by their ideological commitments.[16] Presumably, his conclusions are not dictated by any such commitments.

Achcar never endorses anything that can be interpreted even remotely as Holocaust Denial; on the contrary, he has the harshest things to say about the deniers, especially when they come from the Arab world. He recognizes the uniqueness of the Holocaust and explicitly rejects comparisons between the Nazis and Israeli actions. But—and this is usually expressed in proximity to the places where he pronounces his great indignation with everything that can be linked to underplaying the horrific nature of the Holocaust—he still does not understand why the Arabs are made to pay for the crimes of others. For he thinks that the State of Israel is the price paid by the Arabs, or the Palestinians, for the crimes committed by the Germans. This, however, is also a major argument of Holocaust deniers, both of the hard-core and softer breeds: the Palestinians are the innocent victims of the Nazi's victims, and it is immaterial whether the Nazi crimes have actually taken place or are just inventions.

Throughout his book, Achcar does not show the slightest indulgence toward Israel. It was clearly born in sin and it has been the "bad guy" ever since it wrought the catastrophe known as *Naqba* on the Palestinian autochthon population by taking the land from its rightful owners. Indeed, Zionism, according to this thinking, has been a criminal project ever since its conception in the womb of European colonialism. Judaism—the victim of this horrible crime we call "Holocaust"—is something altogether different from "Zionism", which either as an ideology or as a political project is a colonialist fact, and our compassion and human empathy with the great—greatest—suffering of the Jews in Europe should not induce in us undeserved indulgence toward the crimes of the colonialist-Zionists.

Three points should be emphasized here: as a proud Arab patriot Achcar nonetheless purports to be deeply concerned with the ways the Arab world has dealt with the Holocaust—that is, on the one hand, with the role Arabs and Islamists play nowadays in the global denial culture, and, on the other hand, with the omnipresence of the denial inside the Arab world. But if this is the case, he has done a very bad, indeed, a counterproductive, job. For his criticism of his fellow Arabs' attitude toward the Holocaust is wrapped in so much apologetics and, in particular, with so much blaming of the Zionists for the Arabs' shortcoming that, in the end, the honest reader of the book is bound to say, of course, who could expect otherwise from the victims of these Zionist hideous crimes? But there is more, and worse. Achcar advanced two, as I see it, false allegations according to which Israel was established as a result of the Holocaust ("the Palestinians pay the price for the Nazi crimes"), and Zionism and the Jewish people are two different things, so one can be anti-Zionist without being an antisemite.

Despite all the positive aspects of Achcar's book, his attitude toward the Holocaust is basically instrumental. That it serves, dialectically as it were, and as a kind of alibi, his comprehensive apologetics of the Arab "narrative" is perhaps understandable, but when one realizes that it might also serve as a radical vilification and denigration of Israel and of Zionism, this is a very different story. There is in fact a typical dialectic here—the more one is pro-Jewish and anti-Nazi, the more one feels free to advance what can be construed as extreme claims about Israel and about Zionism.

This is not the place to try to refute the two principles upon which Achcar bases his anti-Zionist criticism. Saying that the Palestinians are also the victims of the Nazi crimes or that Zionism is not an authentic Jewish phenomenon is both absurd and outrageous. But what deserves consideration here is not the content of his claim but the fact that it can be considered as part of normal, even respectable, academic discourse. That the (political) correctness of Achcar's treatment of the Holocaust and its denial leads, permits or just accompanies this kind of discourse is precisely my point. As distant as Achcar is from the Mufti, both agree that the dispossession of the Palestinians of their land was a kind of unjustifiable and unforgivable robbery. Even if, for pragmatic reasons, as a sort of realpolitik, the Arab world eventually agrees to come to terms with the Zionist fait accompli, this will apparently never change Achcar's opinion on the fundamental and irrevocable *illegitimacy* of the Zionist project.

Is it reasonable to speak of Achcar in the context of a discussion of Holocaust Denial? Can one push the limits of this phenomenon so far as to include also Achcar's indictment of it? Does his book qualify for the title of "non-denying-denial"? Insofar as the surface text is concerned, the answer is, of course, no. But if one looks below the surface as I have attempted above, one finds there the old antisemitic delegitimizing topos. Like other forms of Judeophobia, Holocaust Denial is not only irrational but also deceitful—the most obvious falsehoods are part of it; indeed, they are its very essence. Finally, we should note here the *intention* of Holocaust Denial: it is meant to hit the most painful and defenseless parts of Jewish—and Israeli—being. To some extent, all these features are present in Achcar's book. But over and above everything else, what places Achcar's book in the ideological space inhabited by Ahmadinejad, Faurisson, Guillaume, Chomsky, Garaudi or the *Neturei-Karta* is that it uses the Holocaust for the delegitimation of Israel.

In Guise of a Conclusion: Reflecting on Old and New Forms of Hatred

There are a few issues which enjoy a similar place in contemporary culture to that of the Holocaust. Holocaust Denial cannot be understood outside this context. This is undoubtedly a major component of its sui generis nature. There are other cases of denial—Turkey's refusal to admit that an Armenian genocide has ever taken place is just one of them. But, curiously perhaps, it does not seem that this denial has turned, at the hand of either extreme right Turkish patriots or left-wing internationalists and universalists, into a systematic argument against Armenian national aspirations, and the latter's insistence that their catastrophe should be recognized has not been turned against them as being a sort of blackmail or justification of their own not always very humanistic conduct. The catastrophes wrought on the Native American peoples, the African slaves or the

Australian aboriginals (to take just a few examples) are not turned against those groups as arguments undermining their different claims.

It has not been my intention to *explain* Holocaust Denial, whether in its hard-core or softer manifestations. Instead of looking for causal explanations, always a hazardous affair, one could look for the permanence of structural features. A certain historical contextualization may be less hazardous and more fruitful. What I would describe as the deniers' "Holocaust obsession" has to be looked at not only in its own right as a phenomenon but also arguably against the backdrop of the multifarious ways in which Jews and Judaism in general have been a major preoccupation for Christian Europe. To say that saying that the rejection of Judaism, either as a religion, or as a culture, or collectively as a people, or as individuals, has been a constitutive element of Christian Europe's religious and cultural identity would not be an exaggeration. Being the source of Monotheism on the one hand; resisting integration into the new, victorious religions and insisting on preserving its own identity on the other hand, it is not too hard to understand that Judaism could not leave either Christians or Muslims indifferent. The seeds were sown with the early church when its founding fathers legitimated the new religion by delegitimizing the old one. Although not always negative, the theological centrality of the Jews in Christian Europe has been the context within which the complex attitude toward the Jews has become sometimes pathological and, at times, even murderous. This has to be kept always in mind when we discuss the hatred of Jews: it is not, and has never been, simply a case of xenophobia or hatred of the "other", as often claimed. Jews were certainly hated as "different", even when they were not *that* different, but there has always been, in the feelings they provoked and the attitudes people have had toward them, this extra element which makes it into a sui generis phenomenon and which is rooted in theology and in the historical rivalry between different forms of biblical or, as it is sometimes called, Abrahamic monotheism and which was in its origin a struggle over legitimacy.

We usually tend to concentrate on the more venomous, malicious and violent manifestations of Judeophobia. But the more interesting, and in the long run perhaps the more dangerous and also morally unacceptable forms of anti-Judaism, is when it is shared and expressed by people who otherwise are irreproachable and often admirable. Some first-rate intellectuals have adhered to older forms of antisemitism, as they do nowadays when it comes to Israel. They do it by investing a great amount of intelligence—also of bad faith—in justifying to others and to themselves the most absurd and immoral positions they take on Jews, Judaism or the "Jewish question" or on Israel. Holocaust Denial in fact reproduces this important structural element of historical antisemitism. In the parallel universe of Holocaust Denial, this is conspicuous especially on the left, as I have argued above. Traditional antisemitism was an invention of the clerics. Now these are the new clerics who repeat the same prescriptions. Like early-day theologians, they do not call for the destruction of Jews, not even of the Israelis. After all, didn't they say explicitly that the Nazi attempt of doing it was a terrible crime? They only say that the dispossessed Palestinians are the rightful owners of the land the Israelis consider as theirs and that they are the victims' victims and the Jews' "Jews". Even now, 60 or 70 years after the event and probably forever, the fact of Israel as a state cannot gain legitimacy. Just as the unheard-of criminality of the old crime of deicide has tainted the Jewish substance with irreparable illegitimacy, so the alleged new colonial-Zionist crime, the theft of Palestinian land, inflicts an ineffaceable guilt and illegitimacy on what was born out of it. This, however, is not necessarily such a great novelty. As in older times, the core of it is the refusal to accord legitimacy to what is arguably the current most significant form of Jewish existence. I said at the beginning of these reflections, such a refusal does not make any rational sense; it is—again as the old theological antisemitism proved to be—nothing other than a license to kill. Usually it is implicit and perhaps not even self-acknowledged by the delegitimizers themselves. But if and when the conditions ripen, as it did under the Nazis, violent antisemitism risks becoming explicit.

Notes

1. BDS stands for Boycott, Divestment and Sanctions; I shall henceforth use this acronym as a term covering all the anti-Israeli and anti-Zionists campaigns.
2. "We Become 'Mainstream': An Interview with Omar Barghouty" (in Hebrew), in: http://mekomit.co.il The interview was translated from the Arabic as Barghouty, an Israeli citizen (he lives in the Jewish-Arab city of Acre), refuses to talk to the Israeli media. About the ideology of the BDS movement, their practices and more pronouncement of Barghouty and other leaders of the movement, see N. Cary & G.N. Brahm, *The Case Against Academic*

Boycott of Israel, Chicago and New York: MLA Members for Scholars' Rights, 2015.

3. See, e.g., an interview from July 2014 in: https://www.opendemocracy.net/transformation/ray-filar/willing-impossible-interview-with-judith-butler. Similar things are said in her (J. Butler) *Parting Ways. Jewishness and the Critique of Zionism*, New York: Columbia University Press, 2012. See also Gianni Vattimo and Michael Marder (eds.) *Deconstructing Zionism: A Critique of Political Metaphysics*, New York and London: Bloomsbury Books, 2014, to which Butler contributed chapters from her book. These references constitute a very small sample of the anti-Israeli pro-BDS literature.
4. See Elhanan Yakira, "Antisemitism and anti-Zionism as a Moral Question", in: A. Rosenfeld (ed.) *Resurgent Antisemitism: Global Perspectives*, Bloomington: Indiana University Press, 2014, pp. 42–64.
5. See V. Igounet, *Histoire du négationnisme en France*, Paris: Édition du Seuil, 2000.
6. I thank Stéphanie Share for letting me consult this fascinating document, and Valérie Igounet for permitting me to quote from it.
7. For a fuller discussion, see E. Yakira, *Post-Zionism, Post-Holocaust. Three Essays on Denial, Forgetting, and the Delegitimation of Israel*, Cambridge: Cambridge University Press, 2010, especially pp. 15–22.
8. See Alvin Rosenfeld, *The End of the Holocaust*, Bloomington: Indiana University Press, 2011.
9. All studies of the phenomenon of Holocaust Denial discuss Faurrison (who died between the time of the Dublin conference and the final writing of this article) to some extent. See, e.g., D. Lipstadt, *Denying the Holocaust: The Growing Assault on Truth and Memory*, New York: Plume 1993, especially in the Appendix; in particular: V. Igounet, *Faurisson. Portrait d'un négationniste* Paris: Denoël, 2012. In what follows, I assume that the basic facts of Faurrison's denial and the "Faurrison's affair" are more or less known, and instead of narrating them again, offer some reflections on their significance.
10. As thought to be by a not-very-sympathetic anonymous reviewer of this essay.

11. A quick look at the web would easily reveal both the extent and the nature of Chomsky's writings on Israel. Doubting the efficacy of the BDS, Chomsky still believes that Israel should be punished, as he says in one of his latest articles, "for its egregious crimes". The point here is not to discuss Chomsky's criticism of Israel but to point to the (probably non-accidental) coincidence of his anti-Israeli attitude and his curious willingness to associate himself with Faurisson.
12. In a 1981 article in *The Nation*, Chomsky describes Thion as "a libertarian socialist scholar with a record of opposition to all forms of totalitarianism". Thion was already, by the time he met Chomsky, and ever more so afterward, a forthright Holocaust denier. Chomsky does not seem to have ever acknowledged this.
13. I have had, under the most surrealist circumstances, the dubious privilege of spending more than half a day with this outlandish person. He taught me all I needed to know about the Holocaust hoax and about how it was invented in order to serve the criminal intentions of the Zionists. I told this encounter with some more detail in my book, op. cit.
14. Gilbert Achcar, *The Arabs and the Holocaust. The Arab-Israeli War of Narratives*, Eng. Tr. G.M. Goshgarian, London: Saqi, 2010 (published originally in French Actes Sud).
15. Jeffrey Herf, "Not in Moderation", *The New Republic*, November, 2010, also points to many factual inaccuracies. Achcar's book, it seems, has already been more or less forgotten since the time of the Dublin Conference.
16. See M. Litvak and E. Webman, *From Empathy to Denial. Arab Responses to the Holocaust*, London: Hurst & Co., 2009; M. Küntzel, *Jihad and Jew-Hatred. Islamism, Nazism and the Roots of 9/11*, New York: Telos, 2007. Achcar snidely questions Küntzel's competence to deal with the question concerning the Arabs on the ground that he does not read Arabic. Given the fact that Achcar has very extensive ruminations about Israel and about Israeli society and given also the fact that he apparently does not read Hebrew (all the Israeli sources from which he draws his knowledge of Israel are translations), this remark is indeed curious.

CHAPTER 15

Ex Malo Bono: Does This Latin Proverb Apply to Holocaust Denial? The Cunning of Reason

Robert Jan van Pelt

Almost 200 years ago, in the wake of the Napoleonic Wars, Georg Wilhelm Friedrich Hegel coined the concept of the *List der Vernunft*, usually translated as "Cunning of Reason." Hegel believed that the idea of Reason unfolded itself in history through the deeds of larger-than-life characters like Alexander the Great, Caesar, or Napoleon. This process was a messy one, and the protagonists who realized Reason in history did not do so on purpose, adopting ideals and a way of life that could be characterized as by any means reasonable. On the contrary, their motivations were low, compulsive, and without restraint, including greed, envy, fanaticism, pride, ambition, vanity, and megalomania. Yet through these self-seeking passions, history was able to realize itself according to its rational design, making the men who are driven by it into its instruments and tools that may destroy old structures that have ceased to be useful but that are themselves also worn down and used up in the process: gear to be discarded

This work was supported by a grant from The Netherlands Institute for Advanced Study in the Humanities and Social Sciences.

R.J. van Pelt (✉)
University of Waterloo, Waterloo, ON, Canada

A. McElligott, J. Herf (eds.), *Antisemitism Before and Since the Holocaust*, DOI 10.1007/978-3-319-48866-0_15

after they had ceased to be useful. "This may be called the *cunning of Reason*—that it sets the passions to work for itself, while that through which it develops itself pays the penalty and suffers the loss."[1]

Hegel's understanding of history as the unfolding of the Reason by means of world-historical individuals has few adherents these days: while it is undoubtedly true that world-historical individuals like Joseph Stalin, Adolf Hitler, and Mao Zedong can be credited as having been the unwitting authors of the contemporary global understanding of human rights, it is also clear that the concept of Reason using such characters ceases to make sense when the level of destruction, both material and human, crosses a certain threshold: by the end of the Second World War, humankind faced for the first time in history the possibility of complete self-destruction—an end of history that, within the Hegelian *Weltanschauung*, cannot be the purpose of Reason. In addition, the two discourses that assimilated Hegel's understanding of the cunning of Reason as a core concept—the Fascist idea of a "Master Morality," first proposed in Friedrich Nietzsche's *Jenseits von Gut und Böse* (*Beyond Good and Evil*), and the Marxist understanding of the historical role of moral evil, first articulated in Friedrich Engels' *Ludwig Feuerbach und der Ausgang der klassischen deutschen Philosophie* (*Ludwig Feuerbach and The End of Classical German Philosophy*)[2]—have been thoroughly discredited by the ruins of National Socialism and Communism.

Yet, when in the late 1990s I became involved in the struggle against Holocaust denial, I wondered if the cunning of Reason might be helpful to understand the possible significance of the attempts of men like Paul Rassinier, Robert Faurisson, and David Irving to erase from the records of man the murder, by the Germans and their allies, of six million Jews. The development of the practice of history since Herodotus, Thucydides, and Polybius has of course produced many great historians, but none of them would have fitted the megalomaniac character of the Hegelian world-historical man of destiny. Nevertheless, when I began to read the writings of Holocaust deniers, I saw the contours of a vast ambition to overturn the common understanding of the history of the twentieth century not by merely changing the perspective on the facts but by eliminating the facts from the historical record. And while I was convinced that their ambition could not but end in ruin, I also wondered if, in a perverse way, they helped history develop as a discipline.

In all of this, I had to hold my nose—or at least initially. When I began to study the arguments of Holocaust deniers, I was disgusted by their lack of morality and ethics. As a historian, I was inspired by the idea concisely formulated by the late Edith Wyschogrod, who once observed that the primary responsibility of the historian is not to the living but to the dead. The historian who senses this responsibility "assumes liability for the other, feels the pressure of an ethics that is prior to her construal of the historical object. Responsibility thus interpreted is Janus-faced: its moral authority is expressed in its disinterestedness, but its psychological force is experienced as a sense of inescapable urgency."[3] This applies to all historians, but especially to historians who study massacres, genocides, and the Holocaust. Yet if the cunning of Reason was at work in the discipline of history itself, I quickly realized that I should not get enervated by the amorality, or immorality, of a Rassinier, Faurisson, or Irving. In his discussion on the cunning of Reason, Hegel stressed that the unfolding of history did not obey the laws of morality. The tools of reason, the world-historical men, "may treat other great and even sacred interests inconsiderately—a conduct which indeed subjects them to moral reprehension. But so mighty a figure must trample down many an innocent flower, crush to pieces many things in its path." Thus the deeds of those who made history could not be judged by the moral standards that apply to the acts of ordinary men. Hegel claimed that it is "irrelevant and inappropriate ... to raise moral claims against world-historical acts and agents. They stand outside of morality. The litany of the private virtues of modesty, humility, love, and charity must not be raised against them." In conclusion, an individual may "for moral reasons resist and for immoral reasons advance the course of history."[4] And thus I decided to give them the benefit of the doubt—not where it concerns the nature and quality of their arguments, which are clearly beyond the pale, but where it concerns the possible significance of those arguments as catalysts in the difficult and sometimes painful process of understanding.

In the following pages, I will identify six instances in which Holocaust denial has, indeed, led to some worthwhile outcomes—instances in which some general good has emerged from this particular evil. I will identify two advances in our understanding of the history of the Holocaust that resulted from the challenge posed by Holocaust deniers. I will argue why the *Bundesverfassungsgericht* (Federal Constitutional Court) of Germany made an important decision when it established that public denial of a proven and generally acknowledged historical fact is not protected by laws guaranteeing freedom of opinion. I will note that the prominence of Holocaust survivors and other eyewitnesses of the Holocaust in, for example, schools and other educational programs can be partly explained as the result of the challenge posed by Holocaust denial. I will discuss how the Irving Trial, held in the High Court of England and Wales in the year 2000, led, for the first time in the 2500-year-old history of history, to a clear articulation of the duties of a historian. And finally, in a somewhat more personal testimony, I'll try to evoke how our day in court "gentled," to paraphrase Shakespeare's King Harry, the historian's condition while returning it to its origins.

Holocaust Denial and the Advance of Historical Knowledge: The Case of the Hitler Decision

Until 1977, Holocaust deniers were invisible to members of the historical profession. Their writings only attracted the attention of fellow cranks. Things changed with the publication of *Hitler's War*, authored by the British historian David Irving. Written in a gripping narrative style, *Hitler's War* was very different from the dry studies that preceded it. Showing a keen eye for the texture of life, Irving had written what purported to be a historical study in the style of a historical novel. The general public loved it. Professional historians were not enthusiastic. They considered Irving's sympathy for Hitler odd, and they were scandalized by the offensive core of the book: Irving's theory that the Holocaust had been initiated behind Hitler's back by men like Reichsführer-SS Heinrich Himmler, SD Chief Reinhard Heydrich, and Wartheland Gauleiter Artur Greiser. While Irving did not deny the Holocaust as such, his thesis that it had nothing to do with Hitler moved him into a gray zone: the murder of six million Jews between 1939 and 1945 had been commonly understood as a state-sponsored genocide. If it had happened behind the back of the seemingly all-powerful head of this state and against his explicit instructions on the initiative of rogue elements, then the destruction of the Jews would cease to be a genocide and become a series of ordinary crimes. Thus, Irving's book did engage in a denial of what makes the murder of six million Jews a genocide commonly known as the Holocaust.[5]

In the introduction to *Hitler's War*, Irving raised this theory in the context of his attempt to "expose the 'unseaworthiness' of many current legends about Hitler." The "most durable" of these concerned Hitler's involvement in the extermination of the Jews. Irving proposed that the killing had been ad hoc, "the way out of an awkward dilemma, chosen by the middle-level authorities in the eastern territories overrun by the Nazis and partly a cynical extrapolation by the central SS authorities of Hitler's anti-Semitic decrees." Hitler had aimed only to deport the Jews to the East, but the Germans there were unable to deal with the arrival of many Jews in the already overcrowded ghettos. "Partly in collusion with each other, partly independently, the Nazi agencies then simply liquidated the deportees as their trains arrived, on a scale increasingly more methodical and more regimented as the months passed." According to Irving, these massacres did not only happen without Hitler's permission: they even occurred in violation of Hitler's express wish that the Jews would be spared. For this assertion, he provided rather flimsy arguments such as that as a pragmatic politician, Hitler would not have approved of moving "millions of Jews" to the East with the single purpose of killing them there, "nor would he willingly destroy manpower, for which his industry was crying out." Significantly, *Hitler's War* contained only two photos. One showed what Irving described in the introduction as the "incontrovertible evidence" for Hitler's alleged protection of the Jews. It is a facsimile page from Himmler's phone log of November 30, 1941. That day Himmler was at Hitler's headquarters. The log recorded that at 1:30 pm Himmler had called Heydrich in Prague. The topic of discussion: "Jew transport from Berlin. No liquidation." Irving did not transcribe it but wrote as a caption "At 1:30 pm the SS chief telephones Heydrich in Prague from Hitler's bunker in the Wolf's Lair, ordering that there was to be 'no liquidation' of Jews." In the main narrative, Irving wrote that "on November 30, 1941, [Himmler] was summoned to the Wolf's Lair for a secret conference with Hitler, at which the fate of Berlin's Jews was clearly raised. At 1:20 pm Himmler was obliged to telephone from Hitler's bunker to Heydrich the explicit order that Jews were not to be liquidated." While Irving had tried to lift the burden of guilt from Hitler's shoulders, misquoting evidence to make his point—the log only referred to "Jew transport" and not to "Jew transports,"—he did not deny that the Holocaust had occurred. To the contrary: he made a number of references to the role of Auschwitz as an extermination camp. Writing about the spring of 1942, Irving stated that the Germans began to round up Jews in France, Holland, Belgium, and Slovakia to send them to Poland. "Upon arrival in Auschwitz and Treblinka, four in every ten were pronounced fit for work; the rest were exterminated with a maximum of concealment." The major object of that concealment was Hitler. "The concealment was almost perfect, and Himmler's own papers reveal how he pulled the wool over Hitler's eyes."[6]

In a review published in *The Sunday Times*, Hugh Trevor Roper, Regius Professor of Modern History at Oxford, demolished *Hitler's War*. He observed that Irving's discussion of Hitler's attitude toward the Jews was highly implausible. The Himmler phone log of November 30 did not refer to the liquidation of Jews in general but to the liquidation of one transport. "One does not veto an action unless one thinks that it is otherwise likely to occur." Irving's interpretation of the log showed his weakness as a historian: "He seizes on a small but dubious particle of 'evidence'; builds upon it, by private interpretation, a large general conclusion; and then overlooks or re-interprets the more substantial evidence and probability against it. Since this defective method is invariably used to excuse Hitler or the Nazis and to damage their opponents, we may reasonably speak of a consistent bias, unconsciously distorting the evidence."[7]

Yet, for all its idiocy, Irving's theory was to have a useful effect: it proved a useful spark to ignite an important historical debate. The fuel for this debate had been gathering for some years, epitomized by works such as Martin Broszat's book *Der Staat Hitlers* (1969), Karl Schleunes' *The Twisted Road to Auschwitz* (1970), and Uwe Dietrich Adam's *Judenpolitik im Dritten Reich* (1972). Martin Broszat, director of the Institute for Contemporary History in Munich, had reconstructed the Third Reich as a maze of competing power groups, rival bureaucracies, forceful personalities, and diametrically opposed interests engaged in ceaseless clashes with each other. He saw Hitler as a brooding and distant leader, who intervened spasmodically. While in theory his power was unlimited, in practice he preferred the role of arbiter, according legitimacy to one or another line of conduct. He was unable to sustain any effort and procrastinated, and hence it is difficult to see any real long-term planning in the Third Reich. Both Schleunes and Adam agreed with Broszat that the Nazi state had been chaotic, that there had been little central planning, and that decisions were the result of diverse pressures. Applied to the anti-Jewish policies that were to become the Holocaust, Schleunes stated that "during the first years of the Third Reich, nobody within the Nazi movement, starting with the Führer himself, could define what the solution of the Jewish problem could be … It is only in the widest sense that the anti-Semitic premises of National Socialism help us to explain the course taken by the great variety of measures concerning the Jews."[8] Adam postulated that "one cannot speak of a coordinated and planned policy towards the Jews …

a global plan concerning the nature, content and scope of the persecution of the Jews never existed."[9] According to Adam, Hitler would have decided only in the fall of 1941 to kill all the Jews. In the early 1980s, the historian Tim Mason was to label Broszat's, Schleunes', and Adam's views as the "functionalist" view of the origin of the Holocaust—in contrast to the (older) "intentionalist" perspective that assumed that a plan to kill all of Europe's Jews had been Hitler's aim since the 1920s and the underlying justification of German anti-Semitic legislation and actions from 1933 onward.[10]

In *Hitler's War*, Irving had created a caricature of the "functionalist" position, and Broszat felt the need to protect his domain. He published a devastating, 36-page critique of Irving's book in the *Vierteljahrshefte für Zeitgeschichte*. He accused Irving of repeatedly distorting the evidence in order to make a case for Hitler and that he had been completely unable to recognize and understand the complexity of historical connections. Himmler's telephone note was a good example. Considering the circumstances of that note, it was clear that Hitler had not given an order to stop the killing of all Jews but that the note "No liquidation" only referred to a single train, in response to speculations of American reporters about the fate of German Jews being sent to Eastern Europe. Yet, at the same time, Broszat accepted Irving's argument that there was no written order from Hitler to begin a genocide of the Jews. However, this did not mean that Hitler had nothing to do with it. Broszat argued that the radical anti-Semitism of the Nazis and Hitler's desire to see a Jew-free Germany had led them to embark on increasingly extreme attempts to expel the Jews from Germany and later from Europe: only when they had failed to do so did they begin to kill Jews as an "*Ausweg aus einer Sackgasse*" ("way out of a blind alley") into which the Nazis had maneuvered themselves by the summer of 1941. "The practice of liquidation, once initiated and established, gained predominance and evolved in the end into a comprehensive 'programme.'" Broszat therefore postulated that there was no need to assume the existence of an "*umfassenden Geheimbefehls*" ("a comprehensive secret order") for the extermination of Jews.[11] It was enough for Hitler to approve these initiatives in conversation. Broszat did not offer any exculpation of Hitler: his anti-Semitism and his will to destroy had been crucial even if it did not explain everything.

Broszat's article had enormous repercussions. It introduced to a wide public a radically new vision of the origins of the Holocaust. It also triggered an important debate among historians. American historian Christopher

Browning observed that there were already too many indications of a most radical solution to the Jewish problem in play before the stalemate of the late fall of 1941, and that what Broszat had labeled as "vague plans" drafted in the summer of 1941 really amounted to a clear extermination program.[12] At the same time, the British scholar of German-Jewish background Gerald Fleming (born Gerhard Flehinger) had begun work on a book he was to publish in 1982 in Germany.[13] Fleming concentrated on the mass execution of Jews in Riga that Broszat had interpreted as the result of improvisation by local officials. Fleming showed that the orders came from Berlin. In 1982, Browning, Adam, Broszat, and others met at a conference at the École des Hautes Études en Sciences Sociales in Paris to compare notes—Irving was not invited. From this resulted a scholarly consensus that confirmed that Hitler probably never issued a written order to kill European Jewry but that his wishes, either as they were uttered directly or indirectly, were nevertheless of key significance in unleashing the Holocaust. The publication of the proceedings remains a major text in the historiography of the Holocaust.[14] Would it have appeared without the challenge presented by Irving's *Hitler's War*? It is clear that Irving's claims had framed the debate, but the participants had already formulated the central questions that concerned Hitler's role before the publication of *Hitler's War*. Irving's book only speeded up a debate that would have happened anyway.

Holocaust Denial and the Advance of Historical Knowledge: The Case of the Auschwitz Crematoria

A second example of the cunning of Reason at work in the historiography of the Holocaust is the research into the construction of the key components of the machinery of death: the crematoria at Auschwitz. Generally, historians had accepted the assumption, made by the "Extraordinary State Committee for the Ascertaining and Investigation of Crimes committed by the German-Fascist Invaders and their Associates in the Oswiecim Death Camp," which had conducted the first forensic investigations after the liberation of the camp, that the four crematoria that had been built in Auschwitz-Birkenau had been designed with the genocide of the Jews in mind. Because the designs of two of these buildings went back to the fall of 1941, the conclusion was that from that date onward, Auschwitz had been planned as a key site in the Holocaust. This consensus was shattered as the result of the only non-historian who participated in the 1982 conference at the École des Hautes Études en Sciences Sociales: the French pharmacist and amateur historian Jean-Claude Pressac. Pressac's presence at that event, and the work he presented and consequently developed, not only responded to the challenge of Holocaust denial but also (and paradoxically) emerged from it.

Pressac had become interested in Auschwitz in 1962, when he had received as a birthday present Robert Merle's *La mort est mon métier (Death is my trade)*, a fictional biography of Auschwitz by Kommandant Rudolf Höss.[15] Merle described the crematoria as "gigantic."[16] Later, Pressac had devoured Jean-François Steiner's novel *Treblinka*. Inspired by his readings, Pressac visited the remains of Treblinka, Auschwitz, and some other camps in 1966. The visit to Birkenau made a great impression on him, but somehow the ruins of the crematoria troubled him: they seemed so much smaller than the buildings Merle had described. In the years that followed, Pressac conceived of a counter-history in which Germany had won the Second World War. The setting of its first chapter was in Birkenau, which, in the post-Nazi victory, had been expanded with enormous new crematoria. Yet as he wrote this fantasy (which he never completed), the question of whether the Auschwitz extermination camp might have been a piece of fiction from the beginning suddenly became headline news in France. At the end of October 1978, the French weekly *L'Express* published an article entitled "À Auschwitz on n'a gazé que les poux" ("In Auschwitz they only gassed Lice").[17] The outrageous title did not reflect the views of the left-of-center magazine that aimed to be a French version of *Time*, nor did it reflect the views of the author of the article, the investigative journalist Philippe Ganier-Raymond. Instead it summarized the views of the 80-year-old Louis Darquier, who, after the war, had been sentenced to death *in absentia* but who had escaped justice by living in comfortable circumstance in Franco's Spain. Most of the French had forgotten about him but not Ganier-Raymond, who had written a book on French anti-Semitism during the Second World War that discussed Darquier's views.[18] In 1975, shortly after the publication of his book, Ganier-Raymond had traveled to Spain to report on the aftermath of Franco's death. In Madrid, he discovered that Darquier was still alive. It took Ganier-Raymond three years to get the by-then-very-feeble Darquier to agree to a meeting, insisting that no tape recorder would be used to record the conversation. The journalist broke the agreement and secretly taped every word. Thus, the

French nation came to possess a full record of the conversation. Darquier described the Holocaust as a product of Jewish propaganda, created as a means to establish Jewish world domination. He claimed that the deportations to the East had been a part of a benevolent scheme to resettle Jews in a new homeland. When Ganier-Raymond ironically suggested that Darquier might as well claim that Auschwitz was the intended outcome of the 1917 Balfour Declaration that had promised the Jews a "national home," Darquier responded angrily: the accounts that Auschwitz had been an extermination camp where a million Jews had been murdered was just Jewish propaganda. "I'll tell you exactly what happened at Auschwitz," Darquier told Ganier-Raymond. "They used gas. Yes. That's true. But they gassed the lice." When the latter responded that even Eichmann had not denied the facts of the so-called Final Solution to the Jewish Question, Darquier repeated once again that it was a lie and asked: "Do you know anyone who has ever seen what they call as gas chamber?" The journalist mentioned the testimonies of thousands of survivors and that he had seen a gas chamber when he had visited the memorial camp in Oswiecim. "Your gas chamber was invented after the event," Darquier responded, adding: "You won't get me to change my mind."[19]

Ganier-Raymond did not ask about the source of Darquier's contention, and the latter did not volunteer it. Nevertheless, it is clear that Darquier relied on an article entitled "Le 'problème des chambres à gaz'" ("The 'Problem of the Gas Chambers'") that had been written by Dr. Robert Faurisson, *maître de conferences* in literature at the University of Lyons II, and published in June 1978 in the extreme right-wing magazine *Défense de l'Occident* (*Defense of the West*).[20] Faurisson's article began on what appeared to be a reasonable note. "No one, not even those who are nostalgic about the Third Reich, thinks of denying the existence of Hitlerite concentration camps. Everyone also recognizes that some camps were equipped with cremation ovens." These had been necessary to cremate the corpses of inmates who had died of infectious diseases such as typhus. Faurisson then noted that "numerous French, British, American, and German authors" dispute the existence of German extermination camps equipped with gas chambers designed for mass killing—terms he put between quotation marks. "The victims would have been men, women, and children whom Hitler had chosen to exterminate because of their racial or religious affiliation. That is what one labels as the genocide.' The most important weapon of this 'genocide' would have been human slaughterhouses designated as 'gas chambers' and the gas used would most often have been Zyklon B (a pesticide based upon prussic- or hydrocyanic acid)." Faurisson contested both the existence of the gas chambers and the genocide of the Jews. Furthermore, leaning on Irving's *Hitler's War*, he added: "[T]he criminal intention which one has attributed to Hitler has never been proven. As to the weapon of the crime, no one has actually seen it." Both the "genocide" and the "gas chambers" were products of allied hate propaganda that had been picked up and preserved by the media. The result was what Faurisson labeled as "the hoax of the century."[21]

In fact, for more than a decade, Faurisson had been developing a conspiracy theory that assumed that Zionists had created the hoax of the gas chamber and the Holocaust to swindle Germans out of enormous sums of money and the Palestinians out of a land and that Jewish control over the media had not only ensured the success of the hoax but also resulted in a noxious limitation of the freedom of opinion of those who had sought to denounce it. Yet, until the Darquier interview, Faurisson, like any other crank, had been unable to publish his ideas in the mainstream press. Darquier's statement that only lice were gassed in Auschwitz created a scandal: as other newspapers sought to weigh in on the matter, Faurisson's ideas became news. On November 16, an article appeared in the socialist *Le Matin de Paris* entitled: "'Les chambres à gaz: ça n'existe pas.' C'est le thème favori de Robert Faurisson" ("'The Gas Chambers: they don't exist.' This is the Favorite Subject of Robert Faurisson"). Faurisson was quoted as saying that the Darquier affair ought to convince the French that the Holocaust was a fiction and the gas chambers were fabrications and proclaimed "that the massacres in so-called 'gas chambers' are a historical lie."[22] Two days later, the daily *Le Monde*, the French newspaper of record, reported that a prosecutor was considering bringing a case against Faurisson.[23] Because the paper had reported on Faurisson's ideas, *Le Monde* was obliged under French law to offer Faurisson the opportunity to publish a reply. On December 29, Faurisson's "'Le problème des chambres à gaz' ou 'le rumeur d'Auschwitz'" ("'The Problem of the Gas Chambers' or 'the Rumor of Auschwitz'") appeared in print. It began with the declaration that "no-one contested the use of crematoria ovens in certain German camps." The high mortality due to epidemics had made those incineration facilities necessary. "It is the existence of 'gas chambers,' true slaughterhouses for humans, which is contested." Faurisson argued that any visitor to Auschwitz or Majdanek could observe that the gas chambers could not have worked because it would have resulted in a "catastrophe" for the perpetrators, who would have killed themselves. Furthermore, it would be impossible to cram 2000 people into a room of 2000 square feet, and it would have been ridiculous to then sprinkle them with pellets of an insecticide. Faurisson argued that the plans that did exist showed that the alleged gas chambers were typical morgues and that the gas would have taken too long to be extracted from the room. Finally, he noted that in all the trials no one had been able to produce German documentation for Bunkers I and II, which were the first gas chambers built in Auschwitz-Birkenau. Faurisson concluded with the statement that "Nazism is dead, quite dead, and also its Führer. Today only the truth remains. Let us dare to proclaim it: The non-existence of the 'gas chambers' is good news for poor humanity. Good news like this should no longer be suppressed."[24]

The publication of such views in the prestigious *Le Monde* seemed to give the denial of the gas chambers an appearance of respectability. What made matters worse was the fact that, fearing the impact of Faurisson's letter, the editors of *Le Monde* had asked for a response from the Auschwitz survivor and Holocaust scholar Georges Wellers, offering him an opportunity to respond to Faurisson with an article printed on the same page as Faurisson's piece. Wellers tried to set the record straight in a piece entitled "Abondance des preuves" ("Abundance of proofs").[25] But the publication of two articles juxtaposed side by side suggested that *Le Monde* was hosting a confrontation between two equally deserving opinions. Unintentionally, Wellers had given legitimacy to Faurisson. In addition, Wellers' article had given Faurisson the right to respond. Faurisson did not hesitate to make use of it, and *Le Monde* printed his reply on January 16.[26] He claimed that he had believed in the gas chambers until he had read the work of French Holocaust denier Paul Rassinier and that he had reflected on the issue for 14 years and researched it assiduously for another four. "I have analyzed thousands of documents … I have searched in vain for a single deportee capable of proving to me that he has seen, with his own eyes, a 'gas chamber.' I certainly did not want an illusory abundance of proofs; I would have been satisfied with only one proof, only one proof. That proof I never found."[27]

When what became known as the Faurisson Affair broke, Pressac had thought about the crematoria for over a decade. For many years, he had his own doubts about the crematoria, but he had not seen the need to do a fact check in the archives. A contrarian by nature, Pressac felt an instinctive sympathy for Faurisson. Then he read in *Le Monde* on February 21, 1979, a statement drafted by the prominent historians Léon Poliakov and

Pierre Vidal-Naquet and signed by leading members of the French historical establishment. Entitled "La politique hitlérienne d'extermination. Une déclaration d'historiens" ("The Hitlerian Policy of Extermination. A Declaration by Historians"), the 1800-word manifesto began with the observation that "at various occasions since the end of World War II, publicists, who sometimes claim to be historians, have questioned the veracity of testimony about the Nazi policy of extermination." While the absurdity of such a challenge of the evidence had been clear to all in the immediate postwar years, the fact that eyewitnesses were dying and that a new generation had grown up which had not experienced the Second World War compelled the signatories to direct themselves to the young who might be swayed by the arguments of those "publicists." "It is for this purpose," they emphasized, "and not in response to anyone, that we are publishing this statement." The historians acknowledged that they belonged to different schools of thought. But they all considered themselves as "humble servants of truth" who were united in the mission, first formulated by the "Father of History" (Herodotus) to ensure that "human events do not fade with time." The "Declaration" continued with a summary of the Nazi policy to exterminate Jews, gypsies, the mentally ill, and others and gave an overview of the broad evidentiary basis of those facts: both eyewitness testimonies and German documents provided ample evidence. It acknowledged that each piece of evidence should always be considered critically. "Textual criticism is one of the fundamental rules of our profession." Yet in the case of the Nazi genocide of the Jews, the totality of the evidence was above suspicion. The last paragraph of the "Declaration" did stress that "everyone is free to interpret a phenomenon like Hitler's genocide according to his own philosophy," and that "everyone is free to imagine or dream that these monstrous deeds did not occur." Yet, as historians, they also felt compelled to note that, unfortunately, the German genocide of the Jews *had* taken place, "and no one can deny their existence without outraging the truth. Do not ask how, technically, such a mass murder was possible. It was technically possible because it happened. This must be the point of departure of any historical inquiry on this subject. It has fallen to us to recall that point with due simplicity: there is not, nor can there be, a debate about the existence of the gas chambers."[28] This final sentence of the "Declaration" conjured up the worst of academic intellectual arrogance, the attitude with which, according to a version of the Black Legend, Aristotelian scholars working in collaboration with the Inquisition would have rejected Galileo's observations and conclusions. It suggested that free enquiry stopped at the threshold of the gas chambers. It made Faurisson into an underdog of free speech opposed by the defenders of the status quo.

Pressac felt insulted by the seeming paternalism of the "declaration."[29] He decided to travel back to Auschwitz, and this time he also visited the archives. There he inspected the drawings of the crematoria. He noticed again that the buildings were remarkably small and that they contained many awkward and apparently illogical elements. Now he also began to doubt the historical record, and on his return to France contacted Faurisson, who, as Pressac had been told in the Auschwitz archives, had seen the same drawings a few years earlier. At their first meeting, the men recognized in each other a kindred soul. "We had both approached the problem in the same way" Pressac recalled seven years later, "through drawings. Something tangible, concrete." The learned professor had no difficulty seducing the mind of the pharmacist. "Nobody sitting down opposite Faurisson and listening to him for one or two hours could fail to emerge from the conversation shaken or completely converted to his cause. He was steeped in his subject, backed up by 200 kg of documents, 200 photographs, 10 years of reading and 4 years of intensive work." But Pressac was puzzled by Faurisson's strategy. "The latter *denies only the homicidal gas chambers*, not the rest: the deportation, concentration camps, sufferings, malnutrition, slave labour, ill-treatment, sickness, epidemics, crematoriums ... The stratagem is that if the gas chambers are demolished, all the rest will follow and be denounced." Nevertheless, Pressac volunteered to become Faurisson's research assistant. It was to be a collaboration of short duration: as he studied Faurisson's arguments in greater detail, and as he made more research trips to the archives of the Auschwitz museum to collect material for the master, Pressac became convinced that Faurisson was wrong. "His theory stood up for only *two days* to a direct historical confrontation with the Museum documents and the Birkenau ruins," Pressac wrote later. He still had many questions concerning how the gassings had worked, but he began to see that their denial was silly and that Faurisson's deductive reasoning was absurd. They broke at the end of 1980. At this time, Faurisson was on trial. Pressac attended the trial and was impressed by the arguments of the attorney Bernard Jouanneau, who appeared on behalf of the International League Against Racism and Anti-Semitism, the organization that coordinated the suit against Faurisson. "*Maitre* Jouanneau made me live an afternoon of poignant reflection, because for the first time he presented an overall picture of the question." More important was Pressac's encounter with Auschwitz survivor Jacques Zylbermine. Initially, Zylbermine was suspicious of the man who had been close to Faurisson, but he must have been disarmed by Pressac's genuine interest in Auschwitz, and he began to tell his story. This marked the final point in Pressac's break with Faurisson. "In the end, it was not the Höss autobiography or the archive documents, the drawings, the original photographs or the ruins of the Krematorium that turned my initial ideas inside out, but the modest and simple testimony of Mr. Zylbermine, as he told me his story in detail during a whole afternoon."[30]

The testimony of Zylbermine had touched Pressac, and Auschwitz had ceased to be an object of some fantasy about a Nazi-dominated Europe or a delusion of a history without a Holocaust. Pressac felt that Faurisson had taken him in, and now Pressac wanted revenge. He contacted Wellers, who had engaged Faurisson in *Le Monde* and who had just published his own response to Faurisson, *Les chambers à gaz ont existé: Des documents, des témoignages, des chiffres* (*The Gas Chambers existed: Documents, Eyewitness Evidence, Numbers*).[31] Wellers believed Pressac had much to offer and asked him to write down his conclusions. Pressac responded with a 20-page paper on his research on the construction history of crematoria 4 and 5. It offered a wealth of new evidence, but it also challenged the existing historiography of the camp, established by the forensic investigators in 1945, which maintained that all of the four Birkenau crematoria (numbered 2, 3, 4, and 5—crematorium 1 having been built in the *Stammlager* or main camp) had been designed from the outset as killing installations. Pressac argued (wrongly as it would turn out) that in August 1942, crematoria 4 and 5 had been designed with the sole purpose of incinerating corpses and that only during their construction had gas chambers been added to the program. Wellers did not know what to do with the paper. First of all, Pressac's argument revealed that Wellers' *Les chambers à gaz ont existé* was already obsolete. This was embarrassing. In addition, Pressac's paper was also unsettling: in historicizing the construction of Auschwitz, Pressac had not only acknowledged that Faurisson had had a point—it was time to look at the evidence more closely—but had the potential to open a Pandora's box. If a little research in the archives showed that an essential part of the historiography was wrong, it was quite possible that more research would yield more troubling results. Finally, there were also real problems with Pressac's work. Focusing on two crematoria, Pressac did not offer an interpretation of their construction history within the context of the general development of Auschwitz in 1942 and 1943. Neither did Pressac consider his conclusions within the context of the historical development of the Holocaust as such. Pressac's refusal to consider the context was based on his desire to try to study the crematoria without any reference to eyewitness evidence and to consider German documents alone—a clear capitulation to Faurisson's twisted argument as to what evidence was admissible and what was not. Wellers concluded that Pressac's work created more trouble than it was worth, and he chose not to respond. When he did not receive a reply from Wellers, Pressac contacted Vidal-Naquet, who had been instrumental in creating "A Declaration by Historians." Vidal-Naquet recognized the importance of Pressac's work, and he arranged for him to speak at the very conference where Adam, Broszat, Browning, and others were struggling with the question of if, when, and how Hitler had taken a decision to unleash the Final Solution. Unable to take part as a regular participant (because he had not registered in time), and not particularly welcome in the general session due to the fact that Pressac had nothing to contribute to the question of the Hitler decision, the pharmacist was given 20 minutes as a "respondent." Pressac used his time well with an illustrated presentation of the genesis and evolution of crematoria 4 and 5. The participants were impressed, and Francois Furet, the organizer of the conference, decided to include Pressac's presentation and its illustrations as an appendix to the conference proceedings—a volume that only appeared in 1985.[32] Realizing that Pressac would see his work published anyway, Wellers decided to make the best of a difficult situation, and he offered Pressac the opportunity to publish his paper in his own *Le Monde Juif*. This did not mean that Pressac had convinced him that crematoria 4 and 5 were originally not designed with gas chambers. Wellers' offer came with a condition: Pressac would get space in *Le Monde Juif* if he agreed that it would be accompanied by an editorial by Wellers that would outline their differences—a kind of "Reader Beware!" As *Le Monde Juif* was the most important French journal devoted to the history of the Holocaust, and as publication of an article in that venue would bring Pressac the recognition and respectability he sought as a historian, he agreed to Wellers' patronizing terms. In September 1982, Pressac's paper appeared with a three-page introduction in which Wellers praised Pressac's "intellectual curiosity" and his "bold sense of independence" and acknowledged that he had discovered "important details that have not been studied before." Yet he added that his conclusions were often "questionable."[33]

Despite Wellers' reservations, Pressac's paper opened a new chapter in the response to Holocaust denial. While Pressac may have been wrong in some of his conclusions, it did not really matter because he presented the material evidence he had discovered and on which his conclusion was based—pictures of the blueprints, photos of the crematoria under construction, notebooks, order forms, and photos of gas-tight doors and windows that remained on the site and which he had inspected. Faurisson had published none of these. It suggested that it was possible to engage the deniers on their own ground. Pressac continued to research and write, now with the support of Holocaust survivor Serge Klarsfeld, who in 1983 offered him a contract for a book that was to include all the evidence he had discovered. *Auschwitz: Operation and Technique of the Gas Chambers* appeared in 1989—remarkably only in an English-language edition published in the United States. A 563-page folio, the new book contained a wealth of photos of all the blueprints of the crematoria, photos of their construction, facsimiles of all the relevant construction documents, and a transcript of the crucial eyewitness testimony of Sonderkommando Henryk Tauber. This time, there was no patronizing introduction but a preface in which the publishers Beate and Serge Klarsfeld expressed their admiration for Pressac. "When we see what an isolated and tenacious researcher like Jean-Claude Pressac has been able to reconstitute, starting his work 35 years after the liberation of Auschwitz, we cannot but regret that it was not possible for Jewish research missions to study the Auschwitz site and its archives in 1945." Of course, in 1945, there were no deniers to trigger such research missions. At that time, the facts were still clear and undisputed. The Klarsfelds recognized that Pressac's book was only a beginning, opening the way "for other researchers to go more deeply into or modify some investigations and conclusions, and go further than Jean-Claude Pressac in the study of some particular problem or other. But we are certain that his book will remain a reference work pointing the way."[34] Indeed, Pressac's book proved to be a landmark, and not only in providing a response to Holocaust denial. In fact, it proved to be a milestone in Holocaust research: for the first time, it became clear that even the death camps, which had always been the core evidence supporting the intentionalist perspective—after all, doesn't the whole concept of a purposefully designed "death factory" not point to an intention to enact a genocide—could also be interpreted from a functionalist perspective. Pressac provided part of the foundation for a reinterpretation of the history of Auschwitz that now shapes the understanding of the history and the historic significance of that camp.[35]

Historical Facts and the Freedom of Opinion

Faurisson reviewed Pressac's *Auschwitz* in 1991. He dismissed it as irrelevant. If the book had "actually presented the slightest proof for the existence of the alleged gas chambers, media throughout the entire world would have resounded with the news. But instead of uproar, there has been silence." Yet, Faurisson did not deny that Pressac's book marked a watershed. "For the first time, an Exterminationist agrees, apparently at least, to a debate with Revisionists on terrain dear to them: that of scientific and technical argumentation; the opportunity to demonstrate the impotence of the Exterminationists on this terrain as well is too good to be missed."[36] Faurisson felt so confident that he and his allies would prevail where it concerned the "scientific and technical argumentation" because of the incredible success of *The Leuchter Report*, drafted in 1988 and published in 1989. If Pressac's folio-sized tome appeared as a Goliath of a publication, Leuchter's publication was exactly the opposite: concise and, as far as Faurisson was concerned, devastating to the claims of the so-called Exterminationists—that is those who maintained that the Holocaust was a historical fact.

Faurisson had been the godfather of *The Leuchter Report*. In 1988, Faurisson had acted as an advisor to Holocaust denier Ernst Zündel when the latter stood trial in Toronto for the crime of "spreading false news." Faurisson suggested that Zündel engage the American engineer Fred Leuchter as an expert witness: Leuchter had serviced execution equipment in American prisons and therefore had credible expertise in the matter. Leuchter was also naive, and Faurisson and Zündel easily convinced him of the merit of their cause. In February 1988, Leuchter traveled to Auschwitz and Majdanek, studied the layout of the crematoria—or rather of what remained of them—and illegally took various samples of the brickwork and plaster, which he brought back to the United States to be analyzed for residual cyanide content by the Alpha Analytical Laboratories in Ashland, Massachusetts. Back home, Leuchter wrote a report entitled "An Engineering Report on the Alleged Execution Gas Chambers at Auschwitz, Birkenau and Majdanek Poland" (which was later published as *The Leuchter Report: The End of a Myth. An Engineering Report on the Alleged Execution Gas Chambers at Auschwitz, Birkenau, and Majdanek, Poland*). Zündel's lawyer submitted it to the Toronto court. In this report, Leuchter calculated the theoretical capacity of the Auschwitz gas chambers based on the completely arbitrary assumption that the maximum load of the gas chambers would have been one person per nine square feet and that it would have taken one week to ventilate the gas chambers after each use. This led Leuchter to the conclusion that the killing capacity of the crematoria during the period of their existence would have been merely 105,688 people. As to the ovens, Leuchter calculated that these could only have burned 193,576 corpses (theoretical) or 85,092 (practical) over the time that the crematoria existed. When, in addition, he found only a minimal residue of cyanide in the walls of the "alleged" gas chambers, he came to the conclusion "that none of the facilities examined were ever utilized for the execution of human beings and that the crematories could not have supported the alleged work load attributed to them."[37]

When Leuchter presented his findings to the Toronto court, Irving was in the courtroom. Irving and Zündel had been on friendly terms since the latter had recognized *Hitler's War* as a major asset in the cause of Holocaust denial, and he had helped to organize lecture trips for Irving in North America. When he received Leuchter's findings, Zündel phoned Irving, told him that samples taken from the walls of the gas chambers showed negligible amounts of cyanide, and asked if he was willing to endorse in court. According to Zündel, Irving responded: "Why did I not think of that myself?" Zündel and Irving agreed that the latter would travel to Toronto, meet Leuchter, read the report, and then decide if he would testify. Zündel recalled that Irving declared Leuchter's forensic investigation as "a stroke of genius by the defense."[38] During his cross-examination in court, Irving publicly embraced Leuchter's conclusions. "I'm very impressed, in fact, by the presentation, by the scientific manner of presentation, by the expertise that's been shown by it and by the very novel conclusion that he's arrived at," and Irving admitted that "as a historian I'm rather ashamed it never occurred to me to make this kind of investigation on the particular controversy." In conclusion, Irving endorsed the report wholeheartedly. "I think it is shattering in the significance of its discovery."[39] Descending from the witness box, Irving had the choice to pack up, return to London, and forget about it. Yet for reasons that I have explored elsewhere, he chose a different route: he decided that Leuchter's Auschwitz was to be his Rubicon, a hinge in his own career, and a turning point in the history of history.[40] From the moment that he left the courtroom, Irving began to aggressively trumpet his own conversion as a world-historical event. He bought from Zündel the right to publish the British edition of *The Leuchter Report*, and he began to work the lecture circuits. The key subject was Auschwitz. "I don't see any reason to be tasteful about Auschwitz. It's baloney. It's a legend," he declared in a speech given in Calgary. "Once we admit the fact that it was a brutal slave labour camp and large numbers of people did die, as large numbers of innocent people died elsewhere in the war, why believe the rest of the baloney? I say quite tastelessly in fact that more people died on the back seat of Edward Kennedy's car in Chappaquiddick than ever died in a gas chamber in Auschwitz."[41]

Irving's remarks were obscene, and given the preponderance of evidence that in Auschwitz more than a million people, mostly Jews, died in purposefully built gas chambers, it violates the common sense wisdom articulated (according to the late Senator Daniel Patrick Moynihan) by Federal Reserve Chairman Alan Greenspan when he ran meetings: "Each member was entitled to his own opinion but not his own facts."[42] Nevertheless, in North America and Great Britain, the very liberal laws protecting free speech allowed Irving to make such statements without the danger of legal problems, but when he accepted invitations to address neo-Nazi crowds in Germany, he and his hosts faced problems, as Holocaust denial is a punishable offense under German law. In 1990, he was arrested in Munich for having claimed that the Auschwitz gas chamber in crematorium 1 was a fake and also having suggested that those of crematoria 2 to 5 had never existed. Of particular importance was the legal outcome of a talk he was to give in Munich on May 12, 1991, as the guest of the Munich-Upper Bavaria branch of the neo-Nazi *Nationaldemokratische Partei Deutschlands* (National Democratic Party of Germany or NDP). The City of Munich had reminded the NDP ahead of time that Holocaust denial was illegal, and invoking the *Versammlungsgesetzes* (Law on Public Meetings), they instructed the NDP that if Irving were to engage in Holocaust denial and, specifically, mention the "Auschwitz Lie," the hosts were obliged to stop him talking and close the meeting immediately.[43] The NPD appealed first to the Bavarian Government, then to the Bavarian Administrative Court, and the Federal Administrative Court, but they confirmed the legality of the order. The NDP then brought the case to the Federal Constitutional Court, claiming that the order violated basic human rights on the grounds that article 5, clause 1, sentence 1 of the *Grundgesetz* (Basic Law) of Germany states that "everyone has the right freely to express and disseminate his opinion in speech, writing, and pictures and freely to inform himself from generally accessible sources."[44] In April 1994, the Federal Constitutional Court ruled that the principle of the freedom of opinion did not give a person the right to deny the

Holocaust. The reasoning of the court is interesting. It recalled that the Basic Law sought to protect opinions, which "are marked by the individual's *subjective* [my emphasis] relationship to his statement's content. [...] They enjoy the basic right's protection regardless of whether their expression is judged to be well-founded or unfounded, emotional or rational, valuable or worthless, dangerous or harmless." Yet the court also noted that "factual assertions are not, strictly speaking, expressions of opinion. Unlike such expressions, most prominent in factual assertions is the *objective* [my emphasis] relationship between the utterance and reality." While the boundary between opinions and statements of fact were not always clear—opinions are, as a rule, based on factual assumptions—the court did state that "protection of factual assertions ends only where such representations cannot contribute anything to the constitutionally presupposed formation of opinion. Viewed from this angle, incorrect information is not an interest that merits protection." Turning to the particulars of the case at hand, the court noted that "the prohibited utterance, that there was no persecution of Jews during the Third Reich, is a factual assertion that has been proven untrue according to innumerable eyewitness accounts and documents, the court findings in numerous criminal cases, and to historians' conclusions. Taken on its own, therefore, a statement having this content does not enjoy the protection of freedom of expression." In order to clarify this statement, the court added an interesting observation. "Therein lies an importance difference between denying the persecution of the Jews during the Third Reich and denying German guilt concerning the outbreak of the Second World War [...]. Utterances concerning guilt and responsibility for historical events are always complex evaluations that cannot be reduced to factual assertions, whereas denial of an event itself normally will have the character of a factual assertion."[45]

To fully grasp the significance of this landmark decision by the Federal Constitutional Court, it is helpful to recall some observations Hannah Arendt has made on the question at stake. Key to Nazism, she has argued, was propaganda, which consistently denied the important of facts in general. "The Nazi impress on the German mind consists primarily in a conditioning whereby reality has ceased to be the sum total of hard inescapable facts and has become a conglomeration of ever-changing events and slogans in which a thing can be true today and false tomorrow." The result of this was not indoctrination, "but the incapacity or unwillingness to distinguish altogether between fact and opinion."[46] This was the core of the Nazi assault on civilization, as Arendt postulated that the basis of all civilization is an ability and willingness to recognize and say "what is." She credited the Greeks with having first recognized that history should be written impartially, with a disinterested aim to describe the truth about the past. "Homer chose to sing the deeds of the Trojans no less than those of the Achaeans [...].This had happened nowhere before; no other civilization, however splendid, had been able to look with equal eyes upon friend and foe, upon success and defeat." According to Arendt, Homer's evenhandedness had inspired Herodotus, "the first great teller of factual truth," the man who through his practice had established impartiality as the center of historiography. Arendt recognized that the inviolability of facts, central not only to historiography but also to judicial proceedings and philosophical and scientific speculation, is in tension with the freedom of opinion necessary for the (often messy) practice of democratic politics as it invites enfranchised citizens to debate what might be aspired to in the future and what ought to be done in the present to achieve this goal. Arendt noted that, while engaged in politics, individuals, groups, or even generations have the right to interpret facts from a particular perspective, they do not have the right "to touch the factual matter itself." And she provided an example that resembles the one given 27 years later by the Federal Constitutional Court in its decision on the limits of the freedom of opinion. "During the twenties, so a story goes, Clemenceau, shortly before his death, found himself engaged in a debate with a representative of the Weimar Republic on the question of guilt for the outbreak of the First World War. 'What, in your opinion,' Clemenceau was asked, 'will future historians think of this troublesome and controversial issue?' He replied: 'This I don't know. But I know for certain that they will not say Belgium invaded Germany.'"[47]

The decision by the Federal Constitutional Court effectively embodied Arendt's insights and enshrined it as a principle of the German legal code. One can invoke the fundamental democratic right of freedom of opinion to debate the meaning of facts, but one cannot invoke that right to debate the very existence of those facts once they have been clearly established. This does not mean that one cannot engage, if one feels so compelled, in the denial of obvious facts. But, like a parlor game or the ranting of a madman, such an action does not deserve the protection of the law: it does not serve the public interest. However, a debate about the meaning of those facts does serve that interest. This was, incidentally, the idea at the core of the declaration of the French historians of 1979—one that they sadly did not sufficiently elucidate at the time.

Survivor and Eyewitness Testimony and Its Institutional Legacy in the Public Realm

Until the late 1970s, Holocaust survivors generally did not speak in public—the public, pedagogical importance given to the testimony of survivors in the Eichmann Trial was an exception to this rule. Today, countless survivors credit their discovery of Holocaust denial as the catalyst to "come out" from the protection of the private sphere to the exposure that comes with speaking in schools and at public commemorations and with compiling oral histories. They saw Holocaust denial as a specific assault on their own integrity. "The story is told of the Jew who, on being captured by the Nazis, was dealt eighty brutal blows by his captors and yet managed to live to tell the tale," Manuel Prutschi wrote in 1989, when reviewing the impact of Holocaust denial on survivors in Canada. Deniers had given them the eighty-first blow, "in a manner more vicious than the survivor could have anticipated. Rather than the survivor's story not being believed because the level of inhumanity was incomprehensible, the story is actually being denied."[48]

At the time that these words appeared in print, David Irving had already begun to mock the survivors as frauds. In 1990, in a speech given in Victoria, British Columbia, he told his audience that survivors enjoyed life on the luxuriously appointed ship MS Holocaust. "There is no shortage of crewmembers or applicants for this particular ship. The only requirement to become a crewmember of the cruise ship 'Holocaust' is that you should be an Auschwitz survivor. And of course there's an inexhaustible supply of Auschwitz survivors. There are millions of Auschwitz survivors now floating around the world, or people who purport to be Auschwitz survivors."[49] A few weeks later, in Toronto, he stated that the discovery of the index cards of Auschwitz inmates in Soviet archives had made it possible to unmask many crewmembers of the MS Holocaust as liars by comparing the number tattooed on their arms, their testimony, and the index cards. "The experts can look at a tattoo and say, 'Oh yes, 181,219 that means you entered Auschwitz in March 1943.' So if you want to go and have a tattoo put on your arm, as a lot of them do, I am afraid to say, and claim subsequently you were in Auschwitz, you have to make sure a) that it fits in with the month you said you were in Auschwitz, and b) that it is not a number which anyone has used before."[50] Such talk galvanized survivors to speak about their experiences. Yet in Western Europe and North America, they also found a society that was ready for them. Since the mid-1970s, the general public had become collectively more open to the psychological needs of others. It had also begun to appreciate the variety of human society, with its implication that each single person, irrespective of gender, race, religion, sexual orientation, or health, has his or her place and purpose. Television had also changed the way people negotiate the relationship between the public, the private, and the intimate. As it began to broadcast the public heart-rending testimonies of victims as a daily fare, it suggested that listening to testimonies of traumatized people and identification with their psychological needs was an important moral duty. Thus, when Holocaust survivors felt challenged by Holocaust deniers to tell their story, they could do so.[51]

Some of the Holocaust survivors who chose to speak about their experiences in order to combat Holocaust denial looked to the future, at a time when they and other eyewitnesses would have died. How to preserve their legacy and their testimonies? From the time of the Faurisson affair they began to prepare, often with the help of their families, friends, and allies, for the creation of permanent institutions that were to be bulwarks to protect the historical truth against the combined assault of the particular forms of denial practiced by men like Faurisson and the general ignorance and indifference of society at large. Anxiety about the inroads Holocaust deniers were making into public discourse—public opinion surveys done in the early 1980s suggested that a fifth of the public were receptive to the arguments of the deniers—prompted the creation of the United States Holocaust Memorial Museum (USHMM) in Washington, D.C. As the plans for the museum and its permanent exhibition developed, Holocaust denial remained a constant point of reference. "To preclude definitively revisionist declarations by anti-Semitic pseudo scholars who try to 'prove' that the Holocaust never happened," founding director Jesajahu Weinberg observed, "the Museum considered it necessary to restrict itself in the choice of its exhibits solely to genuine artifacts and documentary photographic material with proven provenance (though the Permanent Exhibition includes eight full-scale replicas, cast in fiberglass, of large objects that could not be transferred from Europe to the United States, but that can always be inspected on the actual site)." He added that "all visual details of the exhibition, as well as all its textual explanations, were thoroughly scrutinized by leading Holocaust historians to ensure their factual accuracy."[52] Faurisson and his ilk had claimed that the discovery of a single discrepancy between eyewitness evidence and material evidence would reveal that Auschwitz had been a fake. The founders of the USHMM did not want to offer deniers any such discrepancy. When the USHMM was dedicated in April 1993, Holocaust deniers demonstrated against the "Jewish Lies" and handed out pamphlets. In his speech, President Bill Clinton explicitly referred to the link between the survivors, their passing, the threat of Holocaust denial, and the purpose of the USHMM:

> We must all now frankly admit that there will come a time in the not-too-distant future when the Holocaust will pass from living reality and shared experience to memory and to history. To preserve this shared history of anguish, to keep it vivid and real so that evil can be combated and contained, we are here to consecrate this memorial and contemplate its meaning for us. [...] Look at the liars and the propagandists among us, the skinheads and the Liberty Lobby here at home; the Afrikaaners resistance movement in South Africa; the Radical Party of Serbia, the Russian blackshirts. With them we must all compete for the interpretation and the preservation of history of what we know and how we should behave. The evil represented in this museum is incontestable.[53]

Holocaust denial also motivated survivors at state, county, and local levels to get together and create archives of video-taped testimonies and programs that support Holocaust education in middle and high schools.

The Objective or Conscientious Historian

Holocaust denial emerged beyond the periphery of the discipline of history. Rassinier was a journalist, Faurisson a literary scholar, and Arthur Butz an electrical engineer. Only Irving could claim with some justification to be a historian. While he had no degrees in history, and hence had not undergone the formal training of a historian, he had been a prolific writer of books on history, and therefore was considered by many to be a historian. He considered himself to be so. Therefore, Irving's conversion to Holocaust denial in 1988 was celebrated by Holocaust deniers because it suggested that, finally, a member of the historical profession had endorsed a revision of history proposed by non-historians. But was he a historian? On January 11, 2000, Richard Rampton QC began his opening statement for the defense in the case of David John Cawdell Irving, claimant, and (1) Penguin Books Limited and (2) Deborah E. Lipstadt, defendants, with the following words:

> My Lord, Mr Irving calls himself an historian. The truth is, however, that he is not an historian at all but a falsifier of history. To put it bluntly, he is a liar. Lies may take various forms and may as often consist of suppression or omission as a direct falsehood or invention, but in the end all forms of lying converge into a single definition, willful, deliberate misstatement of the facts. Mr Irving has used many different means to falsify history: invention, misquotation, suppression, distortion, manipulation and not least mistranslation, but those all these techniques have the same ultimate effect, falsification of the truth.[54]

The challenge to Irving's claim to be a historian, verbalized by Rampton on that January day, resulted in a much better understanding of the nature and limits of the historian's practice and can be defined as a fourth example of something good to come out of the evil of Holocaust denial.

The trial was the result of a legal action brought by Irving against the American historian Deborah Lipstadt and her publisher Penguin Books. When in the wake of Leuchter's testimony Irving went on the road to propagate the non-existence of the Auschwitz gas chambers, he had become the poster boy of Holocaust denial: as a widely published writer on the Second World War, his endorsement of the extreme position first articulated by Faurisson mattered. American scholar Deborah Lipstadt recognized this. In her book Denying the Holocaust, published in 1993, she defined Irving as "one of the most dangerous spokesman for Holocaust denial." She contended that, "familiar with historical evidence, he bends it until it conforms with his ideological leanings and political agenda." Initially, Irving chose to ignore the book. But when, in 1996, Lipstadt proved successful in convincing St. Martin's Press to cancel publication of Irving's biography of Goebbels, Irving decided to hit back. In July, Irving announced: "Prof. Lipstadt is about to receive a writ from me for her tract *Denying the Holocaust* which she has foolishly started peddling within the jurisdiction of the British Courts." And on September 5, 1996, he issued a writ of summons, triggering with this an action in which Lipstadt and Penguin Books, which had published Denying the Holocaust in the United Kingdom, would have to either settle with Irving or prove that the statements that Irving considered libelous were justified. Lipstadt and Penguin Books chose the latter option, and the result was a court case that mobilized an enormous amount of resources and that led to an important consideration of the definition of what makes an objective historian. Irving, after all, had claimed that the accusation that he was a falsifier of history was libelous, and it was clear from the beginning that, when driven into a corner, he might admit errors in his judgment but that he would not admit that he had set out consciously to lie about the past when, in 1977, he exonerated Hitler or when, in 1988, he endorsed Leuchter. Therefore the defense team (in which I served as an expert witness on matters pertaining to Auschwitz) articulated an understanding of what makes an "objective historian," a concept that was to allow the court to assess Irving's historiographical methods and, as far as the defense was concerned, distortions. Within the English legal tradition—or for that matter in any legal tradition—no such concept had ever been formulated, and therefore the court could not invoke precedent in this matter. The historian Richard Evans, who was the expert witness on Irving's historiography, articulated in his expert report the core issue: do Irving's historical writings and speeches conform to some minimum standards of historical scholarship?

> That is, in other words, does Irving give a reasonably accurate account of the documents he uses; does he translate them in a reasonably accurate and unbiased manner; does he take into account as many other relevant documents as any professional historian could reasonably be expected to read and cite when he is using one particular source to substantiate an argument; does he apply consistent criteria of source-criticism to all the original material he uses, examining it for internal consistency, its consistency with other documents, its provenance, the motives of those who were responsible for it, and the audience for which it was intended; are his arguments, his statistics, and his accounts of historical events consistent across time and based on reliable historical evidence; does he take account of the arguments and interpretations of other historians who have examined the same documents; and does he, in other words, advance his arguments in a reasonably objective and unbiased manner?[55]

Evans' questions framed the defense team's counterattack on Irving and convinced Mr. Justice Charles Gray, who echoed them in his landmark judgment when he concluded in a key passage that "Irving has misstated historical evidence; adopted positions which run counter to the weight of the evidence; given credence to unreliable evidence and disregarded or dismissed credible evidence."[56] A key concept in Gray's judgment was that of the "objective historian," which he sometimes qualified as the "objective, fair-minded historian," a "honest-minded objective historian," a "serious historian," or—occasionally—as a "conscientious historian." Writing in the *Yale Law Journal*, Wendie E. Schneider summarized Gray's understanding of what makes an "objective historian" in a code of conduct for historians:

> (1) She must treat sources with appropriate reservations; (2) she must not dismiss counterevidence without scholarly consideration; (3) she must be even-handed in her treatment of evidence and eschew "cherry-picking" (4) she must clearly indicate any speculation; (5) she must not mistranslate documents or mislead by omitting parts of documents; (6) she must weigh the authenticity of all accounts, not merely those that contradict her favored view; and (7) she must take the motives of historical actors into consideration.[57]

While the concept of the "objective historian" had dominated the Irving trial, Schneider suggested that the alternative of the "conscientious historian," which Gray had used in a key passage of his judgment,[58] would be more useful in the long term, especially in the North American legal context. Noting that "the quest for absolute historical objectivity has been called into question convincingly," Schneider observed that "the idea of objectivity is not at all central to Gray's standard. [...] The components of Gray's standard do not, in fact, call for the historian to be without personal opinions or inclinations; they merely require him or her to make a balanced assessment of the evidence."[59] In conclusion, Schneider suggested that the "conscientious historian" would not only serve to evaluate the validity of historical research within a legal context but also serve a pedagogical function in the education of future historians. Certainly in the dynamic universe of Wikipedia, the latter purpose has been recognized in the entry on "historian": the preamble to the entry itself provides a substantial exposition of Gray's concept and Schneider's interpretation of it, defining for the world at large—at least at this time—and, perhaps more importantly, for aspiring historians, the task and moral obligation of the historical profession.

The Battle That Gentled the Historians' Condition[60]

Evans articulated the standard to which Irving should be held in the relative seclusion of his study in a Cambridge college. Gray reworked it for his judgment in the relative seclusion of his chambers in the Royal Courts of Justice, and Schneider reflected on its larger meaning far away from the battlefield. Reading their reflections, it is easy to forget that the concept of the "conscientious historian" arose in the middle of a fierce and pitiless war about the truth that did not allow for a negotiated settlement between the opponents but could only end in the destruction of one of the sides. Rampton clearly announced the unrelenting character of the encounter in his opening statement, and it brought an intellectual excitement to the proceedings, which included only very few exchanges concerning jurisprudence and almost wholly focused on the presentation and forensic examination of the evidence for many well-established facts and also some newly discovered ones. Many who sat through the proceedings discovered the excitement of doing history. On April 12, 2000, the day after Gray pronounced his judgment, *The Independent* noted in a leading article that "the cogency of the testimony presented by the defence" had vindicated "the great liberal principle, enunciated by John Stuart Mill, of the marketplace of ideas in which false coin is tested and replaced by true."[61] In a tough editorial, *The Irish Times* applauded the fact that Irving's defeat did not occur under a "hail of rotten eggs and the shouting down of his message by strident adolescent voices," but resulted from "the clinical, forensic examination of his credo, a calculated and methodical destruction of his untruthful version of history."[62] And *The Guardian* pronounced that "truth is no shining city on a hill."

> It has to be worked at; the credibility of those who claim to express it is critical. Even a casual reader of the case reports could quickly see how painstaking genuine historical scholarship is; it builds detail upon detail, avoiding casual inference and thin deduction. Eventually, a plausible narrative is pieced together but even then it has to withstand the slings and arrows of competitive scholars. And the Holocaust is now hot history. Due, in part, to the persistence of the deniers, academic effort has been redoubled. Among the many Irving assertions to be comprehensively demolished was the suggestion that thought police prevent open challenges to received historical wisdom. It is precisely because of the historians' efforts from the early 50s onward that there is now no room for doubt, despite the false trails and the lacunae left by a Nazi bureaucracy as assiduous about destroying the signs of its crimes as realizing the final solution. Other jurisdictions make denying the Holocaust a crime. After this case, we can rely on empiricism and the sheer weight of evidence.[63]

"We can rely on empiricism and the sheer weight of evidence." I had to smile when I read these lines that morning of April 12 as I sat in a carriage of the London Underground on my way to Rampton's chambers for a goodbye before boarding my return flight to Toronto. When 20 years earlier I had begun work on my doctoral dissertation, I had chosen a topic within the somewhat vaguely defined field of intellectual history because I was fascinated by the formation and transformation of ideas and opinions. And while I understood that I was obliged to treat these notions as facts to be established through the analysis of written, painted, sculpted, or built texts—the topic of my dissertation was the idea that the Temple of Solomon has been an *imago mundi*—I did not focus on the question if the designers of that temple had actually sought to create a building that provided a symbolic representation of the world. Within the context of my doctoral research, it did not actually matter if that temple had existed or not. And my own path to the courtroom in London had also begun with an interest in the meaning of the crematoria for our understanding of architecture, but not with a forensic focus on the facts of the crematoria, and the evidence for those facts. Yet as I read the literature on the crematoria, I discovered the writings of Faurisson and Butz and the forensic investigations of Leuchter. The negation of what I always assumed to be well-established facts got under my skin in a way the obviously awful historical material did not: I could read Auschwitz *Kommandant* Rudolf Höss's or *Sonderkommando* Filip Müller's accounts of the operation of the gas chambers without flinching, but became literally nauseous when I read Faurisson's denial of it. So, at that time, I just chose to turn my back to it. I thought I had better things to do than engaging obvious nonsense.

But like the gardener who tried to escape from the angel of death by running to Isfahan, I could not escape the encounter with the deniers. After completing the more speculative *Architectural Principles* and a more empirical *Ortsgeschichte* of Auschwitz, based on extensive archival research, I was pulled into the forensics of Auschwitz when in late 1997 filmmaker Errol Morris asked me to participate in his non-fiction feature *Mr. Death: The Rise and Fall of Fred A. Leuchter Jr.* and when in early 1998 Lipstadt, Evans, and lawyer Anthony Julius approached me to join the defense team in the libel case brought by Irving. And what I discovered when I put my teeth into the material was the delight and excitement any person must feel when he or she goes back to the basics of his or her profession or trade. And a fact is the basic element of history.

In addition, I rediscovered what had motivated me to become fascinated with history to begin with: a very personal gain that seems to offer an exact reversal of the legal maxim that states that *lex citius tolerare vult privatum damnum quam publicum malum* (the law would rather tolerate a private wrong than a public evil). Growing up in the Netherlands in the late 1950s and 1960s and descending from a family of beach combers, I dreamed not of becoming a historian but a sailor, to be more precise, a salvor, that is, a crewmember of one of the strong ocean-going salvage tugboats that had been a source of pride to all Dutchmen since the beginning of the twentieth century. I was both fascinated and horrified by the fact that large and proud ships can so easily disappear below the surface of the ocean, leaving at best an occasional piece of wreckage washed ashore as a clue to the catastrophe that had occurred. Reading about maritime disasters and salvage operations on the high seas, I became attuned to the idea of contingency, and when I realized that historiography and not maritime salvage was to be my profession, I remained interested in the radical contingency of every historical fact. The concept and urgency of "salvage" came to shape my own understanding of the primary work as the historian: before he or she interprets facts, he or she must prevent those facts from sinking into an ocean of oblivion because, once they disappear below the surface, they cannot be recovered. When I began to study the Holocaust, initially focusing on the history of Auschwitz, my self-understanding of being a salvor increased. The Germans had worked hard to kill witnesses and destroy material evidence—both documents and crucial buildings—before they abandoned the camp to the Red Army, and those few who were left to testify did not have the words to do so because, as Elie Wiesel, André Neher, and Jean Francois Lyotard have so convincingly argued, Auschwitz had also destroyed the language to describe it.[64] And then, of course, there was the challenge posed by the manner in which the chief instrument of the genocide, the gas chamber, prevented the possibility of direct eyewitness evidence. Buchenwald survivor Jorge Semprun reflected on this some years ago. "There are of course survivors of Auschwitz," he noted, and he immediately added: "but there are no survivors of the gas chambers."

> No one can tell us that he was there, no one could ever, through the truthfulness of his story, make us say: It is as if I was there! All the massacres throughout history have spared survivors, direct witnesses: they were there. Our imagination, our compassion, our anger also while listening to their stories may make us say: It is as if I were there! Hundreds of thousands of Jews of all social conditions, all ages, men and women, children and elderly people are dead in the gas chambers, and no one can testify. We have the proofs, but not the testimonies. In humanity's collective memory,

> legendary or historical, fable or document, there will always be this ontological vacuum, this lack of being, this appalling emptiness, this infected and poisonous wound: no one could ever tell us that he has been there.[65]

But yet, it was the apparent trace shown in images of the inside of a gas chambers, which I saw for the first time as an undergraduate student, which suggested that, perhaps, Semprun might have been wrong. Jean Resnais's and Jean Cayrol's *Night and Fog* showed me an ordinary, empty room. "Nothing distinguished the gas chamber from an ordinary block," the narrator told me. "Inside, what looked like a shower room welcomed the newcomers." Then a close-up of the concrete ceiling. It seemed uneven, perhaps even scratched. The narrator continued: "The only sign—but you have to know it—is this ceiling, dug into by fingernails. Even the concrete was torn."[66]

These seemingly "impossible" aspects of the historiography of Auschwitz pulled me into the topic. So when first Morris and later the Penguin-Lipstadt team offered me two major opportunities to engage Holocaust denial in general and Auschwitz denial in specific in two very public forums, I finally not only realized that it was an integral part of the history that I had studied, but also that it connected me back to my own very contingent beginnings as a historian and to noble origins of all historiography: the recognition of a trace left by another human in the sand (or in the concrete) or the testimony of the man who saw the trace and, who later, tells his mate: "I saw, on the beach (or ceiling), the imprints of man's feet (or fingers). I saw it, with my own eyes." This, then, filled me with energy, joy, and ultimately deep satisfaction when I prepared my expert report and when I testified in the court. And I admit that it was a worthy adventure, undertaken with the best of companions: Rampton, Lipstadt, Evans, Julius, and the others. And, yes, at times I remembered King Harry's exhortation on the eve of Saint Crispian's day when, looking in the future, he noted "Old men forget; yet all shall be forgot,/But he'll remember, with advantages,/What feats he did that day."[67]

I may have been well prepared, and my analysis of the evidence, and not Irving's wild speculations, carried the day. Nevertheless, I continued to feel the sting of the offense embodied in the willful falsification of history, one that had made me write those angry words a decade earlier. Therefore, when my testimony had come to an end, I decided to return to Auschwitz—a journey to touch base. "Walking the killing fields once again, I was once again reminded of the power of the place, and the absurdity of Irving's arguments," I wrote a few months later as I prepared my memoir of the trial.

> Everything did fit together: the stories of the eyewitnesses, the documents in the archive, and the place itself. But for all its power, the landscape of Birkenau appeared vulnerable also. Surveying the ruins, I felt a sudden pride for having been allowed to represent the history of that place in the British High Court. It was the pride a captain of an ocean-going tug must feel as his ship approaches the bright yellow line of the Dutch coast, with a priceless salvage in tow.[68]

Popular television shows like the 1960s' Gerry and Sylvia Anderson's puppet show *The Thunderbirds* or, more recently, BBC's *Rockface* and the Weather Channel's *Coast Guard Alaska* suggest that a trained rescuer may enjoy if not the reputation, then certainly the experience of having chosen the most noble of human vocations. And a maritime salvor may share in most of the rescuers' pride and, at times, in a decent bounty also. But the fight against Holocaust denial has taught me that the historian's profession is, as the saying goes, not for sissies either and that it fulfills a key role in society when it establishes the facts of the matter and defends, when called upon, in the public realm, the facts that matter. And for having provided both a reason and an opportunity to improve our practices and our understanding of the nature and the dignity of the historical profession, I acknowledge, as a historian, the paradoxical debt my profession owes to Faurisson and his ilk.

Notes

1. Georg Wilhelm Friedrich Hegel, *Reason in History: A General Introduction to the Philosophy of History*, Robert S. Hartman trans. (Indianapolis and New York: Bobbs-Merrill/The Library of Liberal Arts, 1953), 43f.
2. Robert C. Tucker, "The Cunning of Reason in Hegel and Marx," *The Review of Politics* 18, no. 3 (Jul. 1956), 272f., 286f.
3. Edith Wyschogrod, *An Ethics of Remembering: History, Heterology, and the Nameless Others* (Chicago: The University of Chicago Press, 1998), 3.
4. Hegel, *Reason in History*, 43, 83.

5. On the use of the term Holocaust, see Zev Garber and Bruce Zuckerman, "Why Do We Call the Holocaust 'The Holocaust?': An Inquiry into the Psychology of Labels," *Modern Judaism*, vol. 9, issue 2 (May, 1989), 197–211.
6. David Irving, *Hitler's War* (New York: Viking, 1977), xiv, 332, 391f., 505.
7. Hugh Trevor-Roper, "Hitler: does history offer a defence?" *The Sunday Times*, June 12, 1977.
8. Karl Schleunes, *The Twisted Road to Auschwitz: Nazi Policy Toward German Jews*, 1933–1939 (Urbana: University of Illinois Press, 1970), 257f.
9. Uwe Dietrich Adam, *Judenpolitik im Dritten Reich* (Düsseldorf: Droste Verlag, 1972), 357.
10. Tim Mason articulated the difference between a "functionalist" and "intentionalist" interpretation of Nazi Germany in his path-breaking essay "Intention and Explanation: A current controversy about the interpretation of National Socialism," in Gerhard Hirschfeld and Lothar Kettenacker, eds., *Der "Führer Staat," Mythos und Realität: Studien zur Kultur und Politik des Dritten Reiches* (Stuttgart: Klett-Cotta, 1981), 23–42.
11. Martin Broszat, "Hitler und die Genesis der 'Endlösung.' Aus Anlaß der Thesen von David Irving," *Vierteljahrshefte für Zeitgeschichte* 25 (1977), 753.
12. Christopher Browning, "Zur Genesis der 'Endlösung': Eine Antwort an Martin Broszat," *Vierteljahrshefte für Zeitgeschichte* 29 (1981), 96–104.
13. Gerald Fleming, *Hitler und die Endlösung: Es is des Führer's Wunsch* ... (Wiesbaden and Munich: Limes Verlag, 1982).
14. François Furet, ed., *L'Allemagne Nazie et le Genocide Juif: Colloque de l'École des Hautes Etudes en Sciences Socials* (Paris: Gallimard, Seuil, 1985).
15. Jean-Claude Pressac, *Auschwitz: Technique and Operation of the Gas Chambers* (New York: The Beate Klarsfeld Foundation, 1989), 539.
16. Robert Merle, *Death is My Trade* (London: Derek Verschoyle, 1954), 241, 263.
17. Philippe Ganier-Raymond, "'À Auschwitz on n'a gazé que les poux,'" interview with Louis Darquier de Pellepoix, *L'Express*, October 28–November 4, 1978, 164–199. An English version is

published as "In Auschwitz They Only Gassed Lice," Appendix I in Carmen Callil, *Bad Faith: A Forgotten History of Family and Fatherland* (London: Jonathan Cape, 2006), 445–462.

18. Philippe Ganier-Raymond, *Une certaine France: l'antisémitisme 40–44* (Paris: Balland, 1975).
19. "In Auschwitz They Only Gassed Lice," in Cahill, *Bad Faith*, 449–50.
20. Serge Thion printed Faurisson's article in his book on the Faurisson affair. See Serge Thion, *Vérité historique ou vérité politique? La dossier de l'affaire Faurisson. La question des chambers à gaz* (Paris: La Vielle Taupe, 1980), 83–89.
21. Ibid., 83f.
22. "Les chambres à gaz: ça n'existe pas," *Le Matin de Paris*, November 16, 1978.
23. "M. Pierre Sudreau demande une enquête sur l'enseignement de M. Faurisson qui nie l'existence des chambres à gaz," *Le Monde*, November 18, 1978.
24. Robert Faurisson, "'Le problème des chambers à gaz' ou 'la rumour d'Auschwitz,'" *Le Monde*, December 29, 1978, 8; as printed in Robert Faurisson, *Mémoire en Défense contre ceux qui m'accusent de falsifier l'histoire/La question des chambers à gaz*, preface by Noam Chomsky (Paris: La Veille Taupe, 1980), 73–75.
25. Georges Wellers, "Abondance des preuves," *Le Monde*, December 29, 1978, 8; as printed in Faurisson, *Mémoire en Défense*, 78–81.
26. Robert Faurisson, "Une letter de M. Faurisson," *Le Monde*, January 16, 1979, 13; as printed in Faurisson, *Mémoire en Défense*, 84–88.
27. Ibid., 84.
28. "La politique hitlérienne d'extermination: une déclaration des historiens français," *Le Monde*, February 23, 1979, 23.
29. Conversation of the late Jean-Claude Pressac with the author in Oświęcim, November 1990.
30. Pressac, *Auschwitz*, 546, 548, 554, 561.
31. Georges Wellers, *Les chambers à gaz ont existé: Des documents, des témoignages, des chiffres* (Paris: Éditions Gallimard, 1981).
32. Jean-Claude Pressac, "Étude et realization des *Krematorien* IV et V d'Auschwitz-Birkenau," in Francois Furet, ed., *L'Allemagne nazie et le genocide juif* (Paris: Gallimard and Le Seuil, 1985), 539–586.

33. Georges Wellers, preface to Jean-Claude Pressac, "Les 'Krematorien' IV et V de Birkenau et leurs chambers à gaz," in *Le Monde Juif* 107 (1982), 91ff.
34. Beate and Serge Klarsfeld, "Preface," in *Pressac*, Auschwitz, 13.
35. See, *inter alia*, Robert Jan van Pelt, "A Site in Search of a Mission," in *Anatomy of the Auschwitz Death Camp*, Yisrael Gutman and Michael Berenbaum eds. (Bloomington: Indiana University Press, 1994), 93–156; Debórah Dwork and Robert Jan van Pelt, *Auschwitz, 1270 to the Present* (New York: W.W. Norton, 1996).
36. Robert Faurisson, "Auschwitz: Technique & Operation of the Gas Chambers—Part I," *The Journal of Historical Review* 11, #1 (Spring 1991), 25, 28f.
37. Fred Leuchter, *The Leuchter Report: The End of a Myth. An Engineering Report on the Alleged Execution Gas Chambers at Auschwitz, Birkenau, and Majdanek, Poland* (Decatur: David Clark, n.d.), 7, 15ff., tables V, VI, and VIII.
38. Ernst Zündel, as quoted in Robert Jan van Pelt, *The Case for Auschwitz: Evidence from the Irving Trial* (Bloomington and Indianapolis: Indiana University Press, 2002), 43.
39. David Irving, as quoted in van Pelt, *The Case for Auschwitz*, 45.
40. On Irving's motivation, see van Pelt, *The Case for Auschwitz*, 45ff.
41. David Irving, as quoted in van Pelt, *The Case for Auschwitz*, 1f.
42. Daniel P. Moynihan, *Came the Revolution: Argument in the Reagan Era* (San Diego: Harcourt Brace Jovanovich, 1988), 159.
43. "BverfGE 90, 241, decided 13 April 1994—1 BvR 23/94—Auschwitz Lie Case (Holocaust Denial Case)" in Deutschland, Bundesverfassungsgericht, *Decisions of the Bundesverfassungsgericht—Federal Constitutional Court—Federal Republic of Germany*, 5 vols. (Baden-Baden: Nomos, 1992–2012), volume 2, part II, 621–3.
44. "Selected Provisions (Art. 1–20) of the Basic Law for the Federal Republic of Germany," in Deutschland, Bundesverfassungsgericht, *Decisions of the Bundesverfassungsgericht—Federal Constitutional Court—Federal Republic of Germany*, vol. 2, part II, xxiv.
45. Deutschland, Bundesverfassungsgericht, "BverfGE 90, 241, decided 13 April 1994—1 BvR 23/94—Auschwitz Lie Case (Holocaust Denial Case)," 625, 627.
46. Hannah Arendt, "The Aftermath of Nazi Rule: Report from Germany," *Commentary* 10, issue 10 (1950), 344.

47. Hannah Arendt, "Truth and Politics," *The New Yorker* 43, no. 1 (February 25, 1967), 49, 83–4, 86, 88, 52, 54.
48. Manuel Prutschi, "Holocaust Denial Today," in Edmond Y. Lipsitz, ed., *Canadian Jewry Today: Who's Who in Canadian Jewry* (Downsview: J.E.S.L. Education Products, 1989), 30.
49. Robert Jan van Pelt, [The Van Pelt Report]: electronic edition, available at http://www.hdot.org/en/trial/defense/van/X.
50. Ibid.
51. Richard Sennett, *The Fall of Public Man* (New York: Knopf, 1977), 259; Annette Wieviorka, *L'ère du témoin* (Paris: Plon, 1998).
52. Jesajahu Weinberg, "From the Founding Director," Michael Berenbaum, *The World Must Know: The History of the Holocaust as Told in the United States Holocaust Memorial Museum*, 2nd edition (Washington D.C.: United States Holocaust Memorial Museum, 2006), xvii.
53. "Remarks of President Bill Clinton at the Dedication Ceremonies for the United States Holocaust Memorial Museum, April 22, 1993," available at http://www.ushmm.org/research/library/faq/languages/en/06/01/ceremony/?content=clinton.
54. In the High Court of Justice, Queen's Bench Division, 1996-I-No. 1113, Irving versus Penguin and Lipstadt, transcripts, day 1 (January 11, 2000), 88f.
55. Richard J. Evans, "David Irving, Hitler and Holocaust Denial," electronic edition available at http://www.hdot.org/en/trial/defense/evans/160.
56. Charles Gray, "Holocaust Denial on Trial, Trial Judgment," electronic edition available at http://www.hdot.org/en/trial/judgement/13.62.
57. Wendie Ellen Schneider, "Past Imperfect: Irving v. Penguin Books Ltd., No. 1996-I-1113, 2000 WL 362478 (Q. B. Apr. 11), appeal denied (Dec. 18, 2000)," *The Yale Law Journal* 110 (8), 1535.
58. Gray, "Holocaust Denial on Trial," http://www.hdot.org/en/trial/judgement/13.24.
59. Schneider, "Past Imperfect," 1540.
60. Paraphrase of Shakespeare, *Henry V*, Act 4, line 2298.
61. "David Irving lost his case—and we can celebrate a victory for free speech," *The Independent* (April 12, 2000).
62. "Holocaust Denial," *The Irish Times* (April 12, 2000).

63. "Truth's sheer weight: Irving was the deniers' best shot," *The Guardian* (April 12, 2000).
64. Elie Wiesel, "Why I Write," in *Confronting the Holocaust: The Impact of Elie Wiesel*, Alvin Rosenfeld and Irving Greenberg, eds. (Bloomington: Indiana University Press, 1978), 201; André Neher, *The Exile of the Word*, David Maisel trans. (Philadelphia: The Jewish Publication Society of America, 1981), 141ff.; Jean-Francois Lyotard, *The Differend: Phrases in Dispute*, Georges Van Den Abbeele, trans. (Minneapolis: University of Minnesota Press, 1988), 56ff.
65. Jorge Semprun, "Une petite lampe s'est allumée dans la baraque des contagieux ....," in Ariana Kalfa and Michaël de Saint Cheron, eds., *Élie Wiesel en Hommage* (Paris: Les Editions du Cerf, 1998), 60–1; as quoted in Caroline Fournet, *The Crime of Destruction and the Law of Genocide: Their Impact on Collective Memory* (Aldershot: Ashgate, 2007), 32.
66. Jean Cayrol, "Night and Fog," in Robert Hughes, ed., *Film: Book 2—Films of Peace and War* (New York: Grove Press, 1962), 252.
67. Shakespeare, *Henry V*, Act 4, lines 2284–5.
68. Robert Jan van Pelt, *The Case for Auschwitz: Evidence from the Irving Trial* (Bloomington and Indianapolis, Indiana University Press, 2002), 487.

Index

Note: Page numbers followed by 'n' denote notes.

A. McElligott, J. Herf (eds.), *Antisemitism Before and Since the Holocaust*, DOI 10.1007/978-3-319-48866-0

Z

Printed in Great Britain
by Amazon

21198497R10244